RESEARCH IN MARITIME HISTORY
NO. 2

FROM WHEEL HOUSE TO COUNTING HOUSE:

ESSAYS IN MARITIME BUSINESS HISTORY

IN HONOUR OF

PROFESSOR PETER NEVILLE DAVIES

INTERNATIONAL MARITIME ECONOMIC HISTORY
ASSOCIATION

ISSN - 1188-3928
ISBN - 0-9695885-1-8

PROFESSOR PETER NEVILLE DAVIES

CONTENTS

CONTRIBUTORS

About the Editor

LEWIS R. FISCHER is Professor of History at Memorial University of Newfoundland. A specialist in nineteenth and twentieth-century maritime economic history, he has published widely on Canadian, Norwegian and international maritime topics and is currently completing a book on shipbroking. Professor Fischer is Secretary of the Canadian Nautical Research Society; Secretary-General of the International Commission for Maritime History; Editor-in-Chief of the *International Journal of Maritime History*; and Editor of *Research in Maritime History*. He has been a friend and professional colleague of Peter Davies since the mid-1970s.

Contributors

ANDREW ARMITAGE is currently completing a Ph.D. under Peter Davies on the economic history of Belfast shipbuilding at the University of Liverpool, where he is a tutor in the Institute of Irish Studies.

FRANK BROEZE is Associate Professor of History at the University of Western Australia. He is President of the International Commission of Maritime History which publishes numerous studies in the history of shipping, ports and port cities. Intrigues by the perspective of the customers of shipping services.

P.L. COTTRELL is Professor of Economic and Social History at the University of Leicester. He took up his first full-time teaching appointment at Liverpool, thus becoming a colleague of Peter Davies. He has taught at Leicester since 1972, during which time he has also been a Bye Fellow at Robinson College, Cambridge, and a Visiting Overseas Professor at the College of Commerce, Nihon University, Tokyo. His continuing research embraces British and European financial and banking history (albeit with the odd splash of saltwater) during the nineteenth and twentieth centuries. In his spare time, Professor Cottrell can occasionally be seen at the helm of a sailing dinghy.

ANDERS MARTIN FON is a Research Associate with the Norwegian School of Management in Oslo and is working on a history of Astrup Fearnley. A holder of undergraduate and post-graduate degrees from the Norwegian School of Economics and Business Administration, he has published on twentieth-century banking in Norway and on the history of the inter-war Norwegian merchant marine.

ROBERT GREENHILL is a Principal Lecturer in Economic History at the City of London Polytechnic. His research fields are British business links with Latin America 1850-1950. He has a particular interest in a variety of maritime and commodity trades.

GORDON JACKSON teaches history at the University of Strathclyde and has published extensively on the history of British ports and whaling. He is currently a vice-President of the British Commission for Maritime History and a long-time friend and colleague of Peter Davies.

ADRIAN JARVIS, an ex-student of Peter Davies, is Curator of Port History at Merseyside Maritime Museum and a part-time tutor in the History of Science and Technology at the University of Liverpool. His interests in the relationship between engineering and management in the port of Liverpool are reflected in his *Liverpool Central Docks 1799-1905* and a number of papers and monographs.

PETER MATHIAS, C.B.E., F.B.A., D.Litt., was an undergraduate and Research Fellow at Jesus College, Cambridge (1948-55); subsequently a Lecturer in the History Faculty and a Fellow of Queens' (1955-67) before becoming Chichele Professor of Economic History at All Souls College, Oxford (1967-87). He returned to Cambridge in 1987 as Master of Downing College. He is an Honorary President of the International Economic History Association (President 1974-78) and currently President of the European History Society (1989-92).

J. FORBES MUNRO teaches Economic History at the University of Glasgow where he is also Clerk of Senate. His research interests lie in the areas of Scottish overseas enterprise and Third World economic development.

FRANK NEAL is a Senior Lecturer in Economics and Social Statistics in the Department of Business and Management Studies at the University of Salford. He is the author of *Sectarian Violence: The Liverpool Experience 1819-1914* (1988) as well as a number of articles on the theme of the Irish in Britain; his present research project is an examination of the economic, social and political consequences of Irish immigration to Britain during the nineteenth century. He studied at Leicester for his first degree and was a post-graduate student in the Department of Economic History at the University of Liverpool with Peter Davies.

HELGE W. NORDVIK is Professor of Maritime Studies at the Norwegian School of Management. In addition to nineteenth and twentieth-century Norwegian maritime history, his research interests include banking and monetary history. He has published widely in both national and international journals. Professor Nordvik is presently an editor of the *International Journal of Maritime History*.

LARS U. SCHOLL is an historian at the Deutsches Schiffahrtsmuseum. A specialist in nineteenth and twentieth-century German maritime history with a particular interest in shipping and shipbuilding firms, he is the author of several books on German marine artists. He is also Vice-Chair of the Editorial Board of the *International Journal of Maritime History* and a Vice-President of the International Commission for Maritime History.

ANTHONY SLAVEN is Professor of Business History at the University of Glasgow and Director of the Centre for Business History in Scotland. He has published widely on the history of shipbuilding and is currently completing a book on the decline of British shipbuilding.

MICHAEL K. STAMMERS is Keeper of the Merseyside Maritime Museum. With wide-ranging interests in nineteenth-century shipping, he has recently completed a book on the Liverpool merchant ship *Jhelum* of 1849, now a hulk in the Falklands, and has written a number of other volumes, including a history of the Black Ball Line of Australian emigrant vessels. He has worked with Peter Davies over the past twenty years on projects such as the Royal Yacht *Mary* expedition.

DAVID M. WILLIAMS, as an undergraduate and post-graduate student at Liverpool, was a fellow student of Peter Davies. He subsequently moved to the University of Leicester where he lectures in economic history. He has written widely on north Atlantic commerce, maritime labour, government intervention and the free trade movement. He is currently Secretary of the British Commission for Maritime History and Chair of the Editorial Board of the *International Journal of Maritime History*.

Introduction

This volume was presented with affection and admiration to Professor Peter Neville Davies by his friends and colleagues at a banquet during the First International Congress of Maritime History in Liverpool, England, on 20 August 1992. The location and timing were by several criteria ideal. Peter not only was a principal organiser of the Congress but also was chiefly responsible for it being held in Liverpool, the city in which he spent his entire academic career. Moreover, it coincided with his formal retirement from the Department of Economic and Social History at the University of Liverpool.

For many scholars in business, economic and maritime history, the opportunity to know Peter Davies has proven very special. This is true intellectually, as Peter Mathias makes clear in his tribute in this volume, as well as in a personal sense, as David Williams' essay testifies. It is rare for an individual to have this kind of impact in both spheres, since being well-rounded is not necessarily a prerequisite to academic life. But it is precisely because Peter has touched so many people both as a scholar and a human being that made this *festschrift* such a pleasure to put together.

The idea of presenting Peter with a collection of works by his friends and colleagues had its genesis in a conversation in the lobby of the Royal Horse Guards Hotel in London in August 1991. I was in London at the time en route to Norway, where I had planned some research. A few days earlier I had phoned Peter in Liverpool, as I often did when I was in the United Kingdom, to see if it would be possible to see him while I was in the country. I really needed to discuss with him some matters pertaining to the International Maritime Economic History Association, of which he was (and is) President, but I must confess that I also cherished the opportunity to see him as a friend. For the past ten months Peter had been in Japan, as a Visiting Professor at Hiroshima Shudo University, and during that time I missed his wise council and friendship. In our phone conversation, Peter mentioned that he would be coming to London with his wife

Maureen to see their son, Simon, who was completing his medical training at a London hospital. Unfortunately, he would only be in the city briefly, since he was due to fly back to Japan for the last two months of his tenure in Hiroshima. He suggested that we might meet at his hotel after breakfast.

Our conversation, which as always with Peter was both wide-ranging and stimulating, lasted for about an hour. When we had touched upon all the obvious topics, Peter indicated that he would like to discuss something of a more personal nature. It was then that he raised an issue about which to that time I had only heard rumours: that he was considering retiring formally from the University of Liverpool in the autumn of 1992. It was difficult to know how to respond. On the one hand, when a colleague reaches his mid-sixties and has devoted as much time and energy as has Peter to his academic career, it is obviously difficult to begrudge him the right to get on with other facets of his life. At this time, he had just delivered to the publisher his manuscript on the River Kwai, upon which he had been working off and on for two decades; this marked the completion of his third book in little over eighteen months. Clearly, he and his family deserved the opportunity that retirement would provide to pursue other interests. On the other hand, it was difficult to envision Peter in retirement. He was devoted to the University of Liverpool, his academic home, and to his profession. And he still had more energy than most people half his age: his role in establishing the IMEHA and the *International Journal of Maritime History*, his recent election as senior Vice-President of the International Commission of Maritime History, and his work in planning the First International Congress of Maritime History all attested to his continuing vigour and vitality. In the end, all I could do was to mouth some platitudes about how it was of course his decision and I knew that he would do what was best. He said that he was still mulling it over in his mind and would let me know what he decided.

I recall leaving Peter that morning and walking past the colourful horse guards down to the Thames. On a bench alongside the river I pondered our discussion. If Peter were to retire--a decision that was still pending--it was obvious that something ought to be done to honour the immense contribution he had made to the profession. It was also clear that if he did choose to retire, whatever might be done ought to occur at the First International Congress of Maritime History, which fittingly would be held in Liverpool. But the idea of planning and arranging anything which would involve heavily-committed scholars and would have to take place in only twelve months was daunting. And it was not completely certain that he would be retiring at that time.

Four people, all of whom I consulted with over the next few days, convinced me that a *festschrift* was perhaps the most appropriate vehicle; all deserve most of the credit for the timely appearance of this book. I spoke first with David Williams, a man whose advice a generation of maritime historians has learned to be impeccable. When I mentioned the possibility of a *festschrift*, his response was that it was not only the right thing to do but that it had to be done. I spoke next to Sheila Marriner, who although retired herself has been in many ways Peter's closest colleague in recent years. She not only reiterated David's advice but also reminded me most forcefully of the strong pride that Peter has always taken in being identified with the Liverpool school of business history; from then on, it was always clear that the theme of the volume had to be maritime business history. Val Dodd, an amazing woman who has for many years been the secretary at the Department of Economic History at Liverpool and whose insights concerning Peter have always been uncanny, not only thought that a *festschrift* was appropriate but volunteered immediately to do all the necessary tasks in Liverpool. Finally, my long-time colleague and collaborator in Norway, Helge Nordvik, also agreed enthusiastically.

But if a *festschrift* were to be produced in little more than a year, it was imperative that contributors be recruited quickly. Fortunately, a number of Peter's closest academic friends were scheduled to attend a conference in Esbjerg, Denmark in a little more than a fortnight's time. While in Norway I drew up a fairly elaborate outline of the format that a *festschrift* might take, in anticipation that I would have to convince those assembled. In the end, of course, I foolishly underestimated the very real depth of feeling that Peter has evoked in colleagues. At a meeting of about a dozen potential contributors held in Gordon Jackson's room in the conference residence, I sat there while one after another extremely busy scholar promised to rearrange schedules to give the *festschrift* top priority. If this meeting reminded me of the genuine respect and admiration that so many in the profession feel towards Peter, this point was underscored even more forcefully over the next several months: it is no exaggeration to say that the number of people who spontaneously volunteered to contribute would have tripled the size of the book.

When we left Esbjerg, the outline of this book was firmly in place. While it was still necessary to contact some potential contributors and to finalize the precise way the volume would be produced, most of the major decisions had been made. The principal decision outstanding was how it would be published. We all recognised in Esbjerg that this would present a potential problem, especially given the forward planning in which publishers must engage. In the end, I recommended to the contributors that we attempt to solve the problem by approaching the IMEHA, since it seemed fitting that the organisation for which Peter had effectively served as midwife ought to be the body which honoured him.

What was less clear was how we could gain the approval of the Association's executive without informing its President of our intent. Fortunately, Gerry Panting, who at the time was Secretary-Treasurer of the Association, is a man of great organisational experience. When I explained to him what we would like to do, Gerry immediately offered to clear the remaining hurdles. I suggested to him that the book could appear in a new series called "Research in Maritime History." Gerry took the request for the new series to Peter for his approval, which was also enthusiastic. Had he known, of course, that one of the first volumes was to be in his honour, I doubt that his approval would have been so positive. Gerry also of course approved the necessary funds for the project.

The result is this volume. While the finished product does not look exactly the way it was conceptualised, what is perhaps most impressive is that all the contributors managed to meet our very tight set of deadlines. This, too, is a tribute to Peter--time after time I have been impressed by a call, letter or FAX from a contributor to assure me that despite other commitments he would do whatever was necessary to ensure that Peter received the best possible volume.

Because Peter's interests have been so catholic, we have tried to reflect this in organising the book. The *festschrift* is divided into four sections. The first comprises an eloquent tribute from Peter Mathias and a delightful and insightful appreciation from David Williams. Although physically separated, Andrew Armitage's bibliography of Peter's published works should be considered part of this section. Together these contributions serve to introduce Peter Davies to readers who perhaps do have not been fortunate enough to know the man and his contributions as well as others. Those who do know Peter well will doubtless subscribe wholeheartedly to Peter Mathias' and David Williams' observations.

The second section of the book salutes Peter's long-time interest in business aspects of British maritime history. Gordon Jackson's essay on Grimsby demonstrates how the intertwining of commercial, maritime and civic interests shaped the development of the port over the past two centuries. Forbes Munro's essay on the Mackinnon group's activities in the Indian Ocean adds to our understanding of the impact of British shipping interests abroad. Robert Greenhill, in his examination of British shipping in Latin America, reminds us not only of the global importance of such transport but also of the vicissitudes that such involvement can have on the firms involved. Andrew Armitage's study of Workman, Clark and Co. shows how the interplay of family and commercial interests within the context of Ulster led both to the rise and decline of the firm and shipbuilding in Northern Ireland in general. Finally, Tony Slaven demonstrates how the failure to develop a market orientation was a primary cause of the post-World War II decline of British shipbuilding.

The third part of the book is devoted to topics in the local maritime history of Merseyside. P.L. Cottrell's essay explores significant developments in Merseyside trade with the Mediterranean, with a special emphasis on the transition from sail to steam. Frank Neal examines the organisation of ship carpenters in Liverpool, demonstrating as well how this affected shipowning and shipbuilding in the port. Adrian Jarvis' contribution looks at the role of Alfred Jones (about whom Peter Davies has written extensively) in the development of the port system on the Mersey. Finally, Michael Stammers writes about Peter's pioneering role in the development of nautical archaeology in the region.

The final section of the book pays tribute to Peter's contribution to the development of maritime history as an international discipline. Frank Broeze discusses the development and operations of conferences in the late nineteenth century, focusing especially upon the port of Fremantle. Anders Fon and I explore shipbroking, a business which has been little examined by scholars, by looking at the development of a major Norwegian shipbroker. Helge Nordvik's essay looks at the rise of an important Norwegian shipowner, Lauritz Kloster. And Lars Scholl explains the way in which a 1920 agreement with American shipowners facilitated the re-entry of the Hamburg-American Line into international shipping after World War I.

The topics dealt with in this volume obviously by no means exhaust the range of subjects that could have been examined. Nonetheless, it is our hope that collectively they make a contribution to the development of maritime business history, a field in which Peter Davies' contributions have been so significant. More important, we hope that in a small way the papers in this *festschrift* demonstrate the respect and regard the contributors feel toward Peter. The debt owed him by maritime history and its practitioners is substantial. In a modest way this book represents an attempt to repay him for his role in making maritime history an exciting and rewarding field in which to work.

Lewis R. Fischer
Oslo, Norway
June 1992

Peter Neville Davies: A Tribute

Peter Mathias

This book stands as witness to the affection and admiration in which Peter Davies is so widely-held. Where a dozen have written in its pages, readers in their hundreds over the world now and in the future will endorse the sentiments which have brought it into existence.

Every department and faculty, every Society and Association needs--and if they are fortunate have--someone to whom others can turn, and whom outsiders can approach: the person who is always there, conscientious, reliable, meriting trust and confidence, whose instinctive answer to a request for help is "yes" rather than "no" or "maybe," who gets things done without fuss or resonance--in short a stalwart and an anchor for any endeavour. Peter Davies is pre-eminently such a person, whether considered in his various positions in the Department of Economic History in Liverpool, as a scholar, an editor, or as the organiser of wide-ranging international commitments. The different chapters of this book reflect the range of his interests and the different phases of his career as an economic and business historian.

The tap-root of Peter Davies's career as an economic historian, and its subsequent flowering, lies in his total commitment to Liverpool. He took his B.A., M.A. and Ph.D. there, became Tutor in 1964 (at the age of thirty-seven) rising through all rungs of the academic ladder to professor in 1990/91; heading the department for a decade after 1979, and running through the gamut of university committees (no less than nine over the years) as a Senate Representative, while offering virtually continuous service as external examiner. On cannot envisage a more firmly anchored career; and on the basis of this have come Peter Davies's wider endeavours.

Since the Second World War, the Department in Liverpool built a strong reputation in maritime history, with a dozen or so major monographs on shipping lines; Francis Hyde, as Chaddock Professor, being ably supported by Sheila Marriner and Peter Davies.[1] Peter also established his reputation in this field of shipping monographs but pressed towards wider horizons.[2] Interests in Liverpool's wider trade links led him "downstream" to a major business history of Fyffes, which explored the international banana trade and the home market in depth for the first time; moving "upstream" he went from shipping enterprise to the shipbuilding industry.[3]

A succession of wider commitments accompanied the steady progress of his research and publications, as others sought the benefit of his experience: Assistant Editor of *Business History* (1968-81); Chairman of the Liverpool Nautical Research Association (1975-78); Member of the Council for Nautical Archaeology (1967-86); Co-founder of the Maritime Economic History Group (1986-90); Committee Member of the Alabama Trust (1987-); Member of the Committee of the Friends of Merseyside Maritime Museum (1980-). This roll-call could be extended.

Two, among many, initiatives deserve emphasis because they show how outward-facing Peter Davies has been, taking his work to wider constituencies. The first concerns the Merseyside Maritime Museum, on the University's doorstep at the revitalised Albert Dock above the pierhead at Liverpool, one of the great set-pieces of urban

---

[1]This bibliography includes F.E. Hyde, *Blue Funnel: A History of Alfred Holt and Co. of Liverpool, 1865-1914* (Liverpool, 1956); Hyde, *Shipping Enterprise and Management: Harrison's of Liverpool* (Liverpool, 1967); Hyde and S. Marriner, *The Senior: John Samuel Swire, 1825-98* (Liverpool, 1967); Hyde, *Liverpool and the Mersey: The development of a Port, 1700-1970* (Newton Abbot, 1971); Hyde, *et al.*, *Far Eastern Trade, 1860-1914* (London, 1973); Hyde, *Cunard and the North Atlantic, 1840-1973* (London, 1975); S. Marriner, *Rathbones of Liverpool, 1845-73* (Liverpool, 1961).

[2]See P.N. Davies, *The Trade Makers: Elder Dempster in West Africa, 1852-1972* (London, 1973; reissued 1980); *Sir Alfred Jones: Shipping Entrepreneur par Excellence* (London, 1978); *Henry Tyrer, A Liverpool Shipping Agent and his Enterprise* (1979).

[3]*Musa Sapientum: Fyffes and the Banana, 1888-1988* (London, 1990). See also *A Study of Trends in the Wholesale Fruit and Vegetable Markets since 1950* (London, 1985), and *The Growth of the Modern Japanese Shipping and Shipbuilding Industries* (with T. Chida, London, 1990).

renewal in Europe. Largely through Peter's initiative and efforts the museum has a substantial academic dimension to its activities, with joint activities, close liaison and advice. A visit is a delight whether for a scholar in maritime history or a family party; and the museum is richer, with a greater depth of significance to the story it tells, more accurate historically and more enjoyable as a consequence of such cooperation. Retaining the confidence of municipal authorities was not the least of the necessary attributes which brought this about.

Liverpool has proved to be a gateway to the world as regards Peter Davies's career, which also deserves emphasis in any tribute such as this. Joint authorship with Professor Tomohei Chida of Aoyama Gakuin University in Tokyo of a monograph on the Japanese shipbuilding industry embodies this international commitment at the personal research level. But bringing into being the International Maritime Economic Association and becoming its first President in 1990 is the crowning achievement of his career in a wider sense. Subjects become institutionalised by stages--from individual research and publications, by way of journals and national societies, seminars and conferences; and thence from the national to the international scene. Maritime history has now passed through all these stages, and Peter Davies has participated in, if not initiated, them all. Apart from the Presidency of the IMEHA, he is Senior Vice-President of the International Commission for Maritime History (affiliated to the Comité International des Sciences Historiques); Chairman of the British Commission for Maritime History and former Chairman of the Editorial Board of the *International Journal of Maritime History*.

In all these ways Peter Davies's achievements as a maritime historian have been formidable. To him and to his work this volume is an affectionate tribute.

Peter Neville Davies: An Appreciation

David M. Williams

An invitation to write an appreciation for a *festschrift* represents both a pleasure and obligation. The pleasure is obvious enough; the obligation lies in the recognition that one is writing not merely for oneself but also on behalf of many others. In this instance those others are the host of scholars, world-wide, who would wish to record their appreciation of Peter Davies' friendship, academic judgement and great contribution to maritime history.

Yet, though conscious of writing for many, and confident that all will wish to subscribe to the sentiments expressed, I must confess to the personal nature of what follows. This short appreciation is neither a biography nor an assessment of Peter Davies' contribution to the world of scholarship, though it contains elements of both. Rather it is a mix of personal reminiscences, comments on some of the influences in Peter's career and observations on Peter's lifestyle and values. Above all, its aim is to emphasise those unique personal qualities which have gained Peter so many friends and so much respect both nationally and internationally.

My sole special qualification for writing this appreciation is that of all Peter's many academic friends, I can claim to have known him the longest--in fact, from the very beginning of his academic career. It is hardly possible to go back farther than one's first day as an undergraduate at university, and it was on that day that Peter and I met. That meeting was the start of an abiding friendship. It must be said that while we came together in a common situation, it was hardly a meeting of equal or similar parties. I was a typical "straight from school" student; Peter was somewhat older, being what would now be described as a "mature student." Nowadays, such students are commonplace. Back in 1958, older students were very much the exception.

Peter Davies' background before coming to university was unusual. After a prelude of National Service--in his case in the army, during which time he gained some experience of the Middle East and its troubles--Peter embarked on a teacher training course at St. John's College, York, the successful completion of which marked the beginning of a career teaching at schools in the Merseyside area. In a sense this was the commencement of a life-long career in the field of education, but only in a partial fashion. Partial, not just because he was to move from the context of the school to the university, but, even more so, because from early days he was to combine a career in business with that of academic life. Before he came to university, Peter had a commercial interest in the world of motorcycle repair and retailing, and this aspect of his affairs was to play a significant role in his non-academic life for many years thereafter. Even discounting his maturity of years, Peter was hardly a typical student when he enroled at the University of Liverpool in October of 1958.

Despite his seniority and his very much wider experience of the ways of the world, Peter had no difficulty coming to terms with undergraduate life. His friendly, outgoing personality, his willingness to participate, and his treatment of all as equals meant there was no question of any "age gap," and to most of his contemporaries Peter was just like any another student. One quality which stood out then, however, and has stood out ever since and been apparent to all who have known Peter, was that of his calmness and level-headedness at all times. Combined with his affability and ever-optimistic outlook, this gained Peter a host of friends among his fellow students, all of whom knew they could rely on him for sound advice and reassurance on any matter. So it has been for friends over the past thirty years.

Reminiscences of student days can very easily assume the dimension of sentimentality and at worst rival the horrors of being subjected to a forced viewing of friends' holiday snapshots or family videos. While accounts of Liverpool in the late fifties and early sixties, when a three-course lunch at any number of Chinese restaurants could be purchased for less than ten pence, where many city public houses refused entry to unaccompanied ladies, where the Cavern was still resolutely purely a jazz club, and where Liverpool F.C. was languishing in the second division, may tantalize, they are very much reflections of a long-gone era and culture. And one notable feature of Peter's outlook and career has always been to keep the past firmly in perspective and instead to focus on the present and future. It is perhaps because of such an approach to life that all who have known him for any length of time invariably come up with the observation that "he is still the same," the years seemingly having had no effect whatsoever! Even so, a few further observations might be permitted on Peter's undergraduate career, if only to indicate some of his academic roots and to point to some of the traits which have featured in his subsequent highly-successful career. Three traits are perhaps worthy of comment: one academic; another entrepreneurial; another, of a less easily defined quality.

It would seem appropriate to commence with the academic dimension. In 1958 Peter entered the University of Liverpool. He enroled in the Department of Commerce and Economics, situated at that time in Abercromby Square, where after a temporary sojourn elsewhere, the Department of Economic History is currently located. It must be an especially pleasant experience for Peter to return and work in the very building where over thirty years ago he commenced his academic career. In the late 1950s, students at Liverpool enjoyed the privilege of being taught by scholars of especially high repute. Peter, myself and our contemporaries had the inestimable experience of being introduced to economics--and this was an era when introductions were real, first-hand introductions, for economics was not a subject taught in schools--from no less than G.L.S. Shackle.[1] Scholar of world eminence that he was, Shackle approached his teaching very much in terms of a mission, and all who enjoyed his lecture courses gained also the commitment of a dedicated teacher. The latter far exceeded any normal sense of duty. Shackle's room was open at any time to all who sought advice and guidance, and open with a genuine welcome. Peter, along with generations of other students, gained inestimably from those personal tutorials with Shackle--even at that time an elderly gentleman--where time and expertise were so freely dispensed that the recipient of such bounties departed naively believing that they had done Shackle a favour in calling on him! Such was

[1]G.L.S. Shackle died only in 1991. Active until the end, he took great interest in Peter's success and would have gained special pleasure from this volume.

Peter's first teacher of economics--a scholar and a gentleman, for once, in every sense of the words. If Peter enjoyed the most excellent of introductions to economics, so too did he benefit from the expertise of those who taught him in the field of economic history.

At that time, Liverpool degrees in economics embraced compulsory courses in economic history, with scope for further history options. Students who chose to follow a historical path were fortunate, for the department was headed by Francis E. Hyde, a scholar of impressive background--Liverpool, LSE and Harvard--who had recently published *Blue Funnel*, soon to be recognised as a seminal study in business history.[2] Hyde's influence was to prove a crucial determinant in Peter's career and pattern of research. Hyde's colleagues included John Harris, soon to be appointed successor to W.H.B. Court at Birmingham; Ian Keil, who subsequently played an important role in the development of economic history at the new University of Loughborough; Sheila Marriner, later to be a long-standing colleague of Peter's and whose important study--*Rathbones of Liverpool*--was about to appear;[3] and Berrick Saul, authority on international overseas trade in the late nineteenth century,[4] who was in due course appointed Vice-Chancellor of York University. It was a rich spread of economic and business history talent that students of that era enjoyed. No wonder that many opted for courses in economic history.

Such comments on the undergraduate path followed by Peter are important, for early courses and academic influences were to affect profoundly the character and direction of his career, both in the short-term post-graduate context and the much longer dimension. It would be very wrong, however, to imagine that Peter's years as an undergraduate were exclusively dominated by academic study. Even then Peter had achieved that balance and perspective between academic work and extra-University activities which were to serve him so well in the years

---

[2]F.E. Hyde, *Blue Funnel: A History of Alfred Holt and Co. of Liverpool, 1865-1914* (Liverpool, 1956).

[3]S. Marriner, *Rathbones of Liverpool, 1845-73* (Liverpool, 1961).

[4]S.B. Saul, *Studies in British Overseas Trade 1870-1914* (Liverpool, 1960).

to come. In this case, the latter took the form of the continuance and development of his business interests. Indicative of Peter's special ability to combine two careers, two lifestyles, two livelihoods--and to do much more as well--was the fact that coincidental with the very day of the commencement of his crucial first-year examinations, he embarked on his first really independent business venture--the launch of Davies and Jones, a motorcycle business, with shop and workshops in Prenton, Birkenhead. That his partner in this venture was abroad--acting as harbour master in a major West African port--only goes to show how Peter's role in the enterprise was one of "on the spot" management and expertise. It goes without saying that this combination of undergraduate examinations and entrepreneurial initiative was attended with success. Even a subsequent robbery attempt on the premises came to nought as the intruder fell foul of the ex-TT rider in Peter's employ. The only damage was to the telephone used to subdue the attacker! Such are the vicissitudes of business! A few other minor diversions apart, Peter's business ventures were to develop and flourish.

As a final observation on Peter's undergraduate days, one episode must suffice. Peter's studies at the University of Liverpool were those of a home-based student living "across the water" in Birkenhead. As such, the journey through the Mersey Tunnel was a daily occurrence. Readers are invited to use their imaginations and to picture the undergraduate Peter, his lecture notes strapped to the pillion seat, clad in goggles, World War II flying helmet and a camel hair coat (which allegedly had its origins in a bale of cloth inadvertently dropped from a dockside lorry), astride his trust Norton. Such regular passages under the Mersey proceeded uneventfully until one fateful day when the heavy file of lecture notes slipped from its moorings. Here was a case of disaster and no turning back; tunnel regulations and the thunder of heavy lorries to the rear ensured progress to the university with a lighter load and heavier heart. All that was possible was a vain appeal to the tunnel authorities' "lost property section." The outcome? On calling at the appropriate office on his return journey later that day, the notes were there, complete, albeit compressed due to the passage of some thousands of tons of freight vehicles. Such an unexpected happy outcome is illustrative of what would seem a feature of Peter's career--that it has been blessed with good fortune throughout. Without doubt, Peter has seemingly possessed the happy knack of being in the right place at the right time in a special way, for his right place has always been the same--the department at Liverpool. That such opportunity has arisen in his chosen location is good fortune, but there is much truth in the adage of making one's own luck, and it is Peter's response to the opportunities that have fallen to him that has determined his career progress. Good fortune, like the biblical talent, only bears fruit if put to use in an imaginative and forward-looking manner.

In noting Peter's positive response to favourable circumstances, it would be impertinent to suggest that this was determined by lessons derived from his studies in economic and business history. Peter's entrepreneurial instincts were honed long before entering academic life; indeed, his entry into the same when he already had professional qualifications and commercial interests bears this out. Even so, as a justification to their own studies, many historians might like to read something into the fact that the subject of Peter's master's thesis (and later a book) was Sir Alfred Jones, "entrepreneur par excellence."[5] Jones was a man whose career epitomised the virtues of creating and capitalising on opportunity.

All of which leads very neatly to Peter's postgraduate career. Following a very solid honours degree, Peter embarked on an M.A. thesis. Given the departmental interest in the business history of shipping and the recently published studies of Far Eastern and Atlantic trades by Hyde and Marriner, Liverpool's West African connection seemed a natural fresh niche for study; Elder Dempster, the major operator, was an obvious subject. When approached, the company was not forthcoming. Moreover, it claimed, its pre-1932 records were but limited, a response not unfamiliar to business historians.[6] In the face of this unpromising start, Peter focused his attention on Alfred Jones.

---

[5]P.N. Davies, *Sir Alfred Jones: Shipping Entrepreneur par Excellence* (London, 1978).

[6]By good fortune, it subsequently transpired that some records did exist! Peter was to utilise these in compiling his fuller study, *The Trade Makers: Elder Dempster in West Africa, 1852-1972* (London, 1973; reprint, 1980).

Very little was known at the time about Jones, other than that his statue graced a plinth at Pier Head and that he was known as the man who introduced the banana into Britain! A few more shrewd observers, however, suspected that Jones was the "real force" behind Elder's rise to prominence. It was this assertion that Peter set out to test. The outcome was a triumph for, despite the absence of in-house records, Peter produced an outstanding master's thesis which revealed Jones to be one of the most effective entrepreneurs of his day.[7] At the same time, Peter developed a long-term interest in (some would say "love affair with") the banana trade, which in years to come was to permit regular research visits to the Canary Islands and most recently his splendid study, *Musa Sapientum.*[8] But all this was very much in the future. As a Master's student, Peter underwent the experience of Francis Hyde's post-graduate seminars in which a motley of students, including Frank Neal, Eric Taplin and myself, were summoned to report on the progress of research. In retrospect, we may have learned much. At the time the demands of a research report every fortnight were occasions of regular trauma, and sometimes required the exercise of much imagination. Peter emerged from such rigours late in 1963 with his M.A. and much else accomplished in the meantime. Indeed, the successful outcome of his first post-graduate degree was the least of his accomplishments. His business enterprises were substantially extended; moreover, he commenced and personally supervised the building of "Cmar," built appropriately on land adjoining the residence of one of Hyde's Blue Funnel Holt family and with footings physically laid by "bad debtors" to Davies and Jones. At Cmar, Peter and Maureen were subsequently to welcome a legion of maritime history colleagues who enjoyed their unstinting hospitality and very real welcome. This last sentence encompasses the most significant event of those M.A. years--Peter's marriage to Maureen, appropriately and literally, Miss Cheshire. As a guest at that happy occasion, it is an

[7]P.N. Davies, "Sir Alfred Jones and the Development of the West Africa Trade" (Unpublished M.A. thesis, University of Liverpool, 1964).

[8]P.N. Davies, *Fyffes and the Banana: Musa Sapientum--A Centenary History, 1888-1988* (London, 1990).

enormous pleasure thirty years on to congratulate Peter and Maureen and to regret that circumstances have prevented a planned return to their honeymoon destination, that seaport jewel of the Adriatic, Dubrovnik.

Following the award of his Master's degree, Peter immediately began a doctoral thesis. His theme, British shipping and West African development, represented a widening and extending of his earlier study.[9] Such research was very much done out of personal interest, pursued part-time as Peter earned his livelihood from his business interests. Indeed, at that time a career in academic life seemed unlikely; when I left Liverpool for the University at Leicester, it seemed that we would be following careers in different fields. But in 1964 the tutorship in economic history became vacant. Peter was, of course, *in situ* as a senior post-graduate student, and Francis Hyde offered him the post. Peter's acceptance commenced a staff tenure he was to hold for a quarter-century and beyond, and brought him closer to Hyde and Marriner, who now became colleagues, close friends and confidantes. In particular, Peter gave enormous and increasingly vital practical support to Francis Hyde, whose vision problems were worsening. Their daily journeys between West Kirby and Abercromby Square (happily now by car) were a source of enjoyment to both. Peter gained immeasurably from Francis's expertise and approach to business and history--a debt acknowledged in many of Peter's own studies. Peter's appointment to the tutorship marked the beginning of a steady progression through the ranks of lecturing staff to a distinguished readership in 1987 and a personal chair in 1991. Along with this progression and an ever-increasing academic commitment came a shift in the balance of his interests between university and business activity; although he was never to abandon his commercial interests, his daily involvement was substantially reduced. And no wonder, for Peter's academic career involved a major expenditure of time and intellectual effort on both the administrative and research fronts. His ability to serve as head of department for a decade in the most difficult of

---

[9]P.N. Davies, "British Shipping and the Growth of the West African Economy, 1910-1950" (Unpublished Ph.D. thesis, University of Liverpool, 1968).

contexts, as well as sitting on a gamut of Senate committees, while simultaneously producing a whole clutch of important studies, reflects his enormous input and output. Peter Mathias' eloquent tribute and the full bibliography elsewhere in this volume testify to the extent of Peter's commitment, industry and achievement.

This *festschrift*, however, is much more than an appreciation of excellence in research and administration. While comprising a collection of significant studies reflecting many of Peter's research interests, this volume is very much a tribute to someone who commands not merely respect for his achievement but, even more so, respect as a person.

In viewing Peter's career over the past twenty-five years there are many features on which comment might be made. One observation is that his entire career has been within the department at Liverpool and effectively he has lived his entire life on Merseyside. Such an observation might suggest a sedentary disposition and limited outlook. Nothing could be further from the truth. Peter is an inveterate traveller, and visits abroad for research and pleasure have been a constant feature of his career and lifestyle. Indeed, a porter at the department, frustrated at fending off enquiries while Peter was away, took to referring to him as Marco Polo! Peter's travels have taken him around the world, but particularly to North America, Africa, the Canaries and the Far East, where his many visits have included posts as visiting professor at the universities of Musashi and Hiroshima Shudo. Such travels have enabled Peter to develop a world-wide circle of contacts, almost all of whom he would describe as friends. And yet enormously widely-travelled though he is, it would hardly be correct to describe him as cosmopolitan. For all his love of visiting new places and meeting new people, Peter is never really far away from home. All who have travelled with him will be familiar not merely with the regular telephone calls to home and department, but with the ubiquitous radio tuned to the BBC World Service in pursuit of news, football and cricket scores. Peter's lifestyle, and even more significantly his values, is firmly and soberly rooted in his Liverpool base of family, friends and department. The security of such a solid domestic and academic base--from which one can journey out but always return to--is perhaps one of the great elements of Peter's success. Few can have achieved such an effective marriage of the local and the international.

That Peter has travelled so widely in great measure reflects the subject and character of his research. Peter's scholarship has always had an international dimension. Primarily, though not exclusively, his work has been on the history of shipping companies and merchant houses, mostly Liverpool-based, which developed interests overseas. Such studies if they are to be done well are not to be embarked on lightly. "The writing of business history is a hazardous occupation," wrote Hyde in 1962.[10] And indeed it is, not least because a focus on decision-making and investment policy involves the need to get beyond the consideration of time, place and context and to consider the thought processes of the individual entrepreneur. Yet for all the hazards, Peter, introduced to the discipline through his Master's thesis and his close relationship with Hyde, has produced a series of impressive studies, notably of Elder Dempster, Tyrer, and Fyffes. In so doing he has continued the tradition and enhanced the reputation of what is sometimes termed the "Liverpool School of Business History."[11] Yet while Peter has been a significant practitioner of the art of the business historian and served for a time on the Editorial Board of *Business History*,[12] he has not been directly associated with the development and promotion of that discipline--an expansion which has seen the establishment of numerous centres of business history in the past two decades. Rather, Peter has lent his energies and experience to another growth area of historical study, maritime history, which has undergone enormous development in recent years. In terms of the number of active researchers, the nature of research, the establishment of new museums and centres of maritime studies, the creation of new

[10]F.E. Hyde, "Economic Theory and Business History," *Business History*, V, No. 1 (December 1962), 1.

[11]The items cited in the footnotes of Professor Mathias's tribute effectively summarise the output of the Liverpool School.

[12]An initiative of the Liverpool School, the first issue of *Business History*, with Hyde as Editor, appeared in 1958.

specialist journals and organisations and perhaps, above all, in the great growth of contact and exchange of ideas between historians in all parts of the world, the last decade and a half has marked a veritable explosion in maritime history. The causes of this are varied, and the individuals who have participated and contributed to it many. But there can be no doubt that Peter, in all sorts of important ways, has been a significant participant in this major development.

In terms of research, apart from his company histories, his major study of Japanese shipping and shipbuilding (with Professor Tomohei Chida) and a host of published papers represent a highly-valued contribution to the literature. Again, his active participation (including diver's certificate) in Nautical Archaeology in the Mersey and North Wales areas, undertaken when that branch of study was still in its relative infancy, testify to his breadth of interest and foresight. The recent discovery of the Alabama, a vessel with a strong Birkenhead connection, has served to revive this early interest. Further, in a Merseyside context, Professor Mathias has already noted Peter's role in assuring the academic dimension of the hugely successful Merseyside Maritime Museum. Such initiatives, albeit based very much in Peter's home territory, were of international significance. Indeed, Peter in the last few years has played an essential role in the international promotion and organisation of maritime history. Long a member of the British Commission for Maritime History, he assumed the Chairmanship in 1989, and a year later was elected to the office of senior Vice-President of the International Commission. More especially, in 1986 it was he, along with his distinguished colleague, Professor Keiichiro Nakagawa, who conceived and convened a special maritime history session at the Ninth International Congress of Economic History in Berne, Switzerland. That meeting led to the establishment of the "Maritime Economic History Group" and its influential *Newsletter*. These proved to be the respective parents of the International Maritime Economic History Association and the innovative *Journal of Maritime History,* now well into its fourth year of successful publication. Fittingly, when the Association was created, Peter was elected its first President. The tenure of such positions of influence and responsibility reflects many things. It represents a recognition of achievement and a vital contribution made. It reveals Peter's continuing dedication and enormous commitment. Above all it testifies to the view of colleagues the world over that Peter is someone in whom they can wholeheartedly place their trust and reliance. Peter Mathias opens his eloquent tribute with the observation that "every Society and Association needs a person who is always there...a stalwart and an anchor for any endeavour." Fortunate indeed is maritime history; more fortunate still are all who count themselves as Peter's colleagues and friends. In part this volume, like any *festschrift*, bears witness to a scholar's achievement. This book, however, represents far more, and in saluting the man and his work, all who have known Peter will have no doubts about the priority.

It is appropriate that the presentation of this volume should be made in Liverpool on the occasion of the First International Congress of Maritime History, a Congress hosted and organised by bodies with which Peter is intimately associated--the University of Liverpool, the Merseyside Maritime Museum, the International Maritime Economic History Association and the International Commission for Maritime History. All are in Peter's debt. But, better still perhaps, it is fitting that the presentation should be made at a gathering of Peter's family, friends and colleagues where he will be left in no doubt as to the warmth of affection and the esteem in which he is held.

Do Docks Make Trade?: The Case of the Port of Great Grimsby

Gordon Jackson

The British coastline is littered with long-lost ports; here and there a "new" one tests the water. Compared with past performance--and ignoring deep-water quays--most of the old major ports are dying or dead. Harwich, Felixstowe and Dover have taken their places, partly because of changes in composition of trade; partly because of shifts in its direction; and partly because of the entrepreneurial skills of those building new ports. Much is made of the importance of port facilities,[1] but historical evidence would seem to show that these are less important than total transport networks and mercantile connections, which constantly change. The purpose of this paper is to trace the relationship between various influences on the rise, fall, rise, fall and rise of the port of Great Grimsby since 1796. It seems appropriate in this volume to consider the "trade-makers" in one of the English ports about which Peter Davies has written.[2]

"A Port of Very Great Moment:" Grimsby Haven Company, 1786-1846

The basis for the construction of Grimsby Haven was, according to Arthur Young, "a speculation, if they succeed, of rivalling Hull as the chief port of the Humber."[3] A more unlikely rival to Hull does not spring readily to mind. A port of some standing in the Middle Ages, Grimsby was a place of ill-repute by the eighteenth century, her only

[1]For instance, see J. Bird, *The Major Seaports of the United Kingdom* (London, 1963), and G. Jackson, *History and Archaeology of Ports* (Tadworth, 1983).

[2]P.N. Davies, *John Sutcliffe & Son: A History of the Company, 1862-1987* (Grimsby, 1987).

[3]Arthur Young, *General View of the Agriculture of Lincolnshire* (London, 1799), 407.

trade in Parliamentary votes, on which too many of her inhabitants depended.[4] In short, it was a dismal place that John Wesley found "no bigger than a middling village, containing a small number of half-starved inhabitants, without any trade, either foreign or domestic."[5]

The new port of Grimsby did not spring from contemporary trade, nor was it planned by merchants or welcomed by shipowners, for both were strangers there. The only factor distinguishing this "rotten borough" from the normal run of small market towns was two members of Parliament, in whose support local men of influence could vent their spleen or build prestige. It was their conflicting interests that stimulated change.[6]

The Parliamentary seats--like much of the borough property--were shared between the Claytons, a Grimsby family which had made money in London trade, and the Pelhams of Brocklesby, leading north Lincolnshire landowners. In 1774, however, the Pelham faction exerted itself to the point of capturing both seats in three successive elections, leaving George Tennyson, legatee of the Claytons, to revive its flagging influence in the borough.[7] The haven scheme was conceived during the ensuing struggle between Tennyson and Charles Anderson Pelham, first Baron Yarborough, when Jonathan Pickernell of Whitby secretly prepared plans for new port which were announced in 1788 in the names of Tennyson's candidates for the next election. Although Tennyson did not secure a seat in 1790 the haven scheme proved popular with north Lincolnshire landowners; for the benefit of their town and country estates, Tennyson and Yarborough shared the two

---

[4]The early history, decline, and corruption of the old borough is admirably told in E. Gillett, *History of Grimsby* (London, 1970).

[5]J. Wesley, *Journal* (4 vols., reprint, London, 1930), III, 251-252, April 1766.

[6]For a detailed examination of the political context, and further references, see G. Jackson, *Grimsby and the Haven Company, 1796-1846* (Grimsby, 1971), chapter 1, and "The Claytons of Grimsby: Local Trade and Politics in the Eighteenth and Early Nineteenth Centuries," *Lincolnshire History and Archaeology*, IX (1974), 43-51.

[7]Three Tennysons married Clayton heiresses, and almost all of both families' property passed to George Tennyson.

seats in the 1796 election, and Tennyson's candidate became chairman of the Grimsby Haven Company which was formed in that year.

The Haven Company might serve as a classic example of landowners pouring money into transport facilities designed to cater for the growing trade of the industrial revolution, though in truth they thought more of diverting trade from Hull than creating their own, a possibility that drew speedy reaction from citizens of the latter where, according to one of the few Hull merchants supporting the Haven Company, "they now begin to apprehend the consequences of Grimsby being a port may be very fatal to the town of Hull."[8] In fact the Grimsby people had no knowledge of trade or ports, simply assuming that a dock would attract trade with no effort on their part, encouraged by the silly if comforting advice from "intelligent friends" in London that "if accommodations are provided, they will not want custom."[9] Uncontrolled enthusiasm produced grandiose plans and general confusion. Pickernell's "port of very great moment" envisaged a massive dock only three acres smaller than all the nation's docks together, with more quay space than London, and costing £125,000.[10] A whittled-down plan still proposed the biggest dock in Britain for around £50,000. Since it was not easy to attract investment of that magnitude in a port without trade, George Babb, clerk of both the town and the Haven Company, whose morals were as devious as his bookkeeping, overstated the returns and understated the cost. In consequence, the 1796 Act authorised insufficient capital (£30,000) even for Pickernell's

---

[8]Grimsby Central Library (GCL), Babb Papers, J.S. Brandstrom, Hull, to George Babb, Haven Company clerk, 6 April 1796. The mayor of Hull had just warned the Dock Company that the Grimsby plans would be "seriously injurious" to the interests of the town; Hull Guildhall, Box 9, No. 5, Sir S. Standidge to Hull Dock Company, 15 March 1796.

[9]Scunthorpe Borough Museum (SBM), Diary of Rev. Dr. J. Parkinson, 23 September 1800.

[10]GCL, Tennyson Papers, J. Pickernell to Alderman S. Parker, 6 November 1787.

less expensive plan. In short, the project was already out of control, reflecting the amateur status of the company's leaders.[11]

The plan was simple. A lock at the high water mark would impound the haven, providing a dock (five hundred yards by one hundred yards and eighteen-feet deep) and a fourteen-foot channel from the end of the dock to the old town, over a mile from high water. Since "any man of common sense without pretending to be an engineer must see in a moment that half [the designs] are superfluous,"[12] Pickernell was dismissed on demanding fees, and supervision passed to a local man of common sense, Alderman Lusby, who failing to excavate mud faster than it collapsed, begged for a proper engineer before it was too late. When John Rennie was appointed in 1798, he solved the problem of how to construct a sea lock on mud, sand and "greasy substance"--a crucial issue in most east coast ports--by floating it on a raft and using "hollow walls," apparently for the first time.[13] Though escalating costs caused the dock to be reduced, the overall scheme was something of which the company might be proud as it looked forward to its own and the town's prosperity.

The first decade of the nineteenth century was exhilarating in Grimsby. Ships once more tied-up within the ancient strand and men of substance walked the streets. Merchants newly arrived from Hull were welcomed with open arms. Brandstrom and Kusel spent £10,000 on "Iron Wharf," and Knox and Hay about half that sum on "Free Port Wharf."[14] Two whaling companies were established. There were less ambitious plans, but the chief intent was to import timber--a speculative venture during the French wars--for north Lincolnshire, or miscel-

---

[11]"Babb calls an oath nothing more than kissing a calf's skin"; SBM, Parkinson, 23 September 1800.

[12]GCL, Tennyson Papers, copy, Babb to Pickernell, 1 September 1796.

[13]C.T.G. Boucher, *John Rennie* (Manchester, 1963), 48-49. In the haven the local yokels--"we are enjineers [sic] in our turn"--still behaved much as they chose; Jackson, *Haven Company*, 18-21.

[14]Jackson, *Haven Company*, 34-38.

laneous goods with greater privacy and price-fixing than was possible in Hull. These and other schemes earned no fortunes and were soon forgotten: timber stores were better placed in Gainsborough on the Trent,[15] and Hull was infinitely better placed to serve the Humber tributaries. The result was predictable: such was the "great deficiency in sea trade" by 1819 that people deserted the dock area "almost like wild fire or as removing from a contagious disease."[16] The Haven Company discovered the hard way that a dock, no matter how good, does not make a port.

Table 1
Vessels Entering and Clearing Grimsby in Foreign Trade
(Five-yearly averages)

	Entrances			Clearances		
Years	No. of Ships	Total Tons	Average Tonnage	No. of Ships	Total Tons	Average Tonnage
1805-09	41.6	9,504	228.5	6.0	1,188.4	198.1
1815-19	50.2	7,397	147.4	9.4	1,010.8	107.5
1825-29	105.6	12,024	113.9	5.6	864.6	154.4
1844-45	50.5	8,881	175.9	18.0	3,346.0	185.9

Sources: 1805-1809: Kings Beam House, Customs 94/22, 214; 1815-1829: Grimsby Custom House statistics quoted in "Report of Commissioners on Municipal Corporations," Great Britain, *Parliamentary Papers* (*BPP*), 1835, XXVI, 2255; 1844: *BPP*, 1845 (206), XLVII, 287; 1845: *BPP*, 1846 (155), XLV, 307; Jackson, *Haven Company*, 92-93.

Customs statistics confirm this view (see table 1). Grimsby attracted less than ten thousand tons of shipping per annum--on average one vessel per week--until the 1820s, when a major

[15]*Ibid.*, 38-42; I.S. Beckwith, "The River Trade of Gainsborough, 1500-1850," *Lincolnshire History and Archaeology*, II (1967).

[16]Jackson, *Haven Company*, 43-46; GCL, Tennyson Papers, J. Squire, Haven Company clerk, to Tennyson, 23 January 1819.

refurbishment was undertaken which itself demanded a large importation of wood. Nonetheless, the haven continued to decay and tonnage entering in 1844-1845 was lower than in 1805-1809. Exports failed to materialise. Coastal trade was depressingly slight. Between 1813 and 1832 an average of twenty-five coasters (1582 tons) entered the port, and sixty (3522 tons) cleared; in 1844-1846 only thirty-seven (2077 tons) cleared. In such circumstances there was little encouragement for "local" shipowners, whose vessels fell steadily from a peak of around ninety-six (4136 tons) in 1816 to forty-nine (1872 tons) in 1827. By 1846 only thirty-six vessels (1321 tons), most of which were Cleethorpes' fishing boats, remained on the register.[17]

With little trade, few ships and almost no industry, the port of Grimsby was a failure. The rude awakening from pleasant dreams was more dreadful because the harsh reality of decay was so obvious at every turn. The company made an operating profit of only £250 in the first decade of its poverty-stricken existence, and if owners of its worthless shares had ever worked out how much they might have expected their investment to yield elsewhere, they would have found that, allowing five percent compound interest, the haven works had cost upwards of half a million pounds before they received a penny. They could survive on their agricultural incomes, but the merchants went bankrupt or returned to Hull. The general population, which had risen from 1524 in 1801 to 2747 in 1811, as young men sought their livelihoods and raised their families, stagnated from 1819. Unemployment was one of the problems declared to the Municipal Corporations Enquiry in 1833, when Grimsby was running counter to the demographic trend in neighbouring market towns. By 1841 one in ten of the population had fled, and one in eight of the houses was empty.

The failure of Grimsby was virtually unavoidable. The Haven Company was an ill-conceived speculation resting on gross ignorance of commercial realities. A dock may encourage existing trade but it was foolish to lavish too much investment on potential trade before its

[17]Registrations for 1813-1827 were taken from Public Record Office (PRO), Customs 36/5, Shipping Accounts. The data for 1846 came from *BPP*, 1847 (588), LX, 139; Jackson, *Haven Company*, 95.

likelihood was fully explored. Hull, with better connections, shipping and wealth, stood between Grimsby and industrial England; north Lincolnshire lacked significant population and produced neither manufactures nor large food surpluses. In fact, as early as 1800 one of the more perceptive shareholders had forecast disaster and its cause: there was, he said, "no communication as at Hull with the country behind."[18] But by then it was too late for second thoughts.

"The Most Eligible Port of the East Coast:" The Railway Port, c. 1850-1914

To a port with no hinterland the railway boom of the 1840s had much to offer. If a dock alone could not create a port, surely a dock and railway combined would do the trick. The new Sheffield, Ashton-under-Lyne and Manchester Railway Company proposed in March 1844 to extend its influence to Gainsborough on the Trent, which had just been made a "port." But the threat of rivals building to the sea coincided with approaches from Lord Yarborough and the Haven Company, and in October the subsidiary Great Grimsby and Sheffield Junction Railway Company (GG&SJR) was formed under the chairmanship of Lord Worsley, Yarborough's son. It immediately began negotiations with the Haven Company (also chaired by Worsley) which, after half a century of poverty, agreed on 5 August 1845 to transfer its property and rights to the railway's Grimsby Dock Company in return for £100,000 in Dock shares and payment of all debts. In July 1846 the various companies merged to form the Manchester, Sheffield and Lincolnshire Railway Company (MS&L), of which Lord Yarborough, the third largest shareholder, became chairman.[19]

---

[18]SBM, Parkinson, 23 September 1800. On 31 December 1801 he returned to this theme: "There is but a confined tract of country behind Grimsby to trade with it."

[19]Details from PRO, Rail, GSS/1/2, Minutes of Meetings, GG&SJR; HDC/1/2, Minutes of Meetings, Directors, Grimsby Haven Company, MSL/1/63, Minutes of Board of MS&L, Grimsby Docks sub-committee. In general see G. Dow, *Great Central* (2 vols., London, 1959), I, 20, 90-93, chapters IX and XIII; Gillett, *History of Grimsby*, chapter xiv; Jackson, *Haven Company*, 51-53.

The men of MS&L were no less enthusiastic than the innkeepers of Grimsby or the landowners of the Haven Company, both of whom stood to gain from railway and urban development. "The docks," reported the Directors of GG&SJR in August 1845, "will undoubtedly make Grimsby the best steam packet and mercantile harbour and shipping port on the Eastern coast: and its importance in this respect, both to Lancashire and the West Riding of Yorkshire, cannot be too highly estimated."[20] The prospectus of the new Dock Company, having blamed past failures on "the want of an internal communication," was sure that "the proposed additional dock accommodation cannot fail to render it by far the most eligible port of the east coast," and Samuel Sidney's *Railway and Agriculture of Lincolnshire* claimed that "after examining these works, and a railway map including not only England, but the opposite shores of the German Ocean, it was impossible to doubt that railway enterprise would make Grimsby a great corn market and a great seaport."[21] It would become "the Hull...of the district." Sidney also expected the railway to stimulate a deep-sea fishery, which of course it did.

Royal Dock, designed by J.M. Rendel (who also built at Birkenhead) was of quite a different order from the old haven, reflecting recent advances in both civil engineering and steam transport. To avoid silting and to reach deep water for large steamers, the dock projected three-quarters of a mile on about 138 acres of enclosed mud flats, and its entrance was constructed behind the largest coffer-dam yet constructed (1500 feet by thirty-two feet), which used ten thousand piles and alone took two years to build.[22] The dock was

---

[20]PRO, Rail, GSS/1/2, 27 August 1845.

[21]B. Lincoln, *The Rise of Grimsby* (2 vols., London, 1913), I, 230; S. Sidney, *Railways and Agriculture in North Lincolnshire* (London, 1848), 24-25.

[22]C. Neate, "Description of the Coffer-Dam at Great Grimsby," *Minutes of the Proceedings of the Institution of Civil Engineers,* IX (1849), 1-23.

as grand as the preparations.[23] Two locks (three hundred by seventy feet and two hundred by forty-five feet) admitted the largest and smallest vessels without wasting time and water, and as a supreme piece of bravado Rendel placed between them his three hundred-foot Hydraulic Tower, holding 147 tons of water, thus showing the world his confidence in his foundations: he had built a house on sand--and it still stands. The tower, designed as an Italianate campanile, was also a superb advertisement for the port. To passing ships it proclaimed Grimsby's advantage: "When a steamer can run into a port as soon as it makes land, and can transfer its cargo to railway waggons, that cargo may be delivered 150 miles off before another steamer can grope its way up the intricate navigation of a river at night."[24] To the world at large the tower was the symbol of modernity: Armstrong's new hydraulic machinery was the first effective power for dock work.

Once again Grimsby had built a fine piece of engineering, years ahead of Hull's Victoria Dock. For approximately £1,050,000 MS&L got a dock of twenty acres, plus a tidal basin of fifteen acres, a five acre timber pond, and some 3600 feet of quay served, like the warehouses, by rail and hydraulic cranes. When it opened in May 1852 the church bells rang, Sunday Schools processed, the poor feasted, and some six thousand people lined the quay to sing "Rule Britannia." But half-way up the Dock Tower flapped a banner born of experience: SHIPS WANTED.[25] Much would depend on the response.

The history of the Haven Company had shown that a dock of whatever quality does not of itself make a port. The shortcoming had been identified periodically as inadequate "back-carriage," which railways would now provide. But was it so simple? The basic question was whether trade grew by itself once internal communications allowed inland manufacturers to deal with a port, or was made by entrepreneurs within the port providing further services--such as shipping--

---

[23]E. H. Clark, "Description of the Great Grimsby (Royal) Docks," *ibid.*, XXIV (1865), 38-61.

[24]W. White, *Directory of Lincolnshire* (Sheffield, 1856), 574.

[25]Lincoln, *Rise of Grimsby*, I, 311.

without which development could not occur. The essence of railway port operation was to link trains and steamers by adequate, efficient port facilities, and though MS&L owned the railway and dock--one better than the Haven Company--there were still doubts about the third essential component. Early high-cost steamers were generally worked as liners from their home ports where high utilisation was assured, and exogenous shipping--whether steam or sail--was not easily attracted to new ports which could not offer good cargoes in both directions.

MS&L fully understood the importance of regular steamers, and before the dock opened had negotiated with North of Europe Steamship Company for weekly runs to Hamburg and Rotterdam in return for a guaranteed five percent profit.[26] Their seven hundred-ton *City of Norwich* opened the dock, and left with cottons and coal within twelve hours, a turnaround time fully expected to bring impatient shipping from Hull. As a further inducement, dues were initially half those of Hull,[27] and occasionally much lower. In 1858, for instance, Brownlow and Pearson of Hull reckoned their S.S. *Leopard* paid dues of £52 in Hull, £33 in London and a mere £2 in Grimsby. Outward charges for identical goods bound for Russia were said to be £25 in Hull and £16 in Grimsby.[28] It was a persuasive argument in favour of Grimsby, and Hull shipowners responded fairly quickly to the assurance of outward cargoes and the demand for imports via MS&L rails. Already by 1855 five Hull shipping companies had established agencies in Grimsby and arranged for their ships to call there occasionally, while the ill-fated Z.C. Pearson set up the Grimsby and Baltic Steamship Company with half a dozen vessels running to Konigsberg and Copenhagen. There were even hopes of establishing lines to Genoa, Leghorn, Constantinople, and Amsterdam: "It is only

---

[26]Dow, *Great Central*, I, 175-176.

[27]PRO, Rail, GDC/1/2, 30 October 1845.

[28]Lincoln, *Rise of Grimsby*, I, 356.

the want of shipping which at present exists," said Lord Yarborough, "that prevents us doing so."[29]

It was this continuing "want of shipping"--despite the use of Hull vessels--that persuaded MS&L to enter the shipping market, establishing the subsidiary Anglo-French Steamship Company in 1856 in partnership with the South Yorkshire Railway Company and a group of French coal merchants, led by Hippolyte Worms, who already had extensive interests in Cardiff and Newcastle. Although its name and connections implied a close interest in the French coal trade, the company was from the start intended "for the advantage of the general continental merchandise trade," and was immediately involved in the latter when North of Europe withdrew from Grimsby on a day's notice in August 1856, thus exemplifying the danger of over-reliance on an external shipping line.[30] Although Anglo-French bought nine steamers, averaging 350 tons, between 1855 and 1857, they were gradually lost or sold--as were Pearson's--until in 1862 there were only six left in the port.[31] In 1859, steamers made only ninety-one voyages from Grimsby, though this compared well with Goole's eighty-two, and creditably with Hull's 536.[32]

Not surprisingly, Hull shipowners lost interest in Grimsby as their own port made increasing demands on their services. In 1864 MS&L, admitting the inability of local commercial interests to provide adequate vessels, obtained an Act of Parliament to purchase its own steamers, starting, appropriately, with *Lincoln, Leeds, Wakefield, Bradford, Sheffield* and *Stockport* in 1866, followed by *Grimsby, Huddersfield, Halifax* and *Barnsley* in the early 1870s. It also bought Anglo-French's four surviving steamers, and appointed John Sutcliffe,

---

[29]Quoted in White, *Directory*, 576.

[30]Prospectus, quoted in *ibid.*; Dow, *Great Central*, I, 176.

[31]Shipping details from Shipping Registers, Custom House, Grimsby.

[32]*BPP*, 1860 (351), LX, 443. For Goole in general see B.F. Duckham, *The Yorkshire Ouse* (Newton Abbot, 1967); for Hull, see J. Bellamy, *Trade and Shipping of Nineteenth Century Hull* (York, 1971).

who had come from Hartlepool in 1862 to manage Anglo-French's fleet, as its shipping agent. Three local steam enterprises,[33] and two independent ventures by Sutcliffe (who was the only substantial sailing ship owner), were either short-lived or completely insignificant. Apart from MS&L, the only shipowner of note was Hough, Laws and Surtees of North Shields, who introduced nine steamers to the port between 1866 and 1874. They, too, gradually lost interest, and by 1886 all their ships had gone. Once again it was left to MS&L to fill the gap with another six steamers in 1883-1886, enabling the firm to run four times weekly to Hamburg. It should be emphasised, however, that Grimsby had found its niche in the near-European trades in which a few regular steamers could do a massive amount of work; capital support for long-haul trades was completely beyond the local community. It is also worth emphasising the role of a small number of shipping agents, of whom John Sutcliffe and Son was the most prominent. Here was a real trade-maker, with widespread connections in the hinterland and on the continent, building MS&L's Hamburg, Rotterdam and Antwerp trade, "a large portion of which," he claimed, "I have been instrumental in bringing to the port."[34] A little later he was extending connections to the Atlantic, dabbling in emigration, and persuading the Hamburg Amerika Line to call at Grimsby on the way to the West Indies.

The 1870s were years of relative stagnation for tonnage using the port, followed by steady growth in the 1880s and 1890s and a massive upward surge between 1900 and 1913 (see table 2). Provision for growth in the 1880s came partly from the new MS&L vessels, partly from a large number of foreign sailing vessels bringing in timber and taking away coal, and partly by the efforts of MS&L to attract other lines with good facilities and more or less guaranteed cargoes.[35] In 1889 Jack Sutcliffe persuaded Thomas Wilson and Sons to divert some of its huge fleet for a weekly service to Copenhagen and Malmo,

[33]Grimsby Steam Shipping Company (1871), Grimsby and London Trading Company (1881) and Grimsby and London Steam Shipping Company.

[34]Quoted in Davies, *Sutcliffe*, 20.

[35]Dow, *Great Central*, II, chapter 8.

followed by routes to Drammen in 1890 and Gothenburg in 1892. In 1890 the Danish United Steamship Company (DFDS) established an Esbjerg service--twice-weekly from 1897--which has remained one of the most consistent of Grimsby's regular trades. Finally, in the 1890s MS&L again stimulated activity by adding another four steamers to the Hamburg and Antwerp services when it was discovered that goods carried by rail from Grimsby to Liverpool arrived in America several days earlier than those shipped directly from the Europe to New York.

Table 2
Tonnage of Vessels Entering Grimsby, 1867-1913
(Averages, '000 tons)

1867-9	285	1890-4	720
1870-4	384	1895-9	869
1875-9	393	1900-4	903
1880-4	463	1905-9	1225
1885-9	565	1910-13	1703

Sources: Great Britain, Parliament, Parliamentary Papers, *Annual Statements of Trade and Navigation*, various years.

Despite this promising "outside" interest, during the 1880s and 1890s there was only one hopeful sign of the development of local shipping, when Henry and Joseph Bennett, the leading timber merchants, began buying steamers in 1887. Altogether they bought thirteen between 1887 and 1906, far larger than MS&L steamers at an average of 1989 tons net and 3065 gross, but by 1903 they had only three or four left and it was again left to MS&L--or, rather, its successor, the Great Central Railway Company (GCR)--to build fifteen steamers to service the great trade boom in the pre-war years.

Grimsby had found that in the absence of a wealthy and established trading community "local" shipping must also be provided by the port-owning authority. As W.H. Bartholomew, chief engineer at Goole, said of MS&L in 1906, "They own the Grimsby docks, and they got those powers [to run steamers] because they had... pretty well shown that without those powers the docks could not fully develop."[36]

It is clear from Table 2 that enough endogenous or exogenous ships were introduced to the port to sustain a rise in active tonnage that eventually justified the hopes of MS&L for its docks. There was initially a much greater rise in the value of exports, from £1 million in 1853-1860 to £19 million in 1872. Thereafter declining international prices halved the value of exports until the end of the century, though volume, and consequently shipping and port activities, were unaffected. In contrast to the situation in Hull, Grimsby's export trade was always more valuable than her import trade, reflecting a greater ability to ship abroad goods sold by manufacturers and handled by agents than to import raw materials or foodstuffs requiring an extensive port-based distribution and sales network. The total value of trade is only meaningful in comparative terms, and the status of Grimsby is best seen in context of the Humber. Total trade in 1913 was worth £37.9 million, roughly double that of Goole but half that of Hull. Grimsby had made her mark as a major port, and amply justified the pride MS&L and GCR took in their achievement, which comes out in *Per Rail*,[37] one of the best of all railway publicity ventures.

The goods constituting the bulk of Grimsby's imports and exports were similar to those of Goole and Hull, though there were important differences. Grimsby had a far better performance in textiles, with the result that the leading items--textiles, machinery, metals and coal--comprised ninety-seven percent of exports by value in 1865, ninety percent from 1870 to 1895 and about eighty percent thereafter. Wool and woollens were by far the most important exports until the late 1870s, when they were surpassed by cotton. Though there was some slight depression in textiles in the 1880s and 1890s, both yarn and cloth more or less doubled in volume between 1890 and 1913, when textiles made up two-thirds of exports. The MS&L link with Manchester was perfect for the north European cotton trade, and it

[36]*Royal Commission on Canals and Inland Navigations*, 1906 (3184), q 3404.

[37]Anon., *Per Rail* (London, 1913), 75-118.

was a matter of some local pride that Grimsby quickly overtook Goole's exportation of woollens, despite the latter's close connections with Leeds. Even more exhilarating was the passing of Hull in woollen exports by 1870. The same inverse trends are found in cottons, until by 1910 Grimsby's exports were almost double those of Hull. Remaining exports were of marginal importance. Agricultural machinery was the principal item in 1860, chiefly threshing machines from Lincoln and engines from Gainsborough, but Grimsby lost out to Hull, chiefly because the lack of open quay space created difficulties in loading large machines.

Coal was never very important in value--at its height in 1913 it represented only ten percent of the total--but it was undoubtedly the chief commodity as far as the physical attributes of the port were concerned, and exerted an influence out of all proportion to its value. In the 1860s Grimsby shipped a mere seventy thousand tons of coal per annum, and some 300,000 tons in the 1870s and 1880s. By 1890 the half million-ton mark was passed, a million tons by the turn of the century, and almost three million by 1913. The rise of the trade was attributed in 1859 to the low dues compared with Hull, and the latter's inadequate facilities for handling coal, but in the end Hull managed to hold her own against Grimsby, despite the latter's easy connections with the South Yorkshire and Nottingham/Derby coalfields. It was simply the case that coal from the north of the field went to Hull, that from the south to Grimsby.[38] Goole had what was left--about half of Grimsby's total in 1913.

The coal trade, more perhaps than any other, had a pronounced effect on the destination of ships leaving Grimsby. The Anglo-French Company was formed chiefly to ship coal to France, and as late as 1870 that country received more ships from Grimsby than any other, followed by Germany, Russia, Holland and Belgium. By the turn of the century, however, the near-European trade had fallen relatively (and the French trade absolutely) as the Baltic countries drew increasingly

---

[38]Hull Guildhall, Papers Relating to 1859 Dock Bill, Evidence of A. Bannister; "Select Committee on Humber Commercial Railway & Dock Bill," 1904, evidence of F.P. Rhodes, q 282.

on the Yorkshire coalfields.[39] The rising trade with the Baltic (eighty-seven thousand tons in 1870 and 1,048,000 in 1913) indicates the extent to which Grimsby infiltrated Hull's special area of interest, but her trade was wider than this--certainly wider than Goole's. Egypt became a customer in the 1870s; South Africa in the 1880s; Spain and the Mediterranean in the 1890s; and by 1913 some seven percent of tonnage went to India, Japan and the Far East, while roughly one ship a fortnight went to Australia, carrying on a trade begun by the appropriately named *Anthracite* in 1853. By 1913 there were no continents and few countries that had not at some time welcomed coal from Grimsby.

Timber was to imports as coal was to exports--immensely bulky, employing many ships, yet accounting for less than ten percent of trade value. The first major expansion came in the 1870s, but the total remained around 275,000 loads per annum until the present century, when it rose rapidly to 420,000 loads, worth £1.1 million, in 1913. Despite its relatively low value, this was the trade that brought most money to the town, for timber was still a commodity in which local merchants--in the true meaning of that phrase--could participate. Sir Henry Bennett was the leader in the field, working in partnership with Joseph Bennett in Louth, who is said to have started the business in 1845 by adapting the family's bone-crushing mill to the milling of sleepers for the new railway and dock works. Other firms followed, including Joseph Chapman and Joseph Hewson, who combined in 1896 and with whom Jack Sutcliffe, with a finger in most economic pies, was associated.[40]

So important was timber that the chief suppliers, Sweden and Russia, were indisputably the chief sources of shipping in the early days. The situation changed, however, as other trades emerged.

---

[39]Near-Europe and the Baltic (including Denmark) took respectively fifty-eight and thirty percent of the shipping leaving Grimsby in 1870, forty-six and forty-two percent in 1890 and thirty-four and fifty-two percent in 1913. Details of trade in the nineteenth and twentieth centuries are taken from the *Annual Statements of Trade and Navigation* and other published Customs returns.

[40]Anon., *Grimsby Official Guide* (London, n.d.), 169, 181.

Australian wool came home in the colliers, and wool and yarn was imported in sufficiently large quantities from Germany to constitute sixteen to nineteen percent of total imports by value in 1900. Germany became the chief source of imports, sending almost a third of the total shipping entering the port in 1913. Almost as important was the developing trade with Denmark and Belgium which, with Germany and Russia, sent the provisions which Grimsby shared with Goole and Hull. Butter, of slight importance until 1880, was soon the most valuable item, representing a quarter of the total in 1910 as Grimsby cemented her close links with Esbjerg. Butter, bacon, eggs, margarine and sugar together contributed a third of imports from the 1890s to 1913. On the other hand, Grimsby made almost no progress with imported fruit and vegetables: the market was well-established in Hull and stayed there. Nor did Grimsby attract many of the meat and wheat trades, although Marshall's mill was adapted for Indian wheat when the first cargoes arrived in 1876, and sufficient barley arrived from the Baltic and Black Seas for W. Soames to style himself as the largest maltster in Britain.[41]

As the European and American trades developed, imports increasingly became industrial goods rather than raw materials. Some had the ancient intricacy of musical instruments, toys, clocks and glass, silks, embroidery and fine leather goods that had always been imported. Others were the sort of things that had once been Britain's monopoly. Metals and machinery were four percent of imports in 1895 and nine percent in 1913, when machinery alone was worth £328,000. Swedish bar iron, always in great demand, had the added attraction of ballasting timber ships and "stiffened" the barges that carried a quarter of Grimsby's traffic upriver into the canal system.[42] The raw cotton trade never grew, despite early shipments from Mobile and Alexandria and the construction of a special warehouse, but cotton yarn and manufactures comprised four percent of imports in 1895 and eleven

---

[41] *Ibid.*, 187; "Select Committee on the Humber Commercial Dock," evidence of J. Pickwell, q 3033.

[42] *Ibid.*, evidence of T. Marston, q 2487. At both Goole and Hull, fifty percent of traffic was water-borne; qq 2481, 2488.

percent by 1910. Grimsby, like Hull and Goole, was beginning to receive industrial goods from both directions. It might be the beginning of a grand exchange of industrial goods that would benefit the port--or a portent of industrial self-sufficiency that could spell disaster for the port.

The "Gateway to Europe:" Stagnation and Revival since 1914

Within little more than a decade the Royal Dock had made Grimsby the fifth port in the country, but continued progress required the alteration and extension of facilities, another of the factors that can boost or break a port. Grimsby was fortunate in that while she lacked the powerful pressure groups found in Hull, she had a far more enlightened--or perhaps simply a richer--dock authority that was willing to spend money to keep in line with expanding trade. For the sake of its rail income it was vital for the MS&L that as much trade as possible should enter England through its port and not be diverted to ports served by rivals. In the 1850s the problem was want of shipping, so ships were engaged; in the 1860s it was want of space, so new docks were planned. Immediate relief was found by diverting the fishing trade into its own easily constructed dock, and in 1868 MS&L began refurbishing the old haven.[43] Since Rennie's lock was inadequate for modern steamers, Union Dock was opened between the haven and Royal Dock in 1879, and for good measure a twenty-six acre westward extension of the old haven dock was completed in 1880 and named Alexandra Dock. Union and Alexandra Docks added almost fifty acres of decent dock space to the existing twenty-five acres of Royal Dock (the original timber pond had been added to the dock), and the latter's superior facilities were saved for those needing them by diverting the less demanding timber trade to Alexandra Dock, which for good measure was also provided with two mechanical coal drops costing almost as much as the excavation of the dock!

The three docks answered the demand until the revolution in shipping technology in the 1880s handed the future to those ports that

[43]Dow, *Great Central*, II, 163-167.

could afford deep docks. It was no detached comparison that showed Hull's new Alexandra Dock, at thirty-four feet, to be eight feet deeper than Grimsby's Royal. The Secretary of the South Yorkshire Coal Owners' Association put the matter succinctly:

> At the present time the docks at Grimsby are not up to date...In order to enable Grimsby to hold its own and to carry on its trade with success under present and future conditions, a deep water dock of some kind somewhere or another is urgently necessary.[44]

MS&L had already considered and rejected such a dock in favour of Alexandra Dock, which at the time was much cheaper and appeared sufficient.[45] This plan was revived in the late 1890s and after delays when the site at Killingholme proved unsatisfactory a bill was presented for Sir John Barry's Immingham Dock in 1904.

When Immingham Dock was opposed by Hull, the Parliamentary Select Committee was told that no less than Grimsby's future was at stake. The existing docks, representatives claimed, "are somewhat antique...and totally unfit for the trade which at present exists and are hampering the trade and preventing its development."[46] George Doughty, the town's MP, spoke of declining growth rates:

> the reason for that is if you take the timber, or if you take the export of coal, we simply have not the accommodation to do any more business. You cannot put more

---

[44]"Select Committee on the Humber Commercial Dock," evidence of F. P. Rhodes, q 267.

[45]Dow, *Great Central*, II, 163.

[46]"Select Committee on the Humber Commercial Dock," opening speech of Mr. H. Lloyd.

> water into a bottle than it will hold. That is the position of the trade of Grimsby.[47]

The Select Committee accepted the evidence, and a race began to open Immingham Dock before the new George V Dock in Hull. Immingham won in 1912.

Immingham was one of the last of the great railway docks, built in the open country at the end of a railway line. There was scarcely a village, and no intention of building one. "The whole thing," said Doughty, "will be like a set of works, a distance away from a town, with good railway facilities and tramway accommodation..., so that people can get backwards and forwards to their work without difficulty."[48] Sir John Barry regarded the green-field site as a necessity:

> the aim now of all modern docks is to have a very great amount of quay space, so that the cargo can be discharged with the greatest possible rapidity, and cargo returned to take the place of the discharged cargo also with the greatest possible rapidity, so that the ship may get to sea and the heavy expenses of working these large ships may be avoided.[49]

Almost 150 acres were devoted to coal appliances and their ancillaries, and a similar amount to timber, though the former was expected to predominate, with a theoretical daily loading capacity of fifty-six thousand tons and sidings for 175,000 tons in 10,600 wagons.[50]

Everything about the dock, it was argued, was massive except the charges, which were "so low that Immingham can compete

---

[47]*Ibid.*, q 38.

[48]*Ibid.*, qq 144, 149.

[49]*Ibid.*, q 321.

[50]Anon., *Per Rail*, 106-107.

successfully with any other port in England."[51] It contained forty-five acres of water, and its lock, at 840 x ninety feet, with a sill depth ranging from twenty-eight to forty-seven feet, could admit the largest ships of any dock on the east coast. Almost overnight, Grimsby had regained a place in the big league. "Immingham," said the GCR,

> comes into the arena equipped with every advantage that skill and experience can devise. It is not hampered with old limitations and inadequacies; it does not need to be "developed" or "improved." It will not have to toil laboriously along on the heels of its advancing trade; it will lead the way and the trade will follow.[52]

The Haven Company itself could not have banked more hopelessly on the tendency of trade to follow docks. The Great War imposed its own peculiar pattern of trade before the "Gateway to Europe" had time to prove itself worthy of great expectations.

By 1913 Grimsby had reached an unprecedented level of commercial activity based on excellent port facilities, extensive hinterland transport, adequate shipping supplies, developing trade routes and reasonable mercantile connections. She had competed with Hull on almost equal terms and survived. The trade-makers had succeeded, insofar as they controlled or influenced the evolution of the port. There is no evidence that they foresaw the speedy ruin of their achievements by yet another factor crucial to the success of ports: the machinations of politicians. The declaration of war instantly severed links with Germany, which sent a quarter of all ships entering Grimsby in 1913, and Russian trade was halted by the Revolution. There was a brisk demand for coal in France, and war materials for the western front, but the war rapidly assumed a more sinister character than its proponents had expected, and its comprehensive nature put a brake on most trades. Tonnage entering Grimsby fell by eighty-three percent

---

[51] *Ibid.*, 95.

[52] *Ibid.*, 107.

between 1913 and 1917, although this is partly because requisitioned ships--likely to be carrying food and war supplies--were not counted. Equally damaging, official concentration of trade raised Hull's share of Humber imports during the war from sixty-seven to ninety percent, and of exports from forty-eight to seventy-six percent.

For Grimsby the politicians' post-war "return to normalcy" was more easily forecast than found. A large part of Grimsby's European trading area was in ruins, or politically unacceptable: Canadian timber, for instance, was preferred to Russian. After a brisk post-war boom both imports and exports collapsed in 1921, while in comparative terms Grimsby did not regain her value share of Humber imports until 1926 and never recaptured her share of exports. The latter now consisted largely of coal, and after the strike of 1926 that also went into decline, despite extensive refurbishment of Royal Dock in 1929 and the introduction of conveyor-fed coal hoists in 1930-1932 by the LNER, of which the Great Central now formed part. Though Grimsby did better in the coal trade than the other Humber ports, she had nothing like the volume envisaged when Immingham Dock was planned: exports in 1938 were 2.94 million tons compared with 2.98 million in 1913. As a measure of the decay, Grimsby's total exports by 1937-1938 were only sixty percent of Goole's!

The slump of 1929, by reducing world prices, ought to have worked in Grimsby's long-term favour, but in fact did not. First, it pushed Britain further towards protection and imperial trade, and European commerce suffered in consequence. There was only one notable exception: Grimsby forged ahead in the Danish bacon trade, which doubled in volume in the 1920s and again in the 1930s. Second, a concurrent reduction in freight rates encouraged shipowners to reduce and concentrate services. Liverpool and London shipping lines dominated transatlantic and imperial trade and were reluctant to break bulk in--or subsequently visit--the Humber. At the local level Grimsby again lost to Hull. The old Great Central fleet had passed on amalgamation in 1922 to the LNER, which claimed to be the largest dock-owning body in the world. It continued to operate steamers twice-weekly to Hamburg and Antwerp and weekly to Rotterdam, but there was little incentive for expansion, and so concerned were all companies engaged in continental short-hauls about under-loading that they joined to form Associated Humber Lines in 1935. It was not a good omen for Grimsby, where only once in the inter-war period did the tonnage of vessels entering the port exceed that of 1913.

The Second World War affected Grimsby in similar fashion to the first. The eastern ports suffered disproportionately, and residual Humber traffic was again concentrated in Hull. After the war Grimsby's exports virtually collapsed when Hull retained the bulk of the coal trade for a decade or more, and textile and other exports withered. Europe was slow to recover, while transatlantic trade remained elusive. As a commercial centre Grimsby appeared to have no greater potential than the railway on which her second birth had depended. Nevertheless, the most clearly pronounced trend in post-war Humber trade has been the shift of emphasis towards the south bank, based on external influences over which Grimsby itself had minimal control.

There were two separate elements in the third life of Grimsby. First, the Great Central's white elephant at Immingham finally came into its own. As part of rationalisation agreements between the Coal Board, British Rail and the Docks Board, it was chosen as one of the few outlets for exported coal. Because of the build-up of Scunthorpe as a major steel producing centre, the importation of iron ore trebled during the 1960s. Given the abundance of flat land, Immingham became both an exporter and importer of motor cars. Moreover, that same land, plus adequate water supplies, attracted substantial industries requiring easy port access. In the 1950s two pigment works, a paper mill, two Courtaulds factories, and Ciba and Fison began importing and/or exporting wood pulp and assorted chemicals; they were joined by ICI in 1965. By then a major new development was under way. The shift from rail to road which should have ruined Grimsby in fact brought two refineries and vast tank farms, together with new facilities for 100,000-ton tankers. Immingham Dock was soon handling more tonnage of goods than the port of Hull. With vast changes in the shipping industry it no longer mattered who owned the vessels, and local merchants played little part in modern trade.

The second and most telling influence, however, has been the political decision to embrace Grimsby's original trading area in Europe. Great ferries sailed from Immingham until they were allegedly frightened away by labour disputes. But European traffic does not automatically demand large vessels, and roll-on/roll-off revitalised Grimsby's town docks, even the Alexandra Dock, which had been more or less moribund for half a century. Grimsby is still a "port of great moment," though not currently "the most eligible port of the east coast."

It would appear from the history of Grimsby--and Grimsby was far from unique--that regular transformation is part of normal port life, though this was not so obvious before the acceleration of technical developments in transport and industry from the mid-nineteenth century. Since 1800 Grimsby has been three different ports, illustrating the ebb and flow of underlying factors in commercial activity. The first was a fiasco; the second a triumph tailing off into war-related agony lasting until 1945; the third appears successful and will remain so until a shift occurs in one or another of the current economic and political variables. Each phase has enjoyed more than adequate facilities. But the first was divorced from real trade and shipping. The second was deliberately integrated with an internal transport system aimed at a vibrant industrial region which it helped to develop, and exogenous shipping was therefore attracted, though merchants were still absent and endogenous shipping had to be acquired by the railway itself. Its success arose not least from the adoption of free trade which liberated European commerce from traditional restraints. Having acquired a full measure of European trade, however, Grimsby's livelihood was ruined by a rampant nationalism that hated her friends. The facilities for the third phase had been in position since 1912, but were of doubtful value until changes in the hinterland and around Grimsby itself after 1945 made heavy demands on Immingham Dock. Nevertheless, long-term success--especially in the Royal and Alexandra Docks--owed much to the further political decision that allowed Grimsby to return to the trades in which there was the greatest expertise.

The moral, already stated several times, is that trade does not automatically follow docks, which answer only one of a variety of needs. Grimsby, for instance, only prospered when entrepreneurs such as the railway companies or the Sutcliffes initiated complex transport operations linking adequate and competitive port facilities with a hinterland containing effective demand and supply; when regular shipping served overseas connections; and when the total system operated within an auspicious political framework at home and abroad. Professor Bird's famous "Anyport" model suggested that ports evolve over time, upgrading facilities in response to economic or technical stimuli; and in most work on the evolution of ports the assumption is that it is bigger docks that matter. Without in any way detracting from the value of good docks, the time has perhaps come to change the emphasis slightly and to examine them not in relation to earlier ones, but rather as one of the many variable economic and political factors which ensured a port's short or long-term success. Of course, there are overlaps between different stages in a port's life, but the history of Grimsby implies not that one port changed its nature several times through internal influences and relationships, but that three distinct and more or less unrelated economic and physical entities occupied the same site, with the crucial influences coming from connections outwards rather than inwards. Although Immingham was hardly further from old Grimsby than, say, King George Dock was from Hull, the GCR was obviously thinking of this relationship when it advertised "Immingham, Grimsby, THE NEW PORT for the World's Commerce."[53] And the initial failure of the new port of Immingham shows once again that ports are only "eligible" in relation to the ebb and flow of the international economy at specific moments in time. What we have studied is not the history of the evolution of a port of great moment, but disparate moments in the history of the port of Great Grimsby.

[53]*Ibid.*, 118.

The "Scrubby Scotch Screw Company": British India Steam Navigation Co.'s Coastal Services in South Asia, 1862-1870

J. Forbes Munro

The 1860s were marked by a gradual spread of steamship lines in the Indian Ocean maritime region. On the long routes from Suez and Aden to India, Australia and the Far East, P&O, the "flagship" of British imperialism in the region,[1] was joined from 1861 by its French counterpart, Messageries Imperiales, which in its steamship lines from Marseilles to Alexandria and from Suez to Singapore, Saigon, Hong Kong and Yokohama expressed the aspirations and elegance of Napoleon III's empire. The two firms politely manoeuvred for passenger traffic and the fine freights--silks, raw silk, opium, bullion and specie--which were the perfect accompaniment for mail and passenger liners.[2] Meanwhile, on rivers, along coasts, and between islands, smaller and less glamorous steamship lines were founded to conduct, on a reduced scale and with more regard to local environmental and economic conditions, the same mix of mails, passengers and relatively high-value cargo carried by the premier shipping firms.

Among the "country cousins" of P&O and Messageries, the British India Steam Navigation Company (BI) held pride of place, rising to dominance in the coasting liner trades of the Indian subcontinent. If, to choose a metaphor, the P&O and Messageries services were the mainline expresses of the Indian Ocean, BI operated branch lines and slower local trains. BI, which was destined to become one of the world's largest shipping concerns by the end of the century,

[1] Freda Harcourt, "The P&O Company: Flagships of Imperialism," in S. Palmer and G. Williams (eds.), *Charted and Uncharted Waters* (London, 1984).

[2] H.L. Hoskins, *British Routes to India* (London, 1928), 413-414; D.A. Farnie, *East and West of Suez: The Suez Canal in History, 1854-1956* (Oxford, 1969), 62-63.

emerged in the early months of 1862 from the financial reconstruction of a smaller and slightly older firm, the Calcutta and Burmah Steam Navigation Co., which had pioneered regular steamer services between Calcutta and the rice and teak-exporting ports of Burma in the late 1850s. BI was a privately-owned limited liability company controlled by a leading Scottish merchant and entrepreneur, William Mackinnon, who hailed originally from Campbeltown in Kintyre. Mackinnon, his nephews and cousins, together with another Campbeltown family, the Halls, owned BI's "godfather" companies--W. Mackinnon and Co. of Glasgow and Mackinnon Mackenzie and Co. of Calcutta. While the Glasgow firm acted as BI's agents in the U.K.--purchasing vessels from Clyde shipyards and arranging for shipments of steam coal from various U.K. ports to south Asia--the Calcutta house functioned as managing agents, responsible for the day-to-day operations of the fleet in Asian waters. BI was therefore an enterprise which combined the commercial acumen of the West of Scotland's expatriate merchants with the shipping and shipbuilding skills of the Firth of Clyde.[3]

The transformation of Calcutta and Burmah into the much larger British India Steam Navigation Company was the result of two alliances forged by William Mackinnon in late 1861 and early 1862. First, he struck a deal with yet another Scottish expatriate firm, W. Nicol and Co. of Bombay, to ensure that Nicol would withdraw from its own tentative entry into steamshipping and throw itself wholeheartedly into becoming agents in western India for Mackinnon's concern. John Fleming and James Nicol Fleming, senior partners in W. Nicol and Co., were brothers from Glasgow who were busy making money from the cotton boom occasioned by the U.S. Civil War and from urban development projects in Bombay. They and their associates were happy to plough some of these profits into Mackinnon's expanding shipping business. Second, Mackinnon secured the support of a

[3]For the origins of BI and its place within the Mackinnon Group of merchant and shipping firms, see George Blake, *BI Centenary, 1856-1956* (London, 1956), 13-71; J. Forbes Munro, "Scottish Overseas Enterprise and the Lure of London: The Mackinnon Shipping Group, 1847-1893," *Scottish Economic and Social History*, VIII (1988), 73-87; and J. Forbes Munro, "Sir William Mackinnon," in A. Slaven and S.G. Checkland (eds.), *Dictionary of Scottish Business Biography* (Aberdeen, 1990), II, 297-301.

powerful Anglo-India statesman, Sir Henry Bartle Frere, in bidding for a series of Indian government mail contracts which were either up for renewal or were going to tender for the first time. Frere was firmly of the view that the reforming government, which had recently taken over from the old order represented by the East India Company, should get rid of the expensive legacies of the Bengal and Bombay Marines and seek instead to foster a privately-owned mercantile marine in India. He therefore threw his considerable weight behind William Mackinnon's mail contract bids. Mackinnon swept the board, obtaining seven mail contracts worth up to a total of £55,000 per annum, which enabled him to achieve his ambition to create the first comprehensive, all-India steamship service. BI was therefore an Indian variant of the predominant pattern of steamshipping enterprise in the Indian Ocean during the 1850s and 1860s, in which guaranteed income from the carriage of mails and the regularity of scheduled services demanded by postal contracts supplied the financial and operational underpinnings of the liner trades. Armed with these contracts, BI began to define and occupy a niche for coasting steamships in south Asia. This paper explores the nature and extent of its business during the 1860s, before the opening of the Suez Canal further transformed the maritime trades of the Indian Ocean.

I

BI's coastal lines around the Indian subcontinent were effectively operated from two port-city hubs. From Calcutta, BI's original base, Mackinnon Mackenzie and Co. managed the lines from the Hooghly River down both sides of the Bay of Bengal, together with the "cross line" which traversed the Bay from Madras to Burma. This was the network pioneered by the old Calcutta and Burma S.N. Co., and was the more "mature" or developed of the two. From the Bombay hub, Wm. Nicol and Co.'s steamer department managed three lines--south toward the Malabar coast, north toward Karachi, and northwest to the Persian Gulf. This western Indian system was notionally under the authority of Mackinnon Mackenzie and Co. as managing agents for the entire BI fleet. However, while there were certainly matters in which Bombay had to defer to Calcutta, notably over the chartering of "spare" tonnage, much of the routine work of running the contract lines and of the more developmental tasks in seeking out new routes in the Arabian Sea fell to the local knowledge and expertise of Wm. Nicol and Co. These two hub cities were also functionally connected (at a time when they had not yet been linked by railways) by BI's steam service between them, which initially ran as a monthly service but was increased to fortnightly in 1864.

In the Bay of Bengal, the lines from Calcutta to Burma--to the ports of Chittagong, Akyab, Rangoon and Moulmein--occupied a sizeable proportion of BI's tonnage. By 1870, with increases in the frequency of the contract services, there were over one hundred sailings per year between Calcutta, Akyab and Rangoon. Because there were no railway connections between Burma and Bengal, passenger traffic went entirely by sea. A traveller on the lower stretches of the Hooghly River would therefore be likely to meet the occasional BI vessel setting out for Burma, "breaking the surrounding silence with the sounds so familiar on the Clyde or Thames, and matted all over like a large aquatic tent, beneath which a sheeted throng of passengers found shelter from the sun."[4] When one such steamer, the *Persia*, was caught in a cyclone off Sandheads at the mouth of the Hooghly in October 1864 and sank with the loss of all aboard except two Lascar seamen, the passengers were eighteen Europeans (including three children) in cabin accommodation and 120 Indians on deck.[5] Fortunately for the company, loss of life on such a scale was unusual. Cargo from Calcutta included re-exports from Europe, mainly cotton textiles and metalwares, together with silk goods from north India and jute gunnies (sacking), intended for the bagging of Burma's rice exports, which came from the emerging Calcutta jute mills. The gunny trade was seasonal, tied to the rice harvest, and the company's steamers experienced competition from sailing vessels going to the Burmese rice ports to load on charter. But by 1869 Mackinnon Mackenzie and Co.

---

[4]John Matheson, *England to Delhi* (London, 1870), 232.

[5]J.M. Hall to W. Mackinnon, 10 October 1864, Mackinnon Papers (hereafter MP), School of Oriental and African Studies, London, Private Letters File 33.

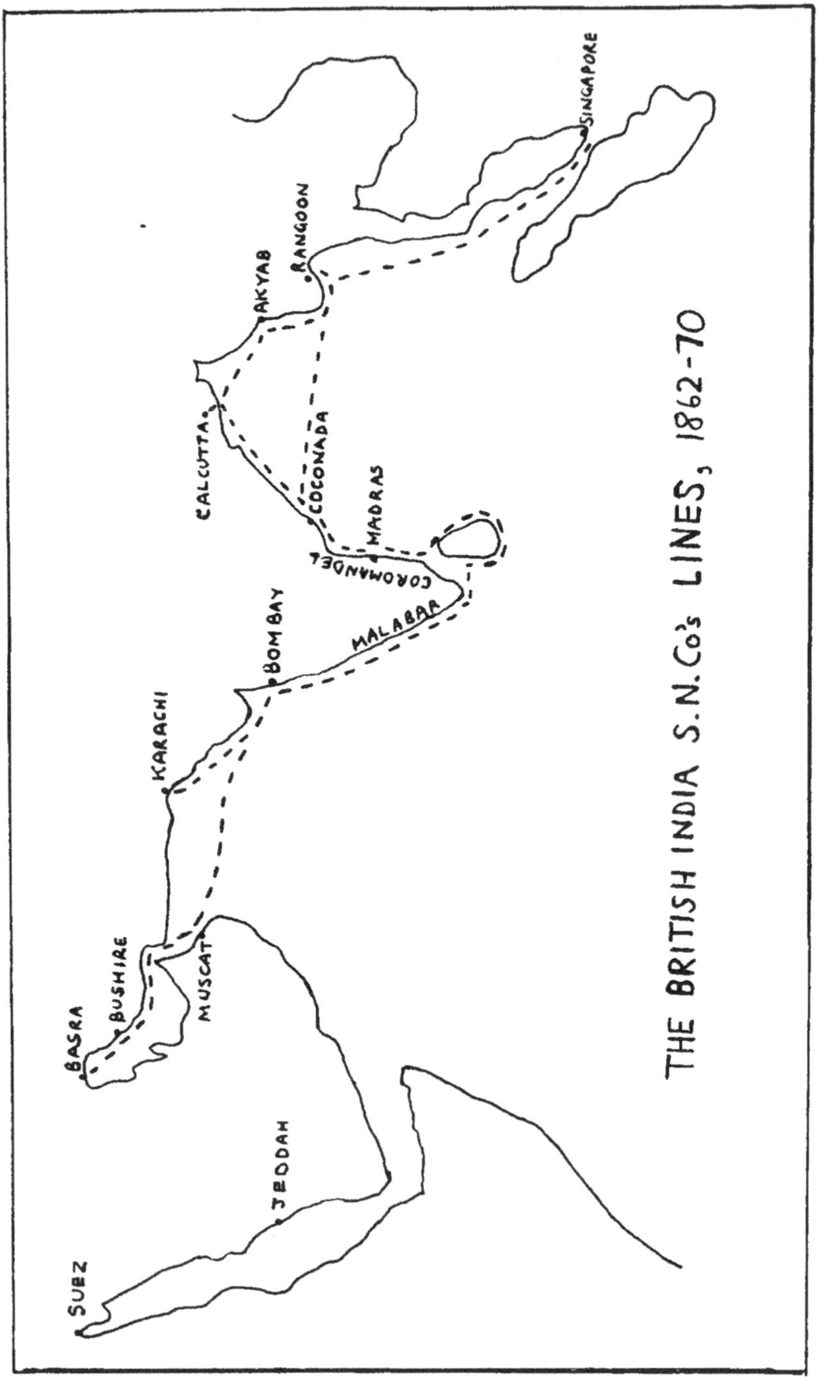
SUEZ
JEDDAH
BASRA
BUSHIRE
MUSCAT
KARACHI
BOMBAY
MALABAR
COROMANDEL
MADRAS
COCONADA
CALCUTTA
AKYAB
RANGOON
SINGAPORE
THE BRITISH INDIA S.N. Co's LINES, 1862-70

had instituted a system of rebates to merchant houses in the rice trade which sent their gunnies to Burma exclusively by BI steamers.[6] BI's cargo trade, however, was still very much a one-way affair (see table 1).

Table 1
Value of Calcutta-Burma Trade Carried by BI, 1868/1869 to 1870/1871 (million rupees)

	1869/9	1869/70	1870/1
Exports from Calcutta	18.1	18.1	16.5
Imports to Calcutta	4.7	6.3	6.3

Source: Proceedings, Financial Department, Separate Revenue, No. 16, February 1873, IOLR, P/667.

The reasons for such disparities were that BI's vessels were simply not suited for the transport of Burma's teak and other timbers, while there was as yet little demand in Calcutta for Burmese rice. When on one occasion the company secretary in Glasgow suggested that steamers from Burmese ports should load bagged rice as ballast, he received short shrift from the managing agents in Calcutta: "we regret that such a course is not practicable as there is no market for Burmah rice here either for local consumption or export."[7] Cargoes from Burma to Calcutta were therefore relatively small loads of miscellaneous mixed goods or sundries. By the end of the decade BI steamers were transporting roughly one-half of all trade between Calcutta and Burma.

At Rangoon, which became something of a secondary hub within the Bay of Bengal system, the steamers from Calcutta over-

[6]Mackinnon Mackenzie and Co. to Secretary, Glasgow, 27 April 1869, National Maritime Museum, Greenwich (hereafter NMM), BIS/6/72.

[7]Mackinnon Mackenzie and Co. to Secretary, Glasgow, 30 November 1869, NMM, BIS/6/72.

lapped with those on the "cross line" from Madras-Bimlipatam to Rangoon. Although this monthly operation carried some cargo--government stores for the Madras Presidency troops in Burma or rice from Burma on the return leg--it was predominantly a passenger service. It offered relatively inexpensive deck passages to migrant workers from south India seeking employment in the docks, wharves, and saw and rice mills of the Burmese ports, and began the connection between south India and Burma which enabled the Chettiar banking and money-lending caste to inaugurate new business opportunities in the "rice frontier" of the Burma delta.[8] Rangoon, more centrally-located in the Irrawaddy delta than the other rice ports, was emerging as the focal point for maritime and commercial activity in Burma, and BI's Rangoon agency became something of a prize.

South of Burma, passenger traffic and cargoes grew thinner and the monthly Calcutta-Singapore line, begun in 1862, failed to justify any increase in frequency. Because of the administrative separation of the Straits settlements from India in 1867, there was a slackening of demand for conveyance of official passengers and government stores, and the fast, direct opium steamers owned by the Apcars and by Jardine Skinner and Co. of Calcutta monopolised the most valuable cargo from Calcutta to Singapore, the opium intended for consumption by the Chinese population of the Malayan peninsula or for re-export to other parts of southeast Asia. Although there were other cargoes--gunnies and cereals from Calcutta, rice from Burma, and spices on the return leg from the Straits--the trade conducted by BI between Calcutta and the Straits was worth only about a fifth of that between Calcutta and Burma.[9] Consequently, James Hall, Peter Mackinnon and Peter Hall, the resident partners in Mackinnon Mackenzie and Co. in

---

[8]M. Adas, *The Burma Delta: Economic Development and Social Change on an Asian Rice Frontier, 1852-1941* (Madison, 1974), 83-102; M. Adas, "Immigrant Asians and the Economic impact of European Imperialism: The Role of the South Indian Chettiars in British Burma," *Journal of Asian Studies*, XXXIII (1973-1974).

[9]Proceedings, Financial Department, Separate Revenue, No. 16, February 1873, India Office Library and Records (hereafter IOLR), P/667.

Calcutta, were much more preoccupied with the affairs of the Burmese lines than of the one to Singapore.

The Burmese lines employed most of BI's older vessels, with the result that the managing agents had to be sensitive to complaints from shippers about the inadequacies of the timetables and from passengers about the standards of catering--even to the more vituperative writers to the English-language press like the resident of Akyab who denounced BI as a "scrubby Scotch Screw Company."[10] They also kept a wary eye on the performance of the agents in the Burmese ports, where during the early 1860s responsibility for the firm's affairs passed from the merchant houses controlled by John Halliday, one of the original founders of the old Calcutta and Burma Steam Navigation Co., to the Bulloch brothers, James and George. The Bullochs were Glasgow merchants, off-shoots of a family with whisky-distilling interests, who ran sailing vessels from London to Rangoon and had been buying their way into Halliday's Burmese businesses. When Halliday finally went bankrupt in 1865, BI took its agency at Rangoon into its own hands for a few months before handing it over to the reconstructed firm of Bulloch Bros. Despite some privately-voiced suspicions that James Bulloch was less than totally devoted to BI's cause, William Mackinnon and his partners were forced to recognise that the Bullochs had become too powerful in the Burma ports to be ignored.[11] From 1865 until the 1930s, BI's shipping activities in Burma would be bound up with the rice-trading and milling Bulloch Bros.[12]

---

[10]Letter of 5 May 1862 in the *Overland Englishman*, enclosure in P. Mackinnon to W. Mackinnon, 9 May 1862, MP, City of Glasgow Bank File 12; J.M. Hall to W. Mackinnon, 11 and 14 August 1863, MP, Private Letters File 29.

[11]P. Hall to W. Mackinnon, 23 May and 10 June 1865, MP, India File 6; BI, Directors' Minutes, 28 December 1865, NMM, BIS/1/2.

[12]James and George Bulloch, whose line of sailing ships from London to Burma would become known as the "Bay Line," were originally from Glasgow, where their brother Mathew still ran the family distilling and whisky wholesaling firm, Bulloch Lade and Co. James and Mathew were both married to daughters of Peter Clouston, a marine insurer who was Lord Provost of Glasgow in 1860-1863. Nevertheless, the Bullochs moved in different social circles from the Mackinnons and Halls and

Above all, the managing agents were concerned to prevent the rise of any possible steam competition on the Burmese routes. The main threat, they believed, was likely to come from yet another Glasgow-based enterprise. Among the several Scottish expatriate firms in Burma was Todd Finlay and Co. of Moulmein, which also had a branch house in Rangoon. The firm possessed a small steamer, the *Ava*, with which it carried goods between the two ports and which occasionally plied between Rangoon and Calcutta, to the irritation of Mackinnon Mackenzie and Co.[13] Todd Finlay and Co. was also the agent for a syndicate established in Glasgow to commence steam-shipping on the Irrawaddy River, the main thoroughfare in Burma, and which late in 1863 purchased the government's four elderly river steamers and acquired a five-year contract for the conveyance upcountry of mails, stores and troops. The Irrawaddy Flotilla and Burmese Steam Navigation Company (IF), established in Glasgow to undertake this contract from 1 January 1865, brought together the mercantile interests of T.D. Finlay and Co., the shipping interests of Patrick Henderson and Co., which operated sailing vessels in the rice trade from Burma, and the shipbuilding interests of William Denny and Bros. of Dumbarton.[14] The emergence of this firm, and the fact that its name implied intentions wider than river navigation, initiated a flutter of concern among the Mackinnons and Halls, and there was some bitterness that Peter Denny, who did so much construction of BI vessels, should be a party to what seemed a rival enterprise. Denny's participation may however have provided William Mackinnon with a lever to bring the IF to an agreement to recognise each other's "spheres of influence" in Burma, for in the summer of 1865 William

---

maintained an independence in business matters as well.

[13]P. Mackinnon to W. Mackinnon, 6, 9 and 13 June 1863, MP, Private Letters Files 27 and 29.

[14]A. McCrae and A. Prentice, *Irrawaddy Flotilla* (Paisley, 1978), 58-66; A.G. McCrae, *Pioneers in Burma* (University of Glasgow, Occasional Papers in Economic and Social History, No. 2, 1986); "A Short History of T.D. Findlay & Son Ltd; East India Merchants, 1839-1951" (typescript, n.d.).

negotiated an arrangement whereby BI purchased two steamers, *Pegu* and *Martaban*, which the Flotilla had built for coasting work, and the IF agreed to limit its coastal activities to the Rangoon-Moulmein route on which the *Ava* already sailed.[15] This delimitation of interests did not fully satisfy either party, and disputes about the running of the *Ava* and the IF's purchase of another coasting steamer, the *Avagee*, rumbled on through the late 1860s. Finally, in 1870 the BI board agreed to buy the Irrawaddy Flotilla's two coasters for £25,000.[16] Thereafter, the two firms settled into harmonious relations, respecting each other's dominant position on coast and on river.

From Calcutta south along the eastern shores of the subcontinent, BI's steamers operated the long coastal line to Bombay. This began as a monthly service in 1863, but proved so successful that the company actually ran it fortnightly for four years before the Indian government agreed in 1868 to increase the subsidy from Rs. 7,500 to Rs. 10,000 per month.[17] Steamers left Calcutta and Bombay on the first and fifteenth of each month and took three weeks to complete the voyage, making fourteen regular calls en route and others by request. Because of the shallowness of the Pamban Channel between Ceylon and India, the steamers went south of the island, calling at either Galle or Colombo. From Calcutta to Ceylon the steamers were effectively under the direction of Mackinnon Mackenzie and Co., while from Ceylon to Bombay they were within Wm. Nicol and Co.'s sphere of influence. This line was much more complex than the Calcutta-Burma lines because in the course of any single voyage the same steamer

---

[15]BI, Directors' Minutes, 27 July 1865, NMM, BIS/1/2; "Memo of Agreement between the B.I.S.N. Co. and the Irrawaddy Flot. and B.S. Coy. Ltd, 2 August 1865," NMM, BIS/6/4; P. MacNaughton to Mackinnon Mackenzie and Co., 9 August 1865, NMM, BIS/6/1.

[16]P. McNaughton to Mackinnon Mackenzie and Co., 28 January, 15 February, 2 and 9 March 1867, NMM, BIS/6/4; BI, Directors' Minutes, 6-7 and 27 October, 3 and 10 November 1869, 1 April and 5 May 1870, NMM, BIS/1/2-3.

[17]A. Monteath, Dir. Gen. of Post Office of India, to Secretary, Financial Dept., 31 July 1868 (No. 108), and Govt. of India to Secretary of State for India, 17 August 1868 (No. 110), Proceedings, India, Separate Revenue, Range 436, XXXV, IOLR.

might be carrying goods over the long distance between Calcutta and Bombay, intermediate passenger traffic and cargo between Calcutta and Madras, and short-distance travellers together with cargo being bulked at the smaller ports for transfer to bigger vessels in the larger ports. A great deal therefore depended on the judgements of the commanders and the various port agents about how much to load and how much to turn away to leave space for cargo or passengers at ports further along the route. In pre-telegraph days, it was not an easy balance to get right, and the early years of the line were punctuated by complaints from shippers and agents about late deliveries or cargo being "shut out."[18] At the first three ports of call south of Calcutta, the Mackinnon Mackenzie influence was strengthened by the placing of its own men in agencies--William Mackinnon's protege Archie Hyslop at Bimlipatam and Vizagapatam, and yet another Hall brother, Stuart, at the important port of Cocanada (modern Kakinada) on the Godavery delta--but south of the Godavery the managing agents had to choose between a variety of existing firms about which they knew little. The key decision was undoubtedly the replacement of Dymes and Co. by Binny and Co. as Madras agents in 1865. Binny, established since 1799 and almost certainly the pre-eminent European agency house in Madras, had been associated with Mackinnon Mackenzie's London "friends," Scott Bell and Co., for so many years that it was perhaps surprising that it had not been first choice as BI's Madras agent. Whatever the reason for the original omission, it was quickly rectified in recognition of Binny's influence over the commerce of the smaller ports of the Coromandel coast, among firms which might in turn become BI agents there, and also its political contacts with the government of Madras.[19] Like Bulloch Bros. in Burma, Binny was now seen as the dominant force in south India.

---

[18]J.M. Hall to W. Mackinnon, 20 February 1864, MP, Private Letters File 31; P. MacNaughton to Mackinnon Mackenzie and Co., 8 June 1867, NMM, BIS/6/4, and 30 April 1868, NMM, BIS/6/6.

[19]J.M. Hall to W. Mackinnon, 24 April and 12 June 1865, MP, Private Letters File 34; *The House of Binny* (Madras, 1969), 1-69.

Table 2
Value of Calcutta-Coast Trade Carried by BI, 1868/1869 to 1870/1871 (million rupees)

	1869/9	1869/70	1870/1
Exports from Calcutta	20.0	15.1	12.9
Imports into Calcutta	3.9	1.6	4.8

Source: Proceedings, Financial Department, Separate Revenue, No. 16, February 1873, IOLR, P/667.

On the Calcutta-Bombay coasting route, BI had rather more competition from sailing vessels and even other steamers than on the Burma lines. Even so, by the end of the 1860s BI steamers represented one-third of all vessels, other than country craft, entering and clearing Calcutta with cargoes to and from Indian ports. The value of goods carried, including treasure, demonstrates that as in the Burma trades BI tended to rely more on higher-value exports and re-exports from Calcutta--cotton goods, silk and silk goods, and jute gunnies--than on lower-value imports--hides and skins, oil seeds and salt--which went by sailing ship and "country craft" (see table 2). The one coastal commodity which could afford steam freights was raw cotton from the Godavery delta and the Coromandel coast, especially during the period of high prices in the early-to-mid 1860s when the "cotton famine" caused by the U.S. Civil War stimulated production and exports in southern and western India. The collapse of that boom in 1865-1866 contributed to the general depression of the rest of the decade and to the slackness in trade about which BI's managing agents complained from time to time.[20] Perhaps surprisingly in light of the distances involved, a relatively high proportion of the steamers' cargo space was taken up by goods travelling between the two terminal ports--for example, forty-six percent of the merchandise imports into Calcutta by

[20]P. Hall to P. Mackinnon, 8 December 1867, MP, India File 6, and to W. Mackinnon, 23 December 1867, MP, Private Letters File 51; Mackinnon Mackenzie and Co. to Secretary, Glasgow, 4 June 1869, NMM, BIS/6/72.

BI steamers from the coast between 1868-1869 and 1870-1871 originated in Bombay. From Bombay to Calcutta, the goods were principally cotton textiles, while from Calcutta to Bombay they were jutes and Benares sugar.[21]

II

From Ceylon north to Bombay, calling at several ports on the Malabar coast as well as at Carwar in the Carnatic, the fortnightly Calcutta-Bombay line became the southern arm of the steamer services managed by Wm. Nicol and Co. To undertake its agency responsibilities--in company literature Wm. Nicol and Co. always received recognition as "Agents in Bombay" just a little below Mackinnon Mackenzie and Co. as the "Managing Agents"--this firm established a separate steamer department, the first effective head of which was Edwyn S. Dawes. The son of a Staffordshire clergyman, Dawes had been employed for some years as a deck officer with P&O before coming ashore to work in its telegraph office in Bombay, where he met William Mackinnon in 1862 and, stressing the need for the expanding BI to adopt P&O's management practices, solicited his support for appointment to Nicol and Co.'s steamship agency.[22] Between 1862 and 1865 Dawes laid the foundations for BI operations in the Arabian Sea, the maritime environment of which was somewhat different from that of the Bay of Bengal. As he quickly pointed out to William:

> We have not the valuable carrying trade on this side that there is in the Eastern and principally from the hardy class of seamen & regular winds on this coast during nine months in the year, & although we shall no doubt

---

[21]P. Hall to W. Mackinnon, 10 June 1865, MP, India File 6; Mackinnon Mackenzie and Co. to Secretary, Glasgow, 2 July 1869, NMM, BIS/7/72.

[22]E.S. Dawes to Lambert, 15 September 1861 and 28 August 1862, and to W. Mackinnon, 27 June and 26 August 1862, Letterbook of Edwyn Sandys Dawes, 1860-1865. I am extremely grateful to Mr. Sandys Dawes for his permission to consult Sir Edwyn's personal papers.

> establish a good carrying trade we shall not I fear be able to run down the native craft as you appear to have done in Bengal. There is a large amount of Govt. work to be done which would be a valuable addition to our receipts altho' it does not pay Govt. to keep up an expensive class of steamer to perform it.[23]

But whether in bidding for government work (mainly troop or specie transport) or in the ordinary coastal trades, BI also faced more competition from other steamships in the Bombay hub than in Calcutta. The same boom of the early-to-mid sixties in Bombay which brought Wm. Nicol and Co.'s partners into alliance with William Mackinnon, and which helped to finance the expansion of BI, also threw up two rival concerns. The first was the Bombay Coast and River S.N. Co., a phoenix reconstituted in 1863 from the ashes of the old Bombay S.N. Co. and which, under the management of J.A. Shepherd, ran a regular line south from Bombay through the many small ports to Cochin. The second was an even more ambitious enterprise, the Bombay and Bengal Steamship Company, which under the management of Stearns Hobart and Co. of Bombay was intended principally to challenge P&O on the Suez-Bombay route but which also sent its vessels east to Madras and Calcutta and therefore competed to some extent with BI's Coast Line.[24] Of the two, the Coast and River Co. gave BI's managers more trouble. While the Bombay and Bengal proved a nuisance between Bombay and Calcutta, putting tramp steamers on the berth to sail two or three days before regular BI departures and thereby diverting cargo away from the mail steamers, and offering attractive rates for through-traffic from Suez

---

[23]E.S. Dawes to W. Mackinnon, 13 November 1863, Dawes Letterbook, 1860-1865.

[24]W.H. Coates, *The Old Country Trade of the East Indies* (London, 1911), 143-145, 146-149.

and Bombay to Calcutta,[25] the smaller firm battled BI's steamers for the trade of the Malabar coast.

The Malabar coast was regarded as a prize by both companies not only because it already had a thriving trade to Bombay in fruits, spices and various timber products transported on country craft but also because it was an emerging centre of European coffee-growing and there were therefore planters' stores and first-class passengers to be carried. But it was also a difficult coast to navigate, especially between June and August when the southwest monsoon blew fiercely from the Indian Ocean and most sailing vessels gave it a wide berth. Dawes would later recall how

> In the year 1862 I went out to Bombay with Mr Mackinnon who gave out his intention of running steamers between Bombay and Calcutta touching at the coast ports. It was pronounced madness by nautical men. The Captain of the P&O steamer said to me, if your friend had passed the coast during the monsoon as much as I have done he would not think of it. Well, towards the end of June when the monsoon was at its height, I sent off the little steamer *Kurrachee*...and from that day to this the steamers have run regularly at all seasons of the year.[26]

What Dawes had established was that small coasting steamers could indeed navigate inshore in the teeth of the monsoon without ending up on the beach, and that BI's Coast Line could therefore function year-round. Nevertheless, the steamers of the 1860s were still unable to beat out of a Malabar port against the full fury of the monsoon, with the result that calls at Malabar ports had to be suspended from 1 June to 15 August of each year.

---

[25]J.M. Hall to W. Mackinnon, 2 February 1865, MP, Private Letters File 34; P. MacNaughton to Mackinnon Mackenzie and Co., 17 October 1866, NMM, BIS/6/3.

[26]E.S. Dawes to Sir Arnold Kemball, 18 September 1871, Dawes Letterbook, 1868-1874.

In the struggle between BI and the Coast and River Co. for Malabar trade and traffic, the Bombay firm made the quicker and more effective start; it was only the introduction of its fortnightly service late in 1864 which enabled BI to compete in frequency and regularity of calls. Even so, rates were driven down--in 1866, for example, BI charged twenty-five percent less for deck passengers and cargo between Bombay and Cochin than for an equivalent journey between Calcutta and Masulipatam--and earnings were squeezed. Time, however, was on BI's side, for the Coast and River Co. was over-capitalised--there had been much issuing of new equity and watering of stock during the height of Bombay's share speculation--and when the bubble burst in 1865, the subsequent tide of liquidations and bankruptcies, which brought down the Bank of Bombay in February 1867, swept over the Coast and River as well. By May 1867, BI was in negotiation for the purchase of Coast and River's business.[27] Although no agreement was reached, William Mackinnon took advantage of the the subsequent liquidation to purchase a couple of its steamers for BI and another two for his Netherlands India Steam Navigation Co. By the end of the decade, BI was alone in the Bombay-Malabar liner trade and was carrying cargo worth an average 1.7 million rupees per annum.[28] Since this was only about eight percent of the total value of Bombay-Malabar trade in mid-decade, however, it would appear that steam had still made little impact on the local country craft.

The line from Bombay north to Karachi was predominantly a mail and passenger service. Indeed, it started in 1863 as an extension of P&O's Suez-Bombay line, the BI steamers waiting in Bombay to carry the "overland" mails and passengers from Britain to Karachi, where it was intended that at least some would travel up the Sind-Punjab rail-river route. Only with the introduction of regular schedules in 1866 did the line begin to take account of local passenger and cargo

---

[27]E.S. Dawes to W. Mackinnon, 23 May and 23 July 1864, Dawes Letterbook, 1860-1865; Coates, *Old Country Trade*, 144; BI, Directors' Minutes, 16 May and 15 August 1867, NMM, BIS/1/2.

[28]Proceedings, Financial Department, Separate Revenue, No. 4, April 1873, IOLR, P/667.

needs. There was little cargo on offer, however, partly because Karachi harbour, despite improvements, had a sand bar at its entrance which confined its use to shallow-draught vessels with small cargo-carrying capacity, but mainly because steamships could not compete in freight rates with the country craft which plied between Sind and Bombay. At the very height of the cotton boom, some raw cotton came down by steamer, but even this was halted by the introduction of government inspections designed to prevent adulteration of raw cotton exports.[29] From time to time the Bombay and Bengal Steamship Co. put steamers on this route to oppose BI, but the practice ceased toward the end of the decade when the combination of the struggle with P&O and the post-cotton boom depression proved too much for the Bombay and Bengal and it too, like Coast and Rivers, went into liquidation. Richard Burton, the explorer, travelling on the line in the mid-1870s, noted sourly that it had "fallen prey" to BI, which charged "the dearest passage of the nineteenth century...How long this absurd monopoly will last is hard to say...The inevitable "canny Scot" rules the roost, and doubtless will fight hard to keep rivals out of the kitchen."[30]

The longest line solely under Wm. Nicol and Co.'s management covered the 1690 miles from Bombay to Basra at the head of the Persian Gulf. This monthly service, which became fortnightly in 1866, originally went via Karachi, but Dawes soon obtained permission to bypass that port and head straight for the Gulf. (The Persian merchants in Bombay objected to the Karachi stop, but it is not clear whether this was for purely commercial reasons or because, as Dawes suspected, as Shia Moslems they disliked travelling in the company of Hindus who used the Bombay-Karachi section of the line.)[31] The first stop was Muscat, the capital city of Muscat-Oman, which was intended to become the main centre for BI operations in the Gulf. But a

---

[29]E.S. Dawes to W. Mackinnon, 28 March 1864, Dawes Letterbook, 1860-1865.

[30]R.F. Burton, *Sind Revisited* (2 vols., London, 1877), II, 11.

[31]E.S. Dawes to W. Mackinnon, 28 October and 27 November 1863, Dawes Letterbook, 1860-1865; E.S. Dawes to Secretary, BI, 20 November 1890, Correspondence, Calcutta Office, NMM, BIS/7/37.

combination of political troubles in Oman in 1866, when the Imam, Thuwaini ibn Said, who had been so helpful and welcoming to the company, was deposed and murdered by his more anti-British son, and Dawes's emergence as victor in an argument within BI over whether it should have a single central coaling station at Muscat for its Gulf steamers or coaling depots at the Bombay and Basra termini, soon reduced the significance of Muscat in the company's plans, and the line became associated principally with the Persian (Iranian) shore of the Gulf.[32] With calls at Bundar Abbas, Linga (Lingeh) and Bushire, the new line tapped southern Persia's maritime trade with India--and for BI's delighted cotton-manufacturing shareholders back in Glasgow held the promise of large new markets for their goods.

A major difficulty, however, was to secure suitable agents in the Persian ports, and the company operated with a succession of temporary representatives until in 1866 Edwyn Dawes, who had left Wm. Nicol and Co. to establish his own London firm, Gray Dawes and Co., took on the Bushire agency. After about a year spent in Bushire, Dawes was replaced by a new junior partner, Robert Paul, and the agencies at Bushire and Bundar Abbas were assigned to the new firm of Gray Paul and Co. Robert Paul, a Glaswegian by origin, had been a clerk in Mackinnon Mackenzie's piece-goods department since the mid-1850s. In 1865, despite "the furious brother of his deserted first love to prevent him from thinking of Glasgow as a pleasant retreat,"[33] he had returned to that city to work in BI's office until a suitable agency could be found for him. Now, like Archie Hyslop and Stuart Hall in eastern India, he was being given the opportunity to use a BI agency as the launching-pad for a mercantile business.

From Bushire, the line went northwest across the Shatt-al-Arab to Basra, the principal port of Mesopotamia (Iraq) which was then part of the Ottoman Empire. British Indian interest in the strategic

[32]A. Johnstone to W. Mackinnon, 25 November 1864, 28 February and 13 March 1866, MP, India File 10; D. Mackinnon to W. Mackinnon, 24 November 1864, MP, India File 10; E.S. Dawes to W. Mackinnon, 21 June 1865, Dawes Letterbook, 1860-1865; J.B. Kelly, *Britain and the Persian Gulf, 1795-1880* (Oxford, 1968), 649-650.

[33]J.M. Hall to W. Mackinnon, 3 April 1865, MP, Private Letters File 34.

significance of this region had been sustained since the 1830s by a Residency in Baghdad, which was supported by two small steamers which plied the Tigris River between Basra and Baghdad under a *firman* from the Ottoman government. In 1861-1862, this river service was privatised as part of the same set of arrangements that brought Indian government contracts to BI, and the two vessels were sold to the Euphrates and Tigris Steam Navigation Co. established by three Irish brothers--Henry, Thomas and Stephen Lynch--who traded in Baghdad and London as Lynch Bros. The mails carried by BI from Bombay to Basra continued upriver to Baghdad on the steamers of the Euphrates and Tigris Steam Navigation Co., which operated a regular cargo service on the Tigris, and arrangements were made between the two companies for through-booking of goods and passengers.[34] So close was the connection between government and private transport at the head of the Gulf that BI's first agent in Basra was actually the Indian government's representative in the town, a man named W.P. Johnston, although in recognition of his official status he was paid a straight fee rather than the more normal agent's commission. When Johnston died in 1869, Lynch Bros. and Gray Paul and Co. at Bushire were rivals for the Basra agency but thanks to the influence of Gray Dawes and Co. upon William Mackinnon, it passed to the latter.[35]

The entry of BI steamers into the Persian Gulf coincided with a generally prosperous phase in the trade between Bombay and the Gulf. Total trade rose in value from 19.6 million rupees in 1860-1861 to 23.3 million rupees in 1868-1869. From Bombay, cargoes were

---

[34]Hoskins, *British Routes to India*, 423-426; R. Owen, *The Middle East in the World Economy, 1800-1914* (London, 1981), 181; T.K. Lynch, *The Navigation of the Euphrates and Tigris, and the Political Rights of England Thereon* (London, 1884), 167-168; Secretary of State to Govt. of Bombay, No. 90 of 16 September 1862 and No. 12 of 17 June 1863, "Selections from Despatches...By the Secretary of State in Council," IOLR, V/6; Euphrates and Tigris S.N. Co. BT31/37919/2241, I, Public Record Office; Stephen Lynch and Co., Baghdad, to W. Mackinnon, 19 August 1863 MP, India File 13.

[35]W.P Johnston to Fleming and Co., Karachi, 18 May 1863, MP, India File 9; E.S. Dawes to G. Mackenzie, 19 November and 17 December 1869, to P. MacNaughton, 7 December 1869, and to R. Paul, 31 December 1869, Dawes Letterbook, 1868-1874.

cotton textiles and metal goods (mainly re-exports from Britain), sugar, cereals, dyestuffs, and substantial amounts of specie, while from the Gulf came dates from Basra, opium, pearls and carpets from Bushire and Bundar Abbas, and raw cotton, silk, wool, grains and horses from both Persia and Iraq.[36] During the cotton boom of the early-to-mid 1860s raw cotton figured more prominently among the imports into Bombay than in the latter part of the decade. The trade carried by BI (table 3) made the Bombay-Gulf line its third most important, after the Calcutta-Burma and Calcutta-Coast lines. In the competition for cargoes between Bombay and the Gulf, BI was apparently more successful against local craft than on the Malabar coast; by 1870-1871 its share was 56.5% of total trade, as against 8.9% for other steamers and 34.6% for "native craft."[37] The reasons for such a relatively early shift from sail to steam are unclear, but probably include Wm. Nicol and Co.'s slashing of freight rates from the Gulf in 1865-1866, as cotton prices collapsed at the end of the U.S. Civil War.[38]

Table 3
Value of Bombay-Gulf Trade Carried by BI, 1868/1869 to 1870/1871 (million rupees)

	1869/9	1869/70	1870/1
Exports from Bombay	4.6	4.9	5.3
Imports into Bombay	7.0	6.2	6.0

Source: Proceedings, Financial Department, Separate Revenue, Nos. 3-4 of April 1873, IOLR, P/667.

The Bombay-Gulf line differed from all the other routes in one important respect. Elsewhere BI acted as a "servant of empire" in that

[36]"Report by Col. Pelly on the Trade of the Persian Gulf," Great Britain, *Parliamentary Papers*, 1871 (456), li.407.

[37]Proceedings, Financial Department, Separate Revenue, Nos. 3-4 of April 1873, IOLR, P/667.

[38]R.G. Landen, *Oman Since 1856* (Princeton, 1967), 98.

its contract lines owed their existence to a well-established imperial order, but in the Gulf the company was an "agent of empire," a tool of the more interventionist "informal imperialism" espoused by Henry Bartle Frere and conducted locally by Lewis Pelly.[39] In providing communications and logistical support for Pelly's Residency at Bushire, BI was associated with his campaign to exert greater influence over the Arab states on the southern shores of the Gulf. Although Pelly was also a small shareholder in the company, there is little evidence that he used his office to advance BI's position other than by generally favourable comments on the company in his reports to superiors. Indeed, his impetuosity and interventionist appetite could be counter-productive for a shipping firm needing a peaceful political framework within which to operate, as was demonstrated by his role in Muscat's political problems in 1866. That the Resident's interests did not always coincide with those of BI and its agents was perhaps expressed most explicitly in Edwyn Dawes's advice to Gray Paul and Co. in 1868:

> Col. Pelly I used to think (*between ourselves*) was perhaps a little too willing to have a collision with the native authorities on the rights of British subjects. Our policy I think must be as far as possible to keep in with the native authorities, as long as we can do so without being subjected to injustice.[40]

There were clearly dangers in too close an identification with the aims and methods of this exponent of imperial vigour.

III

Nonetheless, the political difficulties of operating along the frontier of British imperial influence in the Gulf and along the shores of the Arabian peninsula were insufficient to constrain BI's managers from

---

[39] *Ibid.*, 86-95, 163-205; Kelly, *Britain and the Persian Gulf*, 500-575, 638-716.

[40] E.S. Dawes to R. Paul, 20 November 1868, Dawes Letterbook, 1868-1874.

being drawn ever more deeply into the maritime affairs of that region. The principal reason for such a development was the need of the company's managers in Calcutta and Bombay to find gainful employment for its spare steamers.

From about 1864, BI's fleet was always somewhat larger than strictly necessary for the performance of its contract services. This was partly because penalty clauses in the contracts obliged it to keep a few spare steamers in hand as a reserve against accidents. Coasting services, involving inshore navigation and frequent calls at small ports, were relatively risky, and strandings on uncharted shoals or sandbanks, or collisions with other vessels entering or leaving port, were common. There were also the hazards of weather, particularly cyclones in the Bay of Bengal. In October 1864, for example, a cyclone devastated shipping in the Hooghly, and James Hall, who witnessed it at Calcutta, described how

> When the cyclone was at its height the fury of it was awful to behold. No living thing appeared able to stand upright without support, and all around seemed wreck and ruin. All the tiers of moorings from Coolie Bazaar to Hawlcoleah...were swept away--clean swept--there is not a single vessel moored stem & stern this morning and there isn't a ship in port unscathed.[41]

Among the many vessels which were dashed against each other or thrown onto the river bank were several BI steamers, and the company had to recruit a team of shipyard workers in Glasgow to go out to Calcutta to repair the damage. In such conditions it was a wise precaution to have a few steamships in reserve. But BI's fleet also expanded as a result of its modernisation policy, which took older vessels off the contract lines, and of its practice of buying steamships which became available in India in order to deprive potential competitors. The re-sale of such excess tonnage outside Indian waters always took some time to arrange--for example, Mackinnon Mackenzie and

---

[41] J.M. Hall to W. Mackinnon, 6 October 1864, MP, Private Letters File 32.

Co. tried to sell the two steamers, *Sydney* and *Australian*, in Japan before managing to get the Egyptian government to take them off its hands in 1866--and meanwhile some profitable employment had to be found for the vessels.

In both the Bay of Bengal and the Arabian Sea there was plenty of trooping work to be done, BI bidding for the business against other steamship owners. Sometimes this involved relatively short charters for the transport of small units, as in the regular reliefs of garrisons in places like Singapore or Aden, and sometimes there were entire regiments to be moved--in 1863, for example, BI steamers transferred the 38th Regiment of Native Infantry from Calcutta to Chittagong, and carried over three hundred men of the 68th Light Infantry from Rangoon to New Zealand.[42] Indeed, such was the scale of trooping work available that one large steamer, the *Asia*, was ordered from Denny in Dumbarton in 1865 with decks arranged to make it particularly suitable for troop transport.[43] All of BI's mail contracts with the Indian government carried a clause permitting the latter to charter its steamers in time of military or civil emergency. Normally, the invoking of such a power would have caused some interference with the company's regular lines, but the first occasion on which it was used, to secure transports for the 1867-1868 Abyssinian Expedition, coincided with a slack period in India's coastal trades, and BI's managers were happy to see the government provide employment for all its spare steamers and a few which were temporarily removed from the contract lines. Nine BI vessels were used in the punitive expedition against Emperor Theodore of Ethiopia, and William Mackinnon, with an eye toward discussions about contract renewals in Calcutta, was keen to see that the company received due recognition, particularly for the way

---

[42]Mackinnon Mackenzie and Co. to Home Department, Govt. of India, 20 December 1866, No. 25 of September 1867, Proceedings, Separate Revenue, Range 437, X, IOLR.

[43]P. MacNaughton to Mackinnon Mackenzie and Co., 8 April 1865, NMM, BIS/6/1.

the separate condensers of the engines were used to supply the troops ashore with fresh water.[44]

A different type of employment for BI's spare steamers was also available to the Bombay agents--the conveyance of Moslem pilgrims to and from Jeddah. This was a seasonal traffic which could begin in October-November in the case of pilgrims who also wanted to spend Ramadan in Mecca, but which was at its peak between February and August. Steamships were in demand for such a trade because the complex wind patterns of the Red Sea rendered it hazardous for sailing vessels. BI first entered the trade in 1864, with a charter to convey a Begum and her party from Aden to Jeddah. Edwyn Dawes believed that William Mackinnon would object on religious grounds to the company becoming involved in this trade, and tried to hide the nature of the charter from the Glasgow office, but finding no protest forthcoming was emboldened to take matters a stage further.[45] He proposed that BI should send one or two of its older, ex-government steamers into the Red Sea to ply between Suez and Jeddah with pilgrims from Egypt and the Mediterranean littoral, thereby persuading one of the Egyptian shipping firms in the Red Sea to buy some of BI's unwanted excess tonnage. The strategy, carried out in the 1865 and 1866 seasons by vessels under the command of Capt. Beyts, BI's senior commander on the Bombay station, proved entirely successful, for in 1866 the government of Egypt, which was also interested in the Mejidiah steamship company which operated in the Red Sea, bought the *Sydney* and the *Australian* for £37,000. As part of the terms of the sale, BI had to agree not to carry passengers or cargo between Suez and Jeddah, except as part of a longer voyage originating outside the

---

[44]Wm. Mackinnon and Co. to W. Nicol and Co., 17 December 1867, MP, Private Letters File 35; P. MacNaughton to Mackinnon Mackenzie and Co., 2, 17 and 25 January, 30 April, 18 June 1868, NMM, BIS/6/6; W. Mackinnon to J. MacDonald, MP, Private Letters File 135.

[45]E.S. Dawes to Capt. Beyts, 28 April 1864, and to J.M. Hall, 11 July 1864, Dawes Letterbook, 1860-1865.

Red Sea.[46] The arrangement, however, left BI free to operate on the Persian Gulf to Red Sea route, and every year from 1865 onwards a BI steamer left Basra early in February, calling at Bushire, Linga, Bundar Abbas and Muscat to pick up pilgrims, returning after the Haj to Mecca. In this regular trip lay one of the principal supports for the idea that BI should introduce an "Arabian" line into its schedules.

The concept was that BI should fit itself around P&O's rapid, direct Bombay-Aden-Suez liner service with an indirect, coasting line from Bombay via the ports of the Arabian peninsula to Aden and from there to Suez with possible calls at Jeddah as well as Suakin or Massawa on the African shore of the Red Sea. William Mackinnon started pressing the case for such a line on the India Office in 1866, with support from Frere's government in Bombay.[47] Although neither the government of India nor the India Office were willing to offer a subsidy, Mackinnon persisted, confiding to a friend that "I have taken a great fancy for this line because it really would bring these old countries once more into living contact with the living world, and open up a highway for every good and civilising influence."[48] If such a statement reveals that, probably under Frere's influence, Mackinnon was beginning to think of steamship lines as more than simply methods of transport and communication, that is as carriers of Western "civilisation" as well as cargo, it could not disguise the fact that there were commercial considerations behind the proposal. The intention was that the line would connect at Muscat (or perhaps Karachi) with BI's Bombay-Gulf contract service for the transfer of passengers and

---

[46]E.S. Dawes to J.M. Hall, 28 August and 7 October 1864, Dawes Letterbook, 1860-1865; P. MacNaughton to Mackinnon Mackenzie and Co., 11 and 25 April, 9 May and 16 September 1865, and 17 March 1866, NMM, BIS/6/1; P. MacNaughton to Mackinnon Mackenzie and Co., 29 July 1869, NMM, BIS/6/9; BI, Directors' Minutes, 27 October 1869, NMM, BIS/1/2.

[47]From Bombay (General Department), 28 April 1866, Confidential No. 53 of 1866, and from Gov. General (Post Office), 16 August 1866, Confidential No. 86 of 1866, *Abstract of Letters Received from India*, IOLR, P&S/19.

[48]W. Mackinnon to J. MacDonald, 29 December 1866, MP, Private Letters File 134.

cargo. The steamers employed in the pilgrim trade demonstrated that there was at least seasonal passenger traffic between the Persian Gulf and the Red Sea, while for potential cargo there was opium from Persia (Iran).

In his early years as an East India merchant, William Mackinnon had shown considerable aversion to the opium trade. On one occasion, for example, he informed his partner, James Hall, that if Mackinnon Mackenzie and Co. ever earned any commission on opium it should not be credited to his (William's) account, adding that "I have great doubts about it, although I would be sorry to say another person was doing wrong in acting differently."[49] By the mid-1860s, however, Mackinnon appears to have accepted that opium might be shipped on BI steamers, for there can be little doubt that the carriage of Iranian opium to Aden for transfer to P&O steamships to Europe or China formed part of the "Arabian line" scheme. During the 1860s, Persia had emerged as a significant exporter of "the drug," its exports doubling in volume between 1860 and 1869. Most of this trade by-passed Bombay, where there was a substantial tax on imported opium, going either overland through central Asia to China or by sailing ship to Batavia for re-export to China and the countries of southeast Asia.[50] The voyage of BI's steamer *Scotia* during the pilgrim season of 1869 (repeated in 1870) established yet another route for Persian opium to the East, for in addition to its passengers it took from Bushire and Bundar Abbas 227 chests of opium, of which 130 were subsequently transferred to P&O and fifty-three to Messageries Imperiales at Aden.[51]

---

[49]W. Mackinnon to J.M. Hall, 23 December 1858, MP, Misc. Commercial File 58.

[50]Memorandum on Persian Gulf by G.C. [Sir George Clerk], 17 July 1868, Political and Secret Memoranda, Zanzibar, Muscat & Persia, 1868, IOLR, L/P&S/18/B2; Memorandum by Ronald Thompson, 6 May 1869, in J.A. Saldana, *Precis of Commerce and Communication in the Persian Gulf, 1801-1905* (Calcutta, 1906), 63.

[51]Saldana, *Precis of Commerce*, 118; Mackinnon Mackenzie and Co. to Secretary, Glasgow, 4 May 1869, NMM, BIS/6/72; P. MacNaughton to Mackinnon Mackenzie and Co., 8 July 1869, NMM, BIS/6/9.

All that remained to launch a regular steamship line along the Arabian coast and into the Red Sea was the matter of a mail contract, which Mackinnon hoped might be obtained through Frere's influence. Frere, who retired as Governor of Bombay in 1867 to become a member of the India Council in London, continuously pressed his view that coastal steamshipping was an important vehicle for maintaining and extending British influence along the western shores of the Indian Ocean, particularly in the Arabian peninsula. For example, in a memorandum for the Secretary of State for India in July 1868, he painted a picture of the coastal steamer as a sort of substitute for the patrolling frigate, providing early intelligence of illegal activities and/or political disorder, as well as being a means of stimulating alternative employment for maritime Arabs who otherwise might become involved in piracy. He continued that

> I have no doubt that the steamers now regularly running from Bombay to Busra have greatly conduced to discourage a revival of piracy since the Indian naval squadron was withdrawn; and I believe that the extension and greater frequency of steamer traffic along the coasts of Arabia and East Africa would tend greatly to check slavery, as well as piracy.[52]

Even such vigorous lobbying, however, had insufficient time to bear fruit before the opening of the Suez canal, which transformed the maritime economics and politics of the western India Ocean.

IV

By the end of the decade, BI had consolidated its position as the pre-eminent shipper of mails, money, passengers and fine cargo around the coasts of India and its near neighbours. Following the breakthrough into public contracting achieved by William Mackinnon in 1861-1862,

---

[52]Memorandum on the Draft of Despatches Regarding the Affairs of Muscat and Zanzibar by H.E.B. Frere, addendum of 20 July 1868, IOLR, L/P&S/18/B2.

BI had developed lines of regular, and gradually more frequent, sailings upon which the travelling public, merchant communities, and local officials at many ports came to depend. Its services contributed in no small way to the quickening pace of commercial life around the seaboard of south Asia in the 1860s, well before the Suez Canal exerted its influence. Yet they did so perhaps less in terms of goods transported than of passengers carried and commercial intelligence conveyed. BI's relatively small, general-purpose steamers, like the coasters of the Firth of Clyde and the Irish Sea on which they were patterned, had limited cargo space for which comparatively high rates were charged; they were in no position to compete with European sailing vessels, or even "native craft" in some waters, for the great bulk trades of southern Asia. On the other hand, the introduction of regular local steamship lines, with defined sailing schedules known to the public, meant an improvement in facilities for those who wished to travel, whether cheaply on the open deck or with the greater comfort of cabins and a dining saloon, and for those merchants dealing in goods for which speed and/or known time of arrival merited the payment of higher freights.

To help manage its extensive operations, BI was obliged to create networks of local agents and sub-agents to foster its interests and mediate with its customers (although its reliance on expatriate Scottish firms for these purposes meant that its activities gave no direct boost to indigenous Indian businesses). It also blocked the rise of a potential rival in Burma, saw off two competitors in western India, and began to feel out the potential for coastal steamshipping around the Arabian peninsula. In the process, BI grew physically and benefitted financially. By 1870, on a paid-up capital of £442,000, it had assets worth £633,788, including twenty-three steamers valued at £441,000, and financial reserves worth £111,444.[53] But of course all of this rested to a considerable extent on the fact that it was favoured by the government of India. Just how much BI owed financially to its mail contracts is indicated by Table 4, which sets out the results of the company's profit and loss account.

---

[53]Balance Sheet, BI, Report of Directors, 1870, Inchcape Archives.

Table 4
BI Profit and Loss Account Results,
1864/1865 to 1869/1870

Year Ending 28 Feb.	Balance Before Deprec. (£)	Depreciation of Steamers (£)	Balance After Deprec. (£)	% Capital
1864-65	82,025	23,690	58,336	24.5%
1865-66	69,485	18,406	51,079	14.9
1866-67	122,273	56,635	63,638	16.7
1867-68	215,625	111,864	103,761	24.4
1868-69	111,454	53,000	58,454	13.4
1869-70	110,959	53,652	57,307	12.9

Source: BI, Directors' Minutes, NMM, BIS/1/2-3.

Although the figures for balances after depreciation of steamers and other equipment cannot be taken as a completely accurate measure of the firm's profitability (because of randomness in the rate of depreciation), they seem to indicate that the best trading years were 1864-1865, at the height of the cotton boom, and 1867-1868, when the government chartered a large part of the fleet for the Abyssinian Expedition. By 1866, the mail contracts were worth a total of £62,000 per annum; given that balances after depreciation significantly exceeded that figure only in 1867-1868, the conclusion must be drawn that BI's profitability, and its ability to pay dividends to shareholders, depended almost entirely upon public funds. When one adds to this the influence on potential passengers and shippers of the fact that BI was the official mail carrier, approved in some way by government, and that government departments tended (although they were not yet obliged) to send passengers and cargo by the mail steamers, it is clear that BI enjoyed significant advantages over non-contract steamship lines. This is not to deny the contribution made to BI's performance by the managerial skills of Mackinnon Mackenzie and Co. in Calcutta and

Wm. Nicol and Co. in Bombay, or the business acumen and shipping knowledge of the chairman, secretary and board in Glasgow and London. Nevertheless, in a maritime environment so far removed from the industrial and commercial conditions which had spawned the steamship, state support was still the vital factor in determining success or failure in the ownership and management of steamship lines.

Bureaucrats, Businessmen and Bananas: The Colonial Office and Shipping Services in the West Indies, 1895-1925

Robert G. Greenhill

The interplay between the Colonial Office and British businessmen around the turn of the last century forms the background of this essay. Although the subject has been well-documented in a number of scholarly books and articles, we still lack an unambiguous definition of the relationship. Wide interpretations are still possible on the limits and the extent of the influence exercised by both officials and entrepreneurs. On the one hand, it is argued that the Colonial Office "had an instinctive dislike of government intervention in economic activity."[1] This *laissez-faire* attitude might explain the preference for leaving the daily tasks of business administration, financing and public works contracts to crown agents, who were not civil servants but independent managers, drawing their remuneration from commercial charges levied on their activities.[2] Similarly, W.G. Hynes has pointed out that at the end of the nineteenth century British merchants, faced by subsidised foreign competitors, experienced great difficulty in pushing a reluctant Colonial Office towards a more active recognition

[1]Robert V. Kubicek, *The Administration of Imperialism: Joseph Chamberlain at the Colonial Office* (Durham, NC, 1969), 139.

[2]Richard M. Kesner, "Builders of Empire: the Role of the Crown Agents in Imperial Development, 1880-1914," *Journal of Imperial and Commonwealth History*, V (1977), 310-330; V. Ponko, Jr., "Economic Management in a Free Trade Empire: The Work of the Crown Agents for the Colonies in the Nineteenth and Early Twentieth Centuries," *Journal of Economic History*, XXVI (1966), 363-379.

of their commercial problems and towards increased official pressure in areas as yet outside the Empire.[3]

On the other hand, Joseph Chamberlain's interventionist policy of awakening the Colonial Office to the commercial needs of the colonies is well-known.[4] His view was that private capital had failed to develop those colonies in particular in which poor communications and transport facilities seemed to impede progress. Further, in a case study published in 1969, V. Ponko, Jr. suggested that Colonial Office policy, if not planned or consistent, interfered with British business, which it regarded as selfish and in need of control in the imperial interest. "Private enterprise...in the British Empire before the First World War," he argued, "thus existed at the mercy of the prevailing organisational structure in the Colonial Office."[5] Businessmen were not given a free hand but had to contend with the "cavalier attitude [of officials] toward the sanctity of investment within the Empire" as well as with foreign competition.

Similarly, the response of businessmen to economic opportunities in the Empire varied widely. Several scholars, while stressing the overambitious nature of the Colonial Office's plans, lay part of the blame for failure at the door of unadventurous British entrepreneurs. "On the whole...," explains Hardy, "the great capitalists do not survive inspection of their dealings with Chamberlain at all well. [They] did not see why they should take the slightest risk...unless a guaranteed

---

[3]W.G. Hynes, "British Mercantile Attitudes towards Imperial Expansion," *Historical Journal*, XIX (1976), 969-979.

[4]S.M. Hardy, "Joseph Chamberlain and Some Problems of the 'Underdeveloped Estates,'" *University of Birmingham Historical Journal*, XI (1967-1968), 170-172. See also S.B. Saul, "The Economic Significance of 'Constructive Imperialism,'" *Journal of Economic History*, XVII (1957), 173-192; H.A. Will, "Colonial Policy and Economic Development in the British West Indies, 1895-1913," *Economic History Review*, XXIII (1970), 129-147; and Andrew Porter, "In Memoriam: Joseph Chamberlain: Review of Periodical Literature, 1960-1973," *Journal of Imperial and Commonwealth History*, III (1975), 292-297.

[5]V. Ponko, Jr., "The Colonial Office and British Business before World War I: A Case Study," *Business History Review*, XLIII (1969), 39-58.

profit could be obtained in advance."[6] Businessmen publicly extolled the virtues of Empire but privately asked for taxpayers' money before proceeding with any project. Sir Thomas Lipton, for example, could not be attracted into the Caribbean without substantial guarantees. Yet Chamberlain's model of tropical estates to develop the colonies and to improve Britain's economic links with them did find an echo among certain businessmen. Alfred Jones[7] invested his time and money in West Africa while such business figures as Cecil Rhodes and Donald Currie, of course, made their fortunes within an imperial context.[8]

The purpose of this paper is to explore the relationship between the Colonial Office and businessmen over the supply of shipping services to the West Indies in the years either side of the First World War. In particular, the essay examines the rivalry between two of the great imperial entrepreneurs around the turn of the century, Sir Alfred Jones, the chairman of Elder Dempster, and Owen Philipps (later Lord Kylsant), who assembled the Royal Mail group of shipping companies. Not only was Jones commercially very active in West Africa but after 1900 began to develop the fruit trade between Jamaica and the United Kingdom. This latter enterprise brought Elder Dempster into direct conflict with Royal Mail, the traditional operator of liner tonnage to the West Indies. The following decade marked the response of Royal Mail, under Philipps' control from 1903, to this unexpected competition. The story touches upon wider issues--the impact of Chamberlain at the Colonial Office, the stimulus to economic activity in the West Indian colonies, a principal example of his underdeveloped estates, and the relationship between officials and entrepreneurs.

The paper is divided into four parts. First, the criticisms of Royal Mail, which led to the Colonial Office offering contracts to

---

[6]Hardy, "Joseph Chamberlain," 185.

[7]P.N. Davies, *Sir Alfred Jones: Shipping Entrepreneur Par Excellence* (London, 1978).

[8]Andrew Porter, *Victorian Shipping and Imperial Policy: Donald Currie, The Castle Line and South Africa* (London, 1986). See also his "Britain, the Cape Colony and Natal, 1870-1914: Capital, Shipping and the Imperial Connection," *Economic History Review*, XXXIV (1981), 554-577.

outside companies, are considered. Then, sections two and three examine Royal Mail's response to the more competitive climate in West Indian trade and shipping. On the one hand, the company fought fiercely to regain its valuable position as contract mail carrier; on the other, it at last developed a stronger commercial presence in the Caribbean. Finally, the development of West Indian shipping services immediately before and after the First World War is assessed before some concluding remarks are made.

I

Since the 1870s the Caribbean, like most trading areas, had enjoyed a rapid increase in tonnage and shipping companies. In 1872 the Post Office recorded only six steamship lines which regularly loaded for the West Indies, yet by 1885 Trinidad alone received fifteen calls each month; the number of steamships entering Jamaican ports doubled between 1876 and 1881.[9] Established shipowners like Harrisons and the West India and Pacific Company, which together operated a weekly service from Liverpool to the Caribbean, turned from sail to steam and extended their calls while newcomers from ports like Hamburg, Rotterdam and Barcelona also sought berths. In addition, tramp tonnage was attracted by the seasonal nature of West Indian exports while merchant firms like Prentice, Service and Henderson ran their own ships. Even small communities in the Caribbean enjoyed more regular calls from companies like Scruttons and the Quebec Steamship Company.[10]

But what suggested more choice and improved services for West Indian business meant cut-throat competition and lower freight rates for shipowners, who responded with measures familiar to most ocean

---

[9]Robert G. Greenhill, "The Royal Mail Steam Packet Company and the Development of Steamship Links with Latin America, 1875-1900," *Maritime History*, III (1973), 71.

[10]Robert G. Greenhill, "British Shipping and Latin America, 1840-1930: The Royal Mail Steam Packet Company" (Unpublished Ph.D Thesis, University of Exeter, 1970), 127-129.

routes before the First World War. They introduced the conference system to raise rates, limit competition and tie shippers to the regular lines, thus cutting out the activities of tramps, which allegedly creamed off business during seasonal peaks. Although formal shipping conferences in the West Indian trades were probably introduced later than elsewhere, temporary, informal business understandings had much earlier origins. Many of these collapsed in the 1880s as commercial conditions in the Caribbean became more difficult while new carriers entered the market. But, in 1896 the major liner companies, including Royal Mail, Harrisons and Hamburg-Amerika, formed a conference administered by a paid secretariat which slowly raised rates, introduced the deferred rebate and cooperated with carriers across the isthmus of Panama.[11] In the West Indies complaints about shipping services may, therefore, have had some justification. The introduction of the conference system had probably hurt local traders, increased freight costs and threatened the islands' economic welfare.

If the level and quality of shipping services in the West Indies just before the turn of the century were regarded as unacceptable, the Royal Mail Steam Packet Company, which had enjoyed an unbroken series of mail contracts since 1840, was generally regarded as the chief offender. Complaints during the Admiralty's administration of the packet service--that payments were too generous, that contracts were not open to tender and that service was poor--were repeated much less after 1860 when the Post Office assumed control. Shorter contracts, which reduced payment and threw open mail-carrying to competition, produced an improved performance from Royal Mail--but not to everyone's satisfaction.[12] The West India and Pacific Company, anxious to remove its rival's established advantages, complained in 1873 that "large subsidies are no longer necessary...in the West Indian trade [and] enable the Royal Mail Company to carry goods at lower

---

[11]F.E. Hyde, *Shipping Enterprise and Management, 1830-1939: Harrisons of Liverpool* (Liverpool, 1967), 56-57. For details of the Conference system see "Royal Commission on Shipping Rings," Great Britain, *Parliamentary Papers* (henceforth *BPP*), 1909, XLVII and XLVIII.

[12]Greenhill, "British Shipping and Latin America," 39-50.

rates than will pay."[13] Black spots in Royal Mail's itinerary continued, for example at Colon where the company maintained its connections for the Pacific coast. Moreover, the principle that West Indian colonies should contribute to the mail subsidy, mooted in 1862 but not applied until 1884, forced Royal Mail to satisfy two paymasters.

Performance of the mail contract, while not exemplary, did on the whole satisfy official requirements, but the same could not be said for the company's commercial services. The fault was not entirely Royal Mail's. Tied to the fixed timetable of a mail contract, the company could not always exploit the business opportunities which attracted a more flexible operator. The few really profitable ports in the Caribbean fell to competitors whose freer schedules enabled them to seek cargo while Royal Mail had to call at the many small islands where traffic was negligible. The sugar trade demanded freights well below those offered by the liner companies. Moreover, the bulk of Caribbean trade was provided not by British West Indian ports but by Central America and Cuba, which inevitably attracted the better shipping, to the irritation of colonial shippers. Royal Mail did, of course, respond to the new market conditions, introducing a freight service in addition to the mail contract and expanding the Caribbean's trading links with New York--although the intermittent nature of operations hardly suggests profitable business. Indeed, in the long-run, yet more sailings merely added to available cargo space and further lowered freight rates.

But despite these responses the impression remains that Royal Mail was somewhat unenterprising, living for its mail subsidy in the Caribbean rather than aggressively developing business. It failed to grasp the opportunity offered in 1888 when Sir William Forward's Atlas Line, subsequently absorbed by Hamburg-Amerika, was up for sale; had Royal Mail purchased, this would have consolidated the company's presence in the West Indian-New York trade. New ships introduced by Royal Mail continued to lack facilities, such as reliable refrigerated chambers, which other companies provided. In 1901, for

---

[13]West India and Pacific Company to Post Office, 30 July 1873, Post Office Archives (henceforth Post) 29, fo. 193/400Z/1874.

example, an explosion on the *Para*, which was equipped with experimental machinery for shipping fruit, led to loss of life.[14] Further, the colonies noted the contrast between the more modern liners the company operated on its South American run and the older tonnage loading for the Caribbean.

Towards the end of the 1890s Royal Mail's performance came under close scrutiny. A Royal Commission appointed by Chamberlain to investigate the West Indian economies reported in 1897 that improved communications would assist the islands' economic recovery and that steamshipping should be "conducted in a manner better adapted to the more pressing needs of the colonies."[15] Lucas, head of the Colonial Office's West Indian Department, minuted in 1898 that Royal Mail, "spoilt by their monopoly," would only undertake additional services "at a stiff figure...without any trouble on their part to develop traffic."[16] Many islands now questioned the value of their contributions to the mail service. Governor Llewelyn of the Windwards considered that the company "have not kept pace with the times...the management is too costly and their methods of business too antiquated."[17] Ferry, the Collector of Customs at Trinidad, told a director that Royal Mail had "few friends in the West Indies," while Jamaican officials noted that "under present conditions the methods of the Royal Mail Company are discouraging or entirely prohibitive to some branches of export trade."[18] Even shareholders held these gloomy

---

[14]Royal Mail Steam Packet Archives, National Maritime Museum, Greenwich (henceforth RMSP), *Report of the Directors*, 30 April 1902; W.E. Smith, "The Fruit Industry of Jamaica," *Proceedings of the Agricultural Society of Trinidad* (1904), 31.

[15]"Report of the Royal Commission on Distress in the West Indies," *BPP* (1898), L, 26-27; *The Statist*, 6 August 1898.

[16]Public Record Office, Colonial Office Papers (henceforth CO), 318/293, minute 5889 (March 1898).

[17]Llewelyn to Colonial Office, 26 February 1902, Post 29, fo. 836/296E/1904.

[18]RMSP, *Gatley Guard Book* (1888); Jamaica to Colonial Office, 21 May 1900, Post 29, fo. 744/182C/1902.

views. "The West Indian trade," one admitted, "has not been worked in a manner which the magnificent beginnings of the Company demanded."[19] Robert Kubicek's more recent judgement is that the Royal Mail was "thought to be detrimental to West Indian progress because of its indifference to development."[20]

Accordingly, to improve communications, introduce competition and diversify the West Indian economy, the Colonial Office in 1899 negotiated two contracts, the general mail service and a new direct line between Jamaica and the United Kingdom to transport fruit. Chamberlain seemed ready to end the postal contract but recognised the outrage that termination would arouse. He simply advised renewal "for as short a period as can be arranged without increasing the present subsidy."[21] Royal Mail, the only tenderer, ratified the contract for five years but clearly resented such casual treatment. Negotiations for the fruit service, however, ignored Royal Mail in favour of a bid from a local producers association, the Jamaica Produce and Trading Company.

When this fell through, Chamberlain turned to Sir Alfred Jones, chairman of Elder Dempster, the company which loaded for the west coast of Africa and which enjoyed close connections with the Canary Islands' banana trade.[22] Jones, with large resources and wide commercial experience, typified the sort of businessman whom the Colonial Secretary in his aim of combining a vigorous use of public funds with private initiative in developmental schemes for the colonies sought for the West Indies. Of similar backgrounds and ideals, self-made, industrious and dynamic, the two men were close friends. Chamberlain attached much importance to an earlier approach from Jones in 1898

---

[19]Report of the Shareholders Meeting, 27 April 1887; See also H. de R. Walker, *The West Indies and the Empire* (London, 1901), 48-66.

[20]Kubicek, *The Administration of Imperialism*, 122.

[21]Colonial Office to Treasury, 13 March 1900, Post 29, fos. 754-5/84D/1903. More detail can be found in Greenhill, "British Shipping and Latin America," 138-142.

[22]Kubicek, *The Administration of Imperialism*, 122; Davies, *Sir Alfred Jones*, 67-68.

and the conclusion of the contract, which the Colonial Secretary negotiated personally, was "a matter of urgency...Nothing should...affect the chances of the success of the Direct Line."[23] Chamberlain agreed terms of £40,000 per annum for ten years in return for a fortnightly carriage of fruit (which Elder Dempster would market) and investment in the West Indian tourist trade. Supported now by powerful Jamaican interests, Jones was keen to fight the Royal Mail which, he claimed, "could never have done for the West Indies what we have done."[24]

Royal Mail, alarmed at this private liaison and surprised by new clauses governing fruit marketing and hotel management, lobbied against an arrangement which put their own general service at a disadvantage, since Elder Dempster would now cream off Jamaica's lucrative passenger and cargo traffic. Even officials seemed surprised. At the Post Office, Buxton Forman could not recall "a case in which the Government has obtained a fresh packet service at the expense of the existing contractors," and Spencer Walpole, the Secretary, considered the affair "a very grave injustice" to Royal Mail which agreed to a contract "without the slightest intimation that another line was to be...trading to the same ports."[25] Chamberlain shrugged off accusations of prejudice, adamant that Royal Mail's contract did not prohibit other arrangements. "Practically," he explained, "[Royal Mail] did not want the contract; what they did want was to stop others getting it."[26] Worse followed when in 1900 a third subsidised line between the Caribbean and Canada's east coast, which also diverted traffic away from services operated by Royal Mail, was awarded to Pickford and

---

[23]Colonial Office to Treasury, 16 March 1901, Post 29, fo. 836/296E/1904. See also letters of 17 March 1899 and 13 March 1900, Post 29, fos. 754-5/84D/1903.

[24]Jones to Chamberlain, 13 October 1901, CO 318/302, minute 36355 (1901); see also CO 318/305, minute 44042 (23 October 1902).

[25]Forman to Ollivier, 26 January 1899, CO 318/297, minute 2339; "Report of the Select Committee on Steamship Subsidies," *BPP* (1902), IX, qq 2434-2438.

[26]CO 318/302, minute 27058. The note appears on a letter to Chamberlain from Sir James Fergusson, one of Royal Mail's directors. See also RMSP, Correspondence re: West Indies Mail Contracts.

Black. Even Chamberlain admitted that although Royal Mail showed little enthusiasm for this route when approached in 1898, "strictly we ought to have given them a chance...but we thought Pickford and Black gave us a better bargain."[27]

II

A palace revolution which brought the more enterprising Owen Philipps to the chairmanship of Royal Mail provided the opportunity for the company to defend a position now threatened by subsidised competitors. At first the new management made little headway. Royal Mail's tender to renew the mail contract due to expire in 1905 unwisely demanded improved terms and a higher subsidy. Alfred Lyttelton, Chamberlain's successor as Colonial Secretary, not surprisingly rejected the tender, arguing that "we should do well without a subsidy"[28] to encourage competition. In 1905 Jones, reported to be "very much interested in pushing the West Indies," was awarded the general mail contract, subject to colonial approval, "on the lines required by the Government...for the money...at its disposal."[29]

This decision betrayed every indication of haste, since the expiry of Royal Mail's 1900 contract was imminent. The Colonial Office had expected Jones to tender earlier and now seized upon his proposal. Royal Mail, on the other hand, whose own tender had been published, felt at a considerable disadvantage against competitors which had submitted a late bid with the benefit of what amounted to insider information. The new directors at Royal Mail were very alarmed. Apart from diversion of the subsidy, still an important item among general earnings, and of trade to an interloper whose poaching in 1900

---

[27]CO 318/300, minute 5054, again in response to a letter from Fergusson to Chamberlain. See also minute 4233.

[28]CO 318/311, minute 38709. See also Post 29, fos. 867-8/122F/1905.

[29]Jones to Post Office, 20 February 1905, Post 29, fos. 867-8/122F/1905.

had not been forgiven, the loss of the mail contract would be an embarrassing blow to their prestige.[30]

The Colonial Office experienced unexpected difficulties when Royal Mail challenged its decision. To outflank Sir Alfred Jones, the directors modified the controversial conditions of the earlier bid, canvassed parliamentary opinion, published "inspired" letters and enlisted support in the Caribbean at meetings convened by their agents.[31] The Post office took fright at the "intrigue which the Royal Mail Company seems to be carrying on," while Jones, already "champing his bit [in his] wroth with the Royal Mail" faced resistance in the West Indies where "things are not moving quickly or smoothly."[32] The islands, accustomed to a say, were dismayed at the Colonial Office's pressure for Elder Dempster, which simply threatened to replace one monopolist by another. The company's reputation among West African shippers and its connections with the United Fruit Company were causing anxiety.[33] In June 1905, therefore, the Colonial Office abandoned its planned contract with Elder Dempster, preferring to let the subsidy lapse in favour of postal payments for the volume of mail carried, as it had considered in 1899, thus throwing open the shipping services to competition.

The advent of a Liberal administration in 1906 offered a convenient moment to consider resumption of subsidies for the mail service which, as questions in Parliament indicated, had seriously deteriorated. Without a subsidy, Royal Mail omitted the smaller colonial ports and severed inter-island communications, not only to rationalise services in accordance with market demand but also, no

---

[30]Much of what follows is taken from Robert G. Greenhill, "The State Under Pressure: The West Indian Mail Contract, 1905," *Business History*, XI (1969), 120-127.

[31]Governor of Windward Islands to Colonial Office, 3 May 1905, Post 29, fos. 867-8/122F/1905.

[32]Buxton Forman to Postmaster General, 25 April 1905, Post 29, fos. 867-8/122F/1905.

[33]Great Britain, *Parliamentary Debates*, 4th Series, CXLV (1905), 909-911.

doubt, to create pressure for a renewed contract. But given the low payment of ships' letter rates for carrying the mails, the company was also in the mood for compromise.[34] In 1907, therefore, the directors agreed to reconnect the smaller islands to the main route from Southampton by a subsidised branch line from Barbados in a ten-year contract at £17,500 per annum, increased a year later to £25,000 in return for doubling the service's frequency.

In 1910 a new transatlantic mail contract was negotiated for £63,000 in the face of Royal Mail's threat to withdraw its main line from all British West Indian ports. Vested interests in Britain and the Caribbean rehearsed their established views about the importance of the direct mail service to "the reviving prosperity of the West Indies." To send the mails via the north Atlantic lines to New York would never obtain imperial approval. The new contract, due to expire in 1917 alongside the intercolonial services, sited the company's headquarters at Trinidad, included provision for refrigerated cargoes and allowed the company sufficient flexibility to develop business opportunities.[35]

III

Royal Mail's management did not sit back once the contract was renegotiated but competed more vigorously for commercial work. At first, of course, fiercer competition (especially from Elder Dempster) and the contract *interregnum* after 1905 compelled the directors to drop the smaller communities of the British West Indies from its main line in favour of the more lucrative outlets in the Caribbean. From September 1905 Royal Mail extended its service from Jamaica to New York, inaugurating a bitter rate war with Hamburg-Amerika, which had recently developed the trade. The company also forged stronger links with Central American and Mexican ports in which the growing

---

[34]Royal Mail to Post Office, 13 July, 17 September and 17 October 1905 and 10 August 1906, RMSP, West Indian Mail Contracts; Post Office to Colonial Office, 10 August 1905, Post 29, fo. 896/75G/1906.

[35]Greenhill, "British Shipping and Latin America," 301-305.

volume of plantation traffic, as well as the renewed construction of the Panama Canal, offered increasing business. Operations were not confined to passenger and high-class goods traffic, as freighters were ordered in 1904 to work general cargo services in the West Indies.[36]

Nor were Royal Mail's expanding business interests confined to shipping. The company began to help the colonies' diversification away from sugar towards a wider range of crops. Cotton shipments remained insignificant before 1914 but cocoa achieved some commercial success in Trinidad and Grenada--although output in these islands was dwarfed by developments in West Africa.

But Royal Mail's major enterprise in West Indian cash crops lay in the fruit industry. Stirred finally by the rebukes of the Royal Commission in 1897 and the subsequent surge in official interest, the company first waived charges incurred by the Imperial Department of Agriculture, established by Chamberlain to support fruit production, and then loaded produce marketed by the Symington fruit syndicate at Trinidad. The head start its rivals possessed at Jamaica, careless handling and the failure to attract official support prevented immediate success for these ventures but from 1903 the directors became "fully alive" to the possibilities.[37] The quality of Royal Mail tonnage was raised, marketing arrangements were improved and loans extended to Symington. Upon his death in 1904, Royal Mail bought and enlarged his business as the British West Indian Fruit Company, purchasing cold storage space in Southampton.[38] Royal Mail steadily increased its presence at Trinidad, where the island's better harbour facilities

---

[36]Details of these developments are found in Greenhill, "British Shipping and Latin America," 309-322.

[37]Philipps to Sir Daniel Morris, 4 December 1903 and 9 January 1904, Post 29, fos. 867-8/122F/1905. Morris was the first imperial commissioner of agriculture at the Imperial Department of Agriculture.

[38]"Colonial Reports (Trinidad)," *BPP* (1906), LXXV, 851-852; CO 318/309, minute 21279 (1903); *West India Committee Circular*, 16 March and 12 October 1903, and 30 August 1904.

encouraged the company to shift its headquarters from Barbados. By 1910 Port of Spain shipped ten times as many bananas as Barbados.[39]

Of course, it is important not to exaggerate Royal Mail's participation in the West Indian fruit industry, which remained largely tied to the American market by carriers like the United Fruit Company. Similarly, the combined crops of Trinidad and Barbados were still much smaller than that produced in Jamaica. Further, bananas from Central America and the Canary Islands enjoyed a much larger share of the British market and a higher reputation for quality than those shipped by Royal Mail. At Barbados, for example, protracted loading in the open roadstead and a lack of refrigerated capacity caused bananas to rot in the holds of the company's steamers.

Royal Mail also helped develop tourism on a commercial basis in the Caribbean, which complemented demand for its shipping services. As early as the 1880s the Quebec Steamship Company had conveyed American tourists to Bermuda and Royal Mail had operated Caribbean cruises, popular with wealthy convalescents. Alfred Jones' enterprise in Jamaican hotel construction and the Direct Line's declared objective to develop tourism brought a new dimension, which created an additional outlet for inter-company rivalry. In 1905 Royal Mail offered cruises from Liverpool to the West Indies in a joint-venture with the Cunard Company. It also invested in hotel projects and stimulated the tourist trade with Barbados, earning hard-won praise even from the Colonial Office. From 1909 Royal Mail broke into the increasingly popular American tourist trade in Bermuda, supported by a network of agents on the mainland, active advertising and new luxury tonnage, eventually forcing the Quebec Steamship Company to sue for peace.[40]

Indeed, the Royal Mail Steam Packet Company responded to the new business conditions in West Indian shipping by pursuing a much more vigorous policy towards its competitors. Pressure from

---

[39]*West India Committee Circular*, 2 and 30 July 1912, and 28 January 1913; S.B. Saul, "The British West Indies in Depression, 1880-1914," *Inter-American Economic Affairs*, XII (1958), 16.

[40]For details see, Greenhill, "British Shipping and Latin America," 318-320.

Moorgate induced Scruttons in 1906 to share cargo sailings from Glasgow, Hull and London to the Caribbean and to pool earnings. In 1913 Royal Mail captured Pickford and Black's expanding service between Canada and the West Indies after a concerted campaign to impress Ottawa, where the subsidy was paid, and to exploit colonial dissatisfaction with existing facilities, thus reversing the defeat suffered in 1900.[41]

Alternatively, Royal Mail's more aggressive stance forced rivals into operating agreements. After a period of vigorous rate-cutting, a truce established a permanent conference among shipowners in the Caribbean in 1904. The resulting advance in shipping charges was noted by the governor of Trinidad in his report that year. By 1907, with the settlement of any remaining differences between the major carriers, the West Indian trades were sub-divided, with members belonging to one or more groups. In 1908 Royal Mail forced a close working arrangement of agreed tariffs, pooled earnings and shared berths on Hamburg-Amerika, to which the United Fruit Company later adhered. Royal Mail abandoned calls at Santa Martha (Colombia) and Haiti in return for a free hand at Trinidad, now the company's headquarters for its West Indian services.[42] Not surprisingly, in the same year the West India Committee noted a serious advance in rates attributable to conference decisions "likely to prove detrimental to shippers and to the several industries of the colonies," a view echoed when officials gave evidence to the Royal Commission on Shipping Rings.[43]

---

[41]*The Times*, 24 March 1906; *Demerara Argosy*, 31 May 1906; Colonial Office to Postmaster General, 4 May 1905, Post 29, fo. 896/75G/1906; *West India Committee Circular*, 18 April and 20 November 1906; Philipps to Owen, 3 December 1909, and Skinner to Philipps, 21 February 1910, RMSP, Canadian Correspondence.

[42]"Report on British Trade with Central America," *BPP* (1913), LXVIII, cd 6969, 421; "Royal Commission on Shipping Rings," *BPP* (1909), XLVIII; Hyde, *Shipping Enterprise and Management*, 56-60; B.O. Hough, *Ocean Trade and Traffic* (Chicago, 1920), 182-183.

[43]*West India Committee Circular*, 29 March 1904.

Royal Mail not only neutralised competitors by means of rate wars and non-price competition based upon the improving quality of its own services but also eliminated rivals in mergers and takeovers. Perhaps the most spectacular example was the move to buy Elder Dempster on the death of Sir Alfred Jones. In 1909 Philipps, together with Lord Pirrie, chairman of Harland and Wolff, the Belfast ship-builders who constructed so much of Royal Mail's fleet, purchased Jones' shares, which gave them a controlling interest in Elder Dempster.[44] Not surprisingly, the Direct Line was terminated at the end of the contract in 1910, freeing Royal Mail from a competitor at Jamaica and offering the prospect of greater traffic and higher rates. But the end of the Direct Line was almost certainly not a unilateral decision based upon Royal Mail's business needs. Elder Dempster's own losses of £400,000, exclusive of deficits on running the hotels, had made the operation commercially unviable.[45] At the same time, Jamaica and Whitehall refused to contribute towards a new fruit contract once Elders and Fyffes, which could exploit their links with the United Fruit Company's banana plantations, established their own European service from the Caribbean.[46]

But Royal Mail's increasingly aggressive approach towards the shipping business in the West Indies was almost too successful in that it raised once again the fear of monopoly. The company, explained one official in 1910, "have secured to themselves the power of controlling the freight and passenger traffic between the United Kingdom and the West Indies...as they have removed their competitors."[47]

---

[44]For details of this development see, P.N. Davies, *The Trade Makers: Elder Dempster in West Africa, 1852-1972* (London, 1973).

[45]P.N. Davies, *Fyffes and the Banana: Musa Sapientum--A Centenary History, 1888-1988* (London, 1990), 122. For a less favourable view of Jones and his companies, see Douglas Hall, *Ideas and Illustrations in Economic History* (London, 1964), 59-93.

[46]Davies, *Fyffes and the Banana*, 123 ff.

[47]CO 318/324, minute 32714 (1910).

IV

The year 1911, when Royal Mail's postal contract was renegotiated, seemed to confirm the company's victory in the long struggle with Whitehall and rival shipowners. Philipps not only had apparently turned the tables on the Colonial Office but also had re-established a firm grip on the colonies after the humiliating defeats of 1900. Given the company's fixed assets in the West Indies, Royal Mail's threats to transfer its Caribbean headquarters to foreign soil or to abandon the colonies altogether might have been a bluff simply to exert pressure on both sides of the Atlantic. But by mobilising support in every influential quarter, exploiting shades of colonial opinion and eliminating the threat posed by Elder Dempster, Royal Mail had recovered the subsidy lost in 1905 and forced officials to renegotiate in private rather than invite open tendering. The company, observed one report, had "successfully held their own [against] departmental stubbornness."[48]

But if the victory was sweet its taste did not last long. Within ten years much of the structure of Royal Mail's operations in the West Indies had been abandoned. The Direct Line had already lapsed and the profound shocks of the First World War and the following slump in both the West Indies and the United Kingdom during the 1920s rendered debates about Royal Mail's performance obsolete. The company abandoned its transatlantic mail services in 1916 and its regular passenger routes to the Caribbean in 1920, withdrawing all but a monthly cargo line and the link between Canada and the West Indies, which still offered reasonable commercial prospects. Apart from the Bermudan venture Owen Philipps, now Lord Kylsant, dismantled his company's association with local industry and ended the coasting contracts by 1922.[49]

The reasons for these decisions are clear enough. Business prospects in the Caribbean for Royal Mail were simply not sufficiently attractive. In the fruit trade Royal Mail could not compete with the

---

[48]*Syren and Shipping,* 11 January 1911.

[49]Greenhill, "British Shipping and Latin America," 330-337.

scale of operations mounted by Elders and Fyffes or the United Fruit Company.[50] The West Indian economy stayed profoundly depressed as the profits from sugar, still the main staple, remained low despite all attempts to reduce costs, increase yields and modernise production methods. Subsidised European beet sugar undersold Caribbean producers, who were further thwarted by reviving protection in the 1920s. The islands, never able to raise much enthusiasm in London's financial markets, continued to suffer severe capital shortages which inhibited the provision of infrastructure, such as railways.[51] The depression which a Royal Commission had noted in the 1890s seemed unending, as the colonies remained vulnerable to falling prices which lowered local incomes. Wartime embargoes on British exports and what amounted to a suspension of luxury cruises reduced outward shipments of both freight and passengers.

Postwar prospects were no brighter. Any advantage from the withdrawal of German tonnage during and after the war was offset by the increased volume of neutral shipping, especially from the United States. The Grace Line and the Panama Railroad Company fleets continued working for the United States Shipping Board after 1918 and the Ward-Munson partnership proved unshakable between Nassau and the United States.[52] Even worse for Royal Mail, any lingering strategic importance of the West Indies colonies to Britain had disappeared and there was no powerful commercial lobby for the islands to press the government into action. The Caribbean had become something of a political and economic backwater. As a Colonial Office

---

[50]Davies, *Fyffes and the Banana*, 126. See also P.N. Davies, "The First Hundred Years: Fyffes and the Banana, 1888-1988," supplement to the *Fruit Trades Journal*, 9 September 1988.

[51]Richard A. Lobdell, "Pattern of Investment and Sources of Credit in the British West Indian Sugar Industry, 1838-97," *Journal of Caribbean History*, IV (1972), 31-53; Saul, "The British West Indies in Depression, 1880-1914;" R.W. Beachey, *The British West Indian Sugar Industry in the Late Nineteenth Century* (Oxford, 1957).

[52]RMSP, New York Correspondence; Greenhill, "British Shipping and Latin America," 333-334.

official minuted, "there is little doubt that it does not pay [Royal Mail] to call at British West Indian ports."[53] With the lack of tonnage during and after the war, as well as the spiralling price of coal into the early twenties, there was a huge opportunity cost in running services to the West Indies when Royal Mail enjoyed better prospects elsewhere.

Indeed, by this time it is almost certainly true that Kylsant was "properly fed up with the West Indies." Petty jealousies, inter-island rivalry and "the same old story of...ingratitude" exasperated the company. "There comes a time," explained John Allsop, Royal Mail's secretary, "when the worm will turn." The Chairman, he continued, "has had a great deal to try him." Local opinion, it seemed, almost resented the company's few successes, but "if steamers were cancelled for want of support," explained Allsop, "a tirade of abuse would sure to be delivered at us."[54]

Further, changes in government policy put paid to any idea of fresh subsidies, since the West Indies did not figure largely in any postwar plans for imperial economic regeneration. Although the general mail service was the subject of an official inquiry in 1919, when the West Indian Shipping Committee urged negotiations, Whitehall would only guarantee three-quarters of any payment.[55] Growing divisions emerged between the smaller colonies, which wanted direct services rather than branch lines, and the larger islands, which did not want to pay the higher cost. British officials now looked only to extricate themselves discreetly. By 1925 Prime Minister Baldwin saw no reason for a special contract paid for by the British taxpayer when

---

[53]CO 318/324, minute 32714 (1910).

[54]John Allsop to Hulbert (Halifax, N.S., agent), 27 March 1925, and to Stewart (Halifax, N.S., representative), 4 and 9 June 1926, RMSP, Canadian Correspondence.

[55]"West India Shipping Committee," *BPP* (1919), XXX, 867-886; *The Times*, 31 October 1919.

"existing facilities for the conveyance of mails are adequate."[56] Finally, the Canadian government, which had extended Royal Mail's contract on no less than thirteen occasions between 1919 and 1926, replaced the company, itself already disillusioned by the failure to negotiate a long-term agreement. In the deflationary spirit of the 1920s, when Whitehall, the colonies and Ottawa all preached retrenchment, abandoning mail payments made useful savings. Events had now convinced Kylsant that there was "not much money to be made by acting for governments."

The surprise is not that Royal Mail effectively surrendered its links with West Indies after the First World War but rather that it stayed so long in an area which clearly offered little business. It is not easy to resolve the paradox but a number of factors might explain why the company did not leave earlier. First, Royal Mail had acquired fixed assets in the Caribbean, an agency network, dockside facilities, hotels and fruit industry connections which could not be easily liquidated. While ships could be transferred to new routes, the tonnage often employed in the West Indies, until the building programme begun by Philipps, was too old for the South American services. The second-hand market or scrap were not necessarily attractive alternatives.

Second, Royal Mail perhaps remained in the West Indies in anticipation of a long-term policy of colonial regeneration of the sort Chamberlain seemed to promise at the turn of the century. If his concept of underdeveloped estates in a partnership between business and government had really born fruit, good commercial prospects might have been anticipated. For example, the Imperial Department of Agriculture in Barbados developed new, improved varieties of sugar cane in an attempt to revive the local economy. It encouraged a partnership of scientific officers and planters. Philipps's investment and construction policy after 1902 seemed to reflect a growing optimism that there would be a return upon capital. If so, it was a case of hope triumphant over experience.

---

[56] *Parliamentary Debates*, 5th Series, CLIX, cols. 2596-2597 and CLXXXVI, cols. 26-27.

But a more important explanation of Royal Mail's reluctance to withdraw might be because the corporate culture at Royal Mail inhibited change even when it was clear that the business environment had changed. Owen Philipps certainly brought a shift in the style of management at the company and modernised its fleets. No longer was Royal Mail associated with the naval ethos which emphasised discipline at sea, the rule book and the mail service. But even he was slow to reorganise the company's trades along strictly commercial lines, which would have meant largely pulling out of the West Indies. In 1911 Philipps claimed the company needed £78,000 per annum to place a fortnightly mail service to the Caribbean on a sound commercial basis but would settle for less "in view of the historic connection between Royal Mail and the West Indian colonies."[57] In a sense the recognition of providing a public service came before the objective of profit maximisation and, in any case, the profits from the South American routes could be used to cross-subsidise the losses in the West Indies. By the 1920s, when British shipping entered a particularly difficult period, such cross-subsidisation could no longer be justified. The mistake was not inadequate investment, as colonial interests suggested, but in not abandoning the West Indies earlier. Those lines that remained, like Harrisons and Elders and Fyffes, operated mainly cargo services to Central America rather than to the colonies.

V

What does this case study reveal about Royal Mail as a company? Its commercial policy in the West Indies offers evidence of two kinds in the debate. On the one hand, the view that the company was a profit-maximising monopolist "with a wolfish instinct to devour everything it could seize upon" commands some support. From 1903 it aggressively resisted competition in what it considered its business preserve and developed backward and forward linkages in fruit production, marketing and hotel management. By exploiting vested

---

[57]Owen Philipps to Campbell, 18 November 1910, and Royal Mail to Post Office, 24 November 1910, RMSP, West India Mail Contracts.

interests in Britain and the Caribbean and threatening to abandon colonial ports the directors were able to reverse unfavourable contract decisions. Eliminating rivals like Elder Dempster through mergers, operating agreements and the conference system increased transport costs and reduced shippers' choice. Royal Mail's powerful position in the Caribbean by 1914 must have made the effects of its subsequent withdrawal all the more damaging. The squabble between Trinidad and Barbados for the company's West Indian headquarters illustrates the firm's importance. Direct communication to the United Kingdom and Central America and investment in dockside facilities and local industry, both of which provided employment, were important advantages for the successful island.

On the other hand, Royal Mail's role as a social force rather than purely a profit maximiser should be recognised. Its contractual demands in 1905 and 1910 have to be set against Philipps's declared policy of assisting the West Indies, the company's sacrifices to perform a network of services no other firm would undertake and the introduction of purpose-built tonnage. Royal Mail subsequently ran new tonnage on the complementary coasting services around the smaller islands which fed the main line, as much to promote corporate image as to make a profit.

What does the episode say of the commercial abilities of officials? While it appears that the Colonial Office was outmanoeuvred in its negotiations with Royal Mail, this does not mean that officials, accustomed to a *laissez-faire*, non-interventionist approach, were inexperienced in their relations with businessmen or unwilling to press them. To imagine the Colonial Office, which knew that the inter-colonial contract and the company's investments tied it to the West Indies until 1917, tamely surrendering a general mail contract in 1911 is to misunderstand the position. The government could have called Philipps's bluff as it waited to extract more favourable terms from the company or until the colonies themselves offered higher contributions, knowing that Royal Mail could not do without the subsidy. Moreover, they realised that the "policy of pressing the Royal Mail" had yielded results.[58] Although, as W.K. Hancock wrote, "imperial sovereignty, with its political processes and its restricted geographical framework, was but little in the minds of the men who found their profit in the great services of shipping and insurance," Royal Mail did respond to the lead orchestrated by the Colonial Office.[59]

The episode may also throw light on wider issues. It suggests that in the end official intervention to improve shipping services in the Caribbean had at best mixed results. Undoubtedly, Royal Mail was stirred into action which, despite the shake-up in the company's management after Philipps took over, might not have happened but for the intervention of Joseph Chamberlain and Sir Alfred Jones. Officials perhaps at last accepted a greater responsibility towards the islands, an attitude which might have succeeded but for events outside their control after 1914.[60] But, on balance, the outcome reinforces recent unfavourable judgements about Chamberlain's ability to interest businessmen in the Empire--in contrast to the views of some of his earlier biographers.[61] "It is clear," explained Hardy, "that the capitalists were not going to provide help where Chamberlain had a right to expect it, for all the popular enthusiasms he might assume in Birmingham."[62] Considering the time and effort expended on the West Indies, little had been achieved.[63] Sceptical of Chamberlain's vision of economic opportunity in the Caribbean, hard-headed businessmen took little

---

[58]CO 318/302, minute 41858, 26 November 1901.

[59]W.K. Hancock, "Agenda for the Study of British Imperial History, 1850-1950," *Journal of Economic History*, XIII (1953), 258.

[60]Ronald Hyam, *Britain's Imperial Century, 1815-1914: A Study of Empire and Expansion* (London, 1976), takes the view that Chamberlain's energy and enthusiasm made a deep impression on the Colonial Office.

[61]Porter, "In Memoriam: Joseph Chamberlain," 293-294.

[62]Hardy, "Joseph Chamberlain," 186.

[63]Ronald Hyam, *Elgin and Churchill at the Colonial Office 1905-1908: The Watershed of Empire-Commonwealth* (London, 1968).

interest in the area. Although the presence of Sir Alfred Jones at Jamaica might have helped diversify the island's economy, the development of the fruit trade would almost certainly have happened without such intervention, given the interest of the United Fruit Company, Elders and Fyffes. Moreover, the very company Chamberlain hoped to supplant, Royal Mail, increased its hold on the West Indies on the eve of the First World War. In the end officials refused to continue underwriting a mail contract and terminated the fruit contract, worsening communication between the islands and the mother country.

Finally, what does this case study add to our knowledge of the relationship between the Colonial Office and British businessmen? Is it possible to determine the limits and extent of the powers available to each side? Kubicek argues that in shipping, as elsewhere, growing commercial complexity and the different objectives of business enterprises made cooperation with government policy difficult.[64] On the one hand, the increasing scale of operations through mergers and the impact of the conference system antagonised shippers and made officials suspicious. On the other, government interference upset profit-maximising businessmen.

But the fact that officials and businessmen took a different perspective does not mean that their ultimate goals were opposed. Political necessity and national interest do not invariably clash with profit-making. Both sides wanted an economically active and prosperous West Indies, the government to relieve the taxpayer and businessmen to increase their turn-over. At times, when the Colonial Office played one company off against another or when entrepreneurs put pressure on officials, the alliance seemed uneasy. But in the game of bluff and counter-bluff there was, in fact, a balance to be struck in the equation of power between businessmen and colonial officials. The Colonial Office was no more in the hands of unscrupulous capitalists than Royal Mail was the helpless victim of interfering officials. Each side needed the other and it was no coincidence that both the Colonial Office and companies like Royal Mail began to lose interest in West Indian shipping at about the same time.

---

[64]Kubicek, *The Administration of Imperialism*, 117-118.

Shipbuilding at Belfast: Workman, Clark and Company, 1880-1935

Andrew Armitage

Conventionally the development of shipbuilding at Belfast has been discussed almost exclusively in terms of Harland and Wolff, one of Europe's largest maritime enterprises. Perhaps this is understandable, for the firm is the last major survivor of merchant shipbuilding in the United Kingdom. Yet Ulster's industrial base looms so large in the convoluted Anglo-Irish economic relationship that all its aspects deserve attention. This study attempts to redress the balance of historiography by examining the meteoric course of another large-scale shipbuilding business on the European periphery: Workman, Clark and Company.

A rare consensus exists among historians as to the economic origins of iron shipbuilding in Belfast.[1] By the mid-nineteenth century northeastern Ulster was fast emerging as a mature industrial region within the British economy; linen textile production had gravitated from the rural domestic context to the urban factory and had supplanted cotton in scale of output. Ireland's post-Famine primary sector was unable to sustain its huge labour force, and Belfast manufacturing was a net beneficiary of the demographic influx that took the city's population from 37,000 in 1821 to 174,000 in 1871. Other causal factors for industrialisation included a dynamic banking mechanism which facilitated the flow of agrarian and merchant capital into the secondary sector, and a proximity, both geographical and cultural, to the industrial regions of Lancashire, Cumberland and central Scotland. But this textile revolution was largely achieved through endogenous factor

[1]J.M. Goldstrom, "The Industrialisation of the North-East," in L.M. Cullen (ed.), *The Formation of the Irish Economy* (Cork, 1969), 101-112; P. Ollerenshaw, "Industry," in L. Kennedy and P. Ollerenshaw (eds.), *An Economic History of Ulster, 1820-1940* (Manchester, 1985), 62-108.

inputs; shipbuilding was another matter. As several English and Irish ports discovered, iron shipbuilding was essentially sustainable only in the presence of a wider industrial base. The decline of London, Cork and Liverpool as centres of shipbuilding reflected remoteness from engineering and the wage effect this engendered.

Although iron shipbuilding first began in Belfast during the 1854 boom, production was initially pursued on a small scale as an experiment in national self-sufficiency, utilising locally-manufactured plates produced from indigenous coal and ore and promoted by large-scale municipal investment in the form of navigational improvements to the River Lagan. Inflated wage costs incurred by the local shipwrights soon rendered business unprofitable, and the failure of this autarkic experiment proved the point of later dependency theorists.[2] Ireland's experience was not exceptional, although relevant parallels have hitherto eluded most historical accounts. Shipbuilding in Denmark progressed along remarkably similar lines, since it was contingent on external raw materials, German investment and "substitute" entrepreneurs. Also evident was the tendency towards monopolistic enterprises characteristic of economies on the periphery.[3]

Edward Harland's appointment in 1855 to manage the Belfast shipyard of Robert Hickson represented a new departure for the industry in Ireland, which had previously catered for domestic demand. In particular, it guaranteed access to cross-Channel markets in Liverpool and to family capital in England where Harland's relatives, John Bibby and Gustav Schwabe, were proprietors of the Bibby Line. Gustav Wolff, a nephew of Schwabe, entered Belfast shipbuilding in 1861 at the behest of the family, but was to a great extent a "sleeping" partner. The Oceanic Steam Navigation Company formed in 1867 by Schwabe and Thomas Henry Ismay was largely conceived as an outlet

---

[2]Goldstrom, "The Industrialisation of the North-East;" M. Moss and J.R. Hume, *Shipbuilders to the World: 125 Years of Harland and Wolff, 1861-1986* (Belfast, 1986), 11-36.

[3]H.C. Johansen, *The Danish Economy in the Twentieth Century* (London, 1987), 6-39; Ove Hornby, "Industrialisation in Denmark and the Loss of the Duchies," *Scandinavian Economic History Review*, XVII (1969), 23-46.

for the new shipyard, and amply fulfilled its purpose; the White Star and the Bibby Lines remained Harland and Wolff's principal clients until the 1920s, Bibby accounting for fifty-one percent of ship tonnage launched in the years 1859-1869. Beyond this, the shipyard's circle of "builders' friends" was augmented by William Pirrie (a partner after 1874), whose investments included the African Steam Ship Company (1878) and the Ulster Steamship Company (1879).[4]

Although it has recently been argued by F. Geary and W. Johnson that major economies of scale and anti-cyclical growth were not realised from this process of integration, none of their statistical results derive from regression analysis and are far from conclusive.[5] The statistical validity of their research is to some extent reduced by the nature of their sources--annual rather than quarterly data. Moreover, in asserting that Belfast experienced cyclical fluctuations of greater amplitude than other United Kingdom shipbuilding districts, Geary and Johnson create a false antithesis. Of the British regions with which Belfast is contrasted, only Sunderland was exclusively a merchant shipbuilding centre and hence comparable; the other two, Clydeside and Newcastle, were also involved in the construction of warships--both for the Admiralty and for export--which itself mitigated cyclical extremes. Unfortunately no adjustment has been made for these discrepancies.

Entrepreneurship and its role in economic development have increasingly become the focus of debate in Irish historiography. If measured by the eulogies of Samuel Smiles, Edward Harland was an entrepreneur of the first rank, for the shipbuilder's business biography, published in *Men of Invention and Industry* (1884), immortalised him. To Smiles he was both engineering genius and pioneer of industrial development in Ireland's retarded economy.[6] In reality, this account

---

[4]F. Geary and W. Johnson, "Shipbuilding in Belfast, 1861-1986," *Irish Economic and Social History*, XVI (1989), 42-64.

[5]Joel Mokyr, *Why Ireland Starved: A Quantitative and Analytical History of the Irish Economy, 1800-50* (London, 1983), 211-212.

[6]Samuel Smiles, *Men of Invention and Industry* (London, 1884), 288-323.

tended to ignore the substantive contribution made to Belfast shipbuilding by William Pirrie, who effectively dominated the firm as well as the industry for half a century after 1874; Harland devoted his final two decades to Conservative Unionist politics, acquiring a baronetcy and a small landed estate in County Leitrim. Pirrie's enlightened approach to industrial relations contrasted starkly with Harland's *laissez-faire* antipathy to collective bargaining; more important, Pirrie appreciated the product implications of an increasingly protectionist world market. Nonetheless, Harland's policy of importing skilled labour from England and Clydeside proved a prerequisite of continuing expansion. One corollary was that existing sectarian monopolies of most shipbuilding trades were exacerbated as skilled employment became ever more closely identified with Ulster Unionism and its adherents. Dependency upon Britain for a supply of craft labour also generated strange distortions in the wage structure of the industry. For example, while platers were paid ten percent above the standard Clyde rate, riveters were paid only two percent above and long-standing and declining trades, such as the ship-rigging, earned less than their Scottish counterparts.[7] Premiums to attract expatriate artisans were easily outweighed by savings accrued from cheap unskilled labour. Seasonal and cyclical migration of skilled workers emerged as a salient characteristic of the Belfast shipyard, and labour mobility appears to have been high, not insignificant in an industry

---

[7]Board of Trade Labour Statistics; Public Record Office of Northern Ireland (hereafter PRONI), 2805/WB/15, Harland and Wolff Wage Books. My own regression analysis confirms the wage-elasticity differential between Belfast and other shipbuilding regions; the relationships between real wages (the dependent variable) and ship construction (the independent variable) for the period 1893-1913, were of the following dimensions:

Belfast	R^2 = 0.84	(Durbin-Watson statistic = 0.97)
Tyne	R^2 = 0.47	(Durbin-Watson statistic = 0.64)
Wear	R^2 = -0.11	(Durbin-Watson statistic = 0.34)
Clyde	R^2 = 0.62	(Durbin-Watson statistic = 0.84)

Calculated by the ordinary least-squares method from data in the *Labour Gazette*. Alastair Reid stresses the cyclical variability of skilled workers' wages in "Skilled Workers in the Shipbuilding Industry, 1880-1920," in Austen Morgan and Bob Purdie (eds.), *Ireland: Divided Nation, Divided Class* (London, 1980), 117-118.

requiring a ratio of skilled to unskilled of around two to one. Indeed, the imperative of retaining local wage flexibility is the most obvious reason why Belfast shipbuilders remained aloof from the Shipbuilding Employers' Federation and chose to negotiate independently.

Despite its considerable scale of production, the backward-linkage effect of shipbuilding was modest within the context of Ulster; an ancillary rope industry was successfully introduced during the 1870s, but the main impact of Harland and Wolff was felt laterally. In 1876, for instance, a new shipyard was established in Belfast by the partnership of Richard Lewis, an expatriate Welsh engineer who had managed the Dublin firm of Bewley and Webb until its liquidation, and John MacIlwaine, one of Harland's own naval architects. Undercapitalization dictated that its success would never extend beyond the market for Irish Sea coasters.

An altogether more impressive initiative was undertaken in 1879, however, when another Harland and Wolff naval architect, Frank Workman, sponsored by family capital, agreed to form a private limited company with George Smith Clark, scion of a leading Glasgow textile and shipowning dynasty. The result, Workman, Clark and Company, was incorporated in April 1880, having been granted eight months earlier a lease on a four-acre shipbuilding site on the County Antrim side of the Lagan.[8] An initial capitalization of £30,000 permitted the immediate employment of 150 craftsmen and ensured that the first tenders to local shipowners were competitive. As table 1 shows, share allocation between the two principal directors was to be equal (thirty-one percent each), with the remaining thirty-eight percent being distributed among the respective families. These proportions were broadly maintained despite the enormous rise in investment required prior to the cessation of family control in 1920. In common with other Belfast shipbuilding concerns, the new enterprise owed

[8]Minutes of the General Committee of the Belfast Harbour Commissioners, XXXIV, 379, Belfast Harbour Commissioners' Archives.

nothing to industrial banking of the type which promoted the province's linen sector.[9]

Table 1
Directors of Workman, Clark and Company, Limited and the Allocation of Shares at Incorporation, 29 April 1880

Directors	Address	Occupation	Share Allocation	Share Value
Francis Workman	Belfast	Shipbuilder	368	£9,200
George Smith Clark	Belfast	Shipbuilder	368	9,200
Thomas Workman	Belfast	Merchant	240	6,100
George Smith	Glasgow	Shipowner	100	2,500
John Workman	Belfast	Merchant	77	1,925
Charles Workman	Belfast	Doctor of Medicine	40	1,000
William Service Workman	Glasgow	Shipbuilder	5	125
James Clark	Paisley	Gentleman	2	50
Total			1,200	30,000

Source: Public Record Office of Northern Ireland (PRONI), COM 40/1/W34, Workman, Clark and Company Papers.

Frank Workman, born in 1856, was a member of a local Presbyterian family of muslin manufacturers and merchants who had migrated to Belfast from Saltcoats in Ayrshire during the early eighteenth century (see figure 2). Fortunately for Workman, his family retained close links with its Scottish kin, several of whom were prominent Glasgow shipowners and builders. Educated like many

[9]Philip Ollerenshaw, "The Belfast Banks, 1820-1900" (Unpublished Ph.D. thesis, University of Sheffield, 1982), 170-193.

members of the industrial bourgeoisie at the Royal Belfast Academical Institution, Frank Workman had entered Harland's drawing office as the traditional "gentleman's apprenticeship" for management. Although more privileged by social origin, George Smith Clark (1861-1935) was also related to several Clyde shipowners: his father, James Clark, a Paisley textile magnate, was also a partner in Clark and Service, a leading firm of shipping managers; one maternal uncle owned the Allan Line of passenger steamers; while another was chairman of George Smith and Sons, proprietors of the City Line (see figure 3). Immediately on leaving Merchiston Castle School in Edinburgh, George Clark commenced his training in naval architecture at Harland and Wolff, where he became acquainted with Workman.[10] Edward Harland clearly regarded the Workman, Clark venture with equanimity if not approval, and in his position as chairman of the city's Harbour Commissioners was able to facilitate his former proteges. Commercial rivalry was not conceivable at a stage when the larger shipyard employed 4,500 and enjoyed an annual output exceeding 15,000 tons.[11]

Notwithstanding the nexus with Scotland's burgeoning shipping market, domestic Irish demand accounted for a sizeable share of the new shipyard's orders. In its first decade no less than twenty-eight percent of merchant tonnage was commissioned by Belfast and Dublin shipowners; their importance as clients is partly explained by the limited capacity of the yard, but to some extent as well by the recessions which beset the industry during the 1880s, notably in 1885 and 1887. Two vessels were completed in the company's first year of business; *Ethel* of 265 tons for David Macbrayne of Glasgow and *William Hinde* of 346 tons for the local shipowner of the same name. The Ulster Steamship Company became a major client for ocean-going

[10]D.S. Johnson, "Francis Workman," in D.J. Jeremy and C. Shaw (eds.), *Dictionary of Business Biography: A Biographical Dictionary of Business Leaders Active in Britain in the Period 1860-1980* (London, 1985), V, 891-893; D.S. Johnson, "Sir George Smith Clark," *ibid.* (London, 1984), I, 683-686.

[11]Minutes of the General Committee of the Belfast Harbour Commissioners, XXXVI, 117-118, 130, and 160, Belfast Harbour Commissioners' Archives.

cargo vessels, while William J. Woodside and Company was the principal purchaser of iron and steel sailing barques for Ulster's coasting trade.[12]

Lacking an engine works, Workman, Clark was forced to rely initially upon the local firm of John Rowan and Sons, which unfortunately had little experience in marine engineering. When this arrangement proved unsatisfactory, subsequent ships were engined by J. and J. Howden of Glasgow, a concern with a world-wide reputation. Although the cyclical recession of 1881-1885 provoked the cancellation of three orders, Workman, Clark was able to surmount the crisis through its connection with George Smith and Sons. The *City of Cambridge* (1882) was at 2,760 tons by far the largest vessel constructed to that point, as well as the first passenger and cargo vessel; a further six ships were commissioned by the City Line for Glasgow's India trade during the 1880s. The value of the Clark and Service connection was shown in the four cargo ships completed for that company in the period 1883-1890. One implicit axiom of Belfast shipbuilding was that the British Admiralty very rarely accepted tenders from shipyards in Ireland. Consequently, in peacetime no warships were constructed in Belfast and no incentive existed to invest in specifically naval-related capital goods.

By 1882 the shipyard's workforce had doubled to four hundred, although a permanent niche in the lucrative Liverpool market was not secured until the 1890s. Even so a fresh injection of capital from shareholders raised the nominal value of the company by fifty percent to £45,000 in 1883. The sources of the new investment generally reflected the directors' interests in the Belfast linen industry: in 1881 George Clark had married the heiress to Henry Matier and Sons, a leading cambric business, and its surplus capital was siphoned into fixed shipbuilding plant, particularly the new electric derrick cranes purchased from William Arrol. Given the "lumpy" nature of shipbuild-

---

[12]Workman, Clark (1928) Ltd., *Shipbuilding at Belfast, 1880-1933* (Belfast, 1934), 5-19.

ing capital requirements, access to these funds was vital to obviate the need for public corporate status and to preserve family control.[13]

Spatial restrictions on the north bank of the Lagan were considerable; whereas Harland and Wolff's shipbuilding site on Queen's Island had been reclaimed from the estuary, Workman, Clark's yard was confined by docks and wharves. In 1891 it was determined that smooth expansion could only be maintained if an engineering department could be established, although this necessitated leasing land adjacent to Harland's on the County Down side of the Lagan. Clark's cousin, Charles Edward Allan (1863-1933), who had served his time at J. and G. Thomson of Clydebank, was engaged as the company's first engineering director, an appointment which extended the client base on the Clyde. Alexander Allan, chairman of R. and C. Allan, agreed that new tonnage should thereafter be commissioned from Workman, Clark. The Allan Line immediately ordered the twin cargo ships, *Ormiston* and *Ormidale* (3560 tons), which were launched in 1893. The need for greater engineering capacity was the main motive for acquiring the shipyard and engine works of MacIlwaine and MacColl (formerly MacIlwaine and Lewis); its management had pioneered the use of steel in the construction of bulk ore coasters and the technologies proved of value to Workman, Clark.[14]

The 1890s were a period of exponential progress in output and investment (see table 2). Unlike the initial period, however, the secondary phase of expansion was based on specialisation in the higher-value sector of the market, in particular in refrigerated shipping. Although Pollard and Robertson assert that Workman, Clark had a major interest in passenger liners, in fact only nineteen were produced

---

[13]PRONI, COM 40/1/W34, Workman, Clark and Company, Ltd. Papers. Cf. Harland and Wolff, which on incorporation in 1885 had an issued share capital of £297,500; Moss and Hume, *Shipbuilders*, 56-57.

[14]Lloyd's Register of Shipping, 1893.

in the shipyard's fifty-five year existence.[15] The era of "new imperialism" and state intervention increased freight rates on most routes, British shipowners benefiting disproportionately from new trade in primary products with South America, Australasia and West Africa. Apart from the long-standing relationship with Clark and Service, none of these shipowners had familial links with Workman, Clark, the majority, like Alfred Holt and Company, Lamport and Holt and Houlder Brothers being Mersey-based (see table 3). Fruit transport emerged as the staple business, and by the turn of the century this rapidly-acquired expertise broadened Workman, Clark's export potential. United States' fruit companies increasingly turned to the Belfast shipyard to supply the demand for transport from their plantations in Central America and the Caribbean. The corollary of changing market orientation was that low-cost, undifferentiated sailing vessels were abandoned as unprofitable. Through the re-investment of accumulated profits, the share capital rose to £360,000 by 1900, an eight-fold increase in less than twelve years.[16]

Such success was considered by most Belfast industrialists to be predicated on imperial free trade and continuing economic union with Britain. But when in 1885 the Gladstonian Liberal Party adopted Home Rule as a solution to Ireland's national question, Liberal entrepreneurs like Frank and Thomas Workman and George Smith Clark were forced to reassess their traditional political allegiance. Parnellite Irish nationalists regarded the industrial preeminence of the northeast as an unfortunate aberration from the agrarian route they espoused as a means to national independence; to republicans it symbolised dependency upon Britain. Perhaps inescapably, Belfast shipbuilding assumed a key role in this debate as Ulster Unionists reacted to the ideological and economic threat inherent in a devolved nationalist government, committed to high tariff policies to foster infant industry in southern Ireland. Protectionism seemed certain to

---

[15]S. Pollard and P. Robertson, *The British Shipbuilding Industry, 1870-1914* (London, 1979), 84-85.

[16]PRONI, COM 40/1/W34.

provoke damaging retaliation from Britain, and so the anticipated process of de-industrialisation ensuing from repeal was stressed to the skilled Protestant workers whose Unionist affiliation might be undermined by the incipient socialist movement. Equally, the challenge to *laissez-faire*, imperial unity and British investments was articulated to English and Scottish audiences with great effect by Unionist businessmen.[17]

Table 2
Workman, Clark Output, 1880-1935

Year	No. of Vessels	Gross Tonnage	Indicated Horse Power
1880	2	800	
1881	5	1800	
1882	5	6000	
1883	8	8900	These vessels not engined by Workman, Clark and Co.
1884	12	9800	
1885	4	7000	
1886	5	8000	
1887	6	3300	
1888	11	10800	
1889	7	18100	
1890	10	15100	
1891	12	21700	
1892	8	22800	8300
1893	9	19000	8100
1894	9	33400	15150
1895	9	34100	19850
1896	12	42900	25000
1897	7	25100	16100
1898	9	53900	31000
1899	7	45500	29950
1900	10	56600	31350
1901	12	53100	33300
1902	12	75800	46900

[17]Henry Patterson, *Class Conflict and Sectarianism: The Protestant Working Class and the Belfast Labour Movement, 1868-1920* (Belfast, 1980), 42-61.

Year	No. of Vessels	Gross Tonnage	Indicated Horse Power
1903	7	44500	27550
1904	12	44200	34000
1905	12	58000	44250
1906	13	65100	49500
1907	12	60900	45650
1908	8	50600	38400
1909	16	88200	76550
1910	8	50100	36300
1911	10	67600	51800
1912	10	83600	53400
1913	11	84700	60200
1914			
1915			
1916	77	259850	198850
1917			
1918			
1919	13	87600	58100
1920	13	80035	55700
1921	13	88558	52250
1922	6	51300	29000
1923	5	40900	26300
1924	9	45800	26550
1925	7	25911	21800
1926	3	26760	15025
1927	6	48911	39450
1928	1	357	450
1929	7	53900	32300
1930	11	54880	48900
1931	3	33300	18200
1932	1	5740	6400
1933	2	13800	12000
1934	3	29000	31000
1935	1	8000	5200
	491	2224688	

Source: *Lloyd's Register of Shipping*, various years; Workman, Clark (1928), Ltd., *Shipbuilding at Belfast* (Belfast, 1934).

Table 3
The Principal Clients of Workman, Clark and Company

Shipping Line/ Managing Company	Gross Tonnage Purchased	Number of Vessels	% of Total Output (GRT)
Alfred Holt and Co. (Ocean Steam Ship Co.)	244,562	36	11.0
United Fruit Co. (Clark and Service)	177,268	37	8.0
Ellerman Lines (City Line)	97,063	13	4.4
Commonwealth and Dominion Line	93,885	11	4.2
Lamport and Holt (Liverpool, Brazil and River Plate Steam Navigation Co.)	89,463	11	4.0
Andrew Weir and Co. (Bank Line)	72,446	12	3.3
James P. Corry and Co. (Star Line)	70,067	8	3.1
T. and J. Harrison	66,850	7	3.0
Royal Mail Steam Packet Co.	65,467	10	2.9
Shaw, Savill and Albion and Co.	53,472	13	2.8
Tyser and Co.	60,845	10	2.7
Ulster Steam Navigation Co. (G. Heyn and Sons)	55,141	8	2.5
Elders and Fyffes (Clark and Service)	50,662	10	2.3
R. and C. Allan/J. and Allan	48,538	9	2.2

Shipping Line/ Managing Company	Gross Tonnage Purchased	Number of Vessels	% of Total Output (GRT)
British India Steam Navigation Co.	46,694	8	2.1
George Smith and Sons (City Line)	44,602	8	2.0

Source: *Lloyd's Register of Shipping*, various years.

Shipbuilders had played a seminal role in Ulster Unionism from its inception as a political movement; Sir Edward Harland was returned to Parliament for North Belfast in 1889, while his partner, G.W. Wolff, represented the other shipbuilding division, East Belfast, without interruption from 1892 to 1910. Following Harland's death in 1895, Frank Workman and George Clark were prevailed upon by the Irish Unionist Alliance to stand for political office; while the former pursued a career in municipal politics, Clark eventually secured election to Westminster from North Belfast, a seat which he held for three years. Undoubtedly this political success represented a form of clientism on the part of shipyard workers who feared the erosion of high-wage industrial employment; with equal certainty it strengthened the legitimacy of the shipbuilders in their confrontation with the trade unions. George Clark emerged as a particularly strident opponent of syndicalism and led the employers' resistance to the Belfast Dock Strike of 1907 called by James Larkin. Conversely, commercial imperatives meant that William Pirrie effected a rapprochement with the Liberal Party; Balfour had initially opposed the formation of the International Mercantile Marine and so provoked Pirrie's defection. Such was Harland and Wolff's fear of Conservative tariff reform that Lord Pirrie was prepared to accept devolution for Ireland and to accommodate constitutional nationalism. Tensions between the two Belfast shipbuilders were exacerbated by their divergent political strategies to the point where long-standing agreements on collective bargaining were abandoned. The outcome was competition within the

Belfast Harbour Commissioners for land and in the labour market for key employees.[18]

George Clark's status within the Ulster Unionist Council (UUC) was enhanced as the smaller shipyard continued to expand as an employer. By 1912 when the third Home Rule Bill was introduced, Workman, Clark had a work-force of nine thousand, and when loyalist resistance to government policy intensified, Clark was among the first to organise his workers within the Ulster Volunteer Force. Nationalist accounts of the 1912 Belfast riots stress his refusal to re-employ Catholic and socialist employees expelled during political violence. Marxist historians have interpreted this attempt to impose sectarian uniformity as an unsubtle if effective attempt to reduce the power of trade unionism in the Lagan industry. Whatever the motivation, Clark became closely involved in preparations to oppose Home Rule by physical force. Appointed chairman of the UUC's arms committee, he superintended the surreptitious importation of German munitions through the shipyard. Small consignments of ammunition were initially spirited in as "black-jointing" but larger amounts were transported as it became obvious that the Dublin Castle authorities were unwilling to prevent it. Had the First World War not intervened, George Clark had been destined to become a senior minister in the province's provisional government.[19] The firm's efforts during the Ulster crisis were amply rewarded after Sir Edward Carson was appointed First Lord of the Admiralty. For the first time Workman, Clark obtained lucrative repair contracts for the navy.

The political instability of 1912-1914 could not eclipse the fact that the Edwardian era was one of immense technological innovation. In 1902 Workman, Clark had begun to pioneer the application of Sir Charles Parsons' steam turbine, and the Allan passenger liner *Victorian* (10,630 tons and 11,000 horsepower) was the world's first turbine-propelled liner when it was launched in 1904 for the north Atlantic routes. In 1912 the firm emulated Pirrie's Burmeister and Wain

---

[18]*Ibid.*, 62-91; P. Buckland, *Irish Unionism* (Dublin, 1973), II, chapter 3.

[19]A.T.Q. Stewart, *The Ulster Crisis* (London, 1967), 77, 96-112, 207-209.

endeavour by purchasing a licence from Sulzer Brothers of Winterthur to permit the manufacture of its diesel engines. The United Fruit Company of Boston ordered its first three refrigerated fruit ships from Workman, Clark in 1904; *San Jose*, *Limon* and *Esparta* were to form the nucleus of the "Great White Fleet." Moreover, in the following year, Elder and Fyffe, the British subsidiary of United Fruit, took delivery of the sister fruit carriers, *Pacuare* and *Zent* of 3891 tons for the Jamaica banana trade.[20] Between 1904 and 1917 the Shaw, Savill and Albion Company also proved a major client for refrigerated ships in its pioneering New Zealand trade in frozen mutton; the *Waimana*, completed in November 1911, was considered one of the finest refrigerated vessels. Most of Lamport and Holt's combined passenger/cargo ships were constructed by Workman, Clark, including the *Vandyck* (1911), *Vauban* (1912) and *Vestris* (1912), all of which were high-quality liners for the New York-River Plate route. Specialisation had radically altered the shipyard's orientation during the first decade of this century: twenty-two percent of output by volume was for the foreign and imperial market in 1900-1909, while the residual interest in the Irish domestic market accounted for only six percent of tonnage.

Discounting repairs to warships, Workman, Clark spent much of the First World War constructing auxiliary vessels for the Admiralty. An important expertise developed in the conversion of the famous "Q-ships," which were intended to combat the U-boat campaign. Boom-defence vessels, steam launches, patrol boats, and sternwheel hospital vessels formed the basis of the order book. A significant innovation was the production of oil tankers for the Navy; the experiment proved successful and the shipyard entered the merchant tanker market during the 1920s. Workman, Clark and Company boasted that, despite the dislocation in the labour force caused by the formation of the Ulster Division, the vessels constructed or repaired approximated one for every day of the war. Although the shipyard lacked any real capacity to produce armour plates, this did not prevent

---

[20]Workman, Clark (1928) Ltd., *Shipbuilding at Belfast*, 25-47; P.N. Davies, *Fyffes and the Banana: Musa Sapientum--A Centenary History, 1888-1988* (London, 1990), 102, 119-121.

it from undertaking repairs to battleships such as HMS *Albemarle*, *Britannia* and *Revenge*, or the cruiser HMS *Hampshire*, on the basis of raw material imports. Wartime labour productivity was high, and the directors revelled in the fact that the company took and retained the world productivity record for riveting.

For the Belfast shipbuilders the rise of Sinn Fein in Ireland after Easter 1916 was an ominous development which threatened the continuation of manufacturing in Ulster. When Lloyd George called an Irish Convention of constitutional parties to meet at Trinity College, Dublin, Sir George Clark (recently raised to the baronetcy) was a senior delegate of the UUC, emerging as the foremost advocate of partition to resolve the constitutional impasse.[21] In the immediate aftermath of the war, however, the Belfast shipbuilders were faced with an even more acute problem: the demand by workers for a reduction in the work week to forty-four hours. Their confidence stemmed from the full-order books enjoyed by both local yards, whereas on Clydeside in 1919 twenty-eight percent of insured shipyard workers were unemployed. When the Engineering and Shipbuilding Trades Federation negotiated a national work week of forty-seven hours, the Belfast members were infuriated. Lord Pirrie demanded military intervention "against the Bolshevik agitators whose aim is to smash the institutions of the country." Demobilisation of former shipyard artisans led to a sharp deterioration in industrial relations as well as increased sectarian animosity; many of those hired to replace existing labour during the wartime boom were nationalists.

It was at this juncture that a decision was taken by Sir George Clark and Frank Workman to divest their interest in the business. In December 1919, the Northumberland Shipbuilding Company of Howden-on-Tyne made an offer to purchase Workman, Clark and Company; the Workman family, which constituted a majority of the shareholders, accepted. The alleged rationale for this manoeuvre was that the firm's fixed and liquid assets greatly exceeded the nominal value of its share capital--plant was valued at £2 million, yet the shares were still at their 1914 level of £1.08 million. In reality, the reverse was

---

[21]R.B. MacDowell, *The Irish Convention* (London, 1968), 89.

the case, for the post-war recession was just beginning and devalued the fixed assets.

The Clark and Allan families were ambivalent toward this take-over, but the *eminence-grise* behind the move, Major Robert Workman, secured the approval of most directors and agreement was reached that the old board would continue in office until the end of 1920. By February 1920 two directors of the Northumberland Shipbuilding Company, Sir John Esplen and Sir Edward Mackay Edgar, had joined the board and in that same month the directors unanimously approved the flotation of a £3 million debenture loan at seven percent interest. Ostensibly the purpose was to promote and develop the activities of Workman, Clark.[22]

Robert Workman, besides being a director of Workman, Clark, was also chairman of the Northumberland Shipbuilding Company, a concern wholly owned by the merchant bank, Sperling and Company (see figure 1). Between 1918 and 1920 Sperling had acquired, under the aegis of Northumberland Shipbuilding, total or majority shareholdings in eight U.K. shipyards, of which three (Workman, Clark, William Doxford and Fairfield Shipbuilding) were of international status. The main motive behind this vast horizontal integration was predatory, at least as far as Workman, Clark was concerned.

What had attracted Sperling to the Belfast firm was its large liquid cash reserves (totalling about £4,000,000) and its strong market reputation for consistently high output; Workman, Clark held the annual world record on two occasions before the war, and in 1918 production had been second only to Harland and Wolff. The Northumberland Shipbuilding Company was heavily indebted to Kleinwort's Bank--which had funded recent acquisitions--and the firm intended to strip Workman, Clark of its liquid assets in order to repay the loan. In subsequent legal proceedings it transpired that Northumberland Shipbuilding had colluded with the original directors of the Belfast shipyard to misrepresent the value of the firm's plant and post-merger cash reserves. The *quid pro quo* for Sir George Clark, Charles Allan

---

[22]Urquhart v. Stracey, *et al.*, in *Northern Ireland Law Reports* (1928); PRONI, D1769/9/1A, Workman, Clark and Company Liquidation Papers.

and Frank Workman involved a payment well in excess of the real value of their respective shareholdings to be met from the £3 million debenture loan that had been floated on the basis of a false valuation.

Figure 1
The Sperling Combine, 1919-24/28

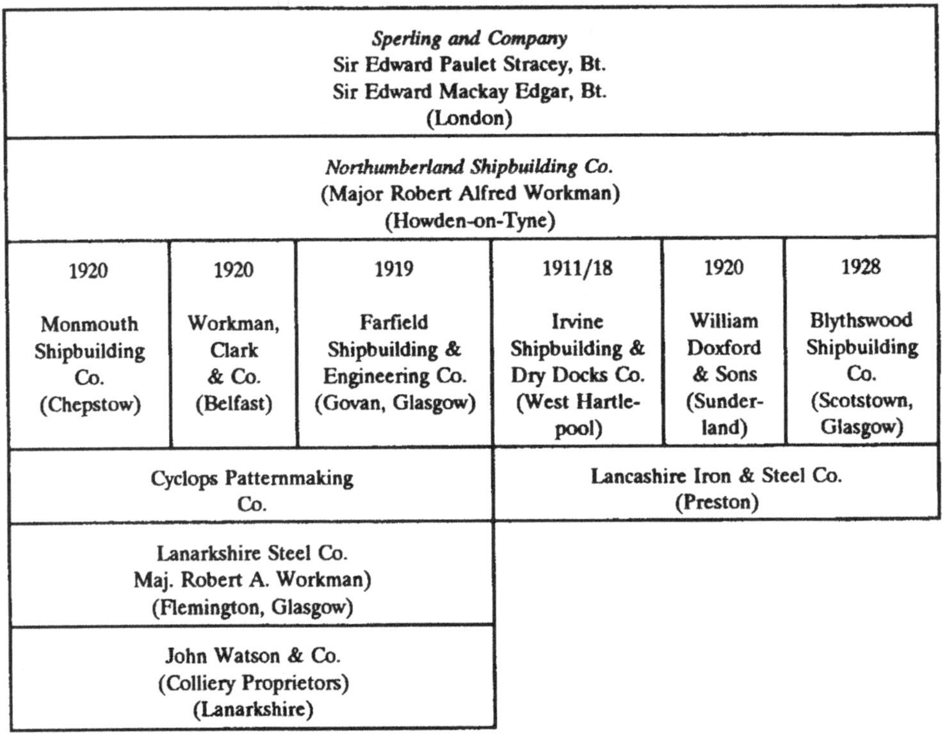

Note: "The Sperling Combine."

Source: PRONI, D 1769/9/1A, Workman, Clark and Company, Ltd., Liquidation Papers; E.L. Jones, *Shipbuilding in Britain* (Cardiff, 1957); F.M. Walker and A. Slaven (eds.), *European Shipbuilding: One Hundred Years of Change* (London, 1983).

Predictably the burden of the interest payments to debenture-holders was intolerable after the sharp downturn of 1922, but the new management insisted the company use its meagre resources to purchase the Lanarkshire Steel Company and its associated group of collieries, John Watson and Company. Apparently the Sperling combine intended to effect economies by securing its own supplies of steel, but if that were the strategy, the outcome was fiasco. During 1920 a loss of 1s. 6d. per ton of consigned output was recorded, but more embarrassing was the discovery that, in Peter Payne's words, "the Lanarkshire Steel Company, for which £25 for each fully-paid £10 share had been paid, did not, and never had rolled plates!" When Workman, Clark and Company later attempted to dispose of the Flemington steel works, inspection revealed that the plant was "unbalanced in lay-out with insufficient furnace capacity," weaknesses which would require capital expenditure of at least £50,000 to rectify.[23]

Moreover, the removal of the shipyard's autonomy contributed to the loss of several major clients, including the Royal Mail Steam Packet Company, Lamport and Holt and Clark and Service. Viewed in the context of the general post-war recession, this explains why output halved from 88,558 to 40,900 tons during the period 1921-1923. Nevertheless, membership of the Sperling group did confer certain marginal advantages in the field of engineering. For example, Workman, Clark was able to cooperate with William Doxford in the development of the Sulzer engine. The *San Benito*, launched for the United Fruit Company in 1921, was the first British-built vessel to be fitted with a turbo-electric motor, while in the sphere of turbine technology the shipyard pioneered "nodal drive," which to a great extent eliminated torsional vibration in ships' propeller shafts.[24]

In 1923 Workman, Clark was unable to pay the full interest on its £3 million debenture and its creditors collectively initiated legal action. The protracted lawsuit against the directors of Sperling and Company and Workman, Clark was financed by a large group of debenture-holders, and its continuation until 1929 seriously damaged the shipyard's commercial reputation. Eventually the House of Lords

---

[23]P.L. Payne, *Colvilles and the Scottish Steel Industry* (Oxford, 1979), 151-164.

[24]J.R. Parkinson, *The Economics of Shipbuilding in the United Kingdom* (Cambridge, 1960), 42-43.

ruled in favour of the plaintiffs that the 1920 debenture prospectus had misrepresented the financial status of the company.[25]

Had Workman, Clark and Company remained in the hands of its original owners, it ironically might have survived the depression of the 1920s, since the creation of the state of Northern Ireland provided the province with a regional government highly responsive to the needs of shipbuilding. The Government of Ireland Act of 1920, which had partitioned the island, devolved limited fiscal powers on the six-county province, although the major tax responsibilities remained with the imperial parliament, thereby constraining the scope for public spending. Despite this, the Loans Guarantee (N.I.) Act of 1922 was even more generous in its extension of credit guarantee facilities to shipowners than its imperial counterpart, the Trade Facilities Act of 1921. Given the dependent nature of the regional economy, intervention by the state did not represent an attempt at the wider management of aggregate demand, even when directed towards a capital-goods industry such as shipbuilding. Consequently, the Ulster Unionist policy of industrial subsidy was regarded with equanimity by the local bourgeoisie, who did not see it as an unwelcome form of corporatism.

Nevertheless, as early as 1923 the government of Northern Ireland clearly had doubts as to the continued viability of Workman, Clark and in allocating credit guarantees it chose to favour Harland and Wolff to the detriment of its smaller rival and the shipyards at Derry and Larne.[26] Workman, Clark had to wait until 1923 to receive an order obtained through the loans guarantee scheme. Eventually a contract was signed with the Bermuda and West Indies Steamship

---

[25]Urquhart v. Stracey, *et al.*, in *Northern Ireland Law Reports* (1929); Clark, *et al.*, v. Urquhart, in *ibid.* (1930).

[26]PRONI, CAB 9A/61/1, Ministry of Finance of Northern Ireland, Shipbuilding Questions, 1922-1932. Belfast shipbuilders and their clients received credit guarantees under the Trade Facilities Act and the Loan Guarantee (NI) Acts aggregating £27.6 million between 1922 and 1929 (seventy-nine percent of the total). British-based shipyards and their clients took the remaining £7.2 million, which represented twenty-one percent. Great Britain, *Parliamentary Papers* (House of Commons) Nos. 31, 32, 43, 98, 179, 215, and 225 (1992-1931).

Company of Furness Withy which operated in the Caribbean cruise market. The order guaranteed employment for 1100 workers, and the luxury passenger liner was, at 19,086 tons, an unprecedented size for Workman, Clark. Despite its reservations, the government acted to furnish additional guarantees requested by the shipowners. The *Bermuda*, valued at £750,000, was launched in 1927, but even the fifty percent rise in production that the project had achieved could not forestall the closure which became certain after the firm was unable to meet its liabilities. As table 4 shows, the effect of the Loans Guarantee Acts on Northern Ireland's productivity was highly detrimental; the priority of the Stormont government was the maintenance of employment in a politically strategic industry (see table 5). The Belfast shipbuilders, especially Workman, Clark, tended to exploit this scheme by employing large numbers of apprentices and labourers.

Although Workman, Clark had left the Sperling combine after its collapse in 1924, the Lanarkshire Steel Company and its unproductive collieries remained a steady drain on the firm's resources until the shipyard went into temporary liquidation in 1928. Unlike the British Trade Facilities legislation, the Ulster equivalent allowed local shipbuilders to take advantage of low-cost, United States steel. Yet Workman, Clark was obliged to support the Flemington works by importing a substantial proportion of it steel requirements from Lanarkshire. Increasingly uncompetitive and desperate for work, the firm resorted to a variety of tactics in an effort to further minimise wage costs. The company's managing director, William Strachan, blamed high municipal rates and unemployment taxes for the inflation of production costs, and pursued this theme frequently with ministers of the Unionist government.[27] In January 1925, Strachan protested: "Not until more factory gates are closed and no money is forthcoming with which to pay rates out of which sheltered men and dole-lifters

---

[27]William Strachan had been Secretary of Workman, Clark between 1902 and 1920, and was its Managing Director from 1920 to 1928, and later of its successor Workman, Clark (1928) from 1928 until 1935. PRONI, COM 40/1/W34, Workman, Clark and Company Papers.

receive their demands, will authorities and men believe that there is a limit to what employers can stand."[28]

Such outbursts seem to have received short shrift from government, despite its strong *laissez-faire* ethos, and Strachan succeeded only in reducing the chances of state assistance. It was quite obvious by 1928 that the Stormont government perceived that a radical rationalisation of shipbuilding was essential to surmount the problems of falling demand. It was equally clear that Workman, Clark had no future in this government strategy. Although in its final months of existence the old firm invested in new welding technology to facilitate its production of bulk oil tankers, the nadir was reached in 1928 when the sole vessel launched was a 360-ton barge for the city corporation.

Table 4
Changes in Shipbuilding Productivity, 1924-1930

	Net Product per Employee (£)			Net Product (£M)		N of Firms	
Region	1924	1930	% change	1924	1930	1924	1930
Greater London	185	239	+29.2	2.554	2.185	68	61
Lancs. & Cheshire	175	182	+ 4.0	2.663	3.115	55	48
Northeast	161	194	+20.5	5.996	7.041	64	59
Clydeside	163	241	+47.9	5.849	7.670	73	57
Eastern Scotland	144	201	+39.6	1.044	1.191	43	27
South Wales	216	224	+ 3.7	1.218	0.977	35	19
Great Britain	169	210	+24.3	22.758	25.920	493	401
Northern Ireland	193	165	-14.5	1.454	1.633	4	2

Source: *Final Report on the Fourth Census of Production (1930). Part II: The Iron and St Trades, The Engineering Trades and the Non-Ferrous Metal Trades* (London, 193 311-326.

[28]PRONI, CAB 9C/11/1: William Strachan to C.E. Petherick (Ministry of Finance), 5 January 1925.

Table 5
Average Rates of Unemployment in Shipbuilding by Region
1924 and 1930 (%)

Region	1924	1930	Change
Northwest	30.4	35.3	+4.9
Northeast	36.3	38.7	+2.4
Scotland	27.3	33.9	+6.6
Wales	34.9	54.4	+19.5
N. Ireland	35.7	24.5	-11.2
U.K.	29.4	32.7	+3.3

Source: *Ministry of Labour Gazette*, 1924 and 1930.

Liquidation abruptly ensued, but Strachan tenaciously organised a consortium of his Scottish shipbuilding and shipowning colleagues, including Lord Inverforth, to re-establish the shipyard. It resurfaced as Workman, Clark (1928) Ltd., but the new enterprise rested on a very slender base--investment by Andrew Weir and Company (the Bank Line), for which Strachan was expected to build oil tankers. Of the twenty-seven ships constructed by Workman, Clark (1928) no fewer than twelve were for Andrew Weir. In the context of the profound slump, the yard performed well to launch 53,900 tons in 1929--the highest annual total since the Sperling take-over. But Strachan's persistent attempts to diversify into civil engineering singularly failed through lack of government sponsorship.[29] New contracts were secured from Norway, both for oil tankers and whaling factories, but despite its participation in the tanker boom of 1930, orders again began to dwindle early in 1935. Considerable friction had developed between Stormont and Westminster over the continuation of loan

[29]Workman, Clark (1928), *Shipbuilding at Belfast*; Patrick Buckland, *The Factory of Grievances: Devolved Government in Northern Ireland, 1921-39* (Dublin, 1979), 105-129.

guarantees which were according an unfair cost advantage to Belfast. English politicians led by Ellen Wilkinson, the Labour M.P. for Jarrow, lobbied for a return to parity; indeed, the British Shipping (Assistance) Act of 1935 specifically excluded Northern Ireland from its "scrap and build" scheme. Workman, Clark (1928) was sacrificed in May 1935 to the National Shipbuilders' Security, a syndicate established in 1930 to eliminate redundant capacity in the industry. Many aspects of the firm's closure resembled a merger with Harland and Wolff: although the larger north yard with its eight slipways was shut, the south yard, engine works and part of the labour force were taken over by Harland and Wolff.[30] Strachan's son, effectively the marketing director at Workman, Clark, accepted a seat on the board of Harland and Wolff, and the smaller company's goodwill was transferred, thereby preserving the Lagan's market share in the tanker business.

It is often stated that it was British shipbuilding's halcyon Edwardian period that was exceptional and not its subsequent long decline. Workman, Clark's case vividly illustrates the point that product innovation, however radical, could never mitigate the cost-effect of a craft labour process. Shipbuilding in Ireland was doubly precarious, existing between two divergent economies, dependent upon expatriate entrepreneurs, partly upon expatriate labour and almost entirely upon cross-channel markets. The meteoric career of Workman, Clark was a barometer of economic development in Belfast; between the wars traditional staples suffered from structural decline as much as from cyclical slump. In the end the firm experienced *de facto* merger rather than complete oblivion. Why did Harland and Wolff survive the great depression when its nearest rival succumbed? The answer lies in the fact that Lord Pirrie had preempted by a decade the predatory mergers which proved so damaging to Workman, Clark. With substantial interests not only in Ireland but also in Liverpool, Clydeside and Southampton, Harland and Wolff maintained its position as the largest unit in the industry. The result was great political influence in Britain as well as Northern Ireland, and it was this leverage which steered the

[30] D.S. Johnson, *The Inter-War Economy in Ireland* (Dublin, 1989), 31-35.; PRONI, D1769/9/1A, Workman, Clark and Company Liquidation Papers.

firm through the collapse of the Royal Mail Group.[31] In the regional context, shipbuilding's importance to the political culture exceeded its declining economic value and ensured a degree of state assistance that was rare outside the command economies of inter-war Italy, Germany and the Soviet Union. But in Northern Ireland's case the departure from financial orthodoxy entailed re-organisation which inexorably moved towards monopoly as the state's role in the industry grew.

[31]Kawasaki in Japan (1927) and Burmeister and Wain (1931) in Denmark were beneficiaries of similar rescue operations by their states because of their scale as employers. See Takao Shiba, "A Comparative Study of the Managerial Structure of Two Japanese Shipbuilding Firms: Mitsubishi Shipbuilding and Engineering Co. and Kawasaki Dockyard Co., 1896-1927," in K. Kobayashi and H. Morikawa (eds.), *Development of Managerial Enterprise* (Tokyo, 1986), 211-229.

Figure 2
The Workman Genealogy

Robert Workman = Elizabeth Boyd
(1749-1836)
(of Saltcoats)

John Workman = Helen Miller
(d. 1846)
(of Belfast)

William Service

John Workman = Maria Watts
(1807-67)
(of Belfast)

Robert Workman = Jane Service
(1804-70) (1815-95)
(of Belfast)

Margaret Service = Sir James Porter Corry, Bt., MP.
(d. 1869) (1826-91)

Sir William Corry, Bt.
(1859-1926)

John Workman, JP.
(b. 1834)
= 1. Elizabeth Grace Coates
= 2. Frances Maria Carver
= 3. Jamina Hughes

Mary Workman (b. 1845) = George Smith

Margaret Murphy (née (Montgomery) = Robert Workman (b. 1842)

William Service Workman (b. 1848) = Margaret Workman Orr

Francis Workman, DL, JP. (1845-1927) = Sarah McCausland (d. 1932)

William Hughes Workman Smith (d. 1915)

Capt. George Marion Workman (b. 1873) = Kathleen Alfred Workman

Maj. Robert Workman

William Orr (1886-1916)

Edward Workman, MC, BA.
Cecil Lindsay

Capt. David = Sarah Workman

Robert Workman Smith

Note: "The Workman Geneaology."

Source: *Thom's Irish Directory, 1920*; M.K. Garner, *Robert Workman of Newtownbreda, 1835-1921* (Belfast, 1969).

Figure 3
The Clark and Allan Genealogy

1830
James Clark (1782-1865) of Paisley — Agnes McFarlance (d. 1836)
George = (1803-76)

1858
Ellen Elizabeth Cory = Robert Clark (1833-1928)
James Clark (1831-1910) — Jane Smith (1837-68)
Janet Smith = Alexander Allan (d. 1892)
George Smith = Margaret Workman (b. 1845)
Henry Matier, JP.

Jessie Georgina = Charles Edward Allan (1863-1933)
Capt. George Smith (d. 1915)

1881
Lt. Col. James Clark, CB, KC, DL, Ma, LLB. (1859-1915)
Sir George Smith Clark, Bt., DL. (1861-1935) — Frances Elizabeth Matier (d. 1929)
1886
Robert Clark (1862-1942) — Alice Matier (d. 1907)
1891
Sir Ernest Herdman, DL. (1856-1952) — Lucy Lambert Matier

1889
Norah Kathleen Clark (d. 1959)

1910
Henry Douglas Clark, MA, BL. (1889-1952)
Sir George Ernest Clark, Bt., DL, MA, MINA. (1882-1950) — Norah Ann Wilson, JP. (d. 1966)

1949
Sir George Anthony Clark, Bt., Dl. (b. 1914) — Nancy Catherine Clark
1946
Colin Douglas Clark, DL, MC, MA. (b. 1918) — Margaret Coleman Threlfall

Note: "The Clark and Allan Genealogy"

Source: *Debrett's Peerage and Baronetage.*

Marketing Opportunities and Marketing Practices; The Eclipse of British Shipbuilding, 1957-1976

Tony Slaven

Market Growth and Changing Market Shares

Between the end of the Second World War and 1958, the output of the world merchant shipbuilding industry rose sharply, from 2.1 million gross registered tons (grt) in 1946 to 9.27 million grt in 1958. During these years Britain retained its position as the world's leading shipbuilder, even though its market share slipped from half to fifteen percent.[1] A recession which began in 1958 lasted until 1961, but thereafter a period of unprecedented expansion ensued. Unfortunately for Britain, it was also an era of continued loss of market share and consequent loss of leadership. While British order books expanded over three-fold to 7.3 grt by 1974, over the same period Japanese orders rose twenty-seven times and Sweden achieved a five-fold increase (see table 1).

These differential rates of growth diminished the market share of British shipbuilders from eighteen to six percent, while the Swedish share declined from fourteen to seven percent; at the same time Japan's portion swelled from twelve to forty-six percent. This change of fortune is even more pronounced if attention is focused on tonnage launched rather than ordered. In 1960 European shipbuilders launched sixty-two percent of the world total of 8.35 million grt compared with just over twenty percent emanating from Japan. At this point the European industry, including Britain, was three times the size of the Japanese. By 1975 Japan alone launched half of the world's total of 35.89 million grt, with European builders contributing less than twenty-nine percent (see table 2).

[1] *Lloyds Register of Shipping*, annual summaries, 1946-1958.

Table 1
Order Books for Mercantile Tonnage, 1957-1976
('000 of Gross Registered Tons)

	U.K.		Japan		Sweden		World
	Total Tonnage	% World	Total Tonnage	% World	Total Tonnage	% World	Total Tonnage
1957	5,734	16.6	5,080	14.7	3,759	10.9	34,511
1958	5,373	19.6	3,784	13.8	3,019	11.2	27,395
1959	4,116	18.4	3,136	14.0	2,790	12.5	22,314
1960	3,296	18.3	2,255	12.5	2,256	12.6	17,975
1961	2,551	13.7	3,537	18.9	2,330	12.5	18,656
1962	2,068	11.3	3,879	21.2	1,985	10.8	18,320
1963	2,374	12.6	5,775	30.6	2,711	14.3	18,890
1964	2,427	11.1	8,146	37.3	2,775	12.7	21,840
1965	2,715	10.6	9,543	37.4	2,475	9.7	25,519
1966	2,835	9.5	11,541	38.8	2,662	8.9	29,762
1967	2,148	6.3	15,043	44.4	2,454	7.2	33,883
1968	2,452	6.0	17,646	43.4	3,001	7.4	40,632
1969	4,634	8.7	18,257	34.2	4,895	9.2	53,332
1970	4,670	7.8	20,662	34.4	5,598	9.3	59,914
1971	4,976	6.0	32,168	39.0	5,969	8.5	82,398
1972	4,569	5.5	35,668	42.9	5,754	6.9	83,170
1973	5,501	5.5	43,783	44.1	9,308	9.4	99,183
1974	7,285	5.5	61,988	46.5	10,980	8.2	133,439
1975	5,907	5.2	48,605	42.9	8,302	7.3	113,349
1976	4,612	6.2	26,811	35.8	5,633	7.5	74,777

Sources: 1957-64: "Report of the Shipbuilding Inquiry Committee, 1965-1966," Cmnd. 2937, Appendix I, figures for December each year.
1965-76: *Lloyds Register of Shipping*, quarterly returns, March each year.

This shift in market shares in a rapidly expanding world market clearly encapsulated a general decline in European shipbuilding in the face of growing Japanese dominance. Within the general European loss of place, Britain slipped from being the major world builder to fifth place in the world--and fourth in Europe behind Germany, Sweden and Spain. By the mid-1970s, in terms of annual profit the British industry was roughly on a par with those of France, the Netherlands and Norway (see table 2).

Table 2
Merchant Tonnage Launched: Percent of World Total
By Country of Build, 1949-1975
(% of World Total Annually)

Country	1949	1960	1968	1975
Denmark	2.7	2.6	2.8	2.7
France	4.9	7.1	2.9	3.6
Germany	-	13.1	8.0	7.1
Italy	3.2	5.2	2.9	2.4
Japan	4.7	20.7	50.8	50.1
Netherlands	5.4	6.8	1.8	2.6
Norway	1.9	2.4	2.9	2.9
Poland	0.2	2.7	2.5	1.7
Spain	10.3	8.5	6.6	6.9
U.S.A.	20.2	5.8	2.6	2.8
Yugoslavia	0.2	1.9	1.7	1.8
U.K.	40.5	15.9	5.3	3.6
World ('000 tons)	3,131	8,356	16,907	35,897

Source: *Lloyds Register of Shipping*, annual summaries.

The nature of Britain's difficulties in the marketplace are clearly discerned if orders are examined according to its two major components, tonnage under construction set against orders on hand but not yet commenced (see table 3). Between 1960 and 1967 the ratio of orders on hand to those under construction was only once significantly above 0.5, indicating a weak position of only having sufficient work on hand to keep the industry operating for six to nine months. Over the next decade, 1967-1976, the order book did lengthen, with the ratio rising to a high of 2.63 in 1974, the 5.27 million grt on order representing three to four years work. This, however, has to be seen in relation to Britain's main competitors. When Britain's ratio stood at 2.6 in 1974, Germany's was 3.0, Sweden's 3.6, and Japan's 4.6. All of Britain's major rivals had succeeded in obtaining longer and larger order books.

Table 3
British Shipbuilding Order Book, 1960-1974
('000 Grt in March of Each Year)

	U.K. Order Book (tons)	Tonnage under Construction	Tonnage not Commenced	Ratio of Not Commenced/ Construction
1960	2,898	1,961	937	0.48
1961	2,427	1,611	816	0.50
1962	2,031	1,359	672	0.49
1963	1,658	1,124	534	0.47
1964	2,301	1,606	695	0.43
1965	2,346	1,517	829	0.54
1966	2,835	1,383	1,452	1.04
1967	2,148	1,497	651	0.43
1968	2,452	1,179	1,273	1.07
1969	4,364	1,657	2,713	1.64
1970	4,670	1,741	2,929	1.68
1971	4,976	1,726	3,250	1.88
1972	4,569	1,836	2,731	1.48
1973	5,501	1,972	3,529	1.79
1974	7,285	2,006	5,279	2.63

Source: Compiled from *Lloyds Register of Shipping*, quarterly returns.

Consequently, during twenty years of unprecedented growth for merchant tonnage, the British shipbuilding industry suffered a serious loss of market share, from eighteen to six percent in orders, and from sixteen to four percent in output. It also experienced a smaller growth in orders and worked with a weaker and shorter flow of commitments than its main competitors, thus providing a less stable production base in a rapid growth phase in world shipbuilding.

The British Market

The nature of Britain's weak market performance can be examined more closely by considering the trends in construction for the two main components of the UK order book. The first is tonnage constructed for UK registration, that is production for the domestic shipping industry; the second, tonnage for foreign registration, which broadly speaking represented tonnage built in Britain for export (see table 4).

Table 4
U.K. Tonnage for U.K. and Foreign Registration, 1958-1976
('000 Grt)

	Launched	For U.K. Registration		For Foreign Registration	
	grt	grt	%	grt	%
1958	1,402	1,064	75.9	338	24.1
1959	1,373	1,257	91.6	116	8.4
1960	1,331	1,185	89.0	146	11.0
1961	1,192	911	76.4	281	23.6
1962	1,073	908	84.6	165	15.4
1963	928	644	69.4	284	30.6
1964	1,043	894	85.7	149	14.3
1965	1,073	937	87.3	136	12.7
1966	1,084	777	71.7	307	28.3
1967	1,298	581	44.8	717	55.2
1968	898	423	47.1	475	52.9
1969	1,039	655	63.0	385	37.0
1970	1,237	1,052	85.0	186	15.0
1971	1,239	844	68.1	394	31.8
1972	1,233	863	70.0	370	30.0
1973	1,017	683	67.1	335	32.9
1974	1,198	954	79.6	244	20.4
1975	1,169	821	70.2	349	29.8
1976	1,500	1,036	69.1	464	30.9

Source: Compiled from *Lloyds Register of Shipping*, annual summaries. Data for 1974 onwards are related to completions instead of launches.

British shipbuilding traditionally built primarily for domestic shipowners, the British market being in large part virtually closed to foreign builders.[2] Prior to 1960 British shipbuilders regularly supplied about eighty percent of all new orders for native shipowners.[3] But from the early 1960s this protected position was weakening. The slippage was especially evident between 1962 and 1966, when foreign builders gained one-third of the British market (see table 5). In fact, 1966 was to be the last year in which British shipbuilders supplied the majority of new tonnage registered in the UK. In the next decade foreign builders supplied as much as three-quarters of all new tonnage for UK registration. The serious penetration of the British market is clearly set out in table 6. In the early 1960s Britain imported roughly two tons of new shipping for every ton exported, but ten years later about seven tons were imported for each exported ton.

This loss of the domestic market by British shipbuilders was not due to an absolute collapse in tonnage built in British yards for domestic owners. Table 5 makes it clear that apart from a low point in 1968 and a high in 1976, annual average new buildings for British owners only fluctuated slightly around an average of about 805,000 grt. In effect, the loss of market share reflected more a failure by British builders to respond to growing demands by increasing output than differences in competitiveness among the shipbuilding nations.

Building for export, however, was not a particular strength among British shipbuilders in general.[4] Export tonnage accounted for as much as half of all UK construction on only two occasions during the period under review, in 1967 and 1968. Tonnage for export normally represented approximately twenty-five to thirty percent of the

---

[2]See Anthony Slaven, "British Shipbuilders: Market Trends and Order Book Patterns between the Wars," *Journal of Transport History*, Third Series, III, No. 2 (1982), 37-61.

[3]This was a typical pattern; all major shipbuilding nations supplied the larger part of tonnage required by their domestic shipping industries. See J.R. Parkinson, *The Economics of Shipbuilding in the United Kingdom* (Cambridge, 1960), chapter 7.

[4]Britain's performance in the export market was weak compared to Japan, Germany and Sweden. See Booz-Allen and Hamilton, *British Shipbuilding 1972* (London, 1973), chapter 10.

British order book (table 4). Critically, however, Britain's export performance weakened in the period 1972-1976 compared to the previous five years, annual average foreign sales declining from 431,000 to 352,000 grt. And this deterioration occurred in a period in which total world tonnage exports rose by more than fifty-five percent. It is clear that Britain's deteriorating market position was consequently related to failures to respond to accelerating demand in both domestic and overseas markets.

Market Opportunities

Not all new tonnage constructed in these boom years was available to Britain's shipbuilders. Many markets were effectively closed in that virtually all tonnage was supplied by domestic production. At the other extreme some countries were completely open in that they had little or no shipbuilding capacity and hence imported almost all registered tonnage. Between these two extremes was a group of competitive markets in which domestic shipbuilders had to compete vigorously with foreigners for a share of home orders.[5] The changing scale and composition of these markets types are shown in five-year periods in Table 7.

In the early 1960s the largest export market was essentially comprised of the Scandinavian countries together with Britain and the Netherlands, followed closely by the open and flag of convenience countries. In the next period the open markets edged ahead in orders leaving the competitive markets just behind, while by the early 1970s, the open markets had become by far the largest source of export orders, with western Europe comprising a second very large market. As a group these countries imported three million grt, some sixty-three percent of their tonnage requirements and one-third of all world tonnage imports.

---

[5] *Ibid.*, 65-66.

Table 5
UK New Tonnage Registration, 1958-1976

	New Tonnage Registered	Tonnage Built in UK	Foreign-Built for UK Registration	
	'000 grt	'000 grt	'000 grt	%
1958	1,349	1,064	285	21.2
1959	1,706	1,257	449	26.3
1960	1,651	1,185	465	28.2
1961	1,314	911	403	30.7
1962	1,477	908	569	38.5
1963	1,082	644	438	40.5
1964	1,126	894	232	20.6
1965	1,231	937	294	23.9
1966	1,257	777	480	32.2
1967	1,303	581	802	58.0
1968	2,432	423	2,009	82.6
1969	2,798	655	2,143	76.6
1970	2,703	1,052	1,651	61.1
1971	3,273	844	2,429	74.2
1972	3,697	863	2,834	76.7
1973	4,176	683	3,493	83.6
1974	3,813	954	2,859	75.0
1975	2,961	821	2,140	72.3
1976	2,148	1,036	1,112	51.8

	Total UK Registration	Foreign-Built	% Foreign
1962-66	6,173	2,013	32.6
1967-71	12,589	9,034	71.8
1972-76	16,795	12,474	74.3

Source: Compiled from *Lloyds Register of Shipping*, annual summaries.

Table 6
Tonnage Launched, Exported and Imported in the UK, 1962-1976
('000 Grt)

Period	Tonnage Launched	Tonnage Exported	% Exports	Tonnage Imported	Export/ Import Ratio
1962-66	5,201	1,041	25.9	2,013	1 : 1.9
1967-71	5,711	2,157	37.8	9,034	1 : 4.2
1972-76	6,117	1,762	28.8	12,438	1 : 7.0

Source: Compiled from Tables 4 and 5.

During these fifteen years the three main market types (closed, open, and competitive) represented eighty-one percent of all world export demand for new tonnage. Tonnage available for export orders outside these markets averaged only 1.5 million grt between 1962 and 1971, and rose to only 3.9 million grt in the last period. Against this, world exports rose from twenty-six million grt in the first five-year period to 104 million grt in the third period 1972-1976. Formerly closed areas had declined as France and West Germany became competitive markets, considerably expanding the opportunities open to British and other shipbuilders. The weakening of British export effort thus has to be seen in the context of rapidly growing export demand and expanding overseas markets.

British Shipbuilding Export Markets

In spite of the enormous growth in export markets in this period, British shipbuilders remained firmly attached to three main outlets, Norway, the open or flag of convenience fleets, and the commonwealth (or former commonwealth) countries (see table 8). These three groups rarely consumed less than seventy percent of British export tonnage, although this apparent stability concealed important shifts in the relative significance of individual markets.

The most dramatic change was the loss of the Norwegian market, which had traditionally consumed up to half of Britain's export tonnage. The UK built over half a million tons for Norwegian owners between 1962 and 1966, but by the early 1970s this had slipped to a mere 144,000 grt, or barely eight percent of UK exports. While some orders by Norwegians might have become for flag of convenience fleets, the loss of this major market reflected Britain's increasing uncompetitiveness relative to Sweden, Germany and, in particular, Japan. Conversely, the open markets, especially Liberia, represented a growth area for British builders, and usurped the position formerly held by Norway. Between these opposites of contracting and expanding markets, the commonwealth and related countries first weakened and then recovered as outlets for British-built tonnage, although these nations were characterized by shifting loyalty and inconsistent orders.

While these shifts may have been the most obvious, it was also clear that the weakest market area comprised the remaining main west European shipping nations, Sweden, Denmark, Netherlands, France and West Germany. Between 1962 and 1976 these countries imported 13.24 million grt, of which Britain's share was barely half a million tons. The main European markets, Britain's closest neighbours, remained largely unexplored by her builders.

Ship Size and Type

The very large growth in ship construction was accompanied by important changes in the size and nature of the product. In 1962 the average vessel launched in the world was 4,400 grt; by 1975 this had increased to 13,639 grt. At the beginning of the period British-built vessels were somewhat larger than average, 5,700 grt as against 4,300 grt in Germany and 3,900 in Japan. This reflected the UK's commitment to building passenger and cargo liners. Only Sweden, already concentrating on very large vessels, deviated especially noticeably from world patterns, with average vessel size of 11,365 grt. By the end of the period, however, the average British vessel of 11,000 grt was considerably smaller than the output of her competitors, as UK builders lagged somewhat in the trend toward bigger ships.

Table 7
New Tonnage Supplied and Registered by Main World Market Areas, 1962-1976
('000 grt)

1962-66	New Tonnage Registered	Supplied by Country of Registration	Tonnage Imported for Registration	% Imports
A. Closed Markets	15,930	15,751	179	1.1
B. Open Markets	8,669	0	8,669	100.0
C. Competitive	19,620	8,681	10,939	55.7
A + B + C	44,219	24,432	19,787	
World Total	53,700	26,781	26,283	

A = France, West Germany, Italy, Spain, USA, Japan; B = Liberia, Greece, Panama;
C = Denmark, Netherlands, Norway, Sweden, UK.

1966-71	New Registrations	By Country of Build	Imports	%
A. Closed	29,202	28,603	599	2.1
B. Open	23,002	0	23,002	100.0
C. Competitive	33,011	11,939	21,072	63.8
A + B + C	85,215	40,542	44,673	
World Total	98,553	44,650	53,900	

A = France, Italy, Japan, Spain, USA; B = Liberia, Greece, Panama;
C = Denmark, West Germany, Netherlands, Norway, Sweden, UK.

1972-76	New Registration	By Country of Build	Imports	%
A. Closed	30,686	29,950	736	2.4
B. Open	50,203	0	50,203	100.0
C. Competitive	52,608	19,525	33,083	62.9
A + B + C	133,497	49,475	84,022	
World Total	159,899	56,005	103,895	

A = Italy, Japan, Spain, USA; B = Liberia, Greece, Panama;
C = France, Denmark, West Germany, Netherlands, Norway, Sweden, UK.

Source: Compiled from *Lloyds Register of Shipping*, annual summaries.

Table 8
Main Markets for U.K. Shipbuilding Exports, 1962-1976

	1962-66 ('000 grt)	1967-71 ('000 grt)	1972-76 ('000 grt)
Total UK Exports	1,041	2,157	1,761
Percentage Share of UK Shipbuilding Exports			
A: Norway	48.4	28.7	8.2
B: Open Markets	14.4	34.3	45.9
Liberia	5.2	19.1	28.7
Greece	4.6	14.0	10.7
Panama	4.6	0.2	6.5
C: Commonwealth and Related	18.0	3.2	16.4
India	4.5	0.4	10.1
Other Commonwealth	10.7	2.3	6.0
South Africa	2.8	0.5	0.3
A + B + C	80.0	66.2	70.5
D: Other European	6.0	18.7	5.5
Sweden	3.0	1.3	0.08
Denmark	0.2	0.7	3.4
Netherlands	-	0.7	1.0
West Germany	2.1	14.7	1.0
France	0.7	1.3	-
E: Residual Markets	13.2	15.1	24.0

Source: Compiled from *Lloyds Register of Shipping*, annual summaries.

The increase in ship size was closely linked to the growing dominance of oil tankers in world construction, the oil tanker share of the market rising from forty-two percent in the early 1960s to over fifty-five percent between 1972 and 1976. By then the largest vessels afloat, the very large crude carriers (VLCCs) for oil and bulk cargoes, were in the 220,000-240,000 ton range. At the peak of the 1970s boom, the tanker and bulk carrier market represented over eighty percent of new tonnage construction. Conversely, the share of general cargo tonnage on world order books declined by more than half, to under ten percent of total tonnage built between 1972 and 1976.

The British response to these developments differed from other major builders. British shipbuilders did not convert to the construction of oil tanker tonnage to the same extent as other nations, especially Japan and Sweden. By the period 1972-1976, oil tankers represented thirty-eight percent of UK tonnage as against fifty-five percent for the world as a whole and sixty-two percent in Japan. Both the large scale and increasing standardisation of the tanker market ran counter to the facilities and practices in many British yards. Among larger vessels, the British market preference was for ore and bulk carriers. Britain also successfully specialised in more complex tonnage markets, such as container ships and LPG/LNG and chemical carriers. Britain also retained a much larger than average share of the general cargo market, with eighteen percent of her order book in this group between 1972 and 1976, double the world average. A traditional pattern of general cargo construction was retained contrary to world trends.

In this period of rapid market changes, Britain moved more slowly than other nations to large ship construction and did not specialise in tankers; instead, UK builders concentrated more on larger than average ore and bulk carriers and general cargo ships. British shipbuilders on the whole did not fully adapt to world trends toward greater specialisation and size, keeping instead a smaller and more varied building pattern. In this context it is clear that as British builders were eclipsed in their domestic market, their export performance remained low key and deeply affected by the collapse of the Norwegian market and the need to depend more on open markets and the unpredictable commonwealth. Moreover, as western European became a large-scale importer, British builders failed to penetrate their nearest market.

All of these weaknesses have frequently been explained by Britain's lack of price competitiveness, by her record of late deliveries, and by her slow response to technological change. While these general characteristics were doubtless of great importance, any explanation of Britain's decline in shipbuilding couched in these terms tends to overlook the root cause of much of her difficulty in this period. The weakness of the British industry was fundamentally linked to the attitudes and priorities of her shipbuilders to marketing. The characteristics of the market posture adopted by British shipbuilders, and their implications in marketing terms, are central to an understanding of the eclipse of British shipbuilding in the 1950s, 1960s and 1970s.

British Shipbuilders: Market Posture

The typical approach of British shipbuilders to the market was historically-determined. For more than a century the market environment had been dominated by the British shipbuilding and the supremacy of the large UK mercantile marine in the world's carrying trades. This conjunction gave British shipbuilders control of the world's largest market for new tonnage.[6]

Within this preferential market environment, links between shipbuilder and shipowner evolved on a customer/builder basis. These client-builder linkages, formal and informal, created for builders preferential access to new orders. For example, Harland and Wolff developed a myriad of such associations, building repeatedly for the Bank Line, Royal Mail, King Line, Elder Dempster, Pacific Steam Navigation Co., and so on. Lithgow on the lower Clyde enjoyed favourable relations with the British and Burmese Steam Navigation Co., Lyle Shipping and Scottish Ore Carriers, among others. Vickers built regularly for the Orient Steam Navigation Co., the Ocean Steam Navigation Co., Furness Withy, Canadian Pacific, and Ellerman. Camell Laird's preferential links lay with Blue Star, Eagle Tanker Co. and Manchester Lines, while Swan Hunter had close links with the Palm Line and the British India Steam Navigation Co. Every British shipbuilder used such "building friends" as the foundation upon which to build its business.[7]

A number of characteristic marketing practices developed from these links. First, the long-standing builder-customer association encouraged marketing and sales to develop on a "personalised" basis,

---

[6]The historical dimension is discussed more fully in Slaven, "British Shipbuilders."

[7]See *ibid.* for a detailed treatment of these linkages.

putting leadership and responsibility into the hands of the managing director or other senior executive to conduct face to face negotiations with shipowners. Senior shipbuilding executives consequently generated what might be called a "contact-network" through which they managed to present their organisation to the external world. This was a role suited to the talents of individually powerful personalities, frequently skilled politically in protecting and developing their company's position.

Second, these personality-based and preferential purchaser links profoundly influenced the building pattern of major British shipbuilders. Building was exclusively to order, customer requirements dominated developments, and yards were obliged to maintain a broad and varied building programme; in other words, they had to be prepared to build almost any type of ship and frequently built a wide variety of vessel types and sizes simultaneously.

These historically-based features obviously meant that few British builders had any conscious product policy about the type of vessel to be produced. The product range of most British yards was fundamentally determined by the range of clients who customarily ordered from them. This client-dominated building pattern was frequently modified by the formal linkages which bound some shipbuilders to other economic activities. For example, in great vertically-combined enterprises like John Browns or Vickers, which linked steel, armaments and shipbuilding, the builder/client relationship was merged with naval shipbuilding, the shipyard essentially being an initial outlet for the special steels, arms and other materials of the organisation. Equally, where shipbuilding companies were heavily involved with shipping lines, as for example the Dennys and the Irrawaddy Flotilla Company, this superimposed a specialist building component on a yard's more general building pattern.

The typical market approach of British shipbuilders, as outlined here, had three characteristics. First, it was client-dependent for the initiation of the contract; second, it was client-determined for the range and type of vessel built; and third, it was personality-based in that the senior executive was responsible for the negotiation of sales. In essence, this may be described as a "passive marketing" strategy, in which the shipbuilder is production rather than market-oriented. In acquiring ship orders, British shipbuilders were essentially "passive contractors."[8]

Having set out the typical features of the marketing attitudes and practices of British shipbuilders, the implications in the context of the market changes set out earlier in the essay can now be reviewed under three broad headings: market appreciation, product choice and market sales strategy.

Market Appreciation

It is an axiom of modern marketing theory that the roots of good marketing lie in an understanding of the market involved.[9] This in turn rests on access to, and evaluation of, detailed current information to construct demand forecasts. For the shipbuilder, a systematic approach to demand forecasting and hence to market comprehension requires the collection and analysis of four main types of information: trade flow, fleet composition and economic trends, and competitor profiles. Together these broadly constitute what may be thought of as market research for the shipbuilding industry.

The analysis of trade flows embodies well-established techniques designed to identify growth trades and routes. In the case of shipbuilding, such analysis is combined with an evaluation of the need for particular types and sizes of vessels to recognise growth sectors. Done systematically, trade flow and fleet composition analysis identifies the salient growth areas for trade, routes, vessels for each shipbuilding nation. Yet throughout the period under review this type of market research was almost non-existent in British shipbuilding. Marketing, as part of British shipbuilding, was investigated by both the Geddes Inquiry in 1965/1966 the Booz-Allen Report of 1972. Between these general studies, two specific marketing enquiries were conducted: one by the management consultants, P.E. Consulting Group Ltd., in 1967

[8]For a commentary on this from the vantage point of the 1960s, see the so-called "Geddes Report," the "Report of the Shipbuilding Inquiry Committee 1965-1966," HMSO Cmnd. 2937.

[9]See Peter F. Drucker, *The Practice of Management* (New York, 1954), 37-41.

for the Shipbuilders and Repairers National Association;[10] the other in 1968/1969 for the Shipbuilding Industry Board by Professor Roland Smith, then Professor of Marketing at the University of Manchester Institute of Science and Technology.[11] Both reports observed independently that the industry undertook little market research and that British shipbuilders, individually and collectively, simply lacked information on markets in a form which provided any basis for sound management decisions. The systematic collection of market data was generally neglected, most shipbuilders relying instead on the informal accumulation of information gleaned mainly from enquiries from shipowners and shipbrokers.[12]

Movement away from this traditional market ambivalence had begun in a small way prior to the Geddes Report. Under persistent government pressure on British industry to improve its export performance, the British Shipbuilding Conference in 1962 appointed an executive in charge of exports, this single post quickly being extended to three export directors whose world perambulations were designed to supplement the soundings of individual firms. This initiative resulted in the establishment of the British Shipbuilding Exports Association Ltd. (BSE) in 1964 to provide an agency for industry "group negotiations" on orders from foreign governments. While BSE had limited resources, its mandate was broad: negotiating export sales, collecting overseas intelligence, and acting as a "credit advisory unit" on terms available in Britain and abroad to aid ship construction. By 1967 it had also begun to prepare special reports on overseas markets visited by its executives.[13] This was followed by fleet

---

[10] P.E. Consulting Group Ltd., *Review of Market Research and Intelligence Requirements and Facilities* (London, 1967).

[11] Roland Smith, *Marketing as Applied to Shipbuilding* (March 1969), National Maritime Museum, SRNA, S42/10/14.

[12] These reports confirmed the views of the Geddes Report of 1965-1966.

[13] "Report of Shipbuilding Board, July, 1967," National Maritime Museum, SRNA, E40/8.

reports on trends in major flag fleets and commodity reports on cargoes such as iron ore. Excellent as this information was, it went largely unused since it focused on general trends, did not dwell on implications for British shipbuilders, and more important, did not attempt to draw out the implications for particular vessel categories. On the whole, shipbuilders found that they could make little use of the information since they still lacked their own market research units which could have related the general information to the specific interests of individual firms. When Roland Smith reported on the Industry in 1969, his view was that only Cammell Laird had developed a market research facility to the extent that it could exploit the flow of information from the shipbuilding industry agencies. Indeed, he thought Cammell Laird so advanced in relation to other British companies that it was capable of providing all its own information.[14]

Trade, fleet and vessel design research and analysis was also initiated in 1966 within the British Shipbuilding Research Association (BSRA) with the formation of a Market Research Section to produce highly-complex and detailed reports without any central guidance. But again, the reports were technically more sophisticated than most firms in the industry required and consequently little use was made of them.

The same pattern of neglect of information is evident in economic trend analysis and in the evaluation of the strengths and weaknesses of competitors overseas. No British shipbuilder appears to have compiled systematic reports on trades, freights, taxes and subsidies, least of all on major overseas firms competing in the same market. Since detailed published information on orders, contract prices and deliveries was readily available on a yard by yard basis, the neglect of such information is remarkable.[15]

The marketing practices of British shipbuilders, in so far as they were influenced by an appreciation of the market, therefore rested not on information, research, or analysis, but on a series of assumptions

---

[14]Smith, *Marketing*; Roland Smith, Report for the SIB, Notes for Discussion, October 1969, National Maritime Museum, SRNA, S42/10/14.

[15]P.E. Consulting Group, *Review*, section 5.

and convictions. At the root of their attitude to marketing lay the conviction that experience taught that shipbuilding markets were not subject to long-term analysis; British shipbuilders appear to have believed that short-term factors, notably freight rates and trade volumes, were the determinants of the flow of orders. Consequently, the collection of market information and the development of related research was unnecessary. Commenting on Roland Smith's report in 1969, Sir John Mallabar, the Chairman of Harland and Wolff, said that he did not need market research. As far as he was concerned, "if you get an explosion in population, you must get an explosion in world trade. This is all I need to know." Although extreme, this view was generally shared within the industry.[16]

The second assumption that underlay this neglect of market information and research was that demand for British-built ships was inextricably linked to the domestic merchant marine, and that this traditional outlet would continue to dominate British shipyard order books. Third, it was assumed that the balance between exported and imported tonnage was stable; it had, after all, been in the twenty to twenty-five percent range of total output throughout the working lives of all British shipbuilders.

These attitudes assumed a continuance of past experience and practice and tied the market expectations of British shipbuilders to a replacement demand from the domestic mercantile marine, in the belief that this demand would remain stable irrespective of changes elsewhere. Yet in the 1960s, increasing international competition, changing technology and rapid economic growth in different parts of the world all contributed to rapid change in the trading and marketing environment for individual shipbuilding firms. Since in marketing terms British shipbuilders operated in general in a poor information environment, they were in no position to anticipate the trends which revolutionised shipbuilding during the decade.[17] British shipbuilders

---

[16]Smith, *Marketing*; Notes for Discussion, National Maritime Museum, SRNA, S42/10/14.

[17]P.E. Consulting Group, *Review*, 7-9.

were reduced to reacting in a laggard fashion to the changing markets of the 1950s and 1960s. The consequence was the collapse in market share outlined earlier in this paper.

Product Choice

Market research and demand forecasting are prerequisites to identify the area or segment of the market in which a firm wishes to specialise. In modern marketing this selection of a market segment is the essential first step to enable a company to choose the product range it is best-suited to provide in its chosen market area. Positive selection of a market area and products--that is the adoption of a clear product policy--are fundamental attributes of modern marketing, which necessitates that the development of the business, planning of investment and allocation and utilisation of resources be governed by market and product policy.[18]

In British shipbuilding market sectors were defined largely by traditional customer-builder relationships. Similarly, it is clear that the selection of vessel types and sizes constructed in any yard was also for the most part historically-determined. Nonetheless, within these general conditions, it is possible to identify three basic product groupings into which the building pattern of most British shipyards may be fitted. In the 1960s these product groupings were: volume producers, typically of low value-added type construction; limited range specialist producers, usually with high value-added content; and full range berth fillers, with a mixture of vessel types.

The volume producers included the companies which by slow growth in scale and long-established specialisation in general cargo construction, concentrated their efforts on a relatively narrow range of basic cargo vessels, depending on sustained high volumes of output for relatively low value-added per unit constructed. This group included the major general cargo builders, notably Lithgow, Connell, Barclay Curle, Hawthorn Leslie, Doxford, Sir James Laing, J. and L.

[18] Smith, *Marketing*, 6-12.

Thompson, Smiths Dock and others. This group represented the most numerous collection of companies in the industry.

The specialist producers essentially emphasised construction of a limited range of specialist tonnage, characteristically with a high value-added. The most obvious adherents to this product policy were the specialist naval builders, Yarrow and Thorneycroft. Also in this group were many smaller yards concentrating on specialist vessels like tugs, dredgers and trawlers. Among these were companies like John Lewis, Richards Ironworks, Simons and Lobnitz.

Among the full range berth fillers, the distinguishing features were principally the lack of any product preference and the habit of building almost any type of vessel. This group could be sub-divided further into two categories of companies. The first, although building across most vessel types, tended to favour the production of higher-value vessels. Notable in this group were John Brown, Vickers and Cammell Laird. All three combined passenger, cargo liner and naval construction, all high value-added vessel groups, with more general cargo building. The Fairfield yard was also in this category, although it did not build passenger vessels. The second sub-division of this group included the full range builders whose major pre-occupation was volume production of lower-value vessels, notably tankers and ore carriers. The main representatives in this product group were Harland and Wolff, Swan Hunter and Stephens.

Although these were the most recognisable production patterns, even among the more specialist producers there was a general rejection of a specific product choice based on specialisation for a clearly identified segment of the market. The assumptions underlying the rejection of market research also favoured the maintenance of this generalised building pattern, which depended mostly on the survival of traditional builder/owner links and the preferential placement of orders by British shipowners in domestic yards. The capture of the home market by foreign builders in the late 1960s exposed the fragility of this traditional policy, and in the emergence of the new shipbuilding groups in the wake of the Geddes Report, some more positive product policy choices began to appear.

The most commonly cited success story of deliberate choice of vessel range and type, coupled with a specific policy to cater for a clearly recognised market need, is Austin and Pickersgill's development of the SD-14 standard cargo vessel.[19] This design combined specific product choice with market identification, selection, and deliberate standardisation of design, all features long rejected as impractical by British shipbuilders. The first two SD-14s were launched in 1967; by 1975 over eighty had been built. The advantages flowing from this positive market strategy were efficient standardised production; better cost control and the production of a vessel at a competitive price; and quick response times to enquiries, since major elements such as hull form, main engine and deck arrangements were fixed and other items were subject only to a limited range of specific options. The remainder of the industry applauded this success, but did not choose to follow it.

Some companies did, however, begin to develop their own brand of product policy. Cammell Laird systematically reviewed its competitive strength in building specific ship types by comparing its own prices with those of competitors using historical prices and dummy tenders. In view of their technical strengths derived from their traditional building patterns, Cammell Laird opted for a product policy specialising in high value-added vessels and a limited range of 20-40,000-ton bulk carriers. This was the most precise product policy based on market analysis undertaken by any British firm in the 1960s. At the same time Harland and Wolff chose to exploit the scale of its Belfast establishment to upgrade its steel working capacity and devote most of its resources to VLCC construction. It did not, however, abandon its general building tradition, and aimed specifically to build smaller vessels as fillers in its major programme. Similarly, Lithgow evolving from its tanker and ore carrier building, decided to invest in facilities to enable it to compete in the VLCC market. Swan Hunter followed this pattern in re-equipping its Wallsend yard, but like Harland and Wolff chose to maintain a full range berth filling strategy as a back-up to its big ship facilities. With the possible exception of Cammell Laird, none of the bigger companies appear to have developed specific product policies in the light of careful market

---

[19]See for example, "Surpertramp: Running the Whitehall Blockade," *Sunday Times*, 10 October 1976.

research. Harland and Wolff, Lithgow and Swan Hunter mainly moved into VLCC construction by following the Japanese and Swedish paths in what seemed to be a growth market. The investment programmes were apparently not founded on any clear market analysis. Moreover, among the major shipbuilding groups, the financially-troubled Upper Clyde Shipbuilders made least progress in the development of product policy, and the smaller yards continued mainly to build as before.

By the early 1970s there had been some movement toward more systematic product policies in British shipyards, but there was neither a general tendency to base these movements on systematic market research nor any convincing evidence that longer-term strategies were being evolved around marketing and product policy. The companies remained substantially product-oriented in organisation and thinking. There is some evidence to suggest, however, that following on Cammell Laird's experience, Harland and Wolff, Doxford, Appledore, Austin and Pickersgill, Scott Lithgow, Swan Hunter and Robb Caledon in various ways cultivated market opportunities more positively. Still, marketing and product policy remained at widely different stages of development and implementation in the industry. For many companies, product choice still lay fundamentally with the customer, and positive marketing based on planned production of selected ship types for specific market areas was still far from the norm.

Market Strategy

The logic of engaging in market research, selecting market segments and adopting a positive product policy is that it should enable a company to develop an effective marketing and sales strategy. The last sequence is a clear identification of customers to whom the planned product range is to be sold. In theory, the successful application of these stages in shipbuilding should enable a company to engage in direct selling through having evolved basic ship designs appropriate to its chosen market sector, and to approach its identified customers in anticipation of requirements. The Japanese certainly exploited this technique in persuading the major oil companies that their requirements could be best met by new generations of ever-larger standardised tankers.

As outlined above, in British shipbuilding customer identification was based mainly on traditional customer/builder associations, and sales to such established customers were vested in the negotiating role of the senior executive of the firm. When confronted with the arguments of the Geddes Committee, and later by the opinions voiced by Roland Smith that marketing and sales required the services of specialised teams, British shipbuilders in general did not believe that any non-traditional sales strategy would work. Sir John Hunter declared that "shipowners will only deal with shipbuilders--marketing directors get pretty short shrift."[20] Sir John Mallabar of Harland and Wolff held that any attempt to deal with marketing and selling through a marketing director and team simply would not work. Ross Belch of Lithgow maintained that the only way to make sales was to have the negotiations in the hands of the senior executives.[21] Consequently, with few exceptions British shipbuilders did not have marketing departments, and few had any marketing functions represented at Board level. The selling of ships was held to be the task of the senior executive, or perhaps the Board.

These two features--dependence on established contacts for customer identification and continuance of the role of the senior executive as the salesman--seriously hampered the evolution of a positive sales policy. Indeed, in the minds of most British shipbuilders there appeared to be little distinction between marketing and selling. Yet the difference is crucial. Marketing involves the development of the company and its resources in line with positively selected market areas and product types. Selling is only the last part of a company's market orientation. Most shipbuilders continued to regard the market as dominated by short-term factors and hence not susceptible to analysis. Equally, they equated marketing with selling, a function which literally stopped when the order book was full. Given such attitudes,

---

[20]Smith, *Marketing.*: Notes for Discussion (1969), National Maritime Museum, SRNA, S42/10/14.

[21]*Ibid.*

the development of a positive marketing strategy involving continuous customer contact was extremely difficult.

In the 1960s these attitudes were maintained in spite of radical market changes. By the 1960s export production was coming to dominate world shipbuilding output and market preferences were changing radically as non-traditional purchasers entered the field. The flag of convenience markets and the new national flag fleets were not susceptible to the old personal contact and preferential builder/client relationships. The old contact network on which British shipbuilders had traditionally relied was being rapidly dissolved by the entrance of aggressive new market-oriented shipbuilders. Nevertheless, British shipbuilders resisted any early abandonment of the old patterns of behaviour.

In the absence of any clearly developed sales or marketing policy, how did British shipbuilders expect to sell their vessels? Marketing theory argues that sales strategies tend to fall into four main types: efforts based on product, price, delivery or credit/finance advantages.[22] While in practice elements of all these policies are likely to be embodied in any sales policy, British shipbuilders were weak in all these areas in the 1960s and 1970s. Most had no clearly defined market or product preference, with the exception of specialist building and the Austin and Pickersgill SD-14. Since resources were spread thinly to support diversified building programmes, price advantage was generally not a sales strategy open to British builders. Moreover, given the endemic labour problems of British yards, marketing based on delivery advantages was a path available to only selected companies like Austin and Pickersgill, Appledore and Robb Caledon. The credit/finance strategy proved workable only in relation to *ad hoc* government initiatives and was not a sound base for marketing.

In view of this, such sales strategies as existed in British yards rested on an older formula which we might describe as the "reputation strategy," in which the effort depended in the end on the overall skills of the builder and his established reputation for good work. This is a

---

[22]See Smith, *Marketing*, 44ff.

production rather than a market-oriented strategy and depended strongly on established customer loyalty.

It is also highly vulnerable, since it is based on customer perception and satisfaction. But in an international environment where clear product and marketing strategies were being ruthlessly developed in line with price and delivery advantages, the British position was untenable. A sales policy based on the "reputation" of builders who had failed to develop a clear product policy was doomed to failure. In Britain's case it is clear that customer perception shifted more rapidly than the self-perception of British shipbuilders. As long-established customers deserted British yards in the late 1960s and early 1970s, builders continued to blame their difficulties on externalities--cheap labour, tax advantages, and unfair credit supports and subsidies enjoyed by their competitors. While the notion that British failures were rooted in a fundamental marketing deficiency was espoused by critics, it was not shared by the industry itself.

Conclusion

This paper has not sought to argue that perceived weaknesses in productivity, price, delivery and credit arrangements were unimportant factors in understanding the decline of British shipbuilding in the 1960s. Rather, it has sought to demonstrate that these features were arguably consequences of a failure to develop a market orientation in a period of rapidly expanding demand. The failure to develop market research imprisoned British shipbuilders in a weak information environment, limiting their ability to identify trends and to plan adaptations. The general failure of British shipbuilders to select market segments and to make clear product choices suited to their own experience, resources and abilities placed yards at a severe disadvantage in competition with foreign builders who developed more positive market and product policies. From this stemmed the inability to perceive the advantages of a positive sales policy based on direct selling to clearly identified customers.

The result of these failures was that British shipbuilding remained production-oriented at a time that successful companies had adopted a market orientation. To do so, of course, involved a long-term strategy which placed market selection and product choice at the heart of the company, its resources and development being planned around these choices. The neglect of company development based on marketing was instrumental in making British companies less efficient in the use of their resources than competitors, who did not squander scarce skills and capital across diversified product ranges. The disadvantages in building times, costs and delivery were cumulatively damaging to the British industry, accelerating its loss of market share, and consigning it to long-term decline. The failure of marketing outlined in this paper was arguably at the root of the inability of British shipbuilders to respond successfully to the challenge from Japanese and European competitors.

Liverpool Shipowners, the Mediterranean, and the Transition from Sail to Steam During the Mid-Nineteenth Century

P.L. Cottrell[1]

> In the year 1851 upwards of twenty-one thousand vessels paid dock dues in Liverpool which had arrived from or sailed to upwards of four hundred ports, scattered over the whole world and serving as outlets for the commerce of every nation which possess anything to exchange in the way of commerce, and which does not exclude foreigners from its inhospitable shores.[2]

After 1800 Liverpool's commerce and shipping, already dominant in north Atlantic trades, began to play a considerable role in other international dealings. This was a result of the interplay of many forces. Liverpool's growing commercial connections with the Orient from 1813 arose initially from the abolition of the East India Company's monopoly. Political, rather than economic, liberalisation was significant in the early development of South American trade from the

[1]Part of the research for this paper was conducted as a SSRC-financed project, "The Supply of Capital and the Economic Development of Merseyside, 1680-1880," directed by Professor J.R. Harris, B.L. Anderson and the author. I am grateful to some of the research assistants employed by the project for transcribing the relevant limited joint-stock company returns (BT31) held at the Public Record Office in Kew. In writing this paper I benefited greatly from the assistance of a number of colleagues, especially Professor J. Armstrong, who shared some of his research notes; D.M. Williams, who provided advice and encouragement; and as always the telling critical eye of M. Vollor. A version of this paper was given to a staff seminar at the University of Exeter, which constituted a useful forum of knowledgable constructive criticism and comment.

[2]T. Baines, *History of the Commerce and Town of Liverpool* (Liverpool, 1852), 840.

1810s. As a port, Liverpool served not only the major industrial districts of southeastern Lancashire and northeastern Cheshire but also with continuing domestic transport improvements--the canal and then the railway networks--came to have an almost national hinterland. With this continuing expansion, Merseyside became the British centre for other trades--the Mediterranean during the 1830s, and the American "west coast" and Australian during the 1850s. This resulted by the 1850s in parity with London, particularly in exports.[3]

In this rise to national prominence in overseas trade, Liverpool remained a port of sail, particularly in terms of its own registered vessels. This was not merely a characteristic of the second quarter of the nineteenth century but, unlike London, persisted until the late 1870s.[4] Yet this is a generalisation: in particular trades, such as the Mediterranean, where the early "unsubsidised" commercial adoption of steam was remunerative, Liverpool shipowners were innovators. The purpose here is to trace this transition from sail to steam in Liverpool's Mediterranean trades. The opening sections review the nature of Anglo-Mediterranean commerce and shipping during the second quarter of the nineteenth century and the emergence of Liverpool as a centre for these trades. There is then a discussion of the adoption of steam by Liverpool shipowners about the mid-century. Here the focus is the constitution and dissolution of the Liverpool and Mediterranean Steam Screw Shipping Co. Further, a continuous thread running through almost the entire paper is the development of the Bibby Line and its move from sail to steam. In all this, a central theme explored

---

[3]On the growth of the port of Liverpool, see C.N. Parkinson, *The Rise of the Port of Liverpool* (Liverpool, 1951); S. Mountfield, *Western Gateway: A History of the Mersey Docks and Harbour Board* (Liverpool, 1965); J.R. Harris (ed.), *Liverpool and Merseyside. Essays in the Economic History of the Port and its Hinterland* (London, 1965); F.E. Hyde, *Liverpool and Merseyside. The Development of a Port 1700-1970* (Newton Abbot, 1971); S. Mariner, *The Economic and Social Development of Merseyside* (London, 1982); V. Burton (ed.), *Liverpool Shipping, Trade and Industry: Essays on the Maritime History of Merseyside 1780-1860* (Liverpool, 1989).

[4]P.L. Cottrell, "The Steamship on the Mersey, 1815-80: Investment and Ownership," in P.L. Cottrell and D.H. Aldcroft (eds.), *Shipping, Trade and Commerce. Essays in Memory of Ralph Davis* (Leicester, 1981).

is the reaction, in terms of business organisation, of Liverpool shipowners to the risks and novelty of investing in steam, which in the case of the Mediterranean trades was from the outset largely the adoption of iron-built, propeller-driven vessels.

Anglo-Mediterranean commerce was an important, but not an expanding, component of British overseas trade during the second quarter of the nineteenth century. By value, between the mid-1820s and the mid-1840s it accounted for about 14.8% of British exports (including re-exports) and ten percent of imports. Until 1815 the Mediterranean had been a traditional source of Britain's imports of raw materials, such as silk, vegetable oil and dyestuffs. This role diminished with the subsequent globalisation of British trade; after 1815, as with European imports in general, the relative importance of traditional Mediterranean products fell markedly. Spanish wool was replaced by Australian, Italian silk by Chinese, and dyestuffs by products from India and the Caribbean.[5] Nonetheless, the expansion of trade with the eastern Mediterranean, the Black Sea and the near East from the 1830s gave a broad stability to Anglo-Mediterranean dealings up to 1850. Growth in commerce with these areas compensated for stagnation or decline in trade with the western Mediterranean. British exports by value to the near East rose from £0.65m per annum average between 1824 and 1826 to £3.038m per annum between 1844 and 1846, while imports increased from £1.154m to £1.798m. This expansion was substantially due to the enterprise of Levantine, especially "Greek," merchants.

Such "Greek" traders, as they were known to the British (though in fact this was a generic description which also embraced Arabs, Armenians and Turks), were largely responsible for the dissemination of British cottons from the Leipzig fairs to southeastern Europe and Russia. It was a commerce that followed from successfully dealing with the legal niceties of Napoleon's continental system and the countervail-

---

[5]For statistical convenience "Mediterranean commerce" has been taken to be British trade with southern Europe and the near East. The calculations are based on the estimates of Ralph Davis, *The Industrial Revolution and British Overseas Trade* (Leicester, 1979), Appendix, 87ff; for commentary, see also 37-38.

ing British orders in Council. Further, the Greek merchant marine, after being nurtured under the Russian flag, from 1815 dominated eastern Mediterranean shipping, especially between Italy and the Levant, and in the export of Black Sea grain.[6]

A major sub-group within this commercial expansion were the Chian Greeks. With the Greek revolt of 1821, they were subjected to a Turkish pogrom in 1822, yet subsequently this island's society generated a number of major mercantile dynasties, which linked the British cotton industry with the markets of the eastern Mediterranean and the Black Sea. In the vanguard were Ralli Brothers, who came to London in 1818 and developed a commercial network which by 1828 also involved branch houses at Odessa, Marseilles, and Manchester. They were followed by Rodocanachi Sons and Co. (relatives of the Rallis), Rocca Brothers, Cassaveti Brothers and Co., Paul and Pater Cababé, and Giustianiani and Nepoti. These were the major firms, but there were many others operating on a smaller scale which collectively constituted much of the mercantile sinews of Mediterranean commerce from Marseilles to the Black Sea, the Levant and Egypt.

The Chians formed a major commercial and financial clan within Europe, playing a role somewhat comparable to those of the Jews and Huguenots. They had been partly forged as a mercantile and financial "alloyed group" by persecution which led to a diaspora, while they were further bonded by inter-marriage and a common cause in nationalism and patriotism. Some had their roots in older established houses in Constantinople, Salonika and Smyrna, while newer men followed the Nile inland to tap markets in upper Egypt and the Sudan, just as their forebears had traced the rivers of the Balkans and southern Russia. Their rise during the second quarter of the nineteenth century was frequently based on reciprocal trade, involving the

---

[6]See Gelina Harlaftis, "The Role of the Greeks in the Black Sea Trade, 1830-1900," in L.R. Fischer and H.W. Nordvik (eds.), *Shipping and Trade, 1750-1950: Essays in International Maritime Economic History* (Pontefract, 1990).

exchange of British cottons for Black Sea grain.[7] By the early 1860s some of these Greeks were constituents of the Liverpool mercantile community, as with Argenti, Sechiari and Co.; Cama and Co.; Franghiadi and Rodocanachi; Frangopulo, Bingham; Lemonius and Co.; P.A. Ralli; and J.P. Schilizzi and Co.[8]

With this expansion of trade along the littorals of the eastern Mediterranean and the Black Sea, especially from the 1830s, direct British involvement also grew, particularly in the Black Sea. A consular office was re-opened at Bucharest in 1826, but a wider official administrative structure only developed in the Danubian Principalities after the Peace of Adrianople and Turkish recognition of Greek independence at the London Conference of 1830. Vice-consulates were then established at Braila and Galatz and British ships were specifically noted off the Danube delta in 1834. Another pointer to this commercial expansion was the opening of British mercantile houses in Allepo from 1835.[9]

Such growth developed from a rather inauspicious background. In 1833 J. Nickols of Nickols, Son and Green, shipowners and brokers in the Mediterranean trade, complained to the Select Committee on Manufactures, Commerce and Shipping of its depressed state. He

---

[7]D.S. Landes, *Bankers and Pashas. International Finance and Economic Imperialism in Egypt* (London, 1958), 24-27; S. Fairlie, "The Anglo-Russian Grain Trade, 1815-61" (Unpublished Ph.D. thesis, University of London, 1959), chapter VI; S.D. Chapman, "The International Houses: The Continental Contribution to British Commerce, 1800-1860," *Journal of European Economic History*, VI (1977), 35-42.

[8]As shown by the fire policies taken out with Sun Fire for mercantile stocks within the port; see P.L. Cottrell, "Liverpool and the Atlantic Economies" (Paper presented to the International Urban History Conference on "Cities of Finance," Amsterdam, May 1991). Some of these Greek merchants moved into steam shipping from the mid-1840s, with the most famous contemporary account being S. Xenos, *Depredations: or Overend, Gurney & Co. and the Greek and Oriental Steam Navigation Company* (London, 1869).

[9]P. Cernovodeanu, "British Economic Interests in the Lower Danube and the Balkan Shore of the Black Sea between 1803 and 1829," *Journal of European Economic History*, V (1976), 118-120; D.A. Farnie, *East and West of Suez* (Oxford, 1969), 11.

maintained that his firm had made no profit on an A1-rated ship of 136 tons, built in 1831 for the Turkish trade, with the financial returns received from this investment merely covering insurance and interest at four percent. Nickols attributed this outcome not to cyclical factors but to competition from the Austrians, Genoese, Danes[10] and Swedes, and to the use of Austrian, Sardinian and Greek vessels under Russian colours in the Black Sea grain trade. Closer to home, Nickols noted that the focus of British Mediterranean trade was shifting from London to Liverpool.[11]

Comparing the relative roles of ports in a particular trade is fraught with difficulties. At least some weight is lent to Nickols's remark that the Mediterranean trade was shifting from London to Liverpool by an examination of the voyage entries in *Lloyd's Register* during the mid-1830s. This is a less than ideal database, given its restricted coverage, but it does reveal in broad terms the relative roles of various British ports for outward trading voyages. It indicates that in 1835/6 at least 595 vessels left for the Mediterranean from a minimum of thirty-seven British ports and the Channel Islands; of these, London and Liverpool were by far the most important, with respectively 216 (36.3%) and 150 (25.2%) of noted departures. Although no great weight can be put on these data, they do point to London still being the greatest centre of the trade, with Liverpool of considerable importance. Other "centres" were the Clyde (twenty-four), Plymouth (twenty-two) and Yarmouth (twenty-five)[12] and their significant but minor roles are supported by a consideration of the

---

[10]See H.C. Johansen, "Danish Shipping Services as a Link between the Mediterranean and the Baltic, 1750-1850," in Fischer and Nordvik (eds.), *Shipping and Trade, 1750-1950.*

[11]United Kingdom, Parliament, *Parliamentary Papers* [hereafter *B.P.P.*], 1833, Select Committee on Manufactures, Commerce and Shipping, evidence of J. Nickols, qq. 5838-9, 5841, 5853, 5855, 5858, 5862, 5870-1.

[12]*Lloyd's Register of British and Foreign Shipping. From 1st July 1836 to the 30th June 1837* (London, 1837).

shipping that carried Mediterranean imports to the Mersey to be discussed later.

A printed summary of the bills of entry of the Liverpool Customs for the first half of 1837 provides *some* indication of the role of imports from the Mediterranean (with the exception of wood) within this port's commerce and shipping.[13] Of the 961 vessels that arrived from foreign ports during these six months, carrying cargoes other than wood, 199 came from the Mediterranean--from Gibraltar in the west to Odessa on the Black Sea in the east. These vessels were generally small, with the most typical being between 100 and 150 tons. They carried the whole range of Mediterranean produce, spanning the alphabet from almonds to yellow berries, normally in the form of mixed cargoes. The nature of the source does not allow any solid estimate of the relative importance of particular products. Brimstone, cotton,[14] currants, "fruits," figs, nuts, olive oil, oranges,[15] tallow and wool were all imported as sole cargoes, while in terms of frequency of appearance, lemons, madder, shumac and wine were also of some significance.

---

[13]*B.P.P.* (1837-1838), XLV, 317; "Returns, from the Customs containing the name of every Vessel arriving with a cargo from a Foreign Port (except timber) at Liverpool..." (5 January to 5 July, 1837). A further reservation over the employment of these data arises from the question of seasonality. My colleague, David Williams, has pointed out that one drawback arising from the period covered by the summary is that the autumn inflow of dried fruits from the Aegean is omitted. This is pointed up by the inclusion of only five mentions of vessels from Zante and three from Cephalonia within the summary.

[14]Liverpool began to import cotton from Egypt in 1824; by 1837 such imports amounted to 25,817 bales, 2.5% of the port's total imports of cotton during the year. D.M. Williams, "Liverpool Merchants and the Cotton Trade 1820-1850," in Harris (ed.), *Liverpool and Merseyside*. On the growth of Egyptian cotton production and its export, see Landes, *Bankers*, and E.R. Owen, *Cotton and the Egyptian Economy 1820-1914* (Oxford, 1969).

[15]More generally, see D.M. Williams, "The Citrus Trade to Britain in the Nineteenth Century" (Paper presented at XVII Congreso Internacional de Ciencias Historicas, Madrid, August 1990).

With respect to ports of origin, there are also difficulties of interpretation. It is evident from the nature of the source that the listed port of lading was probably the chief port of loading within the Mediterranean for any particular vessel, but ships may have called at a number of other ports not listed.[16] Moreover, some Mediterranean ports, such as Marseilles, were major entrepôts.[17] Hence the frequency of any particular port in the source can only be treated as indicative. Such a broad picture shows that the Adriatic (Venice two mentions, Trieste fourteen), the Ottoman Empire (Constantinople two, Gallipoli six, Smyrna thirteen, Alexandretta two), the Black Sea (Odessa eight) and Egypt (Alexandria nine) were by the late 1830s already of some importance. Indeed their frequency of listing in aggregate as ports of lading is on par with all western Mediterranean ports--Spanish, French and western Italian. Despite the limitations of the source, what clearly emerges is the importance of Sicilian ports (in aggregate fifty-five) and in particular Licata (fifteen), Messina (thirteen) and Palermo (sixteen). These ports supplied a range of cargoes, frequently mixed,[18] which suggests that they acted as entrepôts and transhipment places. Sicily, however, was the source of brimstone, the Mediterranean product which occurs most frequently (fifty-nine mentions) in *all* the Mediterranean vessels' cargoes itemised in the summary. It may be that if Liverpool had a particular characteristic in Anglo-Mediterranean trade, it arose from the import of Sicilian

---

[16]Only one vessel in the summary is indicated has having called at two Mediterranean ports--it is one of the first entries and its precise composition may be due to a clerical error or confusion over the rules for compiling the summary. One probable general example of the problem is provided by cargoes from Gibraltar, which were declared in the summary to be gums, nuts, "oil," wine and wood, although it is possible that such products were transshipped through Gibraltar from southern Spain.

[17]According to the listing, Marseilles was the port of lading for brandy, brimstone, cotton, olive oil, madders, sugar and tallow, of which brimstone, cotton, madders and sugar, and also possibly tallow were unlikely to be of southern French origin.

[18]Anchovies, barley, barrilla, brimstone, lemons, hides, pozzolana, "oil," olive oil, oranges, pumice, shumac, sulphur, wheat and wine.

brimstone.[19] Sicily held a global monopoly over the supply of sulphur during the nineteenth century and it accounted for about two percent of total British imports from Italy during the second quarter of the nineteenth century, third in importance after silk and olive oil.[20] Sulphur was vital to the growing chemical industries of south Lancashire, firmly within Liverpool's hinterland.

When used in conjunction with the relevant volume of *Lloyd's Register*,[21] the summary also provides a view of the shipping involved in Liverpool's Mediterranean trades. It has been possible to identify positively 140 vessels, some seventy percent of the 199 listed in the summary. On this basis, the most typical vessels entering Liverpool from the Mediterranean were either brigs of 150 to 200 tons (15.5% of *all* entries from the Mediterranean) or schooners of 100 to 150 tons (12.5%). Much of the tonnage was of relatively recent construction, with sixty-nine percent of *identified* vessels during the first half of 1837 having been built during the previous decade and a further twenty-eight percent during the decade 1817 to 1826. Nearly all--86.5%--were of domestic construction,[22] with the major building places being Yarmouth (15.6% of the total number of *identified* vessels), Liverpool (9.9%), Sunderland (5.6%) and Plymouth (4.25%). The rest were predominantly built in the minor ports around the coast of the British Isles.[23] If there was any regional concentration, it was the southwest,

---

[19]Apart from other Sicilian ports--Catania and Girgenti--brimstone was also shipped to Liverpool from Marseilles (a relatively frequent cargo) and Naples.

[20]I.A. Glazier, V.N. Bandera and R.B. Berner, "Terms of Trade between Italy and the United Kingdom 1815-1913," *Journal of European Economic History*, IV (1975).

[21]*Lloyd's Register* (1836).

[22]Foreign-built vessels had largely been constructed in either the Mediterranean (seven vessels) or the Maritime provinces of British North America (seven).

[23]In terms of major ports, apart from Liverpool, one vessel each had been built at Bristol, Dublin, Glasgow and London.

where 9.9% had been launched, in addition to those constructed at Plymouth.[24] Such diffusion may be attributable to a number of factors--particularly both the relative ease of construction of "small" vessels on river banks and in creeks at a time when iron played little role in shipbuilding, and the "openness" of the trade, which did not generally require any particular type of vessel. Further, it would seem that Mediterranean voyages were for many vessels one leg in a complex pattern of annual movements, often involving participation in both the British coastal trade and foreign shipments. Still, one exception has to be made about these broad generalisations: the fresh fruit trade, which required speedy vessels and an ability to beat against the wind, was largely undertaken by schooners.

The regional pattern of ownership of vessels entering Liverpool from the Mediterranean during the first half of 1837 was broadly similar to the diffused nature of their construction. This is understandable given the relatively small size of the craft, which did not represent sizeable capital investments. They were registered at forty ports in the British Isles, as well as in Jersey and at six foreign ports. The major British ports played a somewhat greater role as places of registration than of shipbuilding,[25] with, for example, nineteen vessels registered at London in the names of seventeen separate owners. Of the "minor" ports, Yarmouth was equally important as a place of ownership as construction: seven Yarmouth owners had fourteen vessels engaged in the Liverpool-Mediterranean trades, of which two were substantial shipowning firms. Moreover, some "minor" ports may have played a disproportionate role: Harrison and Slade of Poole had three vessels

---

[24]These were Brixham (one vessel), Bideford (three), Devonport (one), Falmouth (one), Fowey (one), Hayle (one), Mevagissey (one), Pill (one), Shaldon (two), Teignmouth (one) and Topsham (one).

[25]The contributions of the "major" ports, excluding Liverpool and London, were: Bristol: Capt. and Co.-- *Hercules* and *Endeavour*, Champlain--*Antigua Packet*, and T. Lewis--*Emerald*; Dublin: Capt. and Co.--*Lady Leitram*, and Palgrave--*Zuleika*; Glasgow: Dounies--*Eleanor Gordon*, and J. Mitchell--*Lisbon*.

in this trade during the six months being considered,[26] while the *Apollo*, owned by W. Brock of Bideford, completed two voyages.

Not surprisingly, Liverpool was the major centre of vessel ownership, with twenty-four registered at the port. There were two patterns of ownership--eleven vessels were in the names of eleven separate owners, while twelve were owned by just two firms--Bibby with eight and Vianna with four.[27] Two shipowning firms, with only one vessel apiece engaged in the trade during the first half of 1837, completed two voyages, which may be an indication of commitment to the trade.[28]

Bibby and Vianna[29] were two of the Liverpool shipowning firms which began regular Mediterranean steam services in the early 1850s, while two of their associates in this venture--Moss and Cotesworth--each owned at least one vessel which during the first half of 1837 made a Mediterranean voyage.[30] Yet if the sample is a reliable guide to relative importance, Bibby during the late 1830s had the largest Liverpool Mediterranean fleet. One of its vessels--the *Mary Ann* (a 147-ton brigantine, built in 1824)--made three voyages during the six-month period, and two others--the brigantine *Emma* (152 tons, built

---

[26]*Convivial*, *Julia* and *Prince Eugene*.

[27]Vianna's vessels were *Carena*, *John Souchay*, *Mischief* and *Tagus*.

[28]Acraman's *Racer* and Worrall's *Ellen Clare*.

[29]From *Lloyd's*, it would appear that Vianna had two other vessels in the Mediterranean trades--the schooner *Laura Ann* (145 tons, built in 1831) and the brig *Mauney* (186 tons, built in 1826).

[30]In addition to the schooner *Water Witch* (144 tons, built in 1831), Moss also owned the schooner *Glynne* (129 tons, built in 1834), which according to *Lloyd's* was employed in the mid-1830s between London and Chester. Similarly, Cotesworth not only owned the schooner *Cintra* (114 tons, built in 1834) but also employed the schooner *Gertude* (132 tons, built in 1834) between Liverpool and Lisbon. This firm also owned the barque *Winwick* (266 tons, built in 1833), which in the mid-1830s sailed between Liverpool and Jamaica: in 1837, it had just taken delivery of the brig *Bella Portena* (238 tons, built at Maryport).

1833) and the brig *Margaret Highfield* (178 tons, built 1828)--each made two Mediterranean voyages during the same period.[31]

The Bibby Line had been established by John Bibby, born in February 1775 on a farm at Eccleston near Ormskirk. He was the fourth of five sons, a circumstance which probably led to his career within the Liverpool mercantile world. By 1795 he worked for James Hatton, an iron merchant and manufacturer of ship's fittings, and Bibby retained an interest in this trade until the 1830s. Like many who ultimately become shipowners, by 1801 John was acting as a ship-broker, in association with William Hall. His transition to becoming a shipowner was very rapid; during the early years of the nineteenth century, he already owned in whole or in part a number of vessels on the Liverpool registry. Further, by 1805 he was working in his own right in ship brokerage. Two years later he established a merchant partnership with John Highfield, who was also involved in the iron trade. The precise origins of this association, which continued until the late 1830s, are unclear and there is some conflict in the available documentary evidence. It may be that their firm grew out of an

[31]The other Bibby vessels in the summary were the brig *Amelia* (200 tons, built in 1826), brig *Bispham* (214 tons, 1826), brig *Ellen German* (176 tons, 1833), *Ellen Highfield*, ketch *Ellen Jenkinson* (162 tons, 1823), and schooner *Fanny Connell* (171 tons, 1827). Neither *Lloyd's* nor E.W. Paget-Tomlinson (*History of the Bibby Line* [Liverpool, 1969]), indicate that Bibby owned the *Ellen Highfield*, but the "construction" of her name--both "Ellen" and "Highfield" (Bibby's co-partner in the 1830s)--is a strong indication that she was a Bibby vessel. Like Cotesworth and Vianna, Bibby also ran to Portugal, employing in the mid-1830s the snow *Henry Hoyle* (207 tons, 1829), barque *Rolstone* (167 tons, 1827), and snow *Warrior* (100 tons, 1833). Bibby was also the owner of the snow *Bootle* (153 tons, 1820), which in the mid-1830s sailed between Liverpool and St. Thomas, and the 187-ton *George the Fourth*. *Lloyd's* gives the rig of the latter as a snow and locates her in the mid-1830s at London, while Paget-Tomlinson (p. 61) describes her as a brig, further stating that she was lost off La Guayra in 1835. The fleet list in Paget-Tomlinson (pp. 60-63) indicates that Bibby also owned the following other vessels during the mid-1830s: schooner *Ann Paley* (166 tons, 1827), ship *Cestrian* (380 tons, 1833), snow *Duchess of Clarence* (247 tons, 1828), snow *Fearon* (152 tons, 1813, co-owned with J. Fearon, who was a tenant of some of Bibby's warehouses in Liverpool); brig *Hardware* (152 tons, 1821), ship *Mary Bibby* (299 tons, 1825), and brig *Nile* (156 tons, 1800).

association in shipowning dating from 1805; certainly between 1805 and 1807 they held shares in seven small vessels, mainly involved in the coastal trade. What is clear is that in 1807 they commenced regular sailings between Parkgate on the Dee and Dublin. Very quickly this service expanded beyond the confines of the Irish Sea, first to the Baltic, in 1817 to the Mediterranean and in the early 1820s to South America. It is not at all evident how Bibby accumulated funds to invest in shipping. If it was from his other activities, these must have been sufficiently profitable to allow this diversification, notwithstanding that the initial maritime investments were in vessels of relatively small size.

In 1821 the shipowning interest was styled John Bibby and Co., although John's business association with Highfield continued. Any ambiguities in the precise constitution of Bibby's merchant and shipowning interests were to a certain extent reflected in the complexities of vessel ownership. Frank Neal's analysis of the Liverpool register revealed that between 1815 and 1835, Bibby had interests in twenty-seven vessels totalling 6,101 tons. Of these he owned three outright, but fourteen were owned in conjunction with Highfield and Bibby, while the remainder were undertaken by Highfield and Bibby with other associates. Between 1829 and 1836 John Bibby and Co. had interests in eighteen vessels.[32]

On the death of the senior John Bibby in 1840, the firm became John Bibby and Sons, being subsequently renamed John Bibby Sons and Co. in 1853, when the major partners were John II and James Jenkinson Bibby. These sons of John I concentrated their shipping interests upon services to Iberia and the western Mediterranean. From 1839 they were run in conjunction with a copper works at Seacombe and other smelting undertakings were later established at St. Helens and Garston.[33]

---

[32]Paget-Tomlinson, *Bibby Line*, 103; F. Neal, "Liverpool Shipping 1815 to 1835" (Unpublished M.A. thesis, University of Liverpool, 1962), 82-87.

[33]Paget-Tomlinson, *Bibby Line*, 3-4.

As in the late 1830s, so during the 1840s much Anglo-Mediterranean trade was undertaken by brigs and schooners.[34] Direct British commerce with the region was further stimulated by the repeal of the Corn Laws, which facilitated the growth of Black Sea grain imports. While in 1842, 123 ships carried such cargoes to British ports, seventeen docking at Liverpool, by 1853/4 British involvement in the trade had risen to 187 ships, although Liverpool's participation had not grown, consisting of only fifteen vessels.[35] Such quantitative indicators militate somewhat against the oft-made argument that it was the repeal of the Corn Laws in 1846 which led immediately to further developments of Liverpool's shipping connections with the Mediterranean. The lack of initial expansion in the late 1840s with the Black Sea may have been compensated, however, by the growth of corn imports from Egypt and the subsequent greater opportunities to import Mediterranean fruit with the repeal in 1853 of the relevant duties on that produce.[36] Yet during the 1850s, Liverpool became a major importer of breadstuffs; such grains during the decade were second only in importance to cotton, the port's staple import. In the 1850s a substantial mercantile community specializing in these international dealings emerged. For instance, Rathbones imported breadstuffs not only from the Black Sea and Egypt but also across the Atlantic and from France. Mediterranean and Russian grain imports were dislocated, though, by the substantial price fall with the end of the Crimean War in 1856.[37]

The inception of British commercial steam services in the Mediterranean from 1840 evolved from the development, with state encouragement and aid, of a steam route to India. This began in 1835 as a monthly mail service, involving overland transhipment at the Suez

---

[34] W.B. Forwood, *Reminiscences of a Liverpool Shipowner 1850-1920* (Liverpool, 1920), 43.

[35] S. Fairlie, "Shipping in the Anglo-Russian Grain Trade to 1870: Part One," *Maritime History*, I (1970), 164.

[36] G. Chandler, *Liverpool Shipping. A Short History* (London, 1960), 87.

[37] S. Mariner, *Rathbones of Liverpool 1845-73* (Liverpool, 1961), 17-18.

isthmus, which continued until the opening of the canal, although eased by railway construction in the 1850s. Initially the first leg to Alexandria was undertaken by Admiralty packets, together with mercantile vessels, involving some use of auxiliary steam. The maritime situation changed markedly from September 1840, when the P&O began a monthly service to Alexandria. In both service and capital investment, this built upon the Peninsular Steam Navigation Co., founded in 1835 to run to Spain and Portugal, which in turn was an extension of the earlier coastal steam shipping interests of the City of Dublin Steam Packet Co., established in 1824. The P&O's service replaced the Admiralty packets, but until 1845, its Mediterranean paddle steamers were wooden, in deference to the Admiralty's continuing prejudice against iron.[38] Of importance to others who set up further steam services was the development of Gibraltar as a coaling station.

The major growth of British steam shipping within the Mediterranean occurred during the 1850s and was shaped to a significant degree by the economic impact of the Crimean War. Military demands resulted in the substantial chartering of tonnage by the government, such vessels being drawn from both the general mercantile marine, including northeast colliers, and the ocean-going steam shipping companies. The effect on the charter market was to sustain for a further three years the rise in freight rates which had begun in 1851, initiated by a cyclical British export boom. This prolonged escalation in freight rates over the first half of the 1850s stimulated the building of iron steam tonnage for short sea voyages, in the Baltic from 1853 and by the closing years of the decade in the Mediterranean. Unlike many of the oceanic routes, these services were not supported by mail

---

[38]Farnie, *East and West of Suez*, 11-16, 27. On the origins of the P&O, see also F. Harcourt, "Ownership and Finance 1820-1850: The Case of Ireland," in J.R. Bruijn and W.F.J. Morzer Bruyns (eds.), *Anglo-Dutch Mercantile Marine Relations 1700-1850* (Leiden, 1991); I am indebted to David Williams for this reference.

subsidies, but being of short duration, fuel consumption was not so critical, thus leaving greater commercial carrying capacity.[39]

Although the general growth of British steam shipping in the Mediterranean was a feature of the late 1850s and the 1860s, Liverpool shipowners, along with others, began such services on a regular basis from the early 1850s. One initiative may have been due to a dinner party hosted in 1849 by W. Miles Moss of James Moss and Co., a firm established in 1815 by a Liverpool ship chandler. Moss and Co. provided regular shipping services to the eastern Mediterranean in the late 1840s, running sailing ships to Alexandria in conjunction with Lamport and Holt. According to the memory of one Liverpool shipowner, Miles Moss brought together at his dinner table all Liverpudlians who had a major interest in Mediterranean shipping. The guest list has not survived, but it likely included representatives of at least two other firms--Bibby and Vianna, Jones--which in conjunction with J. Moss and Co. used sailing packets to provide a regular service with sailings every ten days from Liverpool to Genoa and Leghorn.[40] The guest list may also have included Papayanni, who had established a shipping firm in the 1840s operating to Malta, Egypt, the Levant and the Black Sea.[41]

Moss used the occasion to give his opinion on the state of the trade. His appraisal is unavailable, but another Liverpool shipowner, Charles MacIver, was at the same time encouraged to enter the Mediterranean steam trade as a result of the repeal of the Navigation Laws, which he believed facilitated Liverpool as a point of transhipment for French and Mediterranean goods destined for America.[42] This liberalisation of trade may also have motivated Moss, who in any case had greater knowledge of Mediterranean commerce.

---

[39]J.R.T. Hughes, *Fluctuations in Trade, Industry and Finance* (Oxford, 1960), 205, 208, 210, 211, 218; Farnie, *East and West of Suez*, 27, 32.

[40]*Gore's Directory of Liverpool 1851* (Liverpool, 1851).

[41]Chandler, *Liverpool Shipping*, 88, 91.

[42]F.E. Hyde, *Cunard and the North Atlantic 1840-1973* (London, 1975), 16-17.

Whatever the spur, Moss announced to guests that he had contracted to build the steamer *Nile* at a cost of £21,000. Moss sought shareholders for the venture, but initially only managed to obtain £12,000 in subscriptions from those around his dinner table. However disappointing the immediate response, this occasion has been regarded as the origin of the subsequent Mediterranean steam lines run by three shipping firms--Moss, Bibby, and Vianna, Jones and Chapple.[43] Bibby may have been the most receptive to Moss' proposal, as during the 1840s it had considered investing in steam and began to operate occasional paddle vessels in the Mediterranean. This experience led them to favour propeller propulsion for a number of reasons--consistency of "drive" whatever the load, better arrangement of space within the vessel, and easier loading and discharge by not being impeded by paddle boxes amidships.[44]

There must always be doubts about stories such as this, especially when they are derived from gossip and written down some seventy years after the event. But Moss' relatively early interest in commercial deepwater steam is clear and was shared by his associates, Lamport and Holt. During the early 1850s Lamport and Holt had also decided to replace sail with steam and was developing some experience with the propeller-driven *Scamander*. Further, in 1851 it sent, in conjunction with Moss, the *Orontes* on its maiden voyage to Sicily, Egypt and Syria.[45] Moss acquired the vessel that same year, but it was in 1853 taken over by F. Chapple, one of his associates in the Mediterranean steam venture. Yet the *Orontes* was not a pioneer. Baines has noted that Liverpool had begun to send screw steamers to the eastern Mediterranean from at least August 1845, when the *Novelty*

---

[43]Forwood, *Reminiscences*, 43.

[44]Paget-Tomlinson, *Bibby Line*, 4. More generally, see B. Greenhill, "An Introduction: The Development of Screw Propulsion for Steam Vessels," in S. Fisher (ed.), *Innovation in Shipping and Trade* (Exeter, 1989), 38-39.

[45]F.E. Hyde with J.R. Harris, *Blue Funnel. A History of Alfred Holt and Company of Liverpool from 1865 to 1914* (Liverpool, 1957), 11.

and the *Levantine* were despatched to Constantinople.[46] There are strong indications that the inception of such services arose in part from growing involvement of Anglo-Greek merchants with British commerce. In 1846, one of their agents, Augustus Mongredien, commissioned the first three iron steamers to run to the eastern Mediterranean and the Black Sea. During the following year he was the agent for the *Osmanli* at Liverpool, after its voyage from Trebizond, Samsun, Constantinople, Smyrna and Malta. In 1850, the *Osmanli* was sold to Vianna, Jones, who were associates in the Moss initiative.[47]

The Moss Mediterranean steam venture was therefore grounded in earlier experience and from its very inception faced competition. At the time of Moss' dinner party a Mediterranean steam service was being operated by the General Screw Steam Shipping Co. (GSSSC) of London, which from 1849 ran between Liverpool, Malta and Constantinople.[48] This service continued until the mid-1850s, represented in Liverpool by the agency of Balfour, Laming and Owen.[49]

If the steam service inaugurated by Moss was not pioneering, it nonetheless marked the future development of regular sailings to the Mediterranean from Liverpool. Further, these were initiated before

[46]Baines, *Commerce of Liverpool*, 672-673. The *Novelty* was a steam auxiliary of three hundred-tons and twenty-five horsepower. On one of her voyages from Liverpool to Constantinople she took 420 tons of cargo; it appears that this particular voyage took place in the early 1840s--certainly no later than June 1842--and therefore before Baines' noting. See B. Greenhill, "The Screw Steamship *Great Northern*," in Fisher (ed.), *Innovation in Shipping and Trade*, 58, n. 16.

[47]Fairlie, "Shipping in the Anglo-Russian Grain Trade," 168, 173.

[48]N.R.P. Bonsor, *North Atlantic Seaway* (Prescot, 1955), 81. The GSSSC was established in 1847 with a nominal capital of £1m under a royal charter obtained by James Lanning, W. Margetson and John Purdue in conjunction with others--see *B.P.P.*, *Accounts and Papers*, LXV (1854), "Returns of all Applications...praying for Grants of Charters with Limited Liability..."

[49]*Gore's Liverpool Directory 1853* (Liverpool, 1853). By 1853 the GSSSC also offered Liverpool traders a steam service *via* London to the Cape of Good Hope, Mauritius, Ceylon, Madras and Calcutta.

any stimulus had been received from the marked rise in freight rates. Moreover, the Moss dinner party led to the emergence of Frederick Chapple as a shipowner within the firm Vianna, Jones, which became Vianna, Jones and Chapple by 1853[50] and brought about a further stage in the development of the Bibby Line, marked by a complete transition from sail to steam during the 1850s.

Although the Moss Mediterranean steam initiative had been preceded by London and Liverpool interests during the second half of the 1840s, the operation of propeller-driven vessels on even such relatively short routes still contained a degree of risk. Consequently those involved with Miles Moss took out some insurance. They did not, however, establish a joint-stock company, like the chartered GSSSC; indeed, compared to London, Liverpool shipowners seldom resorted to limited liability for steam shipping services before the 1860s and 1870s.[51] Instead, the Moss consortium initially operated its steamers through a joint pooling operation called the Liverpool and Mediterranean Screw Steam Shipping Co. (LMSSSC). There are strong indications that the agreements establishing this "company" went beyond the integration of services and the sharing of freights to encompass the cross-ownership of the vessels involved. Certainly the complexity of the underlying understandings and relationships behind the LMSSSC gave rise to litigation in the mid and late 1860s, by when the various parties involved largely operated independently.[52] Apart from the reasons already outlined for such close co-operation between the three shipping firms involved in the LMSSSC, there was one other--competition. This came not only from the established Liverpool service of the GSSSC but also from two newly-founded concerns--the Levant Steam Shipping Company (LSSC), represented in Liverpool by H. Dixon

---

[50]During the 1830s Chapple had been a shipbroker with the Liverpool firm Haskayne, Chapple and Co.; see *Gore's Liverpool Directory 1839* (Liverpool, 1839).

[51]See Cottrell, "The Steamship on the Mersey" and S.R. Palmer, "Investors in London Shipping 1820-1850," *Maritime History*, II (1972).

[52]See "Moss v. The Anglo-Egyptian Navigation Company Limited," *The Weekly Report*, XIV (1865), 150.

(probably W. Henry Dixon) and the Anglo-Italian Steam Navigation (AISNC), represented by M'Kean, M'Larty and Co.

It is difficult to establish firmly the nature of these two firms which also embarked upon regular Liverpool-Mediterranean steam services in the early 1850s, employing propeller-driven vessels. Both companies named their vessels in advertisements;[53] when ownership is traced, some suggestions can be made concerning the firms' constitution and composition. But these can only be tentative as, apart from the effect of the chartering of vessels, there are other problems in using such an approach to identify those involved. These arise from the separation between the ownership of vessels and their management by agents, while being further complicated by services being apparently provided by companies. Company is an ambiguous English term and the day-to-day use of "company," or "Co." in a firm's title may not necessarily mean the existence of an underlying proprietary, partnership, or corporate entity, whether an unlimited company as under the 1844 legislation, or a chartered concern as before 1855.

In 1851 the LSSC publicised its service as being provided by the screw steamers *Brigand*, *Pirate*, *Astrologer*, *Pioneer* and *Lancer*, operating twice a month to Constantinople, calling en route at Malta. None was registered at Liverpool; instead, they appear (with the exception of the *Lancer*) on the Glasgow register on 1 January 1851 as owned by the Glasgow and Liverpool Steam Shipping Co. (GLSSC), a "company" style used by G. and J. Burns.[54] Yet it would appear from the published summary registration data that the *Brigand*, *Pioneer* and *Pirate* were paddle steamers, while, according to one authority, the *Pirate* was transferred in 1851 to David Hutcheson and Co. for the west highland steam ship trade.[55] Of the four steamers so traced, only the *Astrologer* clearly meets the LSSC's description in its advertisements, being an iron screw steamer of 598 gross tons, although registered by

[53] *Gore's Liverpool Directory*, various years.

[54] *B.P.P.*, 1851 (196) LII, 229.

[55] C.L.D. Duckworth and G.E. Langmuir, *Clyde and Other Coastal Steamers* (Glasgow, 1939), 14, 109.

the GLSSC at Glasgow on 15 June 1850. But there is further conflict in the available evidence, as *Lloyd's Register* gives the ownership of the *Astrologer* as Lewis Potter and Co. of Glasgow, agents for the Dublin and Glasgow Sailing and Steam Packet Co.,[56] although confirming the steamer's use in the Mediterranean trade. Some of this ambiguity arises from the common practice of the replication of vessel's names within "fleets," while other confusion stems from the nature and constitution of the GLSSC.

Duckworth and Langmuir, the pioneering historians of Clyde steamers, only list the *Brigand*, an iron screw steamer, as operating under the agency of W. Sloan from 1858, but more recently Langmuir and Somner have shown her to have been built in 1848 for the GLSSC, passing to Lewis Potter and Co. in 1854.[57] Contemporary documentary evidence also indicates that the GLSSC in 1848 owned the *Pirate*, a *"screw steam vessel"* (my emphasis), valued at £8,500 and acknowledged that the *Pirate* and *Brigand* "were employed [in 1850]...in trading between Liverpool and certain ports in the Mediterranean Sea and in the seas and waters adjacent thereto."[58] This certainly confirms the directory evidence, while leaving the *Lancer* and the *Pioneer* as the only untraced screw steamers of the initial LSSC fleet.

The continuing repetitive use of vessels' names and the transfer of steamers between services and registered owners, arises from the nature of the GLSSC. This was a Scottish co-partnership in which the Burn brothers were heavily involved, although largely as agents, since they only held four of the company's shares. The largest shareholders were W.S. Dixon (nineteen), Lewis Potter (nine) and D.J. McLellan (seven). There are strong grounds for assuming that the W. Henry

---

[56] *Ibid.*, 33.

[57] G.E. Langmuir and G.H. Somner, *William Sloan & Co. Ltd., Glasgow 1825-1968* (Kendal, 1987), 12.

[58] National Maritime Museum, CST 38/6. I am grateful to Professor John Armstrong for transcribed notes from this document.

Dixon of Liverpool listed as owning six shares in this company was the same as H. Dixon, the Liverpool agent for the LSSC.[59]

By 1853 the LSSC was also operating the *Arabian*, *Grecian* and *Persian*. Once more, in the case of these iron screw steamers, there is a conflict in the evidence regarding ownership. The 598-ton *Grecian* was registered at Glasgow by the GLSSC in November 1850 and the 655-ton *Arabian* was so registered on 3 March 1851. Yet *Lloyd's Register* indicates the owner of the *Arabian* as Lewis Potter of Glasgow and the *Persian* as being owned by Lewis Potter of Liverpool, although confirming the steamers' connections with Liverpool and their use in the Mediterranean trade.

One resolution of this conflict in the evidence would be that the LSSC, as the LMSSSC, was a pooling operation, drawing steamers from a number of owners, although grouped under the umbrella of the GLSSC, together with other associated western Scottish coastal steam ship "companies." In the case of the LSSC, this involved the transfer of steamers between the GLSSC and the shipowning shareholders which constituted the latter company. Further, it may be that at least in part the Mediterranean service of the LSSC was initially provided by wooden paddle steamers, before the completion of a "full" iron propeller-driven fleet. A suggestion for the change in the particular ownership of steamers run under the name of the LSSC during the early 1850s may be the inception of MacIver's competitive regular Mediterranean service from 1851. The agents for MacIver were Burns and MacIver and the venture only became legally-constituted as a co-partnership under the British and Foreign Steam Navigation Co. in 1855. There was yet a further partial change in ownership of the LSSC's steamers from mid-1852, when Dixon, the "company's" Liverpool agent, began to acquire some of the LSSC's vessels, beginning with the *Persian* on 10 August, followed by the *Astrologer* on 16 May 1853 and the *Arabian* on 25 May 1853.[60]

---

[59] *Ibid.*

[60] However *Lloyd's Register of British and Foreign Shipping. From 1st July 1857, to the 30th June, 1858* (London, 1858) still shows the *Persian* as being owned by Potter and Co. of Liverpool.

There is similar evidence of ownership that points to the AISNC as also being a pooling venture, comparable in nature at least to the initial stages of the development of the LSSC. In 1851 the AISNC named the vessels that provided its monthly screw steam service to Genoa, Leghorn, Messina and Palermo as the *Genova*, *Livorno* and *Levantine*. The *Genova*, of 520 gross tons, was an iron screw steamer registered at Glasgow on 19 September by M'Kean and Co., which was probably connected with the "company's" Liverpool agents, M'Kean, M'Larty and Co. The 494-ton *Livorno* was also a Glasgow- registered iron screw steamer, but owned by A. Galbraith, while the 283-ton *Levantine* was a London-registered (1 August 1849) iron paddle steamer, owned by Cunliff and Co.[61]

From the beginning, the development of Liverpool's steam connections with the Mediterranean was marked outwardly by a high level of competition, with regular timetabled services in 1851 being offered by four companies--the GSSSC of London; the LSSC, represented in Liverpool by H. Dixon; the AISNC, the Liverpool agents of which were M'Kean, M'Larty and Co.; and the LMSSSC, the consortium shipping "company" constituted by Bibby, Vianna, Jones, and Moss. Further, there were also the occasional Mediterranean steam voyages of the *British Queen*, chartered by Charles MacIver. Competition there undoubtedly was, and this increased with the later "full" MacIver service, but there may have been factors moderating its cutting edge.

During the development of the coastal steam shipping trade over the second quarter of the nineteenth century, trade-sharing agreements had been struck to moderate the effects of competition, such as that between MacIver and Burns in 1835 for Glasgow-Liverpool services.[62] With respect to the regular steam voyages to the Mediterranean from Liverpool in the early 1850s, there is some circumstantial evidence which may be indicative of at least a temper-

---

[61]*B.P.P.*, 1851 (196), LII, 229.

[62]Hyde, *Cunard*, 15; see also J. Armstrong, "Conferences in British Nineteenth-Century Coastal Shipping," *Mariner's Mirror*, LXXVII, (1991) 55-56.

ing, personal link between the LSSC and the LMSSSC. Thomas Martin during the early 1850s was involved in the provision of a regular packet service to Lisbon with Bibby, Vianna, Jones, and a third firm, Cotesworth, Wynne and Lynne. Martin also had been the Liverpool agent for the GLSSC, one of the initial providers of steamers to the LSSC[63] and in 1848 held a single £60 share in the GLSSC.[64] Such a relationship is very tenuous, but what is clear is that initially the LMSSSC did not compete directly with the LSSC. The LSCC's steamers ran to Constantinople *via* Malta, whereas the initial steam route chosen by the LMSSSC was to ports on the west Italian coast *via* Sicily. On this route, the LMSSSC was only in competition with the smaller steam fleet of the AISNC, while the consortium of Liverpool shipowners behind the LMSSSC had considerable knowledge of this trade, accumulated through their sailing interests of the second quarter of the century. Indeed, Bibby, with Vianna, Jones and J. Moss, continued to run a regular sailing packet integrated service to Genoa and Leghorn alongside that of the steamers of their LMSSSC. By the mid-1850s there is further evidence indicative of collaboration between the "companies" that provided Liverpool-Mediterranean steam services, in that two of the LMSSSC's steamers--the *Albanian* and the *Euphrates*--were advertised for Italian Adriatic ports by both constituents of the LMSSSC (Bibby and Moss) *and* Burns and MacIver. Yet there is also one indication of a contrary direction with respect to competition, arising from the early 1850s intermediate Sicilian service of the LMSSSC. This "company's" steamers called at Messina and Palermo, but Vianna, Jones, together with James Moss, jointly under their own names, also advertised a direct steamer line for these ports.[65]

Liverpool was an early entrant into the provision of steam shipping for the Mediterranean, a relatively "short" service route, which in many respects meet the criteria which have been highlighted in

---

[63]Duckworth and Langmuir, *Clyde Steamers*, 7.

[64]National Maritime Museum, CST 38/6.

[65]For route provision, see *Gore's Liverpool Directory 1851* (Liverpool, 1851).

Knick Harley's general analysis of the transition from sail to steam. These were the importance of passengers, high value/low bulk products dominating the "hold cargo," a recognised premium for speed and regularity, light and variable winds in the Mediterranean, and a return cargo frequently consisting of perishable fruit.[66] Furthermore, Liverpool's innovation was for shipowners not only to adapt steam but also to apply the propeller and iron, both relatively novel even in the 1850s. As early entrants they reaped substantial rewards and fortuitously benefited from the six-year rise in freight rates from 1851 to 1856, which they could not have foreseen when they made their initial investment calculations. Yet there were other innovative elements in Liverpool's behaviour which do not quite adhere to the "Harley amalgam" of explanatory factors. One was the importance of sulphur in Liverpool return cargoes, a low-value freight which did not require speed (and which may have constituted the Mediterranean's opportunity "ballast" freight). Another was the cost of coal at Mediterranean ports, given that the littorals of the Mediterranean and the Black Sea were not rich in coal deposits. By the end of the 1850s there was a major British coal export trade to the Mediterranean to fuel the newly-established railways as well as steamers. Nonetheless, in commissioning steamers Bibby until the late 1860s used "lifting screws," a device which allowed the steamers to make full use of their additional sails, particularly when running before the wind.

Lastly, it is clear that investing in steam had risks. These were insured against, but not by resort to the chartered company before 1855, nor by the general availability of limited liability thereafter. Rather the Liverpool application of steam to Mediterranean routes during the 1850s involved "pooling agreements" which went beyond mutual timetabling and shared freights to the provision of vessels. Indeed, there are tenuous indications that this approach went as far as vessels being shared between at least two of the four outwardly competing "companies" for traffic on one of these new steam routes.

[66]C.K. Harley, "The Shift from Sailing Ships to Steamships, 1850-1890: A Study in Technological Change and Its Diffusion," in D.N. McCloskey (ed.), *Essays on a Mature Economy: Britain after 1840* (London, 1971), 221-222.

Overall, through these various arrangements, competition was moderated until at least the late 1850s, thus providing a benign market environment for the initial stages of technological innovation on shipping routes between Liverpool and the Mediterranean.

The LMSSSC's initial fleet of propeller-driven steamers was brought together during the second half of 1850. The 304-ton *Osmanli* was registered at Liverpool by F. Chapple on 28 May 1850, while the 267-ton screw steamer *Rattler* was registered by J.J. Bibby on 28 October 1850. Moss's *Nile*, also a screw steamer of 525 gross tons, came on to the Liverpool register on 13 November 1850.[67] Unlike the *Nile*, the *Rattler* was not a new vessel. It had been built by R.J. Lecky and Co. of Cork, where it was registered on 24 September 1846 under the ownership of T.S. Reeves and Co. In November 1847 it was bought by William Law, Ogilby and Co. of London. Before being employed in the Mediterranean, the *Rattler* made one voyage in 1850 from Holland to Liverpool.[68] Bibby's acquisition of the *Rattler* had been guided by Edward Harland, who was completing his apprenticeship with Robert Stephenson and Co. Harland had been brought to Bibby's attention by Gustav Christian Schwabe, a Liverpool commission merchant and junior partner within Bibby's shipping interests from the 1840s. There were links of marriage between the Harlands, the Schwabes and the Dugdales, reinforced in the latter case by mutual business interests in northwestern commerce. Such relationships of business and friendship subsequently extended to embrace the Bibby family. On the one hand, they led to Bibby acquiring its steamers from Harland and Wolff from 1859 until 1870 and investing in the Belfast yard for a limited period between 1871 and 1872, while on the other, the Dugdales became minority shareholders in Bibby's steamers from the 1860s.[69]

---

[67]*B.P.P.*, LII (1851), "A return...of the whole of the registered steam vessels of the U.K. on 1 January 1851."

[68]*B.P.P.*, 'A return of the number and tonnage of British steam vessels which entered the ports of the United Kingdom from France, Holland and Belgium in 1850.'

[69]M. Moss and J.R. Hume, *Shipbuilders to the World. 125 years of Harland and Wolff, Belfast 1861-1986* (Belfast, 1986), 14-15, 22.

Bibby subsequently passed the *Rattler* onto F. Chapple in 1853, an indication of the business and capital ties within the LMSSSC.[70] Another manifestation of the inter-relationships of ownership within the LMSSSC was the transfer in 1852/53 of the *Calpe* from Bibby to George Louthean and Cross, who in 1851 were constituents of the LMSSSC, and later in 1853 were involved in sailing packet services to Lisbon, Genoa and Leghorn in association with Bibby, Vianna, Jones and Chapple, J. Moss, and Cotesworth, Wynne and Lynne.[71] Similarly in 1853 the *Orontes* was transferred from W.M. Moss to F. Chapple.

The steam venture by Moss and his associates to the Ligurian and Tyrrhenian seas, provided in 1850/51 by the *Arno*, *Tiber*, *Nile* and *Osmanli*, proved immediately successful. As a result, the constituent shipowning firms behind the LMSSSC acquired three new iron propeller vessels in 1851, followed by a further ten between 1852 and 1855 (see Appendix I).

The success of the LMSSSC also led some of its associated shipowning companies to initiate independent steam services to Iberia and additional Mediterranean ports. Bibby, with its junior partner, G.C. Schwabe, established its own steam service to Portugal in 1853, while the following year it began to run to the eastern Mediterranean. This began in a "transitional form," being initially under the "umbrella" of the LMSSSC and employing steamers owned by Moss.[72] This Levant initiative by Bibby in 1854 appears in practice to have been a transfer of the service run by James Moss and Co. in 1852/53 to Alexandria and Syria via Sicily, with the *Nile*, *Orontes*, *Scamander* and the *Pactolus*. A steam service to the eastern Mediterranean brought

---

[70]I am grateful to Robin Craig for the precise registration information, which also showed that the vessel was not the *Rattler* which had been built at Sheerness in 1843 for the Admiralty and took place in the propeller versus paddle propulsion trials.

[71]*Gore's Liverpool Directory*, 1851 and 1853. This conflicts with the fleet list drawn up by Paget-Tomlinson, *Bibby Line*, 64, which shows Bibby retaining ownership of the *Calpe* from 1852, when it was built by J. and G. Thompson of Glasgow, until it went missing in 1868.

[72]Paget-Tomlinson, *Bibby Line*, 4-5.

Bibby into public competition with the LSSC, whose ships were now largely owned by H. Dixon, its Merseyside agent.

Other local competitors also embarked upon eastern Mediterranean steam shipping, with Papayanni acquiring his first steam vessel in 1854.[73] Further, MacIver's venture with the *British Queen* during the early 1850s led to the development of a full, regular service. In 1851 the *British Queen* was fully taken over by Cunard, with its continuing Mediterranean sailings supported by the *Margaret* and the *Shamrock*, and Burns and MacIver acting as agents to the steamers. This growing service from 1853 involved five new screw vessels, beginning with the *Balbec*, *Melita* and *Phoebe* running *via* Gibraltar and Malta to eastern Mediterranean ports, such as Constantinople, against the LSSC and the GSSSC. In 1855 the British and Foreign Steam Navigation Co., a co-partnership of Burns, MacIver and Cunard, was established to organise and control the capital involved in the Mediterranean service. MacIver's initiative ultimately led in 1857 to the operation of the *Etna* from Liverpool and Southampton to Malta and Alexandria, connecting *via* the Suez isthmus with the European and Australian Co.'s short-lived service to Colombo and Australia.[74] As well as an expansion in the number and range of Mediterranean steam services from Liverpool, the LMSSSC's direct rival, the AISNC, widened its service to include Civita Vecchiai and Naples on the western Italian coast, as well as Marseilles.

During the mid-1850s such an expansion was warranted by the general cyclical upswing in trade and more particularly by the repeal of the fruit duties in 1853 and the economic effects of the Crimean War. For instance, Bibby steamers were chartered by the government for trooping, an experience which appears to have subsequently affected the design considerations for new Bibby tonnage in the 1860s. On the supply side, vessels such as MacIver's *Andes* and *Alps* demonstrated that screw cargo/passenger steamers had sufficiently low

[73]Chandler, *Liverpool Shipping*, 88.

[74]*Gore's Directory*, 1853; Bonsor, *Seaway*, 15-16; Hyde, *Cunard*, 17-18.

running costs to compete successfully with sailing packets.[75] Nonetheless, new Bibby steamers were equipped with "lifting screws" until the late 1860s, an indication of a continued reliance upon the wind to reduce direct running costs and to maximise carrying capacity by minimising the size of on-board coal bunkers.

By 1856/57, the peak of the cyclical expansion of the 1850s, there had been a substantial expansion in the provision of steam services from Liverpool to the Mediterranean, coupled with some change in the shipowners and agents which provided them. (see Appendix II) There was one case of total withdrawal--the GSSSC--while the name "AISNC" had been dropped, although that "company's" service to the west Italian coast *via* Marseilles was still being continued through the agency of M'Larty, now in partnership with Lamont.[76] It would appear that the LSSC's services had developed to such an extent that it required representation in Liverpool through two agencies. Dixon continued to act for the "company," but only for its services to Constantinople, the Levant and Syria, while Fowler and Dagnall were now the agents for the runs to Constantinople, Salonica and Smyrna. Similarly, Burns and MacIver were now representatives for two Mediterranean routes, to the Italian Adriatic ports, as well as the original Turkish service, with both involving a call at Le Havre. The new Adriatic service shared the steamers *Euphrates* and *Albanian* owned by the LMSSSC "group," and was also advertised by Bibby and Moss as a new eastern Italian line. Such collaboration underscores the moderation of competition. A totally new departure was the provision

---

[75]Bonsor, *Seaway*, 15.

[76]During 1852 and 1853 this firm also ran the Canadian Steam Navigation Co., following the receipt of a contract from the Canadian government. But due to opposition from the Board of Trade, it was unable to incorporate through a royal charter the London, Liverpool and North American Screw Steam Ship Co. In 1853 M'Kean & M'larty had also acted as Liverpool agents for the Anglo-Brazilian S.N. Co. See Bonsor, *Seaway*, 77; *Gore's Directory*, 1853.

of steam sailings to Spanish Mediterranean ports by two new entrants, G.H. Fletcher and Co. and Bahr, Behrend.[77]

By the mid-1850s the LMSSSC appears to have become even more complex in terms of the provision of services by the various constituent shipowning concerns. The "company" provided a service to western Italian ports, but the shipowners who formed the consortium also offered other services, both jointly and independently. Bibby and Moss ran a service to Sicily and the Adriatic in what appears to have been collaboration with Burns and MacIver. Independently, Moss offered a service to the Levant and Egypt, as did Vianna, Chapple, albeit with different intermediate ports of call: Gibraltar for the former and Malta for the latter. Furthermore, by 1856/57 the constituents of the LMSSSC offered a range of steam services to Portuguese ports involving some of their other associates, with the *Cintra* being run by G. Louthean and Cross and the *Douro* by Cotesworth, Wynne and Lynne.

During the late 1850s the LMSSSC was dissolved, with Bibby being the principal legatee. The reasons for this are by no means clear, but the 1857 crisis and the experience of some other providers of shipping from Liverpool may be suggestive. This points to liquidity problems for some firms. For instance, Burns faced cash difficulties by 1856 which became acute with the onset of the 1857 crisis. This resulted in Burns pushing for a termination of its shipping interests with MacIver and Cunard from September 1856, ultimately leading to George and James Burns retiring from the British and Foreign on 30 September 1857 and George Burns leaving the British and North American Royal Mail Steam Packet Co. on 24 August 1859.[78] More generally, the 1857 crisis had a particularly severe impact upon the Liverpool mercantile community. This may have been responsible for Dixon transferring the interests of the LSSC to Bibby, although this

---

[77]This firm was founded in the late eighteenth century by a Dane and as with so many shipowning concerns had a pre-history in shipbroking. See Chandler, *Liverpool Shipping*, 82.

[78]Hyde, *Cunard*, 18-19.

transaction only led to the acquisition of one of the LSSC's steamers--the *Crimean*--in 1857.

Almost from its inception, and probably arising from the nature of its constitution, the affairs of the LMSSSC had been marked by transfers of steamers among the various shipowning entities behind the "company." In 1857--a timing which may be significant--Bibby outwardly took over the *Frankfort* and *Maeander* (and probably also the *Milan* and *Braganza*) from F. Chapple.[79] These may not have been outright sales as Chapple continued to have an ownership interest, possibly an eighth, in some Bibby steamers during the mid-1860s, sufficient for him to use as collateral for raising a loan in London. The ending of the arrangements behind the LMSSSC became overtly clear in 1858, when Bibby entered into a collaborative agreement with the P&O for the provision of steam services to Alexandria. This was due to the completion of the railway across the Suez isthmus, which dispensed with the camel caravans of the "overland" section of the steam route to India, thus increasing the cargo capacity of this transhipment section.

The alliance with the P&O was possibly responsible for Bibby taking over the *Cairo* from Chapple in 1859, while further tonnage was acquired during the same year from Papayanni--the *Boeotia* and the *Ionia*.[80] The Bibby fleet was also augmented by new tonnage built by Harland and Wolff, which supplied a ship a year from 1859 until 1864. Bibby's orders to Harland and Wolff may have played a decisive role in the calculations of Edward Harland that had led him to acquire the yard at Queen's Island from Robert Hickson during the autumn of 1858. The first contract was for three cargo vessels, each of about 1,500

---

[79]This perspective arises from the fleet list, with commentary, drawn up by Paget-Tomlinson, *Bibby Line*. The summary registry details still show on 1 January 1859 F. Chapple, with others, as the owners of the *Frankfort*, *Milan* and *Braganza*, while the *Maeander* was under the name of W.M. Moss. Such confusion probably arises from the inter-ownership of these vessels under the LMSSSC, and Chapple certainly retained minority interests in them until the mid-1860s.

[80]Once more there are differences between the summary registration data and the fleet list in Paget-Tomlinson, *Bibby Line*, particularly with the *Boeotia*.

gross tons--the *Venetian*, *Sicilian* and *Syrian*--not yet quite "full" steamers, as they were equipped with "lifting screws." This order was completed by April 1860 and the commercial success of these steamers, together with the personal and financial link between the Liverpool shipping firm and the Belfast shipbuilding enterprise provided by Schwabe, resulted in Bibby ordering in 1860 a further six vessels, each of about 2,000 gross tons (*Grecian*, *Italian*, *Egyptian*, *Dalmatian*, *Arabian* and the *Persian*).

With this second order, Harland applied ideas that he had been developing since the early 1850s, namely to increase the length of the vessel without adjusting the beam in order to augment carrying capacity. Stiffness was maintained through the vessel being constructed as a box girder, formed by the installation of an iron upper deck. These "Bibby coffins," as they became known, also had innovative rigging--pole masts, fore-and-aft--and steam winches and braces to undertake heavy lifting. Economy in operation was also increased by the use of an improved version, involving rubber rings for packing, of Hall's surface condenser. This allowed sea water to condense exhausted steam, thereby permitting the recycling of "contained" fresh water within the vessel's engine and eliminating salt corrosion. Aspects of these ideas were also applied to some of the older vessels within Bibby's fleet, with the *Tiber* and *Calpe* each being lengthened in 1861 by ninety feet to increase carrying capacity while also saving on the costs of new construction. Moreover, such innovations were incorporated in the building in 1862 of new, smaller, steamers for the Iberian trade--the *Castilian* and the *Catalonian*, each of 607 gross tons.[81]

Just as it is difficult to establish a rank order for British ports in the Mediterranean trades in the mid-1830s, so there are comparable problems regarding the establishment of a similar perspective at the end of the 1850s. A careful use of the voyages noted in *Lloyd's* can, however, provide an indication. These data point to at least 870 vessels departing for the Mediterranean from British ports and the Channel Islands in 1859/60, of which eighty-six (9.8%) cleared Liverpool and

---

[81]Moss and Hume, *Shipbuilders*, 18-20, 507.

forty-nine (5.6%) London.[82] Although this may show that Liverpool had become the national centre for the Anglo-Mediterranean *general* export trades by the late 1850s, in terms of the frequency of itemisation of voyages in *Lloyd's*, the focus of British shipping movements to the Mediterranean was the northeast coal ports of Shields with 217 listings (24.9%). In marked contrast to the mid-1830s, the outstanding feature arising from an examination of *Lloyd's* is the incidence of voyages not only from Shields but also from a whole range of northeast and south Wales coal ports--in all totalling 528 (60.7%).

Because of the nature of availble contemporary published statistics, it is difficult to establish clearly the quantity of coal exported to the Mediterranean by the close of the 1850s. One estimate would be of the order of 1.25m tons, equivalent to 17.6% of total British coal exports.[83] In 1860 nearly two-thirds of British coal exports was despatched from some five ports--Newcastle (Shields), Hartlepool, Cardiff, Newport and Swansea--of which by far the most important were Newcastle and Cardiff. Those that went to the Mediterranean and the black Sea not only provided bunkering services for steamers plying there, but also supplied railways, gas works and rising domestic and industrial consumption. In the case of south Wales, its rise to dominance as the centre for the British coal export trade was almost totally related to meeting the demand for marine steam. This followed from the Admiralty trials of the 1840s which had proved the superiority of south Wales steam coal for this purpose. The geographical position of the field meant that the majority of south Wales coal exports went

---

[82] *Lloyd's Register of British and Foreign Shipping. From 1st July, 1860 to the 30th June 1861* (London, 1861).

[83] Based on *B.P.P.*, 1861 [2894], CX.1, *Annual Statement of Trade and Navigation, 1860*. The problem arises from exports to both France and Atlantic coast and the Mediterranean. French "Mediterranean" imports of British coal have been taken to be a third of total French imports, namely 15,991 tons out of 47,974 tons. Similarly Spanish (and the Canaries) "Mediterranean imports" have been taken to be half of total imports from Britain, namely 187,368 tons out of 374,736 tons. Otherwise the estimate is the aggregate of British exports to Russia (southern ports), Sardinia, Two Sicilies, Austria, Greece, Turkey, Egypt, Algeria, Gibraltar, Malta and the Ionian Islands.

to France and the Mediterranean--these markets taking sixty-nine percent of such exports *in 1880.*[84]

The *Lloyd's* data also provide an overview of the nature of shipping clearing Liverpool for the Mediterranean, but given the incomplete coverage of the source, it cannot help us to be more precise. Omissions are particularly marked in the case of steamers. For sail, this source captures seventy-five vessels, of which the most typical were brigs of 151-200 tons (nine), schooners of 101-150 tons (nine) and brigantines of 101-150 tons (nine). Although this was little different from the mid-1830s, there was clearly a move to somewhat larger vessels, pointed up by the use of barques, of which seven were of 301-350 tons and three greater than 350 tons. One much greater change was the utilisation of Canadian-built vessels--twenty-four in all. In terms of fleets, the only one clearly revealed is the "Z line," the specialist fruit vessels of Glynn and Sons of Liverpool, which included the brigs *Zegri* (111 tons) and *Ziska* (260 tons) and the schooner *Zigzag* (119 tons).[85]

Using *Lloyd's* in this way only leads to the identification of eleven steam vessels clearing Liverpool for the Mediterranean, four of which were owned by Bibby. Perhaps one indication of the scantiness of *Lloyd's* coverage is that six of these vessels were steam assisted, being noted as "AP," while a further two were relatively small, each of 116 tons and with sixty horsepower, both owned by the Spanish government. Some greater flesh on the bare outlines provided by the *Lloyd's* data can be gleaned from work undertaken on the Customs Bills of Entry by David Williams, originally for the specific purpose of analyzing British imports of citrus fruits.[86] In 1860 this shows that nineteen steamers were involved in bringing fruit to the Mersey from the Azores, Iberia and the Mediterranean; of these, thirteen were

[84]M.J. Daunton, *Coal Metropolis: Cardiff 1870-1914* (Leicester, 1977), 7-9.

[85]See Chandler, *Liverpool Shipping*, 89-91.

[86]I am very grateful to David Williams for his tabulated transcriptions of the Liverpool Bills of Entry for 1860. For the background to this material, see D.M. Williams, "Citrus Trade to Britain."

Bibby steamers, the majority of its fleet of twenty-two vessels. One, the *Calpe*, although outwardly a "Bibby steamer," was being operated under the agency of Cotesworth, one of Bibby's former associates in the LMSSSC. The data indicate an operational division within the Bibby fleet in 1860, with four steamers, mainly the oldest, being allotted to the Luso-Iberian trade, running to Oporto, Lisbon and occasionally St. Ures. Five other steamers provided the service to western Italian ports and Sicily, while two others served Adriatic ports. By inference it would seem that the rest of the "Bibby fleet" constituted the service to the eastern Mediterranean, the Levant and Egypt. The cargoes carried from the western Mediterranean by Bibby steamers were, as in the mid-1830s, mixed, with consignments of citrus fruit lying in the holds alongside brimstone, copper, dried fruit, nuts, paper, shumac and wheat.

The expansion of Britain's dealings with the eastern Mediterranean received a further stimulus during the first half of the 1860s through the economic consequences of the American Civil War. The search for alternative supplies of raw cotton focused British trade and investment upon the Middle East--especially Egypt--and India. The "cotton famine" had a clear impact upon British trade from 1862, with the most dynamic export markets being Turkey and the Middle East, to which British exports by value increased by 105.3% between 1862 and 1866, albeit from an initially low base. Similarly, imports from Turkey and the Middle East expanded in value terms to a greater extent than the overall increase of British imports between 1860 and 1866--52.9% as opposed to 40.2%.

The general trade boom between 1862 and 1866 went hand in hand with a growth in British steam tonnage. Investment in steam around mid-century was affected by the inception of an inventory cycle. The expansion in the general use of steam during the first half of the 1850s led to something of a glut of such tonnage by the middle years of that decade. Generally, however, that glut had disappeared by 1859. Thereafter, until 1865 the annual number of steamships constructed in British yards increased by 154.6%, while the annual volume of steam tonnage launched rose by 372.6%.

The pattern of Bibby's further acquisition of steam tonnage between 1859 and 1864 coincided with the general expansion of the

British steam fleet. Bibby placed regular orders for new steamers from 1859 with Harland and Wolff. This process continued with the commissioning of the *Douro*, a 528-ton cargo ship which was delivered by the builders on 21 November 1864. Its size (as well as its name) indicates that it was destined for the Luso-Iberian service. Here Bibby was no doubt aided by its associates on the Alexandria route--the P&O--relinquishing its Iberian service in 1862.[87] In part the *Douro* replaced the vessel of the same name acquired by Bibby in 1853, which was sold in 1862 for blockade-running, as was also the *Minho* of 1854. Such sales no doubt assisted in financing the continued expansion of the Bibby fleet and were indicative of some of the economic effects of the American Civil War and the "cotton famine." The *Euphrates* of 1854 and the *Boeotia*, acquired from Papayanni, were also sold during the mid-1860s, but not for such speculative purposes, while the *Corinthian* of 1855 was lost in 1864, as had been the *Catalonian* in 1863, one of the first two Luso-Iberian steamers to have been built by Harland and Wolff.[88]

The other constituents of the LMSSSC continued to provide Mediterranean steam services after the dissolution of the consortium between 1857 and 1859. It appears that James Moss & Co. during the early 1860s worked their steamers in conjunction with their former associates of the early 1850s--Lamport & Holt--and with Papayanni.[89] Like Bibby, Miles Moss expanded his fleet during the mid-1860s, acquiring eleven iron screw steamers between 1860 and 1865, also turning to Harland & Wolff for some of this new tonnage, taking delivery in February 1865 from Belfast of the *Sesostris*, a cargo ship of 2053 gross tons.[90] It seems that Miles Moss was once again the

[87]Farnie, *East and West of Suez*, 63.

[88]Paget-Tomlinson, *Bibby Line*, 64-68.

[89]Chandler, *Shipping*, 149.

[90]*Atlantic* (1860 {built 1857}, 1309 gross tons); *Memnon* (1861, 1209 gross tons); *Isis* (1862, 1725 gross tons); *Lotus* (1863, 589 gross tons); *Cecile* (1863, 563 gross tons); *rosetta* (1864, 972 gross tons); *Luxor* (1864 {built 1853}, 1420 gross tons); *Gunga* (1865,

mainspring of this new grouped enterprise during the mid-1860s, as Papayanni acquired no new vessels before 1867, persisting with four steamers of the 1850s, including the original *Orontes*,[91] and Lamport & Holt had only one vessel--the *Talisman*, 738 gross tons, 80 hp, of 1860, first registered at Liverpool in 1864, and which from its description in the summary registration details would appear to have been a steam auxiliary.

The dissolution of the LMSSSC seems not to have checked Chapple's career as a shipowner, for in 1858 he registered the newly-built *Forwood* (587 gross tons) at Liverpool. By the mid-1860s, in association with Dutton, Chapple was a shipowner in both London and Liverpool and decided to use the favourable, although speculative, financial environment provided by the "cotton famine" to establish a limited company for his shipping interests--the Anglo-Egyptian Steam Navigation Co. (AESNC). It appears that he embarked upon this venture in May 1864, at the height of the bull market in raw cotton. He was unable to persuade the Imperial Ottoman Bank to become fully involved with his company; the most that this institution was prepared to do was to acquire a minority interest of five hundred shares, but only if it became its banker and representative in the Levant and at Marseilles. This lack of support led Chapple to put his plans for incorporation on hold. With the fall in raw cotton prices after the autumn of 1864, as it became clear that the Civil War would end in an Union victory, Chapple now approached a London finance company--the International Financial Society (IFS)--for a loan. The sum involved was £75,000 for one year, secured by Chapple's continuing one-eighth interest in the Bibby fleet of twenty-two steamers. The transaction was completed on the basis of discounting finance bills.

The successful loan arrangement resulted in the IFS acting as an issuing house for the AESNC. However, with the fall in cotton prices and then the decline in activity on the London capital market

1201 gross tons); *Thebes* (1865, 2068 gross tons); *Krishna* (1865, 1355 gross tons); *Sesostris* (1865, 1966 gross tons).

[91]The others were *Arcadia* (1855, 1089 gross tons); *Laconia* (1856, 1151 gross tons) and *Agia Sofia* (1857, 1437 gross tons).

during 1865, all that the IFS' directors were prepared to do was "simply...their best to ensure it" rather than to "guarantee the successful formation of the Company." The company was to be established on the basis that Chapple's own steamers were worth at least £180,000 and that the vendors, with their fellow directors, would maintain their shareholding of 10,000 for at least a year. Initially Chapple balked at these terms and approached the Egyptian Commercial and Trading Co. (ECTC), possibly not realising that this company was connected with the IFS. The outcome of the tangle of negotiations was the joint promotion by the IFS and the ECTC of Chapple's shipping company in March 1865. Its main assets were seven vessels including the *Rhone* of the Bibby fleet, one hulk and two lighters, which were to be acquired by the company from Chapple and his partners for £275,000, paid in cash and shares. The success of the promotion, which had initially boded well, was ultimately dashed by a legal action brought by Moss, Chapple's former Liverpool associate of the 1850s. This led first to the IFS deciding that Chapple and Dutton were unfit to serve as directors, managing agents, or ships' husbands. Moreover, Chapple and Dutton were disbarred from receiving payment in shares arising from the goodwill of their partnership, but rather were now required to provide sufficient funds to meet the ten percent dividend payment stated in the prospectus. Lastly, the ultimate failure of the public issue resulted in the IFS, the ECTC, and their stockbrokers--Cazenove--holding a substantial number of AESNC's shares.[92]

The 1866 crisis led to the Chapple loan and the shares of the AESNC becoming illiquid assets of the IFS. The status of these assets was also affected by continuing litigation brought by Moss. By June 1866 the IFS was the largest shareholder in the AESNC, owning 46.9% of it shares, while simultaneously maintaining the company with short-term finance. During the latter part of the 1860s the IFS bought further shares from its own financial associates, Dutton's heirs, and on the open market. This resulted in the IFS holding eighty-seven percent of the company by July 1873. Between 1869 and 1873 the AESNC,

---

[92]P.L Cottrell, *Investment Banking in England 1856-1881. A Case Study of the International Financial Society* (New York and London, 1985), I, 195-199.

operating from the offices of the IFS, made profits of £6,000 per annum, after allowances for depreciation on total assets of £85,000. But with the cyclical downturn of the mid-1870s, the company once more required short-term financing and the IFS decided to liquidate it.

In 1868 the IFS also acquired the equity of redemption on Chapple's pledged interest in the Bibby line. This allowed the IFS to sell Chapple's former one-eighth share in the *Meander*.[93] Further disposals by the IFS of Chapple's other former interests in Bibby steamers took place in the early 1870s, when they were ultimately acquired by Frederick Leyland.[94]

Just as the 1857 crisis appears not to have unduly affected Bibby, the 1866 financial turmoil also seems to have left the company unscathed. In 1867, possibly benefiting from cyclically depressed construction costs, it took delivery of a further three ships from Harland and Wolff--the *Istrian*, *Iberian* and *Illyrian*, each of 2,877 gross tons. Unlike some Bibby vessels built in the early 1860s, these were rigged to benefit from sail assistance, thus obtaining the maximum reduction in operating costs and the largest carrying capacity. Consequently they had mixed square and fore-and-aft rigs, while the *Istrian* also had a "lifting screw." At about three thousand tons, and as "long" ships at four hundred feet, their construction had necessitated an investment by Harland and Wolff of £1,500 in lengthening and strengthening ways and other equipment, but the Bibby contract returned Harland and Wolff to profitability in the mid-1860s.[95]

This expansion of the Bibby fleet continued throughout the cyclical slump in the British economy during the late 1860s. In 1868 the tug *Camel*, built at Dumbarton, was acquired and in early 1869, Schwabe placed an order with Harland and Wolff for a further three four hundred-foot vessels, beginning with the *Bavarian*. As in 1866/67,

---

[93]This may have been an initial step to allow Bibby to dispose of the *Meander* in 1868. See Paget-Tomlinson, *Bibby Line*, 66.

[94]Cottrell, *Investment Banking*, 440-443.

[95]Paget-Tomlinson, *Bibby Line*, 12; Moss and Hume, *Shipbuilders*, 26-27.

this Bibby order greatly assisted the Belfast concern financially.[96] Yet while it was being completed, the ownership of the Bibby Line began to be considerably reorganised. This arose from both external and internal factors. The opening of the Suez Canal in 1869[97] brought an end to the 1858 collaborative agreement with the P&O and, although this could have been foreseen, it seems to have resulted in Bibby having surplus tonnage. Overcapacity went hand-in-hand with problems of managerial continuity. The sole family managing partner since 1864 had been James J. Bibby. He was now fifty-seven, but his son Frank was only thirteen and his other young immediate relatives had already embarked upon mercantile careers. During the ensuing three years a discussion took place within the firm over future strategy; one immediate result was that Schwabe was informed that there were no further investment opportunities for him in any new Bibby tonnage.

This did not put an end to Schwabe's career as a Liverpool shipowner. Just as the Moss dinner party may have led to the inception of a Liverpool steam line in the early 1850s, so an after-dinner game of billiards may have been the environment in which Schwabe established with Thomas Ismay the basis for the Oceanic Steam Navigation Co., legally founded on 6 September 1869. Schwabe had already discussed this project with Harland and Wolff, and Edward Harland subsequently made a small investment in the company. More important, the Belfast shipbuilders agreed to supply tonnage at cost plus a four percent commission, beginning with an order for five 420-foot, four thousand gross ton steamers at a price of over £110,000 each.[98]

Schwabe's departure left Frederick Leyland as the only other active partner in Bibby besides James J. Bibby. He argued, like

---

[96]Moss and Hume, *Shipbuilders*, 28.

[97]For a wide-ranging general discussion on the immediate impact of the opening of the canal, see Farnie, *East and West of Suez*, 81ff.

[98]Moss and Hume, *Shipbuilders*, 28-29; see also W.J. Oldham, *The Ismay Line* (Liverpool, 1961), 29. The "billiard" story comes from Forwood, *Reminiscences*, 40, the same source as for the Moss dinner party.

Schwabe, that Bibby should now enter the north Atlantic trades, but apparently James J. was initially reluctant, given the competitive nature of the route. It may be that Leyland attempted a buyout as early as November 1869; certainly the IFS was approached at that time by someone interested in acquiring Chapple's former shares in the Bibby steamers still held by his financial institution. The IFS agreed to sell at £55,000 a share, while leaving £20,000 as a loan for a year at eight percent secured by the vessels. This transaction fell through and between 1870 and 1872 the IFS contributed £10,000, its proportionate share, to the re-fitting of some of the Bibby steamers. While the IFS was forced to retain the Chapple loan on its books for a further period, it was being serviced by gross profits of £8,000 per annum on the Bibby shares, which covered interest charges debited at £6,000 per annum and left a balance sufficient to meet the refit costs.[99]

Frederick Leyland finally succeeded with his plan in January 1873, taking majority control of the Bibby fleet, with James L. Bibby retaining only a minority shareholding. Leyland acquired Chapple's former interest in the *Cairo* from the IFS in 1874, when he promptly sold the vessel. Subsequently Leyland took over the rest of the former Chapple interest in the steamers from the IFS.[100] Leyland continued to run the Bibby steamers in the Mediterranean, but also from March 1876 began to put them onto the Atlantic. The route chosen was to Boston, where the competition was weakest. Cunard served this American port, but not in a concerted fashion, while the only other competitor was the Warren Line of Geo. Warren and Co., which employed chartered tonnage for its service. Leyland decided to use the four hundred-foot steamers built in 1867--the *Istrian*, *Iberian* and *Illyrian*--which he equipped in 1877 with compound engines. This service was increased in frequency from fortnightly to weekly, taking

---

[99]Cottrell, *Investment Banking*, II, 440-441.

[100]*Ibid.*, II, 440.

cargo and bringing back live cattle to purpose-built docks at Birkenhead.[101]

Of the Bibby vessels that Leyland acquired, in 1874 he sold the *Danube* and the *Cairo*. Any carrying capacity lost through these sales of aged tonnage was quickly made good, as Leyland contracted for five new steamers with Liverpool builders for delivery in 1874.[102] These were followed during the mid-1870s by a further four orders to Liverpool shipbuilders.[103] Over the same period two former Bibby steamers were lost--the *Rhone* and the *Grecian*.

The Bibby Line until 1873, and the Leyland thereafter until 1880, were run like many other Liverpool shipowning enterprises as private partnerships, with their shares being shares in ships rather than shares in an enterprise.[104] But from 1878, Liverpool shipowners of both sail and steam began to organise their vessels as "single ship companies," with each ship being registered under the name of a separate limited company. Liverpool shipowners were not alone in pursuing this corporate path, but in the late 1870s and early 1880s they were in the vanguard compared with their peers in other ports. Consequently, 126 of the 171 shipping companies registered with the Registrar of Joint Stock Companies between 1878 and 1881 were Merseyside concerns, largely of the "single ship" variety. The main reason for this sudden change in corporate organisation appears to have been to acquire further safeguards against the financial consequences of collision at sea. In such circumstances with a "single ship" company, all that a third party could litigate against was the ship involved and the "single ship"

---

[101]Bonsor, *Seaway*, 332-333.

[102]*Cyrenian* (1433 gross tons, built by Bowdler); *Cyprian* (1432, Bowdler); *Lesbian* (1562, Royden); *Ligurian* (1561, Royden); and *Lisbon* (664, Royden).

[103]1875: *Athenian* (1619 gross tons, built by Royden); 1876: *Algerian* (1757, Bowdler); 1876: *Alsatian* (1765, Leyland); and *Andalusian* (1763, Leyland).

[104]See Cottrell, "Steamship on the Mersey;" on ship shares more generally, see R. Davis, *The Rise of the English Shipping Industry* (London, 1962) and R. Jarvis, "Fractional Shareholding in British Merchant Ships with Special Reference to the 64ths," *Mariner's Mirror*, XLV (1959), 308-11.

company which owned it, not the rest of any fleet, and there would be little in the kitty if the "single" ship had been heavily depreciated.

Frederick Leyland began to convert his fleet into "single ship" companies from 20 May 1880 and the registration papers provide further evidence regarding the ownership of the former Bibby vessels, as well as the new tonnage Leyland bought after 1873. Shares in Leyland's single ship companies did not have convenient financial fractions, but at first glance had unwieldy denominations, like £56, £91, £258, and £313. Actually these were sixty-fourths--ship shares--and so shareholdings in Leyland's "single ship" companies mirrored the original distribution of ship shares after the demise of Chapple's interest. Generally, this evidence confirms that F.R. Leyland was the principal shareholder in the vessels. What is of some interest are the minor holdings. In all the vessels owned by Leyland in 1880, including those built after 1874 and on the stocks in the early 1880s, members of the Bibby family--James Jenkinson Bibby (1813-1897), now residing at Shrewsbury, John Bibby (II) Sr. (1810-1883) who described himself as a J.P., and John Bibby (III) Jr., a Liverpool copper merchant--held shares. Furthermore, the Bibby's former associates also continued in the early 1880s to retain minor interests in the case of vessels built or acquired before 1869.

Broadly there were three patterns of minority interests, which for convenience can be named after three vessels--the *Egyptian* of 1861, the *Arabian* of 1862 and the *Cyprian* of 1874. In the Egyptian pattern of share distribution, Schwabe held one thirty-second, with James Dugdale owning one-sixteenth and John Dugdale one thirty-second.[105] In the case of the *Arabian*,[106] Schwabe held three thirty-seconds and James and John Dugdale, one-sixteenth and one thirty-second, respectively. In the *Cyprian* pattern, the most common in terms

[105]PRO, BT31/2653/14107. Common also to the *Castilian* of 1862 (BT31/2652/14104), the *Bavarian* (BT31/1652/1401), the *Iberian* (BT31/1653/14108), the *Illyrian* (BT31/2653/14109), all of 1869, and the *Bohemian* (BT31/2652/14102) and the *Bulgarian* (BT31/2652/14103) of 1870.

[106]PRO, BT31/2652/14099. Common also to the *Persian* of 1863 (BT31/2654/14114), and the *Istyrian* of 1869 (BT31/2653/14110).

of number of vessels involved,[107] there was no Schwabe or Dugdale minority interest, which confirms the point that Schwabe in 1869 was told that there were no further opportunities for him to invest in new "Bibby" ships.

Although regular steam services from Liverpool to the Mediterranean developed rapidly from the early 1850s, after a "trial" period from the mid-1840s, some steam vessels, like many of those owned by Bibby, relied upon sail to a some degree; even in the case of newly-commissioned tonnage, this persisted on into the mid-1860s. Technological change, even in the apparently favourable environment of the Mediterranean, was a gradual process and many early Liverpool screw iron steamers were of an intermediate type. Some of the initial fleet were regarded by Lloyds's surveyors as steam-assisted, being noted as "AP," while subsequent vessels were equipped with "lifting screws." Although there were the fortuitous exogenous shocks of the Crimean War in the mid-1850s, with its trooping requirements, and the economic consequences of the "cotton famine" in the mid-1860s, there was not a rapid once-and-for-all technological transformation of Merseyside steam shipping to the Mediterranean. As on oceanic cargo routes, sail retained its advantages, even if only as an additional means of propulsion in the case of mid-century Mediterranean steamers. Further, sailing packets could be run on a regular base and continued to be, even after the arrival of the steamer, as with the fleets of Bibby and its associates to the western Italian coast. Bibby only took delivery of its last sailing vessel--the *Melbourne*, a Canadian-built (1856) ship of 1,212 gross tons--in 1858, although she ended her days in the 1870s as a coal hulk at Gibraltar. However for some particular Mediterranean cargoes, such as fruit, steam had an advantage.[108] Other cargoes--of

---

[107]PRO, BT31/2653/14105. Common also to the *Cyrenian* (BT31/1653/14106), the *Lesbian* (BT31/2653/14111), the *Ligurian* (BT31/2653/14112), and the *Lisbon* (BT31/2653/14413), of 1874, the *Athenian* of 1875 (BT31/1652/14100), the *Algerian* of 1876 (BT31/2651/14096), the *Alsatian* (BT31/1652/14097) and the *Andulisian* (BT31/2652/14298) of 1876. The *Douro*, acquired by Bibby in 1863, also shared this pattern of distribution of ownership (BT31/2673/14265).

[108]Williams, "Citrus Trade to Britain."

the "Suez" transhipment variety, such as bullion to the east and oriental silks to Europe--could afford the premium of mid-century steam freight rates.[109] Such a gradual transition can be explained further by the factors relating to the cost of coal. Liverpool's adoption of steam for Mediterranean services had largely taken place before the perfection of compound engines, which came in the 1860s, whereas steamers in the Mediterranean were dependent upon supplies of exported British coal.

If the technological transformation was evolutionary rather than revolutionary, so also was Liverpool's corporate response. The port's initial Mediterranean lines were run as pooling operations, with investment undertaken through traditional ship shares. This arrangement appears to have had a platform through the prior concerted sailing packet services such as to the western Italian coast, but with steamer pooling it may have been taken a stage further through the inter-ownership of vessels involved, as with the LMSSSC. Such tightly drawn organisational devices, however, seem only to have been used in the 1850s. Thereafter, collaboration continued, as between Bibby and the P&O from 1858 to 1869, and Moss and Papayanni during at least the 1860s, but it now applied to the provision of services rather than to the underlying capital investment. In the case of Bibby, when Leyland finally adopted limited liability in the early 1880s, it was not to expand the potential for financial investment but to contain the financial consequences of misadventure.

In all this, Bibby appears to have been a classic example of a shipowning interest during the first half of the nineteenth century. It grew out of merchanting and shipbroking, while its undoubted success in sail, measured by the size of its fleet in the 1830s and 1840s, provided the resources to adopt steam, but in graduated stages from the 1850s. Ultimately the family's other business interests meant that there was a problem of succession from the late 1860s. One minor and active extra-family partner--Schwabe--was turned away, to establish rapidly another major line, Oceanic. It then took three years of debate

---

[109]P.L. Cottrell, "London, Paris and Silver, 1848-1867," in A. Slaven and D.H. Alderoft (eds.), *Business, Banking and Urban History* (Edinburgh, 1982), 130.

before the next stage of the enterprise took shape under Leyland. Such problems of transition may have been eased, if Bibby, like some of its London counterparts, had adopted the corporate form earlier, either by royal charter before 1855 or subsequently by the registration of a limited company. Yet they were not alone in facing problems from the late 1860s--they also confronted Cunard, another shipping partnership in the late 1870s, and, the royal chartered P&O. As well as generalities, there were also the importance of personal links. In the case of Bibby, its particular link, through Schwabe, was to Harland and Wolff. This appears to have been of benefit to both parties: Bibby obtained Edward Harland's expertise and new ideas, while Harland and Wolff received major orders at fortuitous times during its initial development as a shipbuilding enterprise.

Appendix I
Liverpool and Mediterranean S.S.S. Co.:
The Initial Fleet, 1855

Owner	Date of Registration or Year of Build	Vessel and Type	Gross tonnage
J.J. Bibby	28 Aug. 1850	*Rattler*, iron, screw	276
	6 Jan. 1851	*Arno*, iron, screw,	669
	10 Sept. 1853	*Douro*, iron, screw* (Schooner, 50 hp)	278
	13 Oct. 1853	*Danube*, iron, screw* (Barque, 160 hp)	829
	29 Nov. 1853	*Rhone*, iron, screw* (Barque, 160 hp)	836
	1855b	*Albanian*, iron, screw	1,035
(with others)	10 Apr. 1854	*Minho*, iron, screw	400
	1854b	*Euphrates*, iron, screw	1,153
	1855b	*Corinthian*, iron, screw	1,170
Bibby and Co.	1852b	*Calpe*, iron, screw	799
	6 Dec. 1854	*Cintra*, iron, screw	516
G.C. Schwabe	1 Dec. 1851	*Tiber*, iron, screw	980
G. Louthean and Cross	1 Jan. 1853	*Calpe*, iron, screw	799
F. Chapple and others	5 Aug. 1851	*Frankfort*, iron, screw	658
	10 Nov. 1852	*Osmanli*, iron, screw	563
	16 Apr. 1853	*Rattler*, iron, screw	427
	22 Oct. 1853	*Orontes*, iron, screw	748
F. Chapple and Co.	1855b	*Milan*, iron, screw	1,053
W.M. Moss	13 Nov. 1850	*Nile*, iron, screw	525
	16 Jun. 1851	*Orontes*, iron, screw	748
	9 May 1854	*Tamaulipas*, iron, screw	485
(with others)	1855b	*Maeander*, iron, screw	974
W.M. Moss and Co.	1855b	*Araxes*, iron, screw	1,156

Notes: b denotes year built; * indicates that the vessel was regarded by *Lloyds* as an iron sailing ship, with steam providing auxiliary power.

Source: *B.P.P.* "Return[s]...of the whole of the registered steam vessels of the United Kingdom..." [annual] 1 January 1852:- 1852, XLIX; 1 January to 1 January 1854:- 1854, LX; 1 January 1855:- 1854-55, XLVI.

Appendix II
Liverpool Steam Services to the Mediterranean, c. 1857

"Company," agents/ constituents; service interval; vessels employed	*Intermediate ports of call*	*Principal ports served*
Levant Screw Steamship Co. (Henry Dixon and Co., merchants and steamship agts.) twice a month Screw steamers: *African*, *Spartan*, *Arabian*, *Persian*	Gibraltar, Malta	Alexandretta, Constantinople, Beirut, and Alexandria
(Fowler & Dagnall, comm. merchants, agts.) Steamships: *Grecian*, *Athenian*, *Circassian*, *Egyptian*, *Armenian*, *Crimean*	Malta, Syra	Salonica, Constantinople and Smyrna
Liverpool & Mediterranean SSS Co. John Bibby, Sons & Co. Vianna, Chapple & Co. James Moss & Co. Geo. Louthean & Co. Screw Steamers: yTiber, *Milan*, *Frankfort*, *Calpe*, *ARNO*	Gibraltar	Genoa, Leghorn, Messina, Civiti Vecchia Naples, Palermo
John Bibby, Sons & Co. James Moss & Co. Screw Steamers: *Danube*, *Euphrates*, *Albanian*, *Corinthian* [see also: **British & Foreign S.N. Co**/ Burns & MacIver]	Corfu Gibraltar	Palermo, Messina Ancona and Trieste

"Company," agents/ constituents; service interval; vessels employed	*Intermediate ports of call*	*Principal ports served*
James Moss & Co. Screw Steamships	Gibraltar	Palermo, Messina, Alexandria, Beirout and Alexandretta
Vianna, Chapple & Co.	Malta	Alexandria, Beirout and Alexandretta
John Bibby, Sons & Co. Vianna, Jones and Chapple James Moss & Co. every 11 days sailing packets		Genoa, Leghorn and Naples
[British & Foreign S.N. Co.] Burns & MacIver every ten days Screw Steamers: *Balbec*, *Euphrates*, *Albanian*	(Havre) Messina and Malta	Corfu, Ancona and Trieste
Burns & MacIver Screw Steam ships: *Karnak*, *Teneriffe*, *Melita*, *Taurus*, *British Queen*, *Alps*, *Lebanon*, *Delta*, *Armininian*, *Balbec*	(Havre) Gibraltar Malta	Syra, Constantinople and Smyrna
Papayanni & Mussabini Screw Steam-ships: *Boeotia*, *Laconia*, *Orontes*, *Ionia*, *Macedonia*, *Thessalia*, *Arcadia*	Malta and Syra	Constantinople and Smyrna
Lamont, M'Larty & Co. every 11 days steam-ships	Gibraltar	Marseilles, Genoa, Leghorn and Naples

"Company," agents/ constituents; service interval; vessels employed	*Intermediate ports of call*	*Principal ports served*
G.H. Fletcher & Co. Screw steamers: *America*, *Europe*		Barcelona, calling at Corunna, Malaga and Valencia
Bahr, Behrend & Co. Screw Steamers: *Ebro*, *Tajo*, *Duero*		Cadiz, Malaga, Valencia and Barcelona
	Luso-Iberian Services	
Cotesworth, Wynne & Lyne John Bibby, Sons & Co. Geo. Louthean & Cross Packets, screw steamers every 11 days		Lisbon, Oporto and Portugal
G. Louthean & Cross Screw Steam-ships: *Cintra* & c.		Lisbon
Cotesworth, Wynne & Lyne Steam-ship: *Douro*		Lisbon
Vianna, Chapple & Co. every 11 days screw steamers		Lisbon, Oporto

Source: Gore's Directory 1857.

Bigots or Patriots?
The Political and Religious Allegiances of the Liverpool Ships' Carpenters, 1815-1851

Frank Neal

By 1851 Liverpool was one of world's greatest seaports. With a population of 375,000 it was the second largest town in Britain outside of London. In addition to its prominence as a seaport, it was also the place of residence of over eighty-three thousand Irish-born persons, the majority Catholic, poor and unskilled. In that year, large-scale disturbances took place between Irish Catholics and Orangemen, as a result of which three people died. The town had already achieved a national notoriety as the scene of bitter disputes between Irish and English, and in the first half of the century the group of indigenous workers most prominent in the street warfare was the ships' carpenters. This paper sets out to describe that conflict and to offer some possible explanations of the phenomenon of these Tory working men.[1]

By the end of the eighteenth century Britain was ruled by some two hundred aristocratic families, members of which dominated both the House of Commons and the House of Lords. The electoral system in this period empowered between ten and twelve percent of the adult male population to vote, a large proportion of whom were landowners.[2] This preponderance of property owners in parliament ensured that both agricultural and more general landed interests would

---

[1]For detailed accounts of the sectarian conflict in Liverpool see F. Neal, *Sectarian Violence: The Liverpool Experience 1819-1914* (Manchester, 1988); P.J. Waller, *Democracy and Sectarianism: A Political and Social History of Liverpool* (Liverpool, 1981).

[2]E.J. Evans, *Political Parties in Britain 1783-1867* (London, 1985), gives a succinct survey of political developments over the period. See also R. Stewart, *The Foundation of the Conservative Party 1830-1867* (London, 1978), particularly part 1.

be protected. Many large towns at the beginning of the nineteenth century had no right to return members to parliament, in contrast to a number of underpopulated rural areas. Exceptions were those towns which for various reasons had been granted borough status. One such place was Liverpool which, at the start of our period, had the right to return two members.[3] Voting power in both borough council and parliamentary elections lay in the hands of a group of men known as freemen. One significant consequence was that a large proportion of the freemen were working-class artisans and labourers, many in the maritime trades. At a time when the majority of the population were disenfranchised, including most of the wealthy emergent middle class, the working-class freemen possessed the vote. Their monopoly of the franchise ended in 1832 with respect to parliamentary elections and 1835 in the case of borough contests.

The arcane system by which the freemen of Liverpool came to possess political leverage in the borough is not the central concern of this essay. Some explanation of the political arrangements is necessary, however, in order to appreciate both the source of the power which this section of the working class came to exercise and the motives which caused them to become embroiled in the bitter political struggles within the town, particularly between 1835 and 1851. Burgages were holdings of land held on lease from the Lord of the Manor and hence burgesses were the holders of such leases. In 1207 King John granted such leaseholders in Liverpool certain liberties and customs of a free borough. In practice this came to mean that the burgesses or freemen came to possess the right to vote in both

[3]A number of studies have examined the pre-reform franchise and elections in Liverpool, together with portraits of the main contenders for office: I. Sellers, "William Roscoe, The Roscoe Circle and Radical Politics in Liverpool, 1787-1807," *Transactions of the Historical Society of Lancashire and Cheshire* (*THSLC*), CXX (1968), 45-62; E.M. Menzies, "The Freemen Votes in Liverpool, 1802-1835," *ibid.*, CXXIV (1972), 85-107; F.E. Sanderson, "The Structure of Politics in Liverpool, 1780-1807," *ibid.*, CXXVII (1977), 65-89; K. Moore, "Liverpool in The Heroic Age of Popular Radicalism, 1815-1820," *ibid.*, CXXXVIII (1989), 137-157. While none of these has analyzed in full detail the surviving poll books, a partial analysis may J.R. Vincent, *How the Victorians Voted* (Cambridge, 1967), 136-139.

municipal and parliamentary elections. Most significant was the fact that they were subsequently exempted from paying certain local taxes on goods passing through Liverpool and some Irish ports. In 1229 Liverpool was granted its first Royal Charter, confirming the privileges of the freemen.

The mechanics of power in this early period of local government were relatively simple. All freemen had the right to meet in an assembly known as the Common Hall, a body which had the power to pass local laws. The elected officials responsible for the day-to-day running of affairs were the mayor and two bailiffs, all subject annually to election by the freemen. A second Royal Charter in 1695 was rather vague in its delineation of the power of freemen and subsequently political power became concentrated in a smaller body of freemen known as the Common Council. By the end of the eighteenth century, this had become a self-selecting oligarchy, predominantly Tory and Anglican in outlook. All freemen still possessed the franchise in both parliamentary contests and the annual elections of mayor and bailiffs, but the candidates for whom they could vote in council elections were restricted to those selected by the Common Council. Whatever the shortcomings of this system, the Corporation of Liverpool in the eighteenth century laid the basis for one of the greatest dock systems in the world.

There were three ways in which a person could become a freeman. A man born of a freeman father was eligible, as was any man who served his time as an apprentice under a freeman. In addition, the Common Hall, and afterwards, the Common Council, could admit anyone to the status of freeman. By 1800 the body of Liverpool freemen consisted of two discrete groups. On the one hand there were a number of wealthy merchants and shipowners, most of whom were involved in the West Indian and African trades, who were members of the Common Council and in effect ran the affairs of the port and borough. For such people there were clear advantages in being a freeman. Their goods were exempt from town dues and they exercised considerable influence on the development of the dock system, the passage of local by-laws and the disposal of patronage available to the borough. In 1787, thirty-seven of the forty-one members of the Council owned slave ships or had substantial investments in the slave trade. Of the twenty mayors holding office between 1787 and 1807, all had interests in the slave trade.[4]

The other much larger group of freemen comprised skilled and semi-skilled workers as well as labourers. Among these artisan freemen, the maritime trades were heavily represented, including ships' carpenters, riggers, sailmakers, ropers, maritime sawyers, anchorsmiths and the like. Of all the maritime trades in Liverpool, the group which came to have the highest political profile was the ships' carpenters. Before proceeding further, however, it is useful to note that in the contemporary literature the terms "shipwright," "journeyman shipwright," and "ships' carpenter" were used interchangeably, while shipbuilders were frequently referred to as "master shipwrights," "master carpenters," or simply "shipbuilders."[5] It has been estimated that by the last decade of the eighteenth century more than one-third of all freemen were employed in maritime trades. For such people, the privilege of not paying taxes on goods passing through the port was irrelevant. Their main privilege was to vote for candidates in municipal and parliamentary elections. If elections were contested, the votes of working-class freemen were bought with drink, food and money. The advantage of this perquisite, however, was somewhat diluted by the fact that many elections were uncontested. For example, following the parliamentary election in Liverpool in 1761, the next contested election was not until 1780.

Such a political system embodied an inherent weakness in that it was suitable only for the running of a small town; the rapid growth of Liverpool as a port during the eighteenth century revealed these structural faults. The number of freemen in the seventeenth and early eighteenth centuries represented a relatively large proportion of the adult population and their interests. At the onset of the nineteenth century, this was no longer the case. The creation of freemen had not

---

[4]Sanderson, "The Structure of Politics in Liverpool," 88-89.

[5]The most important contemporary source of information on the shipwrights and their trade association is contained in the evidence given to the Select Committee on Artisans and Machinery of 1824 and contained in its *Fourth Report* (hereafter, *SC 1824*).

kept pace with the growth of population and so they were increasingly unrepresentative of the people of Liverpool. By 1812 the total number of freemen represented about three percent of the population. Their small numbers notwithstanding, the dock system developed under the direction of freemen, both shipowners and merchants, who possessed great commercial acumen. A particular source of opposition to the Common Council was the large number of wealthy merchants who were not freemen and were thus excluded from the exercise of political power in the borough. To add to their chagrin, the majority of the vote-wielding freemen were working class, with no wealth or position in the town. Menzies estimated that by 1812, between sixty and seventy percent of the electorate were of the lower class of freemen.[6] The majority of wealthy merchants and shipowners excluded from power shared the same ideology as the small oligarchy on the Common Council; what they wanted was a share of power. Despite this congruence of economic and political interests, there were points of conflict between the ins and the outs. The membership of the Common Council at the end of the eighteenth century represented overwhelmingly the interests of the West Indian and African trades, which resulted in a large amount of municipal effort and money being put into the sustaining of those interests at Westminster. This was reflected in the choice of parliamentary candidates and in the organising of petitions and other pressure group activities. After the abolition of the slave trade in 1807, the concerns of these people became less important, as trade with America and the Far East mushroomed.

National and international events during the last quarter of the eighteenth and the first quarter of the nineteenth century conspired to rattle severely the nerves of the British establishment. The American War of Independence, which began in 1775, was followed by war with France and rebellion in Ireland. Simultaneously, the domestic scene was marked by a rising tide of opinion in favour of political reform.

---

[6]Menzies, "The Freemen Votes in Liverpool," 88-89. This seems not unreasonable given the occupational distribution of the freemen who actually voted in the 1806 election; see Appendix A. The term "lower class" as used by Menzies, however, is rather open to different interpretations.

Such demands came not only from the rapidly growing number of wealthy merchants, traders and manufacturers excluded from power but also from some sections of the aristocracy. This movement for change was manifested in petitions, pamphlets, meetings, books and private correspondence. The increasing volume of criticism of the existing political arrangements did not, however, represent a homogeneous body of opinion but rather reflected a wide spectrum of views, from demands to tinker with existing arrangements to an insistence on the substitution of universal male suffrage, and in more extreme cases, the abolition of the monarchy and the proclamation of a republic. Added to all these causes of concern was a growing volume of industrial unrest: the opening decades of the nineteenth century witnessed violent attacks on factories, machinery and occasionally manufacturers.

While political alliances had not yet coalesced into modern political parties, among the restricted electorate and power brokers there had emerged two distinctive groupings, Tories and Whigs. Any understanding of Liverpool politics in the nineteenth century must be based on an awareness of the place of religion in the national political arena. At the most simplistic level, Tories were characterised by a conviction in the need to defend and preserve established institutions, in particular the monarchy and the Church of England. From this followed an unwillingness to grant full civil liberties to non-Anglican denominations, an attitude frequently accompanied by a detestation of Roman Catholicism, which was seen as a foreign religion and politically subversive. By contrast, those aristocratic families comprising the Whigs were committed to maintaining the supremacy of parliament against the arbitrary exercise of monarchical power; in effect, a determination to limit the power of the throne and the influence of the court. In keeping with this libertarian streak was a desire to dismantle restrictions placed on dissenters and Catholics. By the onset of our period, the terms "reformers" and "radicals" had been added to the political lexicon. Generally, the former was used to describe those who wanted to alter the voting system fundamentally, in contrast with the latter, who campaigned for more fundamental changes.

In late eighteenth-century Liverpool the majority of the wealthy freemen councillors were predominantly, but not exclusively, Tory and

Anglican, their wealth earned in slaving and the African and West Indian trades. These established families included the Gregsons, Aspinalls, Branckners, Cases, Gildarts, Norrises and Tarletons. The non-freemen reformers included William Roscoe, William Rathbone, William Rushton, the Reverend John Yates, William Wallace, James Cropper and the Reverend William Shepherd. The Rathbone family were timber merchants and shipowners in Liverpool. The epithets Liberal, reformer, or radical were applied to them, depending on the political climate. It was from this group that the Liverpool campaign for the abolition of the slave trade emanated.[7] These reformers formed an anti-Corporation political opposition, as did many non-freemen merchants who, while Tory and Anglican, resented the power of the Council. Local Whig included the Lords' Sefton and Holland, the Earl of Derby, the Heywood banking family, Stephen Backhouse and others. It was against this background that the votes of freemen were sought by the contenders for power. Before 1832, the voting patterns of freemen were a shifting mosaic. Indeed the studies undertaken so far of pre-reform parliamentary elections indicate no consistent political bias. After this date the freemen shipwrights and others clearly on occasion voted in their own interests. Yet a difficulty for them was that the system of voting was public and so a man's preference would be known to his employer. As the Tory merchants and shipowners on the Council provided work for shipwrights and other maritime tradesmen, they could on occasion dictate the voting preferences of their employees. Nonetheless, as the well-being of the trade of large merchants and shipowners was also in the best interests of maritime workers, there was a certain mutuality of interests. Samuel Holmes, a builder and employer on a large scale, and also a leading member of the Liverpool Conservatives, stated in 1833 that "...I have always been of the opinion that a West Indian merchant in Liverpool

---

[7]For a description of the Corporation of Liverpool's response to the abolitionist campaign, see F.E. Sanderson, "The Liverpool Delegates and Sir William Dolben's Bill," *THSLC*, CXXIV (1972), 57-83. See also K. Charlton, "James Cropper and Liverpool's Contributions to the Anti-Slavery Movement," *ibid.*, CXXIII (1971), 57-80.

is rather a formidable opponent at an election, for they employ so many shipwrights."

The parliamentary election of 1806 demonstrated, however, the independence of the freemen when they felt strongly about an issue or were bribed sufficiently lavishly.[8] The two Tory MPs, Colonel Gascoyne and General Tarleton, stood and were opposed by William Roscoe, a leading reformer and a long-standing critic of the slave trade. This fact alone should have resulted in Roscoe's defeat, but the two Tory candidates were personally disliked and the Corporation had been employing non-freemen on some of its work. Local Whig aristocrats, the Earl of Derby, Lord Sefton and Lord Holland, backed Roscoe who took the seat from Tarleton. Table 1 below indicates the voting pattern of the freemen voters in the maritime trades, men who one might have felt threatened by the proposed abolition of the slave trade. Each freemen had two votes.[9]

Of the 919, 453 gave their vote to Roscoe, 352 of them voting for him alone, a sure sign of support whatever the motives. Among the shipwrights, 148 of the 246 (sixty percent) voted for Roscoe, 112 being single votes. Roscoe spent £12,000 on the election, most of it on bribes, and so his votes cannot unambiguously be interpreted as support for reform, although he did promise to champion the rights of freemen. In the 1807 parliamentary election Roscoe was decisively beaten in what turned out to be a "No Popery" election, a contest in which he incurred the hostility of unemployed seamen and the Anglican clergy. In the

---

[8]The details of this campaign are described in Sellers, "William Roscoe." For Holmes, see the "Report of the Select Committee on Liverpool Borough Elections," Great Britain, Parliament, House of Commons, *Parliamentary Papers* (hereafter *BPP*), 1833, (583), X, 357.

[9]I have studied the results of this poll by loading the data from the 1806 poll books onto dBase III+ and carrying out an analysis of the election results. This is part of a project involving a detailed examination of all the available Liverpool poll books. One objective is to discover the residential pattern of the freemen voters.

1832 election the maritime trades supported the Conservative candidates, Lord Sandon and Sir Howard Douglas.[10]

Table 1
The Voting Pattern of the Freemen in Maritime Trades Who Voted in the Liverpool Parliamentary Election of 1806

	Number of Paired Votes Cast			Single Votes		
Occupations	Gascoyne & Tarleton	Gascoyne & Roscoe	Tarleton & Roscoe	Gascoyne	Tarleton	Roscoe
Shipwrights	33	23	13	24	41	112
Sailmakers	19	4	1	16	10	23
Boatbuilders	15	3	1	4	9	6
Blockmakers	18	3	1	7	10	34
Mariners	14	5	3	16	12	27
Ropers	57	19	4	30	18	50
Pilots	9	1	-	4	5	9
Coopers	56	10	5	22	15	88
Anchorsmiths	1	4	0	0	0	1
Ship' Chandlers	1	-	1	0	0	2
	223	72	29	123	120	352

Source: 1806 Poll Books.

Despite this support Douglas, the Conservative, was not elected, the victors being Sandon and Ewart; a significant proportion of the electorate threw its weight behind the Liberals. Thornley, as an American trader, was not popular with the shipwrights. In the parliamentary election of 1835, the freemen shipwrights

[10]Vincent, *How the Victorians Voted*, 137.

overwhelmingly voted for Sandon and Douglas, this time securing the election of both Tory candidates.[11] It was after 1835 that the shipwrights became more closely involved in Tory politics, particularly in municipal affairs, and were drawn into conflict with the Irish.

Table 2
The Voting Pattern of the Voters in the Maritime Trades Who Voted in the Liverpool Parliamentary Election of 1832

	Total Votes Cast			
Occupation	Ewart (L)	Thornely (L)	Sandon (C)	Douglas (C)
Master Mariners	14	9	24	16
Mariners	57	51	71	59
Sailmakers	61	47	86	76
Pilots	11	6	34	23
Shipwrights	61	39	320	287
Total	204	152	535	461

Source: J.R. Vincent, *Poll Books: How the Victorians Voted* (Cambridge, 1967), 137.

The Whig administration which came to power in 1830 ushered in a period of rapid and fundamental election reform. The Reform Act of 1832 gave the borough franchise to all householders paying a rent of £10 per year, thus increasing the size of the electorate and diluting, though not removing, the political influence of the freemen. The 1835 Municipal Corporations Act laid down that members of town councils were to be elected by ratepayers, further weakening the influence of the freemen, and also required boroughs to appoint a watch committee and set up a police force. A crucial consequence of the 1835 Act was that council elections had to be held each year, thus necessitating the tightening of party organisation. It was this single fact that initiated a

[11] *Ibid.*, 138-139.

period of bitter street conflict between ships' carpenters and Irish Catholics; municipal elections were now fought unambiguously along party lines. The stakes were particularly high in Liverpool, where the docks generated huge revenues and membership on the dock committee was a highly sought prize. Municipal confrontations reflected national party concerns; on the one hand the Conservatives used the slogan "Church, King and Constitution," while the Liberals and Reformers, cool towards King and Church, were keen on free trade and favourable to concessions towards non-Anglicans. Last, but most significant, the Liberals were sympathetic to the grievances of the Catholics in Ireland. In Liverpool this was to prove their undoing.

From 1835 to 1841, the main driving force behind Liverpool Conservatism was Hugh McNeile, an Irish Anglican priest of great ability and charisma. Together with other Irish Anglican priests in Liverpool, he organised the opposition to the triumphant Liberal borough council, which was swept to power after the passing of the 1835 Act. By 1841, the Conservatives gained unchallengeable control of the council, and in that year won the two parliamentary seats. Their success was due to the sheer energy and drive of the Anglican clergy, who were ceaseless in their efforts to organise voter registration and to politicise the newly-enfranchised electorate, in the main the lower middle-class "shopocracy."[12]

In addition, they re-doubled their efforts to win the support of the freemen. Protestant and Conservative Operative Associations were founded; lectures and leaflets distributed; Church halls put at the disposal of Conservative speakers; and a stream of propaganda successfully identified Liberals as pro-Catholic, friends of England's enemies, and hostile to the Church of England. The patriotism of the working classes was invoked and harnessed to Conservative ends. The kind of behaviour by Liberals which incurred the odium of Conservatives and Orangemen is illustrated by an incident which occurred a few months later. In 1835, the Liberal administration had set up a select committee to investigate Orange Lodges in Great Britain and Ireland. A promi-

---

[12]For a detailed treatment of the "No Popery" campaign at this time, see Neal, *Sectarian Violence*, chapter 2.

nent member of that committee was the Reformer MP, Joseph Hume. The *Liverpool Mercury* of 9 October reported that Hume visited friends in Liverpool and that William Rathbone, Laurence Heywood, and other leading Liberals in the borough called on Hume to congratulate him on exposing the existence of Orange Lodges in the army. The onslaught on Liverpool Liberalism must be seen in the context of both the endemic anti-Catholicism of Victorian England and heavy Irish immigration into the borough. The 1841 census revealed that over forty-nine thousand Irish-born persons lived in the city. The number residing in South Toxteth ward, where many carpenters lived, was 1769, with another 4354 in nearby Great George ward, and 2775 in North Toxteth ward. In 1851, the number of Irish in South Toxteth alone was 4558.[13] In the absence of any published analysis of the occupations of the Irish immigrants contained in the census returns, we do not know to what extent they posed an economic threat to Liverpool's ships' carpenters and others, but clearly some of the immigrants must have been in maritime trades.

Any resentment on the part of the indigenous population towards the immigrant Irish was exacerbated by the existence of the English Orange Order. The success of English Orangeism in appealing to sections of the working classes must be seen in the light of the phenomenon of popular loyalism. The Conservatives were very successful in the nineteenth century in monopolising the language of patriotism.[14] Founded in 1807 in Manchester, at the height of establishment fears of insurrection, it was modelled on the Irish organisation and quickly became popular among certain sections of the unskilled

---

[13]*Ibid.*, tables 9 and 11. For a study of the role of steamships in transporting the famine Irish to Liverpool, see F. Neal, "Liverpool, The Irish Steamship Companies and the Famine Irish," *Immigrants and Minorities*, V, No. 1 (March 1986), 28-61.

[14]Neal, *Sectarian Violence*, chapters 1 and 2; F. Neal, "The Manchester Origins of the English Orange Order," *Manchester Region History Review*, IV, No. 2 (Autumn/Winter 1990/1991), 12-24; H.Cunningham, "The Language of Patriotism, 1750-1914," *History Workshop*, XII (August 1981), 8-23; A. Booth, "Popular Loyalism and Public Violence in the North West of England, 1790-1800," *Social History*, VIII, No. 3 (October 1983), 285-313.

English working class in the north of England. It offered comradeship, the advantages of a benefit society in many cases, and the enjoyment of the patronage at the disposal of the middle-class manufacturers, mill owners and merchants who provided the leadership. By copying the Irish tradition of having a July 12 procession to celebrate Williamite victories in Ireland, it incurred the ire of Irish Catholics and violence usually accompanied such events. The Order made its first public appearance in Liverpool in 1819, and a serious riot ensued, caused by Irish Catholics. In the subsequent court case, the persons giving evidence against the Irish prisoners were John Jones, a shipwright, Thomas Walters, a cooper, and Hugh Crowther, a customs officer. In Liverpool, membership of the Orange Order ultimately overlapped with participation in the various operative associations which came into being at this time. More particularly, in Toxteth ships' carpenters became a significant element in the local Orange lodges. Most of the shipbuilding operations were sited in the south end of the port, as were the timber yards. The majority of ships' carpenters lived near the shore, and their residential clustering was centred on Grafton Street.

On 12 July 1835, a large number of Irish went on the rampage in Liverpool. This violence was triggered by the belief that an Orange procession was to be held. This was not the case, but the rioting was of an extremely serious nature, involving police and Irish Catholics.[15] In October 1836, the Liverpool Conservatives gave a dinner for their working-class supporters. The Liberal *Liverpool Mercury* saw the event as part of the Conservative campaign to win over the lower orders. Reporting the event, it commented sourly on the amount of drinking that took place and the presence of "carpenters, ropers and other greasy rogues."[16] It was the 1837 parliamentary election in which antagonism between ships' carpenters, "greasy rogues" and Irish Catholics came to the notice of the general public. The sectarian overtones of the political battle emerged early in the campaign. On 3 July the Catholic Defence Association in Liverpool met to discuss ways

---

[15]Neal, *Sectarian Violence*, 55-56.

[16]*Liverpool Mercury*, 28 October 1836.

of meeting the non-stop attacks on Catholicism. The *Liverpool Mercury* urged all Catholics voters not to vote for a Tory.[17] The Conservatives saw the issues as the defence of church, monarchy and constitution against the depredations of Lord Melbourne's government. On the day before polling started there were clashes between Tory and reform supporters. On polling day many Irish Catholics wore Liberal colours, and attacked Conservative supporters and polling booths. Large numbers of ships' carpenters, who lived principally in Toxteth, attacked reform supporters and any Irish they met. The press reports agreed that Irish supporters of the Liberals initiated the fighting, but that the carpenters were equally willing to indulge in acts of physical violence. In the country as a whole, the Liberals won but in Liverpool both Conservative candidates were returned. In his victory speech the Conservative candidate Lord Sandon told his audience that:

> You have set a good example to the whole country which I trust the whole country will follow, an example of sincere and earnest attachment to Protestant institutions and earnest attachment to our ancient constitution, to the hereditary privilege of the House of Lords, and the hereditary privileges, which as freemen, you possess yourselves. There is one peculiar element of our success to which I look with no small satisfaction [: t]he deep sincere religious feeling which existed in the town.[18]

Following the parliamentary election, McNeile and the Anglican clergy redoubled their efforts to bring about victory in the municipal elections. Central to this objective were the votes of the freemen. Though the 1835 Act had increased the total number of those eligible to vote in local elections, the freemen voters were still a significant element. For example, in 1837, the number of voters enfranchised on

---

[17] *Ibid.*, 7 July 1837.

[18] The speech was widely reported in the press; see, for example, *Liverpool Mail*, 27 July 1837; *Liverpool Courier*, 26 July 1837.

the basis of household rent was 10,252, while freemen votes totalled 3197.[19]

The antagonisms between ships' carpenters and Irish Catholics soon re-surfaced. It was a carpenters' tradition to hold a procession on May 29 to celebrate the restoration of Charles II. As the event approached in 1839, the 1837 election had clearly not been forgotten. Days before the procession, rumours circulated that the Irish planned to attack the carpenters. Simultaneously, in the Irish areas it was said that the carpenters would wear Orange colours. When the parade was held, there was no trouble during the actual march.[20] The geography of the area was such that Grafton Street, the centre of the carpenters' residences, was only four hundred metres from New Bird Street, Crosbie Street and Blundell Street, where many Irish lived. After the procession, gangs of young carpenters went to these streets and commenced to attack houses. Large-scale fighting broke out in a number of streets and the police, under Michael Witty, the head constable, had difficulty controlling the situation. In one of the shipbuilding yards, carpenters drove Catholic labourers off the docks. In subsequent reports on the disturbances, it was alleged that the carpenters used the tools of their trade as weapons and that Tory politicians had financed the carpenters' drinking, paying off debts incurred in the 1837 election. An insight into a contemporary view of the nature of the problem is provided by an article in the *Liverpool Albion* of 3 June 1839:

> ...Unhappily, however, passions of animosity have been excited by the previous proceedings amongst two large parties of our working population, the ships' carpenters who have ever been the tools of the Tory candidates for the honour of parliamentary election in this town, and the poor Irish, who are naturally on the other side of the

---

[19] *Liverpool Standard*, 31 July 1840.

[20] The events surrounding the carpenters' procession were extensively reported in the local press; see *Liverpool Albion*, 3 June 1839; *Liverpool Mail*, 4 June 1839; *Liverpool Journal*, 1 June 1839.

> question, and who, from necessity in a strange and somewhat 'unfriendly' country as regards workmen, are thrown upon the lowest scale of labour. Independently of the fact that the carpenters are comparatively rich and numerous as a body, they have for years been nurtured and formed into a sort of Orange combination, ready on any emergency of a Tory adventurer offering himself as a representative of them or rather of those who cajole and bribe them, to burst forth from their graving docks and ships' bottoms, with deadly weapons in their hands, and mustering, like a regiment a thousand strong to carry the town vie et armis.

These disturbances were quite serious and much damage was done to homes. Its main significance, however, was to indicate that relations between Irish and carpenters had not improved. Such clashes made it easier for the Conservatives to enlist the support of the freemen, the hatred of the Irish spilling over into anti-Liberal sentiments. In part these arose from Liberal dalliance with Irish nationalists. The *Liverpool Albion* suggested that Tories engineered the clashes by spreading rumours. After these disturbances the process of politicising the shipwrights was taken a step further.

By September 1840, there already existed a fisherman's branch of the Protestant Association and on September 23 McNeile received a petition from a group purporting to represent the shipwrights, stating their intention to form a branch of the Protestant Association and asking him to be chairman:

> We, the undersigned members of the provisional committee, beg leave to inform you that the shipwrights of this town, desirous of being united in the defence of our Protestant Constitution, the safety of which is so much endangered by the open violence of professed friends,

> have determined in forming a branch of the Protestant Association for Toxteth Park...[21]

The majority of shipbuilding operations took place in the south end, and most of the timber yards were there also. For example, the yards of Grayson, Wilson, Mottershead, Humble and Milcrest and Clarke and Nickson were on the land between Salthouse dock and the river. At the side of these were numbers 1, 2 and 3 graving docks. This site was within easy walking distance of Grafton Street. Even nearer to Grafton Street, about five hundred metres removed, were the yards of John Dawson, William Dickenson, Peter Chaloner, Joseph Steel and Thomas Royden. They were situated between the Queens dock and the river, together with graving docks number 4 and 5 and Duncan Gibb's timber yards. Heading the signatures to the petition was Duncan Gibb. He was a major shipowner in Liverpool and probably the largest timber merchant in the area. As such he would be a source of employment to shipwrights. He was also a leading member of the Conservative party and a Protestant activist. Another signatory was Joseph Crisp, a leading Liverpool Orangeman. McNeile accepted the offer to become chairman. The episode clearly illustrates the growing identification of the shipwrights with the Conservative cause.

On 29 September 1840 a meeting of shipwrights, coopers and other artisan freemen was held to discuss further the establishment of the Shipwrights' Protestant Operative Association. It was addressed by a number of leading Liverpool Conservatives, including Samuel Holmes and John Shepherd, with McNeile in the chair. The speeches provide a classic example of the ability of Conservatives to appeal to the nationalism and patriotism of the working classes. Councillor Whatham, in reference to the 1837 election, reminded the meeting that had it not been for the Shipwrights' Association, Liverpool probably would not have two Conservative MPs. He then went on to praise the shipwrights, sailmakers, coopers and ropers, expressing the hope that they would continue to defend the British constitution. Presumably, he

[21] *Liverpool Standard*, 30 September 1840.

meant that he hoped that they would help to return more Conservative candidates in the future. Samuel Holmes told the freemen:

> If the Church of England remains much longer on the defensive, she is gone--for it is an axiom in warfare that a besieged city eventually must fall; but if the garrison is strong enough to make a sortie and repel the aggressors, it is secure. That is now the position of the Church of England.[22]

The effect of the propagandising efforts of the Protestant Operative Societies and Orange Lodges was to shape the feuds and antagonisms of the artisan and labouring classes into something like a coherent ideology. In so doing, Conservative orators managed skilfully to interweave both economic and religious arguments. Under Protestantism, trade and wealth had increased. The British constitution, unwritten as it was, guaranteed the equality of all Englishmen before the law and protected their hard won rights and liberties. Central to this admirable state of affairs was the Church of England--the church of all Englishmen--which imparted a spiritual dimension to public life. Attacks on the Church of England were not only attacks on England's spiritual legacy but also on the very core of the political arrangements which had served Englishmen so well. Into this ideology was injected a defence of landed interests and their hostility to free trade. The Corn Laws protected landed interests, the core of Conservative support, while the Navigation Laws secured to British shipowners the carrying trade in inter-empire trading. A further cause of hostility to the Liberals was the fact that, under O'Connell, over seventy Irish representatives in parliament kept Liberal governments in office from 1835 to 1841.[23]

From 1840 onwards, ships' carpenters became increasingly involved in violent clashes with Liberal supporters. In January 1841,

---

[22] *Ibid.*

[23] Stewart, *The Foundation of the Conservative Party*, 159.

H.G. Harbord, a prominent Orangeman, led a gang of carpenters to break up a meeting in support of free trade.[24] On 31 May, the ships' carpenters again held their annual procession in honour of the restoration of Charles II. Participants included shipwrights, blockmakers, and other maritime tradesmen. They were escorted by three hundred police because there was a not unnatural fear of an Irish assault, a constant concern after the 1839 riots. The shipwrights went to Christ Church, where the sermon was preached by Fielding Ould, an Irish cleric and Orangeman. In fact there were no disturbances but the general perception was that the Irish would be hostile to the shipwrights.[25] Soon thereafter, the animosity between the carpenters and Irish was again brought to public attention. During the first week of June, a meeting was held in the south end to support the Anti-Corn Law Association. A large crowd attended, including many Irish. A number of ships' carpenters appeared and barracked the speakers, attracting the hostility of the Irish. Some carpenters on leaving the meeting smashed the windows of St. Patrick's Catholic Church, an incident which caused great anger among the Irish. At another Anti-Corn Law meeting the next day, even larger numbers of Irish attended and attacked several people. After the meeting the windows of St. James' Anglican Church in Toxteth were smashed.[26] The following morning a crowd estimated at two thousand, comprised principally of ships' carpenters and their allies, marched from the graving docks towards the town centre. On being stopped by the police they said they wanted a deputation to attend the mayor, seeking protection from the Irish.[27] This series of confrontations was in fact an escalation of tension, which subsequently spilled over into widespread violence

---

[24]*Liverpool Albion*, 8 January 1841.

[25]*Liverpool Mercury*, 4 June 1841; *Liverpool Chronicle*, 4 June 1841.

[26]Neal, *Sectarian Violence*, 57.

[27]Liverpool Record Office, Watch Committee Minutes, 12 June 1841, Report from M.J. Whitty, Head Constable.

between carpenters and Irish Catholics in the elections the following July.

The confrontations between ships' carpenters and Irish at the meetings of the Anti-Corn Law Association need to be viewed in the context of a vigorous and virulent campaign waged by Conservatives in Liverpool. This opposition to the free traders managed to blend economic and religious arguments into a coherent defence of England's religious and economic heritage and was remarkably successful in persuading the artisan classes that free trade would harm their interests. The flavour of Conservative meetings is exemplified by the Protestant Operative Association's gathering at the York Hotel in February 1841 to petition against free trade. In the chair was Daniel Ledson, a warehouse owner. In his speech to the assembled working men he asked them "Are we not banded together to defend the institutions of our land? Are we not banded together to defend our Church? Yes, and we will defend our national Church because she is the holy, the just, the tolerant, the pure Church."[28]

At another meeting of the Protestant Operative Association on 7 June 1841, the *Liverpool Standard*, the most extreme Protestant newspaper in the town, claimed that the main speaker should say that "the true intention of the present government, which, covered by the wild cry of liberality, is really and truly, to suppress Protestant principle and re-establish Popery in this land." The same meeting was addressed by Joseph Crisp, a prominent Orangeman in Liverpool. He told the audience that in Ireland seven Protestant clergymen had been murdered but in England, where Catholics were outnumbered sixteen to one, no Catholic priests had been killed.[29] The effect of this non-stop flood of anti-Catholic propaganda can only be guessed at, but events during the 1841 general election indicate that the Protestant working class had absorbed some of the venom. The Whig administration went to the country and lost, in part paying the price for its flirtation with Irish nationalism. What is certain is that any potential

---

[28]*Liverpool Standard*, 5 February 1841.

[29]*Ibid.*, 8 June 1841.

Liverpool MP had to woo the carpenters. On 28 June, for example, a pre-election meeting of an estimated one thousand ships' carpenters was held at Bond Street, presided over by Thomas Price, himself a ship's carpenter. The meeting was addressed by the two Conservative candidates, Lord Sandon and Mr. Cresswell.[30]

Tuesday, 29 June, was nomination day for the candidates, Walmsley (L), Palmerston (L), Sandon (C) and Cresswell (C). From the outset there were clashes between rival supporters. On election day (30 June) there was serious rioting, particularly in the south end, between Irish Catholics and ships' carpenters and their supporters. The characteristic dress of the carpenters was a blue jacket and throughout the day many carpenters were beaten up. In turn, roaming gangs of carpenters attacked both Irish and Liberal supporters. The police were severely extended and almost lost control of the situation. The Irish knew the public houses popular with ships' carpenters and attacked them. In turn some houses occupied by Irish were stoned by carpenters. In one case a publican and shipwright, John Casement, repulsed an Irish attack on his house, shooting four Irishmen and one woman. By any standards of Victorian urban disorder the riots were serious and brought to a head the antagonism between shipwrights and Irish Catholics, particularly in the Toxteth area. One Conservative supporter died from injuries received in the fighting. The Conservative candidates won the election but the events badly damaged inter-communal relations. On the day after polling day, there was panic in the predominantly Irish Catholic Lace Street area in the north end when rumours spread that ships' carpenters were gathering to march on their streets. The rumour was unfounded but when the police went to disperse the crowds a constable was shot by a drunken Irishman.[31] The election result, a victory for the Conservatives, reflected an even greater identification of the maritime trades with the Conservatives, as shown in table 3.

---

[30] *Ibid.*, 29 June 1841.

[31] Neal, *Sectarian Violence*, 57-59.

With reference to the election violence, the apportionment of blame by the press reflected the political complexion of the individual paper, although in general both Irish and carpenters were allocated equal responsibility. The *Liverpool Albion*, in commenting on the disturbances, expressed a commonly-held view among the uncommitted. In describing the unfolding sequence of events, the *Albion* stated:

> ...At length, soon after the close of the poll, numbers of shipwrights, who have been persuaded by the 'No Popery' orators of Liverpool, to consider themselves the natural enemies of Irishmen, committed a series of acts of violence in various parts of the town.[32]

Table 3
The Voting Pattern of Those in Maritime Trades in the Liverpool Parliamentary Election of 1841

Freemen	Candidates			
	Walmsley	Palmerston	Sandon	Cresswell
Stevedores	6	6	3	3
Pilots	1	2	65	65
Sailmakers	27	25	85	82
Shipbuilders	4	44	18	18
Shipwrights	67	62	350	346
Shipbrokers	8	7	13	11
Shipowners	6	6	13	13
Totals	144	112	547	538

Source: Vincent, *Poll Books*, 139. Of the 825 votes cast by Shipwrights, eighty-four percent went to Conservative candidates.

[32] *Liverpool Albion*, 8 July 1841.

The constant intertwining of political, economic and religious issues by Protestant propagandists is well illustrated by a leader article in the *Liverpool Standard* several months after the Conservative victories. The *Standard* was warning its readers not to relax their Protestant vigilance just because a Conservative administration was in power:

> That Manchester, Salford, Bolton, Stockport, etc, with one third of their populations composed of Irish Roman Catholics, and to a man voting in accordance with the dictation of their priesthood, return exclusively anti-Corn Law candidates to Parliament, is to be attributed solely to the power which Popery has elected for herself, even here in England.[33]

The proportion of Irish claimed for the towns quoted were shown to be nonsensical by the 1841 Census, but the effect of a non-stop stream of such claims had its effect on working-class perception of the threat posed by Irish immigration.

In Liverpool, the confrontation between Irish and shipwrights occurred again in July 1842. A deputation of Orangeman approached the mayor for permission to hold a July 12 procession. He suggested they should abstain in view of the probability of disorder, and on 25 June the borough magistrates passed a resolution disapproving any such procession.[34] The Orange deputation seemed to accept this and recommended the Lodges not to march. The Toxteth Lodges, which had the highest membership of ships' carpenters, refused to obey their leadership and threatened to parade. On the day, the police were at full alert as several thousand Irish gathered in the north end, threatening to march to Toxteth to stop any Orange processions. Irish dockers went on strike and joined the crowds in Vauxhall, where the police

---

[33] *Liverpool Standard*, 5 November 1841.

[34] Public Record Office, HO45/249D, John Shaw Leigh to Sir James Graham; *Liverpool Mercury*, 1 and 8 July 1842.

contained them. Throughout the day, the Irish attacked men they thought were carpenters and several were severely injured. A crowd of an estimated two thousand carpenters and supporters did parade, resulting in clashes with Irish Catholics in Toxteth.[35]

While the events in 1841 and 1842 seemed to mark the height of street fighting between shipwrights and Irish Catholics, they were not the end of Orange-Catholic conflict in Liverpool. Just how many carpenters were Orangemen we simply do not know and the numbers engaged in the violence in the streets suggest that other Protestant workers were involved. There is evidence that the shipwrights were open to argument on the merits of free trade and that their position on the issue was not unreasonable. On the 21 February 1844, a meeting of shipwrights took place, attended as well by members of other maritime trades, to hear an address by members of the Anti-Monopoly Association. One shipwright expressed the view that although the existing monopolies were bad, the system worked well for shipwrights. Colonial "slop" ships coming to Liverpool were so badly built they needed repairs each voyage and, repair work was all the shipwrights had. By implication, if the carrying trade were thrown open, the shipwrights would suffer.[36] The protectionist case, however, was already doomed and despite this reasonableness an element among the carpenters continued to provide the muscle for Conservative intimidation of opponents. The question of why the shipwrights acted the way they did remains.

Any attempt to understand both the actions and motives of the ships' carpenters in Liverpool must take into account the economic environment in which they had to sell their labour. Like any other form of labour, their earnings were determined by the forces of demand and supply operating in the labour market, and these in turn reflected conditions prevailing in the markets for the finished product, shipbuilding and repairing. In studying the Liverpool maritime labour

---

[35] *Liverpool Albion*, 18 July 1842; *Liverpool Mail*, 14 July 1842; *Liverpool Mercury*, 15 July 1842.

[36] *Liverpool Albion*, 26 February 1844.

market it is crucial to keep in mind that both the market in newly-built vessels and ship repairing was, and still is, international. Liverpool shipowners in the period did not have to purchase vessels locally, nor have them repaired on the Mersey. Similarly, shipowners elsewhere had a wide choice of suppliers and repairers. Factors determining the choice of a builder when commissioning a new vessel would include the relative importance the potential owners placed on quality versus price. In Liverpool, labour costs were a significant proportion of total costs.

The demand for any form of labour is determined by the marginal physical product of the labour and the price of the finished product in the market. In the case of a ship, the revenue earned was determined by freight rates over the life of the asset. Thus, falling freight rates worked backwards into the demand side of the labour market. Similarly, in the case of ship repairing, the willingness of shipowners to maintain their assets in a good state of repair depended on freight rates. In 1816, for example, a number of Liverpool merchants informed the Shipwrights Association that wages would have to be reduced in consequence of a fall in freight rates. This precipitated a two-week strike before a compromise was reached.[37] On the supply side, the number of shipwrights willing to work and the amount of time they were willing to toil could be influenced by a powerful trade association. To the extent that a workers' combination could enforce apprenticeship regulations and a closed shop, its power to control wage rates correspondingly increased. Additionally, the demand for labour could be increased by imposing restrictive practices. The marginal productivity of labour depends on the ratio between capital and labour in a given state of technology. Equally important, investment in capital equipment usually involves long amortization periods. Such decisions, although they affect the productivity of labour, were the preserve of the shipbuilders rather than the shipwrights. Keeping such factors in mind, attention will now be turned to the local shipbuilding industry.

---

[37]*SC 1824*, evidence of Samuel McCall, shipwright and Vice-President of the Liverpool Shipwrights' Association.

Space does not permit a full analysis of shipbuilding on Merseyside, although this writer is at present completing such a study. It seems plausible to assume initially that there was some relationship between the number of vessels built and the demand for ships' carpenters, and also a similar relationship between the tonnage of vessels entering the port and the volume of repair work. Let us first look at the issue of shipbuilding. Table 4 illustrates the output of newly-built vessels in the years preceding the period under review.

The period 1787 to 1808 includes some disturbed years in international relations which affected Britain's trade, principally during the war with France. In the twenty-two years there were only four in which the output of Liverpool yards exceeded five thousand tons. With respect to the employment generated, by 1804 the number of shipwrights in Liverpool was estimated at 327 plus 160 apprentices, making a total of 487. For the nineteenth century there is no complete series on the tonnage built at Liverpool. Table 5 below depicts the period 1814-1849 and has been constructed from various sources. In addition, it refers to wooden vessels registered at Liverpool. From 1838 onwards iron vessels were also being built in the port.

Table 4
The Number and Tonnage of Vessels Built at The Port of Liverpool 1787 to 1808

Year	Number	Tonnage	Year	Number	Tonnage
1787	44	5731	1798	11	2201
1788	40	5139	1799	24	5708
1789	26	3166	1800	23	4430
1790	27	4737	1801	27	4584
1791	18	2393	1802	18	2761
1792	30	3509	1803	19	3122
1793	18	2137	1804	10	2165
1794	18	2635	1805	25	1989
1795	12	1463	1806	9	1787
1796	34	5175	1807	7	771
1797	20	4749	1808	9	610

Source: R. Stewart Brown, *Liverpool Ships in the Eighteenth Century* (Liverpool, 1932), Table III, 22-23.

Table 5
The Number and Tonnage of Wooden Ships Built and Registered at Liverpool Over the Period 1814 to 1849 Inclusive

Year	Number	Tonnage	Year	Number	Tonnage
1814	23	3846	1832	17	3342
1815	18	3286	1833	12	2445
1816	18	2565	1834	17	3995
1817	16	1898	1835	20	5759
1818	18	2462	1836	17	3946
1819	11	1898	1837	8	1042
1820	15	4458	1838	13	4191
1821	14	2175	1839	14	3293
1822	18	3053	1840	18	5870
1823	17	3517	1841	12	3729
1824	27	5778	1842	12	3221
1825	18	3957	1843	14	3509
1826	17	4258	1844	6	2262
1827	9	1933	1845	8	3286
1828	13	2459	1846	12	3195
1829	16	4251	1847	14	3365
1830	15	2901	1848	10	3218
1831	14	2511	1849	7	2229

Source: For 1814, *Accounts and Papers, 1814-15* (279) VII. For 1815-1820, from F. Neal, "Liverpool Shipping in the 19th Century," in J.R. Harris (ed.), *Liverpool and Merseyside: Essays in the Economic History of the Port and its Hinterland* (London, 1969), 170. For 1821-49, see *Report of the Shipbuilding Committee of the Liverpool Borough Council (1850)*.

In only three of these years did tonnage exceed five thousand tons and the overall picture is one in which the local industry failed to develop. We do have data on all vessels built at Liverpool, irrespective of where they were registered. Table 6 covers the years 1820-1832, and also includes the tonnages for Sunderland and Newcastle, by way of contrast. The inferences to be drawn are basically unchanged. The tonnage built did not increase significantly compared to Sunderland

and Newcastle. From 1838, iron built vessels began to make their appearance in Liverpool yards, signifying the beginning of the end for ships' carpenters (see table 7). This relative stagnation in building through 1849 stands out when placed against the growth in tonnage entering Liverpool.[38] For example, in 1816, 1340 ships entered Liverpool, representing 300,673 tons. In 1845, the corresponding figures were 4045 and 1,406,541. Thus, the number of vessels increased 301% over the thirty-year period while the tonnage increased by 468%. Over the period, the correlation coefficient between tonnage built at Liverpool and tonnage entering was only 0.186. Thus, there is no linear relationship between the two variables. Yet it seems plausible to argue that an increase in the volume of shipping using the port indicates an expansion of trade and hence a need for more vessels. It is not only plausible but reasonable to argue so. But Liverpool shipowners and merchants did not need to purchase vessels in Liverpool, and the evidence strongly suggests that they met much of their requirement for tonnage by purchasing new ships elsewhere, in particular in British North America. Table 8 shows the sources of North American vessels registered at Liverpool between 1842 and 1846, a period in which the Liverpool ships' carpenters were becoming increasingly worried about their job prospects. Nearly all this tonnage from British North America, and registered at Liverpool, was owned by local men.

It can be seen that this source alone provided more tonnage than the Liverpool yards over the same years. The official returns do not make clear whether or not these colonial-built vessels were new, but evidence elsewhere suggests that they would be. Initially, they were registered in the colonies, many being purchased by Liverpool owners and subsequently transferred to the Liverpool register without having

---

[38]The figures in table 5 for the years 1820-1832 do not agree with those contained in Appendix 1 of the *Report* of the Select Committee on Manufacturers, Commerce and Shipping, (1833), 718, entitled "An Account of the Number and Tonnage of Ships built at each of the Principal Ports of the North of England in each year from 1820-1832 inclusive." The reason for this is that the figures produced by J.A. Tobin, chairman of the Shipbuilding Committee, refer to vessels built and registered at Liverpool, thus omitting those built at Liverpool but registered elsewhere. I am at present constructing a complete series of vessels built in Liverpool, 1815-1890.

first been used for any trading venture. Take the case of the 441-ton barque *Galatea*, built in New Brunswick in the summer of 1849 and on completion registered at Saint John on 21 September 1849. She was purchased by John Jardine and William Tee, merchants of Liverpool, and transferred to Liverpool in February 1850.[39] For all practical purposes, she was a newly-built vessel on her arrival in Liverpool. If one defines a colonial vessel as new if built within a period of less than one year of its registration at Liverpool, then the importance of British North America to Liverpool shipowners and merchants becomes very clear. Given the alternative sources of vessels, both in North America and the northeast of England, the ability of ships' carpenters to force up wages and maintain employment was limited by the elasticity of demand for the finished product. In 1850, the borough council set up a committee to investigate what was described as the decline of shipbuilding on the Liverpool banks of the Mersey.[40] As table 9 indicates, in that year, 41,405 tons of newly-built shipping was added to the Liverpool register, ninety-nine percent of it Liverpool-owned.

Of the total "new" tonnage (using the definition proposed above) of 41,405 tons, two-thirds came from British North America. The contribution from the Liverpool yards was 3474 tons, representing 8.4%. In the case of British-built vessels in Table 6, the figures refer only to vessels built in 1850. It is of course possible that the Liverpool yards supplied new vessels to owners at other ports during the year, but this is unlikely given the total output figures given in table 2 and the fact that the council had set up an enquiry into the parlous state of the Liverpool industry.

Without going into details, the major factors influencing the uncompetiveness of builders on the Liverpool side of the Mersey were principally the relatively high labour costs and an inability to provide

---

[39]Liverpool Registers of Merchant Ships, No. 73, 1850. These are kept at the Merseyside Maritime Museum.

[40]The proceedings of this committee were fully-reported in the local press during September and October. Official copies of the report do not seem to have survived. For very detailed press coverage, see *Liverpool Mercury*, 10, 13, 17, 20 and 24 September and 1 October 1850.

vessels of the size the market required. The high labour costs were in turn the result of both the system of short leases of land to the builders and restrictive practices on the part of the Shipwrights' Association. The issue of leases resulted in a lack of space to spread out timbers, thus increasing labour costs. Even more significant was the unwillingness of builders to invest in long-term labour-saving equipment, such as steam cranes and saws, as well as fixed-assets in the form of buildings. Many of the most important builders had to move several times within short periods. The lack of investment in new technology ruled out increases in labour productivity in local yards, thus making it even more difficult for Liverpool builders to overcome cost disadvantages relative to the northeast and North America. Labour costs were a significant element in the total cost of a ship. For example, Liverpool sources in 1850 estimated that the total cost of a first-class Liverpool-built ship of five hundred tons burthen, to be classed A1 for from ten to twelve years, was £9800; of this, labour costs accounted for thirty-six percent, the same as the cost of timber.[41]

During our period, repair work was of major importance in maintaining the demand for shipwrights. It might be supposed that this was related to the volume of shipping entering the port; as this was steadily increasing, then so should have the demand for shipwrights and related tradesmen. Although this was generally true, there was no simple relationship between the volume of traffic and the demand for repairs. Unfortunately, we simply do not know the volume of repair work undertaken by the shipbuilders or the shipwrights using the public graving docks. We do know that shipowners had a choice of where they sent their vessels for repairs. For example, American vessels were frequently repaired and maintained in their home ports and so generated little work in Liverpool. In 1822, of the 136,650 tons of shipping entered inwards at Liverpool, 114,825 tons, or eighty-four percent, were foreign vessels from the US, and the majority of these were American vessels. In 1826, the comparable figure was seventy-

---

[41]*Liverpool Standard*, 16 July 1850, contains a long leader on the local shipbuilding industry.

eight percent.[42] For this reason American ships and Liverpool merchants in the American trade were not popular among maritime tradesmen. From the perspective of master shipbuilders, a deleterious consequence of the public graving docks was that journeyman shipwrights would take on repair work, thus denying the builders the volume of work necessary to hold a permanent labour force in their yards. Shipbuilders giving evidence to the 1850 enquiry into the state of shipbuilding at Liverpool claimed that their costs of production were influenced by the small areas of the land leased to them by the corporation, with obviously adverse consequences for investment in fixed-assets and the cost of labour.[43]

Table 6
The Number and Tonnage of Vessels Built at Liverpool, Sunderland and Newcastle, 1820-1832

Year	Liverpool		Newcastle		Sunderland	
	No.	Tons	No.	Tons	No.	Tons
1820	18	4329	17	1953	60	7560
1821	14	2583	19	2641	48	6464
1822	25	3588	30	4599	39	6571
1823	21	3986	23	3292	55	11278
1824	38	6449	33	6142	70	15184
1825	31	5552	57	12390	98	20818
1826	33	5999	46	6892	84	16055
1827	13	2797	37	5374	81	13597
1828	17	2935	41	6000	71	13743
1829	18	4497	50	8287	78	15096
1830	21	3346	31	5530	74	15132
1831	27	3727	53	8762	104	20954
1832	23	4553	51	9012	109	24519

Source: *Select Committee on Manufactures, Commerce and Shipping* (1833), Appendix No. II.

---

[42] HC, *Accounts and Papers*, 1826-1827 (343), XVIII, 301, "All Ships Entered Inwards at the Port of Liverpool from the United States of America, 1822-1826, inclusive."

[43] *Liverpool Mercury*, 10 September 1850, Liverpool Council Report on Shipbuilding, evidence of Thomas Royden, Peter Chaloner, Robert Clarke and Joseph Steel.

The barriers to entry in any labour market can take various forms. Possession of a skill in short supply relative to demand protects workers, particularly if the skill is expensive to acquire. Yet skill *per se* is neither a necessary nor sufficient condition for high earnings. Where a skill is plentiful, then a union can try to create barriers to entry by enforcing an apprenticeship system, a closed shop and/or restrictive practices. These can be achieved by agreement with employers or by use of force. Beyond the control of workers is the appearance of new technologies or materials which render their skills obsolete. In 1810, the ships' carpenters had formed the Shipwrights' Benefit Society.[44] In 1824, one of its senior officers claimed it was established to provide assistance for members in sickness and old age. In fact the Combination Act of 1799 and its amendments in 1800 made it necessary to adopt the form of a Friendly Society to avoid prosecution. All available evidence suggests that by 1824 the members of the Shipwright Society in Liverpool operated as a trades union and did so openly after the 1824 Combination Act. Reference has already been made to the estimated 487 shipwrights in Liverpool in 1824. The 1841 Census records 267 "shipwrights and carpenters" under twenty years old and another 1226 over that age. The 1851 census dropped the term "carpenter" and recorded 321 "shipwrights and shipbuilders" under twenty and 1887 twenty or older. Thus, in the first half of the nineteenth century, the number of men describing themselves as shipwrights increased five-fold.

In 1824 John Cain, the Society's Secretary, stated that there were 837 members representing virtually all the time-served shipwrights in Liverpool. The Shipwrights' Society operated a closed shop during the first quarter of the nineteenth century. This was enforced vigorously, the Liverpool men displaying a ferocious objection to outsiders looking for work on the local waterfront. On occasion, violence was used to discourage such interlopers. For example, Samuel McCall, a Society official, reported that some Welshmen and Irishmen were driven out of town. These men had formed a gang and presumab-

---

[44] *SC (1824)*, evidence of John Cain, secretary of the Shipwrights Benefit Society, 19 March 1824. See also evidence of John Kirwan and Samuel McCall, 17 March 1824.

ly used the public graving docks.[45] The men also enforced manning levels of which the shipbuilders did not approve, using the tactic of walking off ships if a builder objected, or on occasion violence. The experience of the shipbuilder, Charles Grayson, will suffice to illustrate the problems. In June 1820 he was repairing the *Milo*.[46] He ordered a carpenter to leave the vessel, as he considered him too drunk to work properly. The rest of the men downed tools and walked off, leaving Grayson to finish the work with apprentices. The men were willing to work on another vessel which Grayson had in dock, but when they insisted that the man who was the cause of the dispute be employed, Grayson complied. On another of Grayson's vessels, the men walked off because they claimed it was a fixed-price job and this would mean they would have to work harder. In August 1821 shipwrights left work on another Grayson vessel following a dispute; in the end, to avoid going out of business, Grayson had to publish a humiliating apology. At this time other builders experienced similar difficulties. There was a consensus among the principal shipbuilders in 1824 that their difficulties in getting the mayor, as chief magistrate, to prosecute carpenters involved in violence was not simply a problem of evidence. They believed that the magistrates supported the shipwrights because of the voting power of freemen and that the Association had Tory allegiances.[47] The builders in general felt the Shipwrights' Association was a burden on their attempts to bring orders to Liverpool. This view was unchanged in 1850 and was repeated again in 1853 during yet another confrontation between Liverpool builders and shipwrights.[48]

---

[45] *Ibid.*, evidence of Samuel McCall.

[46] *Ibid.* The information in this section is taken from the evidence of Kirwan, McCall and Cain.

[47] *Ibid.*, evidence of Liverpool shipbuilders.

[48] *Liverpool Mail*, 29 October 1853, carried a long account of a meeting between shipbuilders and shipwrights to settle yet another dispute, this time over wages and the employment of men from outside of Liverpool. Thomas Royden suggested a head-on confrontation with the shipwrights to settle once and for all who ran the building yards.

Table 7
The Number and Tonnage of Iron Vessels Built and Registered at Liverpool 1838 to 1849

Year	Number	Tonnage	Year	Number	Tonnage
1838	2	452	1844	3	538
1839	1	280	1845	4	1294
1840	2	190	1846	4	1558
1841	3	639	1847	3	471
1842	1	67	1848	1	449
1843	0	0	1849	2	145

Source: Liverpool Borough Council, *Report on Shipbuilding, 1850.*

Table 8
The Number of Colonial Built Vessels Regisered at Liverpool During the Years 1842-1846 Inclusive

	New-foundland		Canada		New Brunswick		Nova Scotia		P.E. Island		Total	
Year	No	Ton	No	Ton	No	Ton	No	Ton	No	Ton	No	Ton
1842	-	-	4	2617	3	2904	-	-	-	-	7	5521
1843	-	-	5	1896	4	1350	1	615	-	-	10	3861
1844	-	-	3	1358	6	3266	-	-	-	-	9	4624
1845	-	-	1	266	5	3325	-	-	2	293	8	3884
1846	-	-	2	1240	2	1615	1	200	-	-	5	3055

Source: House of Commons, *Accounts and Papers* (1847), LX.

A monopolist can fix the price or regulate supply; what he cannot do is dictate both price and quantity. This simple economic truth the Liverpool shipwrights learned the hard way. In attempting to enforce a closed shop, they tried unsuccessfully to control the labour supply. But the apprenticeship system was breaking down, and employers were hiring apprentices in preference to journeymen. The Society's early aggressive posturing had been supplanted by a more conciliatory tone by 1842. That August, a meeting of the Operative shipwrights met in Liverpool:

> ...to consider the just right of the men belonging to Liverpool to employment in preference to strangers...if the merchants of the town understood their own interests, they would go hand in hand with the men against the system of apprenticeship carried on in Liverpool, as the merchants were charged the same rate of wages for a boy who had not been a week at the trade, that was charged for a man and it could not be expected that the work of the boy could be compared to that of the man.[49]

Table 9
The Tonnage of Newly Built Ships Registered at Liverpool During the Year 1850

Place of Building	Tonnage	Place of Building	Tonnage
New Brunswick	14751	Barnstaple	623
Canada	7090	Bideford	285
Nova Scotia	3919	Bridport	811
Prince Edward Island	1427	Plymouth	131
Liverpool	3474	Littlehampton	230
Maryport	1716	Isle of Man	221
Workington	1188	Winsford	193
Scotland	1454	Northwich	130
N.E. England	1561	Runcorn	89
Channel Isles	1089	Gathurst	46
Belfast	1177		
		Total	41605

Source: *Liverpool Registers of Merchant Shipping*, 1850.

[49]*Liverpool Mercury*, 2 September 1842.

There is no doubt that economic distress generally was increasing during the 1840s, and the secular decline in the fortunes of the ships' carpenters was exacerbated by the cyclical depressions. Faced with underemployment it is not surprising that individual members of the Association reacted violently to any attempt by the masters to bring in strangers. In November 1842 a number of non-freemen repairing and building vessels were assaulted by shipwrights. The victims and the shipbuilders took out warrants against the ships' carpenters involved. In one incident, a man had a rope put over his head and was dragged along the ground, nearly being asphyxiated. The *Liverpool Mercury*, ever hostile to the carpenters and Conservatives, in reporting the court cases, admitted that times were hard and that there was real distress, but it blamed the carpenters for supporting the Conservatives:

> These poor short-sighted men, have for a long time, been the dupes of a party who by their restriction on trade have cramped our commerce and of course, thrown hundreds, nay thousands, out of employment. They [carpenters] were warned in time of the foolish course they were pursuing, but the tempting bribe and the influence of strong drink prevented them from paying any attention to this warning ...they are now reaping the fruits of their own folly and venality, many of them being dependent on the parish for relief and employed in breaking stones for the highways.[50]

William Rathbone, one of Liverpool's leading Reformers addressed an Anti-Monopoly meeting in the borough in January 1844. He said that in his capacity as magistrate he had to sit in Toxteth and hear cases of men who had not paid their local taxes. He claimed it was the most painful duty he had ever had to perform. Among the 130 cases which came before him were ships' carpenters, sailmakers,

---

[50] *Ibid.*, 11 November 1842. For further assault cases, see *Liverpool Chronicle*, 26 November and 17 December 1842.

ropemakers and others who were desperately poor. One young man told Rathbone he had not worked for four months, yet was being asked to pay the poor rate. His household goods were confiscated.[51] In August 1847, the ship *Endymion* was launched at the yard of Peter Chaloner in Baffin Street. Chaloner stated that of 1600 shipwrights in Liverpool, "not more than 200 of these men received constant work at five shillings a day." It is important to recognise that adding to the distress in Liverpool was the influx of famine Irish; in 1847, 296,000 landed, of whom 116,000 were paupers. During 1847, the burden of the poor rate increased significantly, partly because of the Irish poor, and the town was devastated by a typhus epidemic, colloquially referred to as the "Irish fever."[52] In such a situation unemployed workers did not have far to look for a scapegoat. Eight years later, Mr. Neill, Secretary of the Shipwrights' Association, claimed that on inspecting the building and repair yards on one Friday in January 1852, he had found only 110 men working out of 1600 shipwrights in Liverpool.[53]

All the available evidence points to the fact that over the period under review here the numbers of men described as shipwrights increased while the demand for their services declined, not simply because of economic downturns but because of the availability of new vessels and repair yards elsewhere at lower prices. Further, insofar as they were carpenters, their skills were becoming obsolete by mid-century. The advent of the steam vessel in 1815 had been followed by a steady development in marine engine technology, creating a new breed of boilermakers and related trades. In 1829, 5849 tons of steam shipping were registered at Liverpool. By 1850, the figure had risen to 11,411 tons.[54] A further technological innovation was the introduction

---

[51]*Liverpool Albion*, 22 January 1844.

[52]Neal, *Sectarian Violence*, chapter 4.

[53]*Liverpool Mail*, 29 October 1853.

[54]P.L. Cottrell, "The Steamship on the Mersey, 1815-80: Investment and Ownership," in P.L. Cottrell and D.H. Aldcroft (eds.), *Shipping, Trade and Commerce: Essays in Memory of Ralph Davis* (Leicester, 1981), table 21.

of iron-built vessels, a development which accelerated the rate of the technological obsolescence of wood. For the present discussion, the most telling statistic is that in 1866, thirty-two iron vessels were built at Liverpool, for a total tonnage of 22,631. During the same year, four wooden sailing ships were built, adding only 469 tons to the total output of the local industry.[55] Thus though wooden shipbuilding was almost extinct, the local industry, including Birkenhead, was expanding in tonnage terms as a result of iron construction. The 1871 census recorded 4143 shipwrights and shipbuilders in the borough of Liverpool. By this date the ships' carpenters were simply not an issue in local affairs.

The secular decline in the fortunes of the ships' carpenters and the situation of chronic underemployment which faced them from 1815 onwards was a factor in their attitudes towards the Irish in their midst. This was particularly the case after 1840. In many countries through to the present, economic hardship among an indigenous population is often blamed on immigrants. In the particular case of the ships' carpenters, such animosity would be more explicable if there were evidence of direct competition with Irishmen in the labour market. Clearly, some of the immigrants were carpenters, and may have sought work in the more specialised spheres of shipbuilding and repairing. Indeed, there is some reason to believe that Irish Catholics did compete. For example, after the carpenters' celebration of Royal Oak Day (29 May) in 1841, John Pheron, an Irish ships' carpenter, was asked by some English carpenters to contribute towards the expenses of the day. He refused and was beaten up.[56]

There is harder evidence of a growing threat in the form of Irish Catholic ships' carpenters. On Royal Oak Day in 1856, ships' carpenters belonging to Loyal Orange Lodge Number 31 met in Liverpool for the annual King Charles II celebrations. In a speech by Brother Clarke, a shipwright, it was claimed that of two thousand ship-

---

[55]HC, Accounts and Papers (1867), LXIII, "A Return of the Number and Tonnage of Vessels above 50 tons Built at Each of the Ports of the United Kingdom."

[56]*Liverpool Mercury*, 25 June 1841.

wrights in Liverpool, "only 350 were not Romanists." He also asserted that Catholic ships' carpenters had recently devoted a day's pay towards the building of a local Catholic church.[57] There is no way to judge the accuracy of such claims, but Clarke and another official of the lodge, Casement, were Orangemen who had been prominent members of the Shipwrights' Association; and even if not true, they believed Protestant shipwrights were under threat from Catholics.

Whatever the role of economic rivalry, it would be wrong to dismiss the expressed concerns of some ships' carpenters over the well being of the Church of England. Among the English working class there was a minority of committed Christians, Anglicans in particular, who were ferocious in their defence of a church which was seen as an integral part of the political arrangements that had made Britain great. These concerns had been inflamed by the "No Popery" campaign in Liverpool between 1835 and 1851, a period spanning not only political reform but also the influx of famine Irish. Yet it is equally clear that the expressions of outraged religious susceptibilities from Anglican pulpits legitimised less respectable shipwrights in their hostility towards the Irish. Such emotions had their origins not only in economic rivalry but also in resentments over the anti-social behaviour of elements in the Irish community, territorial claims, and a genuine but crude English nationalism, which saw the Irish as disloyal and traitorous. In addition, the pressure of living in overcrowded slums, particularly in summer, gave rise to violence between young men from both sides. Territorial gang claims were probably involved. Grafton Street was adjacent to streets, such as Crosbie Street, Jordan Street and New Bird Street, in which many south end Irish lived. The boundary was Parliament Street. In addition to such factors, there was the Orange Order and its institutionalised coat trailing on July 12, the endemic English anti-Catholicism and simple xenophobia. One can only surmise at the relative importance of these influences. After 1851, the reporting of street warfare between shipwrights and Irish became a thing of the past. Like old soldiers the ships' carpenters simply faded away, while the numbers of Liverpool Irish increased. The private battles of the

[57] *Liverpool Herald*, 31 May 1856.

shipwrights were simply part of a larger Catholic-Protestant conflict in Liverpool which lasted well into the present century. This episode in Liverpool's history serves to remind us that the maritime history of a port must include the communities that ships and shipping activities bring into being. Similarly, social historians must place the history of such communities in the context of the maritime environment in which they existed. Maritime history encompasses more than ships.

Appendix A
The Occupational Distribution of the 2247 Freemen Who Voted in the 1806 Parliamentary Election in the Borough of Liverpool

Accountants	3	Coopers	196
Anchorsmith	6	Cordwainer	7
Attorney	2	Corkcutter	6
Baker	36	Corndealer	1
Banker	6	Cornfactor	1
Banker's Clerk	3	Currier	3
Barber	8	Draper	3
Baronet	1	Druggist	4
Barrister at Law	1	Dyer	2
Basketmaker	2	Enameller	2
Bedsteadmaker	1	Engraver	2
Blacksmith	20	Esquire	30
Blockmaker	73	Farmer	2
Boatbuilder	38	Filecutter	2
Bookbinder	1	Flaxdresser	1
Book-keeper	54	Gardener	3
Brassfounder	4	Gentleman	30
Brazier	22	Gilder	1
Breadbaker	3	Glassmaker	2
Breeches Maker	3	Glazier	2
Brewer	3	Governor of the Workhouse	1
Bricklayer	52	Grocer	21
Brickmaker	1	Gunmaker	11
Broker	16	Gunsmith	6
Brushmaker	7	Hairdresser	15
Butcher	39	Hatter	26
Cabinetmaker	87	Hoopmaker	1
Calico Printer	2	Hosier	1
Captain R.N.	1	Husbandman	1
Carpenter	4	Insurance Broker	1
Carter	1	Ironfounder	2
Carver	6	Ironmonger	16
Carver and Gilder	1	Jeweller	1
Chairmaker	3	Joiner	73
Chandler	5	Joiner & Cabinetmaker	1
Cheesemonger	1	Labourer	5
China Manufacturer	4	Lathcleaver	2
Clerk	8	Letter Case Maker	1
Clockmaker	3	Linen Draper	1
Coachmaker	3	Liquor Merchant	1
Coachman	1	Locksmith	1
Medical Doctor	1	Shopkeeper	1
Marble Mason	4	Silversmith	3
Mariner	77	Slater	19

Mason	13	Slater & Plasterer	4
Mathematician	1	Smith	16
Mercer	2	Soapboiler	5
Mercer & Draper	1	Stationer	2
Merchant	194	Staymaker	5
Miller	1	Stonemason	2
Millwright	4	Sugarbaker	2
Minister	1	Surgeon	4
Nailor	5	Tailor	24
Painter	35	Tallow Chandler	10
Pawn Broker	3	Tanner	2
Pilot	28	Timber Merchant	1
Pipemaker	4	Tinman	8
Plasterer	14	Tobacconist	25
Plumber	9	Town Clerk	1
Plumber & Glazier	7	Turner	3
Pocket Book Maker	2	Upholder	12
Porter Dealer	1	Victualler	4
Potter	32	Waggoner	1
Printer	7	Watch Case Maker	2
Rear Admiral	1	Watch Engraver	2
Rigger	1	Watch Spring Maker	3
Roper	178	Watch Tool Maker	4
Saddler	15	Watch Gilder	1
Sailmaker	73	Watch Maker	17
Sailor	1	Wheelwright	3
Salt Proprietor	1	White Cooper	1
Sawyer	6	Whitesmith	10
Servant	1	Wine Cooper	1
Ships Chandler	4	Wine Merchant	1
Shipwright	246	Woollen Draper	1
Shoemaker	46	Yeoman	2
		No data	3

Source: See text.

Alfred Jones: Integration and Adversity in Liverpool

Adrian Jarvis

Alfred Jones was not a man who showed excessive human kindness towards his competitors, and this paper is certainly not an attempt to whitewash his character. Those who desire a eulogy are referred to the 220 column inches of his obituary in the *Liverpool Courier* of 14 December 1909. It may be, however, that his behaviour in seeking to control integrated activities in and adjacent to the Liverpool South Docks[1] is less unscrupulous than appears at first sight. The continuing and impressive growth of tonnage through the port of Liverpool towards the end of last century creates the image that shipowners were being provided with services at prices they would grudgingly concede were reasonable. In such an atmosphere of sweetness and light, cornering territory and integrating porterage, stevedoring, cartage, warehousing and oil milling seem highly aggressive.

That picture is erroneous: the services provided for shipowners may have been better than in some other ports, but they were not good. The shipowner had to fight to get what he wanted and needed for working his traffic. He had two principal "opponents," both of whom could reasonably be expected to see the provision of services for men such as Alfred Jones as central to their own business interests. That, however, was not how things happened.

The Mersey Docks and Harbour Board (MDHB)

For much of the period of Alfred Jones' control of Elder Dempster, the Dock Board was a highly ineffective body which allowed its meetings and those of its standing committees to become occupied with discussions of trivia to the exclusion of the issues at the heart of

[1] P.N. Davies, *The Trade Makers* (London, 1973), 124-125.

the relative decline of the port.[2] This was probably partly both the cause and effect of the absence from its membership of some of the best business brains of the time, including Alfred Jones. Yet among the trivia and indecision of the Board, there are some consistent lines of policy, one of which had an important bearing on the activities of Elder Dempster.

Ever since the widespread adoption of screw steamers, owners had exhibited a strong desire for appropriated berths in the docks. The higher costs and greater speed of discharge of steamships made faster loading and unloading both desirable and achievable, but only if the ship could go straight to a full-length side-on berth on arrival. Despite the huge expansion of the docks in terms both of water area and quay lengths, there was no time before 1914 when the Board could allocate the length of appropriated berths the owners wanted.[3] The extensive modernisation programme undertaken by A.G. Lyster under the 1898 Dock Act caused only the last of a sequence of problems created by major engineering works in the South Docks, necessitating frequent removal and exchange of appropriated berths.

In these circumstances, the Board's policy, which was probably wise, was to try to prevent any one shipping company from gaining control of an area. This was effected by providing berths which were not adjacent and by moving firms around. If a company were so fortunate as to be granted extra space it would almost invariably be by moving to a different dock rather than by the extension of an existing berth. In 1892, for example, Elder Dempster moved from Brunswick to Queens, having held the former berth for only two years.[4] It was not until 1909 that the firm finally acquired the location at West

---

[2]A. Jarvis, *Liverpool Central Docks 1799-1905* (Stroud, 1991), chapter 6.

[3]The MDHB "Berth Papers" chronicle the struggles for berths firm by firm.

[4]Docks and Quays Committee (D&Q), 12 December 1890, Maritime Records Centre (MRC), Merseyside Maritime Museum. There followed prolonged pestering for more space, and the move to Queens was approved by D&Q on 22 June 1892. On 6 July 1892, D&Q debated, but did not adopt, a proposal that Elder Dempster be requested to stop its constant requests for additional space.

Toxteth and West Harrington which it would occupy until 1963.[5] Every such change involved knock-on effects on firms holding other berths, which rippled up and down the Dock Estate, creating vast amounts of work for the Board, its standing committees and its staff (who included twenty-eight clerks to service the committees).[6] However jaundiced a view one might take of the Board's conduct of its business, it is unlikely that these regular shake-ups resulted merely from stupidity or indecision.

The Board never let slip an opportunity to show who was in charge. The most trifling alterations made by tenants at their own expense were required to be "to the satisfaction of the Engineer" and Elder Dempster was not the only firm to be peremptorily informed by the Docks & Quays Committee that their dustbins were to be removed.[7] All building maintenance was undertaken by the Board under the control of the Engineer, even in cases where the work was both urgent and trifling, such as clearing blocked gutters which caused water damage to cargo.[8] When Elder Dempster wished to instal a water supply to feed the boilers of its donkey cranes, the work was required to be done at its own expense, to the approval of the Engineer and subject to removal "whenever they may be called upon." In that case the ground had to be made good to the satisfaction of the Engineer.[9]

This policy had a number of undesirable consequences for shipowners, not least the amount of time spent by principals or senior staff in arguing with the Board over matters of little importance.

---

[5]By which time it was complaining that the transit sheds, "state-of-the-art" in 1883, were outdated. D&Q, 13 November 1963.

[6]The rules for the Architects' Competition for the new Dock Offices (1905) detail staff accommodation required; "Worked-Up Paper" (WUP) 93/1, MRC, Merseyside Maritime Museum.

[7]D&Q, 21 February 1883.

[8]See, for example, D&Q, 21 June 1893.

[9]D&Q, 18 November 1892.

Alfred Jones spent many a day this way, often attempting to gain services which the outsider would have expected him to be able to take for granted.[10] But a much more serious problem lay in the question of any sort of specialised facility. The idea of moving companies from dock to dock was only feasible when the facilities required or provided (the two were frequently rather different) were equally suitable for all trades. It was for this reason that Vestey Brothers had a long and bitter struggle before they got a cold store alongside a berth: previous cold stores had been in a variety of inconvenient places, such as the Albert Dock Warehouses, where access was via a forty-five foot half-tide entrance--a tight fit for a present-day ferry. Nelson Brothers, on the other hand, got the cold store fairly easily, but were refused an adjacent appropriated berth and had to depend on the unofficial co-operation of the Harbour Master.[11]

Alfred Jones was by and large very successful in getting what he wanted from the Board. Clearly this was in part because he was a forceful and effective negotiator and partly because the Board could not ignore his influence in the Chamber of Commerce. Most of the time the Board took little notice of representations from the Chamber, but any major financial or engineering problem--of which there were generally several--produced the equivalent of electoral "baby-kissing" when the Board needed the Chamber's support for a Parliamentary Bill.[12] It may be noted in passing that the common assumption that Board members had fingers in every pie and ears attuned to every grapevine is incorrect with regard to the Chamber: surprisingly few men were prominent in both.

---

[10]In 1882, for example, it took three attempts to get the floor of the shed at N. Coburg asphalted. D&Q, 5 April, 10 May and 20 September 1882.

[11]For a more detailed discussion of some of these problems, see Jarvis, *Central Docks*, 117-119.

[12]The great 1873 Dock Act, for example, was preceded by the publication of the proceedings of the Special Committee to Consider Dock Accommodation, which was really a trawl for witnesses to give evidence before Parliament. Liverpool Record Office (LRO), H 387.1 MER.

Figure 1: Interior view of Alfred Jones' Warehouse: the queen post trusses indicate that the building has not been fundamentally altered.

A more compelling reason, perhaps, is that Elder Dempster were an almost ideal customer. Because its ships were trading in an area where there were no large modern docks, they were neither exceptionally large nor particularly demanding as to berthing. That is why the firm was able to continue to use the obsolescent Coburg Dock until 1898.[13] To a Board permanently short of funds for modernisation, a large and highly profitable traffic which could enter a rather wretched little dock was the stuff of which dreams were made.[14] Elder Dempster's prolonged use of premises at the even more dismal River Craft Dock was money for very old rope, even before the question of cargo-handling has been considered. Because most of the cargoes were going to or from places innocent of modern methods of cargo-handling, they were largely capable of being handled with ships' tackle. Unlike some other owners, Elder Dempster was not given to churlish complaints about the excellent hand-cranes put in fifty years ago or frivolous suggestions that hydraulic cranes would be nice. While it must be admitted that on one occasion it did ask for two hydraulic cranes at Brunswick, the firm did not generally make a nuisance of itself.[15]

For the same reasons, the cargoes were usually easy to handle: the constraints at the other end favoured traditional bags, barrels, boxes, and bales. Requiring no special facilities, they could be handled at almost any berth, with the result that berth-swapping was relatively more acceptable to Elder Dempster than to some other owners. More important, perhaps, than actual stevedoring or lumping was the ease of porterage, for historically it was always the porters who were the

---

[13]The company clung to its office there until 30 June, though the ships had moved to East Queens. D&Q, 12 July 1899.

[14]For some financial effects of engineering problems, see A. Jarvis, "G.F. Lyster and the Role of the Dock Engineer, 1861-97," *Mariner's Mirror* (1992, forthcoming).

[15]The application was successful; D&Q, 20 August 1890.

bottle-necks.[16] Quayside paving and shed floors of good quality and repair were about all that was needed, although there were numerous occasions on which complaints were necessary about the lack of even this rudimentary facility.[17] This enhanced throughput and hence dues income, to the great pleasure of the Board. Although it will be suggested below that it may not have fully understood the importance of quayside work, this is immaterial in this context.

COBURG DOCK AND SURROUNDINGS c.1890

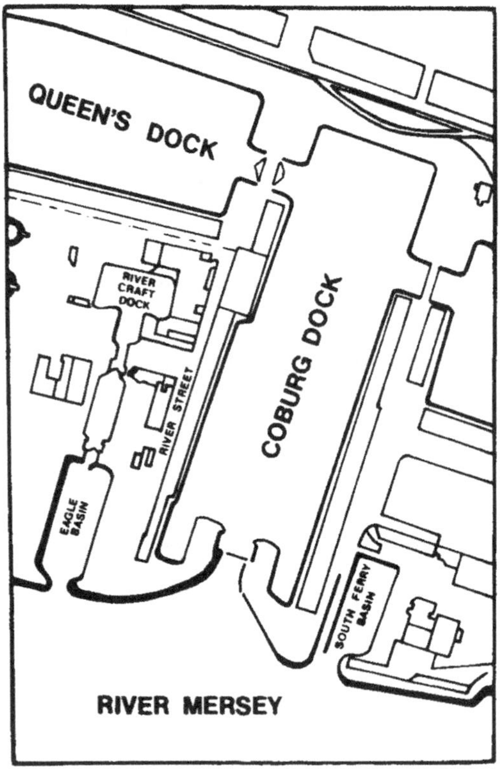

[16]J. and J.B. Hartley, *Report of the Dock Surveyors on a Proposed Plan of High Level Railway upon the Quays of Liverpool Docks* (Liverpool, 1853) gives an authoritative explanation of the prerequisites of efficient quayside working.

[17]For instance, Elder Dempster wrote to D&Q on 19 September 1896 complaining about the quayside paving at Coburg.

Figure 2:: Exterior view of Alfred Jones' Sefton Street Warehouse, May 1992.

What is beyond reasonable doubt is that Alfred Jones did. Probably the clearest expression of his views of the importance of effective quayside working in order to achieve quick turn-round may be found in his testimony to the Royal Commission on the Port of London.[18] This raises the question of whether his integration of activities around Coburg and Brunswick Docks was inspired by greed for money and/or control, as John Holt alleged,[19] or whether he was merely doing his best to overcome certain disadvantages. The Board's policy of attempting to prevent control of quaysides was bound to produce a reactive attempt to gain control. This could take the form of attempting to acquire tenure over any relevant property which might become available, as when Alfred Jones secured the site of the newly-demolished Coburg Hotel.[20] It might also take less legitimate forms, such as parking large numbers of vehicles owned by his Liverpool Cartage Company on River Street in positions that made it difficult for other carters to carry on their business. The Liverpool Cartowners Association complained about this tactic several times without gaining any sympathy or action from the Board.[21] The reason was probably that cartowners were generally believed to be extortionists at best and at worst habitual thieves: whether this was justified is hard to tell, but it was the image rather than the reality which mattered. What cannot be disputed is that the best way of guaranteeing a steady stream of empty carts arriving while a ship was discharging was to own the carts.

---

[18]Great Britain, Parliament, House of Commons, Parliamentary Papers (hereafter BPP), 1902 (1152), XLIII, 240-246, qq. 4832-5005.

[19]Memorandum by John Holt, quoted in P.N. Davies, *Sir Alfred Jones* (London, 1978), 59-60.

[20]D&Q, 13 April 1881.

[21]D&Q, Memorial from the Cartowners Assn., 13 August 1884. There were further complaints (21 April 1886) and a vote that "the matter be allowed to drop" (26 May 1886). More complaints were made on 29 October 1887 (no reply was made) and on 7 November 1887. Finally, on 23 November 1887, the Board resolved that "The Secretary [is] to inform them that the Committee are not prepared to take any action in the matter."

But the carts were only one stage of the process: the porters had to be in the right place at the right time and in sufficient numbers, and the general discontent with the master porterage system suggests again that the best way to get the job done properly (and to save a vast amount of paperwork as well) was to do it yourself.[22] Only if the porters and the carters worked properly could sufficient quay and shed space be kept clear for the flow of goods. The same applied to warehousing. There were effectively no public general warehouses on the Dock Estate: the few that had been built were alongside quays inaccessible even to the relatively modest Elder Dempster vessels.[23] If those imports which were to be warehoused had to leave the Dock Estate, the best place for them to go was to a building close to the berth, roughly level with the quayside, where work was scheduled specifically to suit the movements of the ships. Such a building was the Sefton Street Warehouse. Precisely the same argument applies to palm kernels and their speedy removal to the African Oil Mill.

One of the great problems of the older docks in the port was lack of quay space. The sailing ships for which they had been designed had relatively tiny hatches, usually at least partly obstructed by large amounts of standing rigging. Steamers could discharge at two or three times the rate of a sailing vessel of equivalent midship section, and the result was often a fearful pile-up of goods on the quayside which crept back until it obstructed the roadways.[24] At West Waterloo, a police-

[22]In 1895 the Chamber of Commerce's Dock Rates Subcommittee resolved that the Master Porterage system's "universally recognised abuses and defects," which were "exceedingly detrimental" to trade, be fully investigated. LRO, 380 COM 2/11/1, 15, 31 January 1895. Alfred Jones was present.

[23]The passage width for Albert Dock was forty-five feet; for Wapping, fifty feet; and for Stanley, fifty-one feet.

[24]Rates of discharge are thinly documented. A letter of complaint from the Liverpool Corn Trade Association dated 19 May 1900 gives figures of 318 tons per day for sailing vessels and 826 tons per day for steamers discharging bagged grain. The by-laws penalised rates of under 300 tons per day.

man was given the specific full-time task of trying to control such hazards.[25] A shipowner who was familiar with the problems of turning ships around would be foolish not to attempt to gain control of sufficient quayside to prevent this happening. In any trade which was vegetable-based, for example, there were definite seasons when every available ship came in with the new season's produce and each wanted to get away for the next cargo. The result could be fearsome congestion, as when Harrison complained of the difficulty of getting to its berth because of eleven Elder Dempster ships in Toxteth Dock, berthed five abreast.[26] The attempt to control sufficient quay space to meet such eventualities was not greed or megalomania, but common prudence.

A preliminary scan of the Elder Dempster Berth Papers gives the impression--if taken at face value--that even such a desirable customer had a fairly rough time getting quite basic needs provided. Minutes, however, can be of varying degrees of fullness, and instances may be found where the minutes relating to dealings with Elder Dempster are much briefer than usual. Meetings, reports, deputations, and memoranda are referred to without any transcription, summary, or even mention of the nature of their contents.[27] This is, of course, a well-known way of concealing what was really happening and one which had been used in some of the disputes in which Harold Littledale challenged the mode of business of the Board.[28] It is very likely that Elder Dempster was benefiting from some clandestine activities, but unfortunately the Committee Support Papers, which

---

[25]D&Q, 25 October 1876.

[26]D&Q, 6 March 1907. These particular ships were in fact idle, awaiting the season.

[27]For example, in late 1890 and early 1891 four consecutive entries in WUP 134 mentioned two letters, "reports thereon," a call for a report from the Engineer, report read, consideration postponed and never apparently taken up. Nowhere was the actual issue--Elder Dempster berths at Coburg--mentioned, and such omissions were not uncommon. D&Q, 3 December 1890, 31 January 1891, 18 February 1891.

[28]For a selection of tactics, see A. Jarvis, "Harold Littledale, the Man with a Mission" in H. Hignett (ed.), *A Second Merseyside Maritime History* (Liverpool, 1991).

would reveal their nature, survive only from the turn of the century. But if there was indeed something going on, it was as a means of gaining good and serviceable accommodation. If it were necessary to resort to subterfuge for such a purpose, that is a condemnation not of the customer but of the Board. It was not until 1890 that a Board member (and perhaps significantly it was one of the few who was also a member of the Chamber of Commerce) stated on the record that while widespread disregard for the Board's customers had been apparent for many years, nothing had been done to correct the situation.[29] Outside the Board, such things were well-known. The *Journal of Commerce*, in welcoming the election of Alfred Holt as Chairman of the Board, took the opportunity to make remarks about his predecessor, the late T.D. Hornby, which form an object lesson in how rude it was possible to be about the deceased within the rules of late Victorian decency.[30]

Railway Connections

Towards the end of last century, the Port of Liverpool showed a marked reluctance fully to exploit railway connections, especially the provision of facilities for direct discharge and loading to and from railway wagons on the quays.[31] Alfred Jones, in common with many other shipowners, not only placed great importance on quick turn-around of his ships but also was willing to sacrifice many other *desiderata*--notably cheapness--in order to achieve it.[32] It might

---

[29]Discussions at Board, 15 January 1891, Verbatim sequence, MDHB Collection, MRC, Merseyside Maritime Museum.

[30]*Journal of Commerce*, 16 August 1899. The *Liverpool Daily Post* of the same date was marginally more polite.

[31]"There are no means of communicating with ships along the quay berths, and all traffic, heavy and light, has to be carted from the railways to the ships." *Engineering* (10 September 1869), 184.

[32]BPP, 1902 (1152), XLIII, 243, qq. 4878-4882.

therefore be expected that the first rail connection to one of his appropriated berths, laid down the middle of his shed at East Queens in 1894, would be followed by a growing adoption of rail haulage. Yet as the consolidation of the cartage wing of his empire shows, this was not the case. An explanation for the reluctance to adopt methods embraced by most of his contemporaries is necessary.

But were such innovations necessarily beneficial? For bags of palm kernels, for example, the case is not clear. A good hydraulic crane could discharge several bags per minute (providing the lumpers could break it out fast enough) of a cargo which needed to be kept tolerably dry, and a well-worked berth would have sufficient cargo emerging from every hatch of the ship to fill a railway wagon in about ten minutes. If a locomotive were kept in attendance, at a cost of around 6s 6d per hour, it was under-employed. The obvious answer was an hydraulic capstan, with which two men could draw a train of wagons along the quay until it was filled, when a locomotive would remove it and replace it with a train of empty wagons.[33] The problem was that where efficient working required co-operation between what we may loosely term dock employees and railwaymen, friction and chaos were generally the result. Not until 1905, when the Board took complete control of its own railway system, did the situation improve.[34]

The continued use of horses and carts might seem a primitive expedient, but in fact had a certain amount to commend it. The cart was a very flexible means of transport, easily re-routed to avoid temporary obstructions and simply diverted from one task to another as circumstances required.[35] The transit shed fulfilled the role of the battery in a motor-car's electrical system by smoothing the peaks and

---

[33]Hartley and Hartley, *Report of the Dock Surveyors*, 5.

[34]For a succinct account, see J. Hughes, "Some Notes on the Growth of the Liverpool Dock Railways," *North Western Society for Industrial Archaeology & History Journal*, IV (1987), 31-38.

[35]Engineering work, movable bridges swung off and general quayside congestion made flexibility important.

troughs in the rate of handling goods, minimising the risk of any phase of the operation grinding to a halt and stopping all the others with it.

There were also engineering reasons for preferring not to discharge directly into wagons. The most common cause of failure of a dock wall was being burst towards the water at about one-third its height by the pressure of the ground behind it. One of the factors affecting that pressure was the load, or surcharge, on the portion of the quayside which lay between the inside face of the wall and an imaginary line rising from the foundation at the angle of repose of the ground (usually about forty-five degrees).[36] Clearly, walls could be built to stand heavy rolling loads like those of a locomotive, but if no definite benefit resulted, the risk was better avoided. The historian should avoid the trap into which Elder Dempster fell when it requested removal of an obstruction to its Coburg berth only to be informed that the hazard in question was a column holding up the shed.[37]

G.F. Lyster, the Board's Engineer-in-Chief, supported the use of railways when he thought them desirable, notably for coal export, but the list of places where he thought them undesirable was long. In 1889 he gave a paper to the Institution of Civil Engineers on "Recent Dock Extensions in Liverpool" and was taken to task in the discussion for his neglect of railway provision. His response is quite informative. He pointed out that Liverpool was a warehouse port and that imported goods "must as a rule" be moved short distances to warehouses, for which railways were of no benefit. He explained that "Most Cargoes" were made up of small parcels, so that quayside sorting was a complex task requiring the traditional transit shed at the water's edge and offering little scope for expeditious loading onto rail vehicles. Much the same applied to export cargoes, and he enlarged on the problems of getting railway vehicles to the right place at the right time.[38] He went

---

[36]For an explanation of retaining walls, see S.P. Timoshenko, *History of the Strength of Materials* (London, 1953), 47-51 and 60-62.

[37]D&Q, 10 January 1883.

[38]G.F. Lyster, "Recent Dock Extensions," *Minutes of the Proceedings of the Institution of Civil Engineers*, C (1889-90), 79-82.

on to reiterate the extraordinary statement he had made in evidence against the Manchester Ship Canal Bill: that he had had to pull up considerable lengths of railway sidings, previously laid at great expense which "were in most cases absolutely never used."[39]

The present writer has in the past questioned Lyster's competence and veracity. In this case Lyster stated that

> Another factor, telling in favour of cartage was that the quays and the streets of the town in their vicinity were very uniform in level, and the paving was generally excellent, so that the traction of road vehicles was so light as to compare favourably with rail traction.[40]

Any engineering student knew that even the best igneous cube setts did not compare in the least favourably with rails: exact values for relative rolling resistances were standard data endorsed by such bygone luminaries as Thomas Telford and Charles Babbage.[41] Some of the older parts of the estate were still paved with beach cobbles, and meetings of the Docks and Quays Committee were frequently pestered with requests from tenants for the installation of asphalt truckways to reduce rolling resistance. The levels of the surrounding roads are another example of economy with the truth, in that from the inland side of the dock road every side street rises, some steeply enough to require the attachment of a chain horse to ease the ascent of heavily-laden vehicles. In the case of the worst uphill routes it was necessary for horse-drawn vehicles to make extensive detours.

On engineering grounds, Lyster's defence of the horse and cart does not stand. But on financial grounds--that the costs of loading and unloading were so much less as to justify the slow and expensive rate

---

[39]Quoted in Sir Bosdin Leech, *History of the Manchester Ship Canal* (2 vols., Manchester, 1907), I, 305.

[40]Lyster, "Recent Dock Extensions," 80.

[41]For a summary of the topic, see W.S. Hele-Shaw, "Road Locomotion," *Proceedings of the Institution of Mechanical Engineers* (1900), 190-193.

of actual travel--he was probably right. Yet neither explanation gets to the point, which is a matter of local politics rather than engineering or commerce. Lyster, unlike the Hartleys, employed the status which came with his very large salary to mix in Liverpool's highest social circles. He was, for example, a shareholder in the Wellington Rooms, described by B.G. Orchard as the haunt "of the best fashionable society" and as the "sanctum sanctorum of our most exclusive families."[42] Those families included three Chairmen of the Dock Board among decision-makers from every sector of Liverpool trade and industry. In such company he was well able to receive and understand messages about the railway industry.

Those messages were not complicated. It was widely (and probably correctly) believed that railway companies were using the regular heavy traffic from ports like Liverpool to finance grandiose policies elsewhere, notably by adjusting rates per ton/mile to what the market would bear rather than operating on a cost plus profit basis.[43] The fact that shipowners operated in much the same way was seen as irrelevant. Railway companies, for their parts, resented people working out freight rates in terms of cost per ton/mile, a figure which they never published because it rendered invidious comparisons too easy to make. When Professor Hele-Shaw cited costs per ton/mile on the Lancashire and Yorkshire Railway in a paper read to the Institution of Mechanical Engineers, its chief engineer enquired somewhat testily about where he had obtained them.[44]

The dislike of Liverpudlians for railway companies was deep-seated. It was, after all, the Great Western Railway which had been midwife at the birth of the competitor port of Birkenhead and had

---

[42]B.G. Orchard, *Liverpool's Legion of Honour* (2 vols., Birkenhead, 1893), I, 51-52.

[43]See, for example, an open letter dated 12 March 1883 to the President of the Cotton Association which alleged that the London and North Western Railway overcharged by a factor of 450%; LRO, 380 COM 2/11/1. But complaints were long-standing; see "Select Committee on Local Charges on Shipping," *BPP* 1856 (332), XII.1, Evidence of H.W. Schneider.

[44]Hele-Shaw, "Road Locomotion," 247.

helped saddle Liverpool with a mountain of debt when the new port failed.[45] Moreover, the London and North Western Railway had developed a competitor port at Garston and adjusted rates to favour its in-house facilities, as well as annexing and modernising the Ellesmere Port docks in order to retain as much of the Black Country trade as possible. At Widnes it tried to sew up the heavy chemicals industry.[46] In 1872, it tried to amalgamate with the Lancashire and Yorkshire Railway, which produced a sufficiently serious threat to Liverpool's trade to compel the Dock Board and the Chamber of Commerce to remain on cordial terms for a whole year.[47] In short, the railway companies played an important role in Liverpool in the 1880s and 1890s: it was that of the pantomime Demon King. Anything in Liverpool's trading activities which fell short of ideal was ascribed to their wicked schemes.

Lyster's attitude mirrored many of the leading businessmen, Alfred Jones among them. They wanted the benefits of railways, but deeply disliked and distrusted the companies which provided them. Jones was not the sort of man to complain about such things from an armchair in the Conservative Club; he was a man to look into ways of improving the situation. Where appropriate, this could be done within his own business empire by centralising control and by integrating his activities in as small an area as possible, in order to minimise the need for rail transport. Perhaps John Holt did have reasons of his own to suggest that Jones's concentration of his cartage company, warehouses and oil mill within a few hundred yards of each other and of his

---

[45]This episode is summarised in F.E. Hyde, *Liverpool and the Mersey* (Newton Abbot, 1971), 83-88, 121-123.

[46]This was made possible by its control of the Sankey Canal and the former St. Helens and Runcorn Gap Railway, which had built the first specifically railway dock in the world at Widnes.

[47]Much of the mountain of paper generated survives in MDHB, Legal C6, MRC, Merseyside Maritime Museum.

appropriated berths was motivated by greed.[48] Yet it is equally possible that it was a sensible counter-measure to the power of the railways.

Alfred Holt's Plateway scheme of 1882-1883 was a fairly well-known attempt to break the railway companies' grip on traffic between Liverpool and the Manchester area.[49] Its disappearance from the scene was only temporary, for on 28 February 1896 the Chamber of Commerce formed a Light Railway Committee to investigate the same problems which Holt had addressed.[50] The City Council and the Mersey Docks and Harbour Board each made contributions of £250, enabling the employment of a full-time clerk. The Chairman was Alfred Jones, and it soon became clear that the Committee would be a sounding board for schemes, some promising and others less so, intended to harm existing railways in southwestern Lancashire. In addition to Holt's scheme, which was resurrected for the occasion, John Woods proposed up-grading Liverpool and other passenger tramway systems to carry freight and building new connections to enable through running to Manchester. In October 1896, the Town Clerk described it as "probable" that this would be implemented. E.R. Calthrop proposed an entirely new narrow-gauge railway to Manchester, which would carry laden team lorries. To the obvious objection that a team lorry weighed over one-third of its average payload, and that one would therefore be hauling an unacceptable amount of deadweight, he argued that the abolition of most of the normal terminal costs of a railway would more than compensate. Colonel Holmes proposed a standard gauge railway which would differ from existing ones was only in that it would be geared to low-speed operation and would not carry passengers, thus allowing drastic cuts in

[48]Davies, *Sir Alfred Jones*, 49-53.

[49]Hyde, *Liverpool and the Mersey*, 137. There was an enabling bill floated in 1883.

[50]Its minutes are in LRO, 380 COM 2/11/1.

signalling costs and the complete elimination of some of the usual fixed costs of a railway.[51]

Not all of the schemes proposed were sound or practical. Professor Hele-Shaw made some fairly uncomplimentary remarks about Holt's Plateway, suggesting that the entrepreneur did not really understand how a railway vehicle was steered by the rails.[52] John Woods' tramway scheme would have provoked ferocious opposition to its nocturnal noise and J. Tertius Woods' scheme for narrow-gauge railways linking existing canal basins and railways failed to tackle the basic problem. On the other hand, S.B. Cottrell, Chief Engineer of the Overhead Railway, examined and reported favourably upon Colonel Holmes' scheme and the Calthrop proposal of a roll-on, roll-off service for lorries could certainly not be dismissed out of hand.[53]

The activities of the Light Railway Committee never bore fruit, but they were neither the first nor the last such venture in which Alfred Jones was involved. Before the Committee's establishment, the Chamber had urged the Corporation to build its own line to Manchester,[54] and before the Committee's final report was published in 1898, he was active in the Liverpool Self-Propelled Traffic Association. That body is well known to transport historians as the organiser of the famous sequence of Liverpool Trials of 1898-1901, which are usually said to have proved that the steam lorry was a practical proposition. But this was not a disinterested research project in practical thermodynamics but rather another manifestation of the determination of Jones and others to cut railway costs wherever they could, in this case in cartage and terminal charges. In this context it should be remembered that, the Liverpool Cartowners Association notwithstanding, the

---

[51]Final Report of the Light Railway Committee, LRO, 380 COM 15.

[52]LRO, 380 COM 2/11/1. Alfred Holt had served his time as a railway engineer, but that had been a long time ago and Hele-Shaw's accusations seem correct.

[53]*Ibid.*

[54]*Ibid.*, entry dated 8 January 1896. Alfred Jones was Chairman.

railway companies were by far the largest horse operators in Liverpool, as they were nation-wide.

In 1904, Sir Alfred was still on the attack. For about forty years, many of the members of the Dock Board had been fixated with the problems of ship-handling to such an extent that they forgot the blindingly simple truth that docks are not for ships but for the goods the ships carry.[55] If the railways were combining against the interests of the users of the port, then goods must be moved some other way. So effective had the railway public relations machine been that canals were largely seen as obsolete,[56] but Sir Alfred was perfectly capable of seeing through such a marketing ploy and urged that attention be given to the improvement of canal transport out of Liverpool.[57] He knew well enough of the heavy investment in large canals in mainland Europe and he was also aware that while improvements to the Leeds and Liverpool Canal and to the means of getting goods to it would not damage the nationwide might of the railways, it would force them to cut prices on routes which were highly profitable. The fact that without any such improvement, the canal remained marginally competitive even after the Great War shows that he was right, but he failed to convince his contemporaries.[58]

The expenditure needed to recover the Birkenhead situation, coupled with the failure of large portions of the works under construction under the 1873 Dock Act to achieve their objectives, led to a continuing inability to provide good modern facilities for the coasting trade because any available funds were always needed to improve

---

[55]This was clearly explained a half-century before in Hartley and Hartley, *Report of the Dock Surveyors*.

[56]Hele-Shaw, deliberately seeking alternatives to railways, did not mention canals at all. "Road Locomotion," 185-190.

[57]He did this in an interview in the *Liverpool Post and Mercury*, 5 November 1904.

[58]Mike Clarke, *The Leeds and Liverpool Canal* (Preston, 1990), 228-229.

facilities for large ships.[59] The coasting trade came low in the list of priorities (indeed, it commonly seems not to have made the list at all) and the reason for its neglect was simple: the dues on coasters amounted to only a few tens of thousands per year. Such a sum would not suffice even to pay the interest cost of the improvements that were needed. A Dock Board conditioned to thinking in terms of ships rather than goods would ponder the problem no further. A customer, like Sir Alfred Jones, who was concerned with goods, saw the matter quite differently. Coasters were not part of the shipping industry, they were part of the distributive infrastructure of the port. If the dues income generated was so small it would be better not to bother to collect it: let the coasters use the port free, in order to provide a better service to the oceanic trades which were making the real money.[60] It is only quite recently that historians have realised that the coasting trade could offer far more serious competition to the railways than could canals or (for a long time) roads: Alfred Jones knew it and said so in 1904. In the process he demonstrated one of the qualities of a great entrepreneur: the ability to cut through decades of accepted "wisdom" to what was actually the point at issue.

By the standards of some of the relatively obscure millionaires who feature in W.D. Rubinstein's pages,[61] Alfred Jones' rise to riches was certainly impressive, but fell rather short of astonishing. His rise to power and influence was another matter altogether, and his vertical integration may be seen as placing power before profit. When he built the African Oil Mill, for example, the recent history of the local seed pressing trade did not inspire confidence. A spate of liquidations in the 1870s had been followed by a decade in which not a single successful new plant was started,[62] and the prospects of upsetting the dominance

---

[59]For some of the problems, see A. Jarvis, *Central Docks*, 122-127.

[60]See note 57.

[61]W.D. Rubinstein, *Men of Property* (London, 1981), 97-101.

[62]W.H. Brace, *History of Seed Crushing in Great Britain* (London, 1960), 139-144, lists the Liverpool mills.

of traditional centres like Hamburg or Hull seemed minimal. But if control was what he wanted, then the very weakness of the Liverpool industry at that time became an advantage. The oil mill remained under the control of his successors until 1916, when it was sold to the Cooperative Wholesale Society, which continued to expand and modernise it until its eventual closure in 1970.

There is indeed a great divide between the behaviour of Alfred Jones in his dealings in Liverpool and the image of the man conjured up by his memorial at Pierhead. Though the expression "strenuous in business" used in the inscription might be euphemistic, he sought to exert control over every aspect of the trades in which he engaged, and not always by very scrupulous methods. The evidence from two areas of his dealings suggests, however, that his methods were not gratuitously aggressive, but were made necessary by those around him. It is possible that had he behaved otherwise he would never have achieved the prominence to qualify for his memorial--or that it might have stood in some other port.

The *Mary* and the *Lady Lansdowne*

Michael K. Stammers

Besides his other scholarly achievements, Peter Davies has played an important role in the study and management of Liverpool's underwater maritime heritage. He has served as the northwestern adviser to the Council for Nautical Archaeology and has represented Liverpool at international conferences of this new discipline. His two most significant achievements are the excavations of the Royal Yacht *Mary* and the paddle steamer *Lady Lansdowne*.

The wreck of the *Mary* was discovered on 11 July 1971. Unknown to each other two groups, comprised of divers from the Chorley and Merseyside branches of the British Sub-Aqua Club, discovered a number of bronze guns on a site close to the Skerries Lighthouse, approximately seven miles off Holyhead, Anglesey. The finds were reported to Peter Davies and it quickly became clear that both were working on the same important site. Within two days Peter had organised the competing groups to work in harness and arranged a panel of historians and archaeologists to identify the wreck and to advise on suitable methods of excavation and recording. He also negotiated with the local Receiver of Wrecks to ensure that the finds were taken to the Liverpool Museum for proper storage.

All went well at first: the pre-disturbance survey was undertaken and a large number of objects on the seabed were mapped. But the lure of bronze guns and the possibility of other precious material was strong, and rivals soon invaded the site, removing a number of items, including some guns which were later recovered. It became clear that a systematic excavation was impossible in the circumstances and the operation had to be transformed into a rescue mission to save the artifacts from looting. From the location, inscriptions on the guns and large number of seventeenth-century coins, it became apparent that this was in fact the wreck of the first English royal yacht.[1]

The *Mary* had been presented by the city of Amsterdam to King Charles II on his restoration to the British throne in 1660. Indeed, two of the cannons recovered bear the city's coat of arms. The vessel has considerable significance, not only because of royalty but also as the first craft designed for leisure sailing in English waters. She did not last long as a yacht and was soon replaced by a series of English-built craft, but she certainly established the idea of yachting as a pastime. Transferred to the Royal Navy for use as a despatch vessel for mail and government servants, she was used extensively on the passage between Dublin and Dawpool at the western end of the Dee estuary. On her last voyage she was sailing from Dublin with a crew of twenty-eight and forty-six passengers, including the Earls of Ardglass and Meath and the latter's son, Lord Ardee. On 25 March 1675, at about 2 AM in thick fog, she struck a rock on an outlying islet of the Skerries and began to sink. As she settled she began to list heavily and her long mast touched the rocks, enabling thirty-nine of those on board to scramble to safety. But thirty-five, including the captain, the bosun and the Earl of Meath, were lost. The remaining survivors endured two days' exposure on the rocks before being rescued.[2]

Besides the ten guns, the site in 1971 consisted of a large area of concretion embedded in a sloping gulley. This concretion, which was gradually excavated over the next twenty years, yielded a rich selection of silver coins, gold jewellery, silver fittings of weapons, and domestic items, such as pewter plates and cutlery. Some of the latter were stamped with the captain's mark. These were all indicators of the wealth and the importance of those on board. Fortunately, due largely to Peter's efforts, most of this material was recovered and kept as an integral collection. Merseyside Maritime Museum has charge of it and

---

[1]For a full account of the discovery see P.N. Davies, "The *Mary*, Charles II's Yacht. I. The Discovery of the Wreck," *International Journal of Nautical Archaeology and Underwater Exploration*, II, No. 1 (March 1973), 59-60.

[2]"G. Place Parkgate and the Royal Yachts," *Transactions of the Historic Society of Lancashire and Cheshire*, CXXXVIII, (1988), 67-71.

a selection of the best items is permanently on display in the Museum's Safe Passage gallery at Albert Dock, Liverpool.

The rescue phase of the excavation lasted until the end of 1972, but it subsequently changed into a more systematic programme under Peter's guidance. He also arranged financial support for the diving group from the Friends of Merseyside Maritime Museum. This lasted until 1991 and it is very much to his credit that a group of volunteer divers was held together over this long period to work carefully on a very difficult and dangerous site.

But perhaps the most important outcome of the *Mary* excavation was its influence on the policy for the preservation of Britain's underwater maritime heritage. When the wreck was discovered, there was no legal protection for it and other wrecks of similar national importance. As a result of the discovery, this problem was brought into prominence in the press and several times in Parliament. Ultimately this led to the passage of the Protection of Wrecks Act of 1973, which empowered the Secretary of State and Trade to designate the site of important wrecks to protect them from unauthorised salvage. The *Mary* was the first of these designated wrecks and the Royal Yacht Mary Archaeological Team under Peter Davies was the first group to be licensed to work on such a wreck.

Peter's investigation of the wreck of the *Lady Lansdowne* was of a different character. The existence of the wreck of an iron paddle steamer lying alongside the banks of the River Shannon at Killaloe had been documented.[3] Its location suggested that it was the remains of the *Lady Lansdowne* of 1833. If this could be proved it would be of great interest not only for the history of navigation on the Shannon but also for the archaeology of the earliest iron boats and ships. The first iron boat may have been constructed as early as 1744, but it was in the first decade of the nineteenth century that a growing number of iron barges and canal boats began to be built.[4] The first iron steamer was

[3]V.T.H. Delany and D.R. Delany, *Canals of Southern Ireland* (Newton Abbot, 1966), 174.

[4]R. Barker, "John Wilkinson and the Early Iron Barges," *Journal of the Wilkinson Society*, No. 15 (1987), 15-16.

the *Aaron Manby* of 1821, which was prefabricated by Aaron Munby of the Horseley Iron Company, Staffordshire. It was assembled and launched on the Thames, crossing the Channel in 1822 for service on the Seine. A second boat was built in 1822-23 and shipped to France for assembly; two more were entirely built there. The same company manufactured the *Marquis of Wellesley*, a twin-hulled boat assembled at Liverpool in 1824-25 for use on the Shannon. A second steamer for the same river was built in Liverpool by the iron founders and engine builders Fawcett Preston and Company in 1829.[5] In 1831, Macgregor Laird built the iron paddle steamer *Alburkah* at Liverpool to explore the possibilities of inland navigation and commerce on the Niger and the Benne.[6] The builder was the second son of William Laird, who was already in business as a boilermaker at Birkenhead. In 1829, Laird Sr. had assembled a prefabricated iron lighter for Charles Wye Williams's Inland Steam Navigation Company to operate on the Shannon in conjunction with the two iron steamers. An order for two more vessels was completed in 1832 and they in turn led to the building of the *Lady Lansdowne* in 1833.[7] She was the fifth English iron steamer built and considerably larger than her predecessors, measuring 133 feet long by seventeen feet abeam.

Peter Davies visited Killaloe in April 1967 to examine the wreck. It quickly became apparent that the only way to confirm the identity of the vessel was to have an accurate survey by a team of divers. On his return to Liverpool, Peter contacted the Liverpool Sub-Aqua Club and recruited eight experienced divers for an expedition which took place early in July 1967. The wreck was first recorded by underwater cinema and still photography. She was then accurately measured, which proved her identity beyond all doubt. It was also established that the paddles, engines, boiler, deck and superstructure

---

[5]J. Grantham, *Iron as a Shipbuilding Material* (London, 1842), 6.

[6]P.N. Davies, *The Trade Makers: Elder Dempster in Africa 1852-1972* (London, 1973), 35-38.

[7]Foster Petree, "J. Charles Wye Williams, A Pioneer of Steam Navigation," *Transactions of the Liverpool Nautical Research Society*, X (1971), 15-16.

were missing. Nevertheless the remaining portion of the hull provided important information about early techniques of iron shipbuilding. A number of artifacts were discovered inside the hull, including brass portholes, fire bars, fire irons, a spanner, a steam valve, a section of lead pipe and mast fittings. The most interesting item recovered was a Cantrell and Cochrane mineral water bottle which contained two pieces of paper with the names written in ink of "John McEvoy Killaloe 30/7/67" and "John Brosnan Killaloe 30/7/67." The names were common in the district and it was possible that the two were responsible for her partial scrapping and scuttling in 1867. The bottle was buried deep in the silt, on the floor of the engine room. It therefore seemed unlikely that it had drifted into the wreck.[8] The bottle and a selection of the other finds have been conserved and displayed in the Laird section of the Builders of Great Ships gallery of Merseyside Maritime Museum where they serve as tangible reminders of the important and largely disregarded role of Merseyside shipbuilders in the development of iron ship construction. Pioneer inland steamers like the *Lady Lansdowne* developed local skills; within ten years of her launch there were three yards building iron sailing and steam ships for deep sea trade. Local expertise and in particular the work of John Grantham, a Liverpool naval architect and shipbuilder, assisted the spread of iron shipbuilding to other industrial centres.

Peter Davies' contribution to nautical archaeology in the United Kingdom has been important--and not just because of his investigations of nationally-important vessels. His enthusiasm and knowledge have influenced sport divers in Liverpool and elsewhere to view shipwrecks through the eyes of an archaeologist rather than a looter. While there is still much to be done in this infant area to educate divers and document key key sites, Peter Davies must be recognised as an important pioneer.

---

[8]P.N. Davies, "An Expedition to Identify and Survey the Wreck of the Paddle Steamer *Lady Lansdowne*," *Transactions of the Liverpool Nautical Research Society*, X (1971), 22-26.

Merchants from Sail to Steam: The West Australian Shipping Association and the Evolution of the Conference System, 1884-1910

Frank Broeze

> The Association is not regarded as a fighting power, but as a very powerful body for maintaining peace...It is not our policy to start an opposition if it can be avoided.[1]

Rarely can one see the conservative conference ideal expressed more clearly than in these simple lines by William Marden, the London manager of the West Australian Shipping Association (WASA). Remarkably, these were the sentiments not of a complacent steamship company director but of the ambitious representative of an organisation of importers in Australia, a country which took little active part in its own overseas shipping. During the next twenty years or so a strong nationalism arose in the country against the supremacy of foreign--predominantly British--shipping, leading to several parliamentary investigations, the adoption of the Navigation Act (1912-21), the establishment of a Commonwealth-owned shipping company and strong support for the Imperial Shipping Committee. The fact that the WASA favoured agreements, conferences, and active cooperation with British shipping interests makes it a remarkable exception.

---

[1]William Marden to West Australian Shipping Association, 18 April 1902 and 16 January 1903, Acc. No. 2478A, West Australian Shipping Association [hereafter WASA], State Archives of Western Australia, Perth [hereafter SAWA].

Indeed, the West Australian Shipping Association was an exceptional phenomenon in world shipping history.[2] It was an organisation of colonial merchants established in response to the complete dependence of Western Australia on a small group of British shipowners and brokers for its main shipping link between London and Fremantle. Formed in 1884 by a group of local entrepreneurs, the WASA boldly entered the loading business at London. After two years of bitter warfare an agreement was signed with the London brokers by which the WASA gained a significant share in the trade and a voice in policy-making. Moreover, its London manager became the combine's secretary. From its platform in the London-Fremantle trade the WASA in due course also became party to agreements covering Liverpool and Glasgow, Hamburg and the continent, and New York. Not surprisingly, many conflicts arose within the WASA as well as between the Association and its partners and between the combined operators and outsiders. The WASA not only was unable to maintain all it had gained but also in 1905 was subjected to what its directors called the "inquisitorial inquiries" of a thorough and well-informed Royal Commission.[3] Yet by 1910, when Marden died, the Association had achieved both internal and external stability. That year thus forms a suitable closing point for the following analysis of its development.

The scope of operations and performance of the WASA, especially when viewed against the failure of many similar organisations

[2]Until 1888 the WASA was a mere association of individuals: in that year it was incorporated as a private company with limited liability as the West Australian Shipping Association Ltd.

[3]WASA to Marden, 1 January 1906; WASA, IX, SAWA. The result of the investigation was the *Report of the West Australian Royal Commission on Ocean Freights* (Western Australia, *Votes and Proceedings* [1905], I). Very little attention was paid to Western Australia by the British Royal Commission on Shipping Rings and the only relevant evidence was given by White Star Line director, H.A. Sanderson (*Report*, [London, 1909], IV, qq. 18512-16, 18523-26, and 18623-30).

elsewhere,[4] was remarkable. Its financial success was revealed by the Royal Commission. Between 1889 and 1904 the Association made profits of £110,000 on a paid-up capital of about £4,000,[5] an average of well over 170% per annum. Amazing as these profits were, they also were paradoxical since they resulted from high freight rates enforced by a closed monopoly of loading brokers--the very situation the Association had been established to fight! From its records it is clear that the leaders of the WASA believed they could most effectively influence freight rates and shipping services in general by taking an active part in them.[6] Whether they were correct to follow this "window" strategy[7] must remain a moot point; what I wish to investigate here is the role of the WASA in its double identity as shippers' organisation and loading broker and on the two main trade routes in which it actively operated: London-Fremantle and New York-Fremantle. It is true that Western Australia, as Australia in general, was notoriously late to achieve the full transition from sail to steam and that its liner trades displayed several quite unique features, such as the inclusion of sailing vessels in conference agreements and the presence of the WASA. Nevertheless, the main findings may have considerable general value

---

[4]Well-known are the failures of the Assam tea merchants between 1875 and 1896 and Lancashire textile exporters in the early 1880s (through the China Mutual Steam Navigation Company) to break the hold of the shipping conferences covering their trades; see Francis E. Hyde, *Shipping Enterprise and Management 1830-1939. Harrisons of Liverpool* (Liverpool, 1967), 71-74; and Hyde, *Blue Funnel. A History of Alfred Holt & Company of Liverpool 1865-1914* (Liverpool, 1957), 70-75.

[5]Western Australia, *Votes and Proceedings* (1905), I; *Report of the West Australian Royal Commission on Ocean Freights and Insurance*, 25.

[6]See, for example, WASA, Annual Report, 1890-1891, WASA, XLVIII, SAWA ; Advisory Board London to WASA, 18 September 1903, WASA, XXVII, SAWA; and the evidence given to the Royal Commission on Ocean Freights by J.H. Payne (*Report*, qq. 1446-47), W. Sandover (q. 3418), and E. Allnutt (q. 4016).

[7]Cf. Keith Trace, *Shipping Links between Australia and Japan: An Analysis of Current Problems and an Agenda for Further Research* (Canberra, 1977), 31.

and validity for our understanding of the operations and dynamics of shipping conferences in general.

First, however, it may be useful to sketch the organisational structure of the WASA. From the beginning, its functions revolved around two poles: its directors in Fremantle and its manager in London (the daily business in Fremantle was run by the Secretary). The five (later seven) directors were elected from the general membership, which by 1890 numbered about fifty individuals and firms. Ten years later, when membership was temporarily closed, there were about sixty-five members.[8] This flexible membership policy proved highly successful. In 1905 the WASA directors estimated that members controlled approximately two-thirds of all freight carried from London and New York to Fremantle. As the remaining third was contributed by a large number of small shopkeepers and others with annual volumes of less than seventy tons each, the directors felt they did not need to worry about opposition.[9] As London manager of the WASA William Marden had two principal responsibilities.[10] First, he operated the Association's shipbroking business, chartering the necessary vessels, advertising, collecting cargoes and supervising their loading and despatch. Second, he conducted all negotiations leading to the agreements which incorporated the profit-sharing arrangements and other methods to regulate competition between the various participants. Strong-willed, shrewd, cool-nerved and meticulous in his administration of the financial affairs of the various combines, Marden rapidly assumed a distinct and prominent "shipping personality." Not surprisingly, this in turn contributed to the adoption of a more independent outlook and stance which at times brought relations with the board close to the breaking point. This led the board in 1901 to

[8]"Register of Shareholders," WASA, XLI, SAWA.

[9]WASA to Advisory Board London, 9 October 1905, WASA, XXX, SAWA.

[10]On 1 January 1903 Marden took his son-in-law W.F. Marden Ranger in partnership in his firm which was now styled W. Marden and Co. For simplicity's sake I shall continue to refer to the firm as "Marden;" from the contents of its correspondence it is evident that the firm's views continued to be shaped by the elder man.

appoint an Advisory Board at London.[11] Marden, interestingly, did not regard this as a hindrance but rather as a more effective means of demonstrating to the directors that he was making the right decisions and that they could leave the interests of the WASA in his hands.[12] In future years the Advisory Board played a significant if controversial role: while it sometimes bypassed Marden to act directly for the WASA board, on occasion it also supported him. In 1905 the Advisory Board refused to carry out the directors' instructions to sack Marden and, through diplomacy, probably saved the WASA from self-destruction.

Since the 1840s the London-Fremantle trade was dominated by W. Felgate and Co.[13] From the early 1870s this firm also acted as the London emigration agents for the W.A. government. Felgate did not own any ships but chartered from a small number of owners, above all J. Wilson and Co.[14] The fleet occasionally included vessels registered at Fremantle, such as the *Amur*, owned by Bateman, Marmion and Pearse, or Walter Padbury's *Bridgetown* and *Charlotte Padbury*. During the late 1870s several new owners entered the trade. C. Bethell and Co. (from c. 1890 Bethell Gwyn and Co.) and Trinder Anderson and Co., both also active in the trade to eastern Australia, were keen to move into the loading business and established a virtual duopoly when

---

[11]WASA to Marden, 5 August 1901, N 16, WASA, V, SAWA.

[12]Marden to WASA, 6 September 1901, N 36, WASA, V, SAWA.

[13]Frank Broeze, *Western Australia until 1869: The Maritime Perspective* (Nedlands, 1984), 1-15.

[14]Graeme Henderson, "From Sail to Steam: Shipping in Western Australia, 1870 to 1890" (Unpublished MA thesis, University of Western Australia, 1977), chapter 5, discusses the shipping trade between Britain and Australia and the founding of the WASA. See also John Bach, *A Maritime History of Australia* (West Melbourne, 1976), 167-171.

financial difficulties forced Felgate and Wilson in 1882 to retire from the business.[15]

The London brokers naturally used their power to bolster freight rates to provide shipping services convenient to them rather than a dozen colonists. They used a fleet of about a dozen sailing vessels, including several regular wool-carriers, supplemented by the occasional chartered vessel. From 1883 they also began to load steamers. Vexed by the high freights charged by the monopolists, a number of Fremantle merchants, led by John Wesley Bateman, founded the WASA.[16] Bateman also planned the Association's strategy: to enter the chartering business in London in opposition to the established brokers and to offer space at lower rates than currently charged, thus forcing the general level downward. The main strategic asset was the ability of the Association's members to control their imports and the power they had to direct them away from the combine's ships to those chartered by the WASA. But success depended on several factors: the ability of the WASA to charter suitable tonnage, the need to control a sufficient volume of imports to fill the ships, the loyalty of the members if the London brokers decided to retaliate and lower their freight rates below those charged by the WASA, and the presence in London of an energetic and capable manager.[17]

---

[15]The two other loading brokers in the trade, Edelsten and Co. and Macnamara, loaded only a few ships and both retired in 1883. Macnamara was bought out and in 1901 still received pay-outs from the combined brokers (Marden to WASA, 20 December 1901, N 68, WASA, VI, SAWA). In their places as minor participants came Anderson Anderson and Co. and Gavin, Birt and Co.; typed memorandum "Western Australia," Mss.13 [hereafter Marden Papers], SAWA.

[16]In the historiography several myths have been perpetuated about the origins of the WASA, and especially about Marden's role. The surviving letters from 1883-1884 between Batemen and Marden (in the Marden Papers) leave no doubt that Bateman took the initiative in the manner while Marden was in England contemplating his future.

[17]For a discussion of the loyalty of the members and the relationship between the WASA and its manager, see my "'A Great Frankenstein': The West Australian Shipping Association 1884-1906," in Frank Broeze (ed.), *Private Enterprise, Government*

By June 1884 Bateman and his group had signed up twenty-eight "bona fide" importers. Of the colony's large firms only those with direct ties to the London brokers and shipowners (Geo. Shenton, J.H. Monger, Parbury Loton and Co., and W.D. Moore and Co.) remained outside.[18] The WASA could now begin operations, but that of course had to be done at London. Two months earlier Bateman had offered the position of London manager to Captain William Marden, a close friend and associate who had decided to retire from the sea.[19] Marden (1843-1910) had considerable experience in the West Australian trade and enjoyed Bateman's full confidence. His task was to charter ships to carry the importers' goods at lower rates than did Trinder Anderson and Co. or Bethell Gwyn and Co. In August 1884 the campaign started when Marden chartered the *Mira Flores* and soon followed with the *Charlotte*. As expected, a fierce rate war developed which proved costly to the WASA and severely tested the loyalty of its members. As Marden later remembered, although some stood firm around Bateman other members were "mere sitters on the fence."[20] In June 1884 Oliver Trinder travelled to Western Australia to crush the colonial rebellion, but if anything his mission served to strengthen the resolve of the WASA members. "We are determined to run it or *bust* as you express yourself," Bateman wrote Marden.[21] Trinder did

---

and Society (special issue of *Studies in Western Australian History* [1992], forthcoming).

[18]Bateman to Marden, 21 June 1884, Marden papers, SAWA.

[19]Marden first visited the colony in 1863 with the ill-fated barque *African* which was wrecked at Geraldton. Since the early 1870s he had sailed regularly between Western Australia, southeast Asia and China, often carrying sandalwood cargoes for Bateman. In early 1883 his *Catherine Marden* was sunk after a collision with a steamer on the Chinese coast and he retired to London.

[20]Marden to WASA, 4 May 1906, N 422; WASA, IX, SAWA.

[21]Bateman to Marden, 15 August 1884, Marden Papers, SAWA.

not help his cause by describing Western Australia as a "d---d swindling hole"[22] and ultimately made the WASA a compromise offer.

The fight, however, was far from over and for some time freight rates plummeted to ten shillings per ton on general cargo (against forty shillings and more before the WASA was founded). Attempts were also made to lure Marden away from the WASA by offers of a steamer's command and "another Plum."[23] Although the Association lost over £450 in its first year,[24] most members accepted Bateman's argument that the benefits of low freight rates far outweighed those losses: "the indirect profit is the actual profit."[25] The WASA's control over a large share of the colony's imports from Britain and its continued chartering of ships in opposition to the London brokers forced the latter to accept its terms. The outcome in early 1886 was an agreement between the WASA and the established brokers which remained the backbone of Fremantle's trade with Britain.[26] Indeed, there were no major disturbances in the London trade until well into the 1920s when the WASA changed over to the Aberdeen and Commonwealth Line.[27]

Instead of fighting the monopolists, the Fremantle merchants had joined them. What they hoped to achieve with this move was expressed in specific terms in the agreement's preamble:

---

[22]Bateman to Marden, 29 August 1884, Marden Papers, SAWA.

[23]Bateman to Marden, 22 November 1884, Marden Papers, SAWA.

[24]Balance Sheet, WASA, 30 June 1885, Marden Papers, SAWA.

[25]WASA to Marden, 11 October 1884, Marden Papers, SAWA.

[26]No text of the agreement has been preserved; the first complete agreement is dated 11 December 1888, after the WASA had become a limited-liability company (the texts of all WASA agreements are copied in WASA, XXXVII, SAWA).

[27]Agreement, 8 October 1928, WASA, XXXVII, SAWA. Ironically, after the break-up of the Royal Mail Group the A&C Line in 1933 came under the joint control of Furness Withy and Co. and P&O, from the latter of which the WASA had "escaped" in 1928.

> [to work] the shipping trade with Western Australia in the most advantageous way *to all those interested or engaged* in it. With this object it is intended to maintain a regular and sufficient supply of sailing ship tonnage on the berth, to distribute tonnage in such a way as to avoid waste, and *to regulate by a just tariff the rates of freight* and dates of departure generally... (author's emphasis)

Together with the London brokers the WASA chartered and loaded the necessary ships and fixed the freight rates. Although the WASA for the time being was to be excluded from the steamer business, it received a certain compensation for goods diverted from sailing vessels (up to a maximum of £40 per steamer). Profits (and losses) were pooled and distributed according to a formula which gave 7/24th to the WASA, with the rest to be distributed between Trinder Anderson and Co., C. Bethell and Co. and Anderson Anderson and Co.

For an understanding of the business it should be stressed that although both Trinder and Bethell owned a number of vessels themselves which as "regular traders" had a recognised entitlement to be chartered and until 1893 received preferential terms, the combine chartered tonnage at market rates. In principle it operated like a modern NVOCC (Non Vessel-Owning Carrying Company), offering a one-way sailing schedule of rough regularity. Ships only sailed when full, but if necessary cargo was bought by the WASA or individual firms to top the holds. The partners also aimed at always having a vessel on the berth, but occasional gaps occurred when regular traders were expected and no outside ship was laid on in the meantime. The profits of the combine came from the difference between the charter price paid for each ship and, after deduction of all expenses, the freight charged to shipper.[28] The situation in the steamer trade was very similar, with the exception that the WASA until 1893 had no

---

[28]This also meant that efficient stowage commanded a considerable premium. Roughly estimated, a sailing vessel could load twice its regular tonnage in freight tons, but careful attention could lead to additional revenue. In 1889, for example, Marden managed to load, on the same draught, one hundred tons more on the *Colleen* than the previous year (Marden to WASA, 20 December 1889, WASA, LV, SAWA).

direct share in it. The loading business in London was divided between the firms according to a complicated formula. The WASA, Trinder Anderson and Co. (TA) and C. Bethell and Co. (CB) each had a ship in turn, while Anderson Anderson and Co. (AA) loaded every sixth ship. The other firms compensated for this by in their turn postponing their entitlement to the next ship. A cyclical rhythm of eighteen ships was thus constructed: WASA, CB, *TA*, *WASA*, CB, AA, TA, *WASA*, CB, *TA*, *WASA*, AA, CB, TA, *WASA*, CB, TA, AA. The reality was even more complicated, as the *Charlotte Padbury* was always loaded by Trinder and the *Annie McDonald* by the WASA. Not surprisingly under these conditions, in 1890 Anderson "somewhere lost a turn" and had to be compensated.[29]

The agreement specifically enabled the combine to operate a deferred rebate system "for the protection of the trade." Moreover, the London brokers were free to return to their customers "an amount which they may consider fair as to put them on an equal footing with members of the WASA." As a shippers' organisation, the WASA returned most of its profits to its shareholders: twenty percent to each according to the number of shares held and sixty percent to the members that had contributed freight to the ships of the combine, according to the amount of freight paid. The remaining twenty percent was paid into a reserve fund. Because these profits were generated from chartering, which required only small long-term investments and modest liquid funds at any one time, the high dividends that so amazed the Royal Commissioners could be paid. Significantly, the spontaneous reaction of several witnesses, when informed of these profits, was to want to join the Association![30]

When in 1896 the combined London brokers entered an agreement with loading firms in Liverpool and Glasgow to regulate the trade to Fremantle from these ports, the WASA retained its 7/24th share of the London proportion of the profits to be divided. In the case

---

[29]Marden to WASA, 2 May 1890, WASA, LVII, SAWA.

[30]For example, W.J. Splatt (q. 1225), and Benjamin Rosenbaum (qq. 1279 and 1283).

of Liverpool that proportion was 43/64th, in Glasgow 35/64th. Should a vessel require loading at both ports profits (or losses) went 30/64 to London, 21/64 to Glasgow, and 13/64 to Liverpool. This agreement also incorporated the indirect trade via Singapore, from where the West Australian Steam Navigation Company (owned by Trinder and Bethell in combination with the Fremantle firms Geo. Shenton and Co., W.D. Moore and Co., and J. and W. Bateman)[31] and the Ocean Steam Ship Company ran steamers to Fremantle. A supplementary agreement was concluded in 1901, and peace was maintained until after the Great War.

After the heat had been taken out of the London trade,[32] relations between the partners were generally cordial. In 1888 the WASA was transformed into a company which on 10 July 1889 reported its first profits of £211.[33] This figure could have been considerably higher but for an unprofitable contract to carry rails and railway material for the Great Southern Railway Company (Albany-Beverley) which the joint brokers had taken up to keep these large volumes out of the hands of outsiders. Their aggressive search for such contracts at competitive levels remained an important tactic of the combine in defence of its position.[34] It also undermined the case of the opposition in the Royal Commission, as the Western Australian government and major contactors in this fashion were able to pay far lower freight rates for mass shipments than those charged for ordinary trade goods.

---

[31]John Maber, *North Star to Southern Cross* (Prescot, 1967), chapter 37.

[32]Marden for a few seasons tried to interest his principals in also taking up the homeward loading of wool to put additional pressure on Trinder and Bethell, but after a few desultory attempts the Fremantle merchants gave up the business.

[33]WASA, LXVIII, SAWA; see also Marden to WASA, 10 October 1889, WASA, LV, SAWA.

[34]See, for example, Marden to WASA, 25 October 1901, N 47, WASA, V, SAWA, regarding the vital importance of capturing a contract for American rolling stock, including Baldwin steam locomotives, for the W.A. government railways.

From the beginning of the combine part of the London-Fremantle trade was carried in steamers chartered by the London brokers. Initially, the WASA was excluded except for a certain compensation paid for cargo diverted from sailing vessels. Although sailing vessels and steamers in principle competed for the outward trade to Fremantle, with the cheaper and bulkier goods generally travelling by sail, there were fundamental differences in the structure of the sail and steamer trades. Sailing vessels were despatched with full cargoes for Fremantle; they either loaded for home in Western Australia with wool--the true "regular traders"--or found return cargoes in Asian or South American ports as had been the rule with most arrivals from Britain since the foundation of the colony in 1829.[35] Steamers, by contrast, had only part of their holds engaged for Western Australia (occasionally goods were taken for Albany as well as Fremantle) and continued with the remainder of their cargo to eastern Australia. Trinder, for example, operated an outward service which ran from London to Fremantle, Hobart and Fiji.[36] Most of the steamers were employed in the London-Fremantle trade (and later also the New York-Fremantle route) as an alternative to going to eastern Australia directly. Their return voyages were also made from eastern Australia, including Port Pirie as well as the large general ports of Sydney, Melbourne, Adelaide and Brisbane, and sometimes New Zealand. For a long time no steamer returned directly from Western Australia and such employment remained exceptional as mail steamers and not ordinary cargo liners later took the Fremantle wool trade away from the regular sailing vessels.[37] The fact that Fremantle to a certain

---

[35]See Henderson., "From Sail to Steam," chapter 5; Broeze, *Western Australia until 1869*; and Frank Broeze, "British Intercontinental Shipping and Australia 1813-1850," *Journal of Transport History*, New Series, IV (1978), 189-207.

[36]Maber, *North Star to Southern Cross*, chapter 29.

[37]Wool from outports, such as Geraldton, Carnarvon, and loading places further north, were increasingly taken by steamer to Singapore and transshipped to Britain. Besides the extensive WASA correspondence see also Christopher Fyfe's excellent *The Bale Fillers. Western Australia Wool 1826-1916* (Nedlands, 1983), chapter 8.

extent received an overflow of steamer tonnage proceeding to the eastern colonies had important repercussions for the London-Fremantle trade as steamers gradually increased their share.

By 1889 Marden pointed out to the WASA that the compensation clause in the agreement with the London brokers left it but a passive player in the steamer trade. The problem for the WASA was that at this stage it was "very difficult to force their [the brokers'] hand, because of the limited amount of steam tonnage required for your ports, there is no opportunity afforded of bringing pressure to bear by putting on a steamer in opposition."[38] He felt, however, confident "to succeed some day in obtaining in this business a fair and proper footing."[39] Marden's tactical problem, how to put pressure on Trinder and Bethell, became more difficult as the steamers in the Australian trade rapidly increased in size, so that there was ever less prospect of a steamer being exclusively loaded for Fremantle.[40] But the rapid growth of the trade in the early 1890s and the control the WASA exerted over Western Australian imports enabled him in May 1893 to conclude a new agreement which also covered the steam trade.[41] As the steamers, however, did not load exclusively to Fremantle the WASA's share of steamer profits was fixed at only twenty percent, about two-thirds of its 29.2% in the sail trade.

During the boom of the following years the WASA reaped rich profits. These increased sharply from £912 in 1894 to over £12,000 in 1897 and until 1904 fluctuated between £8,500 and £15,000.[42] The tremendous boost given to Western Australia's population, consumption, production and construction of all kinds through the gold discoveries in the Yilgarn, foremost the rich Coolgardie and Kalgoorlie

---

[38]Marden to WASA, 29 November 1889, WASA, LV, SAWA.

[39]*Ibid.*

[40]Marden to WASA, 8 June 1894, WASA, I, file 1, SAWA.

[41]WASA, XXXVII, folios 16-21, 9 May 1893, SAWA.

[42]*Report of the Royal Commission on Ocean Freights*, appendix VI.

fields, was translated into unprecedented demands for imports. The building of its new harbour (opened in 1897)[43] enabled Fremantle gradually to lose its reputation as a slow and dangerous port. But as steam was replacing sail as the main vehicle for the import trade the overall share the WASA obtained from its profits steadily diminished. In 1897/98 steam overtook sail when nineteen steamers arrived from London against eighteen sailing vessels.[44] These were halcyon days for Western Australia and the country in general. Several new companies moved into the trade. The entry of the White Star Line was smoothed with an agreement restricting it to calls at Albany at rates to be fixed in arrangement with the combine.[45] Also Alfred Holt's Ocean Steam Ship Company, which in 1900 began direct sailings from Liverpool and Glasgow to Australia, was accommodated in an "exceedingly satisfactory" agreement.[46] By contrast, German competitors always caused concern. Two German steamship companies operated to Australia, the subsidised Norddeutscher Lloyd (North German Lloyd, NDL) of Bremen and the Hamburg-based Deutsch-Australische Dampfschiffahrt-Gesellschaft (German Australia Line, DADG), which threatened to divert cargoes from London. Although agreements were concluded with the German lines in 1897 and 1898, the latter also including the indirect trade via Singapore,[47] the WASA was thoroughly alarmed when the DADG agent in London suggested to Bethell Gwyn "a

---

[43]Patsy Brown, "Western Australian Merchants and Political Agitation: The Struggle for Fremantle Harbour in the late 19th Century," *The Great Circle*, XII (1990), 73-94.

[44]Director's Report for the year to 30 April 1898, WASA, XLVIII, SAWA.

[45]Marden to WASA, 6 October 1899, WASA, IV, file 3, SAWA. See also Trinder to Marden, 20 November 1901, WASA, VI, SAWA.

[46]Marden to WASA, 9 November 1900, WASA, V, SAWA.

[47]WASA, XXXVII, folios 30-34 and 39-41, SAWA. The agreements in the continental trade with Australia, including W.A., are covered in Otto Harms, *Deutsch-Australische Dampfschiffs-Gesellschaft, Hamburg* (Hamburg, 1933), chapter 8.

combination in Hamburg and London to smash the Association."[48] Although this danger was averted by personal diplomacy,[49] the DADG always loomed threateningly over the horizon.[50]

The irony of the *modus operandi* of the London brokers and the WASA was that they made their best results during the years of shipping depression, when charters were cheap and plentiful, whereas boom times caused acute problems. As changes in freight rates lagged behind fluctuations in the shipping market, 1902 and 1903 yielded record profits, while the Boer War reduced profits to the lowest levels since 1896. In December 1900, at the height of the Boer War, the combined along with Birt Potter and Hughes (which as successors to Gavin Birt and Co. had gained a place in the combine)[51] was forced to purchase the iron barque *Desdemona* to maintain sailings.[52]

At the same time the brokers had been unable to obtain a steamer: "we are somewhat in a hole, rates are going up considerably and there is difficulty in obtaining suitable tonnage."[53] As the disputes in the New York trade (see below) suggested, many of the issues turned around control of and/or access to steamer space. Evidently, the WASA had to seek a more active and larger share of steamer traffic. At the same time, the accumulated profits in its reserve fund (well over £10,000) gave it the means to underwrite new initiatives.

From the late 1890s two major, mutually-reinforcing trends had become visible in British shipping which forced the WASA's hand. The

---

[48]Marden to WASA, 24 February 1899, WASA, III, file 2, SAWA.

[49]Marden to WASA, 6 October 1899, WASA, IV, file 3, SAWA.

[50]See, for example, Marden to WASA, 22 November 1901, N 60, WASA VI, SAWA.

[51]The new firm resulted from the amalgamation of the interests of Allport and Hughes, John Potter and Co., and Gavin Birt and Co.

[52]Marden to WASA, 15 December 1899, WASA, IV, file 2, SAWA.

[53]*Ibid.*

first was a process of concentration,[54] most spectacularly exhibited by the formation of the Morgan Trust and evidenced in the Australian trade by Bethell and Birt Potter and Hughes' Federal Steam Navigation Company, its subsequent alliance with Houlder Brothers and Turnbull Martin and Co. in the Federal-Houlder-Shire Line, and the purchase of Geo. Thompson's Aberdeen Line by the White Star Line (itself part of the Morgan Trust). Second, many steamship owners began moving into the loading business or, conversely, brokers joined forces with owners or began to build up their own fleets. Typical was the establishment by William Lund and Co. of the Blue Anchor Line. Both trends combined in the Federal Line. The net effect of all these developments was that considerable pressure mounted on "pure" loading brokers like the WASA for which the right to participate in combines and conferences could easily be denied by the new breed of powerful steamship owners. By early 1903 Marden had crystallised the main elements of the strategy he believed the WASA needed to follow. Rejecting options like expanding the WASA's loading business into the eastern states' trade, Marden believed that the Association's best chances lay in "forming a West Australian Line in conjunction with our London friends, using the steamers either from New York or this side [London] as required."[55] Although at the time the market for steamships was depressed, Marden believed that future investments would be safe and profitable.

The WASA Board in Fremantle was sufficiently impressed with Marden's ideas to send Director Alfred Sandover to work out the details of the Association's plunge into shipping. As Sandover soon realised, the WASA had no choice if it wished to remain a force in the trade. The London brokers recognised that it was "essential that they should not be dependent upon chartered boats, and that it is absolutely

---

[54]Frank Broeze, "Distance Tamed: Steam Navigation to Australia and New Zealand from its Beginnings to the Outbreak of the Great War," *Journal of Transport History*, New Series, X (1989), 15.

[55]Marden to WASA, 16 January 1903, N 186, WASA, VII, SAWA.

imperative that they should make a start with owning their own steamers."[56] They would go ahead, irrespective of any action by the WASA. If the WASA stayed out, its "interest in the steamship trade would be very much reduced, or possibly cancelled altogether."[57] But the brokers could not exclude the WASA if it were interested, and "once admitted as such our position should be practically assured." The investment would retain the WASA's presence in London and its capability to influence events:[58]

> As long as the Association has an interest in this business they are naturally listened to in their suggestions for reductions in freight, but directly the Association is out of the trade we should have the greatest difficulty in getting freights kept to a fair level.

The return on this investment, of course, could not be expected to exceed that of any other sound shipping enterprise, but the main purpose was to maintain the WASA's presence in the trade; to be admitted was "more important than the matter of ultimate profit."[59]

The Board acknowledged that the sailing vessel was rapidly being phased out (the last was chartered by the WASA in January 1906) and had no hesitation in taking up the twenty percent share in the new Australind Steam Shipping Company which the London brokers, confirming the WASA share in steamer profits, were willing to give. Shareholders unanimously backed the policy and the decision to finance the required £30,000 from the reserve fund and a new share issue.[60] The Federal Steam Navigation Company, which had resulted

---

[56] Sandover to E. Allnutt [Chairman, WASA], 3 July 1903, WASA, XXVII, SAWA.

[57] Advisory Board London to WASA, 18 September 1903, WASA, XXVII, SAWA.

[58] *Ibid.*

[59] Sandover to Allnutt, 3 July 1903, WASA, XXVII, SAWA.

[60] WASA to Advisory Board London, 14 December 1903, WASA, XXVII, SAWA.

from a similar strategy decision of loading brokers, served as a clear example to the WASA and its partners. It financed its expansion after the initial investment entirely from cash flow. Paying no dividends for several years,[61] by 1904 this company had built up a "a fleet of eleven cargo-passenger vessels of the most modern type."[62] The strategic plan for the Australind Co. foresaw a gradual increase of its fleet to six steamers. Its capital of approximately £150,000 would be called up successively for the financing of its first three vessels while the further three steamers were to be paid for out of profits, with a modest dividend being paid to shareholders.

Between 1904 and 1906 this strategy was implemented as in regular succession the *Australind*,[63] *Ashburton*, and *Arrino*, all of about 5,500 gross registered tons (grt), were introduced. Within a few years they were followed by the *Armadale* and *Ajana*. While the vessels were conceived as sisterships, there were considerable improvements in the *Ashburton* compared to the *Australind* in performance and appearance --at least that part which symbolised the determination of the WASA to possess an active stake in steam shipping. Instead of the "abortion" on the *Australind*'s funnel, the second steamer sported a representation of the West Australian flag with a proper "black swan" in the centre.[64] Although there were occasional problems with the regularity of service and homeward employment of the Australind vessels, they had cemented the place of the WASA in the London-Fremantle trade. Later, when the company came into the sphere of the New Zealand

---

[61]Sandover to Allnutt, 3 July 1903, WASA, XXVII, SAWA.

[62]Maber, *North Star to Southern Cross*, 255.

[63]Not to be confused with the *Australind* of 1886, with which the West Australian Steam Navigation Company had opened its steamer service between Fremantle and Singapore.

[64]Advisory Board London to WASA, 11 August 1905, WASA, XXX, SAWA. Directors described the *Australind*'s swan as a "monstrosity;" WASA to Advisory Board London, 23 October 1905, WASA, XXX, SAWA.

Shipping Company and the P&O, the WASA's position remained secure.

The experiences of the WASA in the New York trade in this period were totally different from those on the London-Fremantle run. In part this was caused by the lower volume of trade and the prominence of case oil, and partly by the different nature of the loading business at New York. Marden had chartered the first ship for the WASA from New York in early 1889 but conflicts with the largest Fremantle importer, Wm. Sandover and Co. (otherwise a perfectly loyal supporter of the Association), prevented any working arrangement being reached until 1894. The main problem in New York was that the loading of sailing ships was not in the hands of professional brokers as in London. Instead, a small group of merchants and commission agents, such as Arkell and Douglas, R.W. Cameron and Co., Henry W. Peabody and Co., and Mailler and Quereau, handled both trade and shipping. Initially, Marden was able to reach agreement with Peabody (Sandover's agents) and Cameron,[65] but the rapid growth of the West Australian trade gave ample opportunity to the other American firms to press their claims. Railway iron and mining machinery in particular created demand for shipping space and, as deadweight cargo of great volume, also made it attractive for steamship owners to enter the trade. Moreover, at New York it was often difficult to charter sail for Fremantle, as few vessels of suitably moderate size were available (the chartering for large ships for more than one part was impossible) and considerable prejudice against Fremantle existed.[66]

---

[65]Marden to WASA, 8 December 1893 and 5 January 1894; WASA, I, file 4, SAWA.

[66]Captain Nourse, for example, whose ships came to America from India with coolies for the West Indies, found Fremantle "unacceptable" (Marden to WASA, 14 February 1896, WASA, I, file 2, SAWA), while for the owners of the *Clock*, Fremantle was "taboo altogether" (Marden to WASA, 30 March 1900, WASA IV, file 2, SAWA).

Out of this interplay of forces originated the first complex agreement in the New York-Western Australia trade, "SAVOY."[67] Signed for a duration of six years, it united ten signatories of vastly different nature:

Table 1
The "Savoy" Agreement, 1899

Signatory		*Share in Pool*
WASA Ltd.		33.75%
William Marden		7.50
Bucknall Brothers		
Federal Steam Nav. Co. Ltd.		
Houlder Bros. & Co. Ltd.		
Henry W. Peabody & Co.	"Cecil"	50.00
Arkell & Douglas		
R.W. Cameron & Co.		
Mailler & Quereau		
London Westralia Group		8.75
	Total	100.00%

Through the active cooperation of its members, Sandover and D. and J. Fowler Ltd., both major importers from New York, the WASA had been able to obtain an even larger share than in the London trade. With its 7/24th share of the London Westralia Group (the London-Fremantle combine) and Marden's share, it stood to receive over forty percent of the profits. Exactly one-half was reserved for "Cecil," the combination of three London steamship companies and four New York merchant houses-cum-loading brokers. The London Westralia Group obtained its share as compensation for giving up the right to carry

[67]The text is in WASA, XXXVII, folios 42-45, SAWA. It was named after the Savoy Hotel where the agreement was concluded on 14 February 1899. Cf. the origin of the name "Davis" for the conference to the eastern colonies; Bach, *Maritime History*, 160.

American cargoes to Fremantle via London; in practise it was pure income for doing nothing. To the WASA Board, which disagreed with several of the clauses of the agreement, Marden responded that "non-acceptance now would certainly result in a disastrous fight against a very powerful combination,"[68] and that "our trade from America would surely in the end have been lost."[69]

A vital ingredient in the creation of this coalition of disparate forces was its assumption of a contract for thirty-one thousand tons of steel plates for the West Australian Goldfields Water Scheme. This, however, was not sufficient to create a permanent bonding of interests and in 1901 "SAVOY" broke up.[70] The crucial factor was that the New York merchants refused to be subordinate to the London steamship owners and became determined to establish their own shipping line.[71] As a result of the high costs of American shipping this could not be achieved with national tonnage but had to involve a coalition with other British shipowners. A rate war, which raged between the Tyser and Federal Lines in the trade between Britain and the eastern states, could thus easily spill over to New York.[72] In June 1900 Tyser advertised that it would load in New York in opposition to the Federal Line and its partners, Houlder and Bucknall. If the WASA did not play its cards right, it was in danger of being squeezed out altogether.[73] But the Association was in a very awkward position. As the WASA had no ships of its own it was totally dependent on the goodwill of its London steamship-owning partners; at the same time,

---

[68]Marden to WASA, 10 March 1899, WASA, III, file 1, SAWA.

[69]Marden to WASA, 20 April 1899, WASA, III, file 1, SAWA.

[70]WASA, III, files 3-6, contain numerous letters on the problems in the American business.

[71]See especially Marden to WASA, 11 May 1900, WASA IV, file 1, SAWA; 2 November 1900, WASA, V, SAWA.

[72]*Ibid.*

[73]Marden to WASA, 4 May 1900, WASA IV, file 1, SAWA.

most WASA members obtained their imports from the United States through the New York agency houses which wanted to break with the British companies. Under these circumstances it was of vital importance for WASA members to maintain a united front in support of these London "friends." Marden and the WASA also considered whether it should open an independent office in New York,[74] but a personal visit by Marden convinced him that there was not enough business to warrant the expense.[75] A cautious policy of trying to maintain good relations with all parties failed dismally and when Tyser and the American brokers organised the regular United States and Australian Steam Ship Company (US & ASSCo), Marden was forced to cast the WASA's fate with the London Group.

On 1 January 1902 the new agreement "LAWS" was signed between all "SAVOY" partners minus the four American brokers. In the new pool the WASA and Marden increased their shares to 35 5/8 and ten percent, respectively, while the three steamship companies received 45 5/8 percent. The London Westralia Group retained its 8 3/4 percent for doing nothing. Significantly, the steamship owners as successors to "Cecil" did retain fifty percent voting power. As a full-scale rate war broke out, which in effect was to last until 1906,[76] the new agreement never worked properly. Several prominent WASA members supported the opposition, including Chairman J.W. Bateman who in consequence was forced to resign. As the Federal Line and its allies regarded the Wets Australian business merely as an adjunct of the larger trade to the eastern states,[77] they refused to match the number of sailings offered by the US & ASSCo. But, at the same time, it became clear to Marden that the WASA chartered its Fremantle

[74]See, for example, Marden to WASA, 22 November 1901, N 58, WASA, VI, SAWA.

[75]Marden to WASA, 7 February 1902, WASA, VI, SAWA; 20 November 1903, N 254, WASA, VII, SAWA.

[76]WASA to Advisory Board London, 13 August 1906, WASA, XXXII, SAWA.

[77]Marden to WASA, 16 June 1904, N 295, WASA, VIII, SAWA.

space from its partners at excessively high rates. Not only was the Association unable to match the rates offered by the opposition, but all it was doing, he claimed, was "to put money in the pockets of our partners."[78]

Although the Fremantle directors tried to contain the trouble, Marden insisted on submitting the WASA claim against the steamship owners to arbitration and attempted to renegotiate the agreement. Convinced that Allan Hughes, the Federal Line's leader, was determined to push it out of the trade,[79] he proposed that the WASA work with both the London Group and the US & ASSCo.[80] The arbitration award fully vindicated Marden's position, awarding the WASA slightly more than it had claimed,[81] but it only served to further worsen the relations between the partners. Partly to solve these questions and partly to negotiate a new contract between the WASA and Marden, Director G.F. Moore travelled from Fremantle to London. Convinced that no agreement could be reached with the steamship owners if Marden were involved, he negotiated without the manager's knowledge. But his inexperience and lack of toughness showed in the resulting understanding (no formal document was signed). Instead of gaining an active voice in the conduct of the trade through participation in the chartering business and a share in the pool profits, the WASA in future received merely a percentage of the freight.[82] As

---

[78]Marden to WASA, 24 July 1903, N 231, WASA, VII, SAWA.

[79]Marden to WASA, 8 July 1904, N 278, WASA, VIII, SAWA.

[80]Marden to WASA, 20 November 1903, N 254, WASA, VII, SAWA.

[81]Marden to WASA, 8 January 1904, N 264, WASA, VIII, SAWA.

[82]The text of the correspondence involved is in WASA, XXXVII, SAWA.

Marden had foreseen,[83] the WASA became marginalised and soon lost its identity in the trade.[84]

Hughes' cancellation of "LAWS" also had dire consequences for Marden, who was entirely shut out from the new agreement and thus lost his independent position and ten percent of the New York profits.[85] Marden applied for an injunction to force the partners to continue to trade under the conditions of "LAWS," but in the Court of Appeals Hughes' extraordinary argument--that "LAWS" had in fact never existed because the London Westralia Group had neglected to sign it--was accepted.[86] Marden then moved to claim damages and ultimately the WASA and its partners paid him £700 compensation for lost income.[87] The differences between Marden and the WASA, however, remained as deep as ever and were publicly aired by Advisory Board member William Sandover in his evidence to the

---

[83]Marden to WASA, 8 July 1904, N 278, and 14 July 1904, N 302, WASA, VIII, SAWA.

[84]See, for example, WASA to Advisory Board London, 25 September 1905, WASA, XXX, SAWA; WASA to Advisory Board London, 12 April 1906, WASA, XXXI, SAWA; and Marden to WASA, 16 February 1906, N 412, WASA, IX, SAWA. The ambitious Hughes made a brilliant career culminating in a long-standing Chairmanship of the New Zealand Shipping Co. The Tyser Line in 1907 strengthened itself through an alliance with the German DADG when that strong company opened a New York-Australia service; *Report of the Royal Commission on Shipping Rings*, IV, qq. 14570-72.

[85]As I have suggested in "A Great Frankenstein," the opportunity to take away Marden's independence was a powerful factor in the WASA's willingness to compromise with Hughes and his fellow steamship owners.

[86]Marden to WASA, 12 August 1904, N 311, WASA, VIII, SAWA. As can be imagined, the court verdict with its insights into an intra-conference fight became a titillating piece of evidence before the West Australian Royal Commission of 1905 and was printed in the *Report*, 28-31.

[87]Advisory Board London to WASA, 3 November 1905, WASA, XXX, SAWA.

Royal Commission.[88] Marden's refusal to reply to some letters of the WASA and his withholding of some WASA funds convinced the directors to terminate the Marden's contract.[89] Fortunately for both Marden and the WASA, the Advisory Board at the eleventh hour was able to achieve some extent of reconciliation. In fact, with the irreversible surrender in the American trade, the successful introduction of the Australind Steam Shipping Company in the London trade, and the collapse of colonial opposition after the Royal Commission, the WASA and its London manager for the first time reached the relative stability of calmer waters.

When Marden died in 1910 he was genuinely respected and mourned by all who knew him.

> The dear old Captain...I know I voice the feelings of not only my co-directors but of every member when I say...that we feel one and all that the success of (the WASA) has been achieved so largely by the energy and ability that he displayed in guiding its business in London.[90]

Marden indeed had been as successful as possible in protecting the interests of the WASA with the weapons at his disposal. Without ships, it was control over cargo that counted. This the WASA members could deliver, as long as they remained loyal. But during the 1890s the *status quo* was strongly challenged by dramatic changes in both shipping and the W.A. economy. While the transition from sail to steam could be managed in the London trade, it made extremely difficult demands on the WASA in New York. Only patient and subtle negotiations could safeguard its position when the local brokers with whom Marden had originally dealt were pushed aside by a new breed of aggressive British

---

[88]See *Report Royal Commission on Ocean Freights*, qq. 3421-39; and Marden to WASA, 9 February 1906, WASA, IX, SAWA.

[89]WASA to Advisory Board London, 14 August 1905, WASA, XXX, SAWA.

[90]A. Sandover to H.F. Marden Ranger, 10 April 1910, Marden Papers, SAWA.

steamship companies and their agents. Against Marden's wishes and judgement, this position was given up after Moore's secret intervention in 1904. Whether he would have been able to do much better is doubtful. By contrast, the WASA successfully made the transition to steam shipping in the London-Fremantle trade, albeit as a minority partner in a London-based company.

Marden always clearly recognised the need to think ahead of developments: "...we have to recognise that steamers will sooner or later call at Fremantle and it will be decidedly cheaper to arrange terms for the future before they have made a start and obtained a footing."[91] And he was always supremely confident that he could achieve satisfactory agreements: "It would not suit the interests of the Association to be pressed into a conflict. They are quite willing to negotiate with me, and I am certain that in the end I can reserve the Association its full share of the loading business..."[92] The very nature of the WASA made it imperative to think about agreements in order to secure its business on a permanent basis.[93] Marden's twin credo was the need for agreements and his conviction that a formula could always be found to satisfy all participants. In order to find that agreement he was willing to play hard: "I like a little fighting, but I also like a little peace."[94] But one had to pick the right ground to fight: "What I want to see is the Association progressing and not frittering away money in useless opposition."[95]

What should be stressed is that Marden operated from an extraordinary base which, if not handled carefully, could easily lead to the total collapse of both the WASA's standing in the trade and the Association itself. The situation of the WASA was all the more

---

[91] Marden to WASA, 22 July 1898, WASA, III, file 3, SAWA.

[92] Marden to WASA, 22 Novmeber 1901, No. 58, WASA, VI, SAWA.

[93] Cf. Marden to WASA, 13 January 1899, WASA, III, file 2, SAWA.

[94] Marden to WASA, 11 July 1890, WASA, LVIII, SAWA.

[95] Marden to WASA, 17 November 1893, WASA, I, file 3, SAWA.

precarious since especially in America but also in Britain the shipping business was revolutionised by new demands resulting from modernisation and the rapid expansion of the economy. This concerned not so much the great increase in ordinary imports as a result of population growth (although these also had to be managed), but more particularly from the huge contracts from mining and major infrastructure works such as the railways and, above all, the goldfields water scheme. For the latter some sixty thousand tons of steel plating and eight thousand tons of steel rods for the manufacture of the pipe was required, and later several thousands of tons of pumps and other machinery. Such huge contracts could make the ordinary flow of commodities pale into insignificance and, if taken up by outsiders, throw the trade wide open. Marden and his partners were prepared to fight hard for these contracts and if necessary to take them at losing rates.[96] As a result few outside steamers gained entry into the trade and those were largely boycotted by WASA members who did not want to jeopardise their deferred rebates. Because Fremantle was relatively small, the WASA operated in an environment where very little could remain secret. When Marden proposed that the Association expand its operations to the eastern colonies, he firmly believed that the import trade there simply contained too many firms to make it possible to form effective shippers' organisations.[97] Moreover, the Fremantle Board kept "in touch" with government departments which were induced to change their orders from c.i.f. to f.o.b. so that they could control shipments and ensure they were carried by ships chartered by

[96]See, for example, Marden to WASA, 18 October 1901, N 45, WASA, V, SAWA, regarding the shipment of rails, wagons and locomotives from New York.

[97]See, for example, Marden to WASA, 16 January 1903, N 186, WASA, VII, SAWA. Cf. the evidence given by E.B. Tredwen to the Royal Commission on Shipping Rings about the [British] Australian Merchants Association (which had not even attempted to come to an agreement with the combined steamship companies) and the Importers' Association of Victoria (*Report*, IV, qq. 14531 and 14614-6).

the WASA and its partners.[98] As Marden emphasised, "it is to the interests of all concerned that they [government] should be treated with the utmost liberality."[99]

The position of the WASA and its British partners in the London trade was so strong that considerable opposition arose within the Fremantle Chamber of Commerce.[100] Soon afterwards, with the full support of the W.A. government, a Select Committee and then a Royal Commission were established to investigate the high freight rates between London and Fremantle. In its report the Royal Commission found that the combine had failed to pass on the benefits from Fremantle's new harbour in lower rates on general imports;[101] in consequence, Western Australia was severely disadvantaged compared to the eastern states.[102] Ironically, the fierce rate war in the New York trade, where the WASA had been reduced to virtual powerlessness, accentuated the gap between what critics believed represented ordinary market rates and those charged by the London monopolists. The Royal Commissioners also discovered that the combine had employed the controversial deferred rebate system without, it appears, informing many shippers.[103] None of the WASA's commercial practices, however, were illegal and despite all criticism nothing changed.

---

[98]Marden to WASA, 18 October 1901, No. 45, WASA, V, SAWA. C.i.f. costs included insurance and freight, leaving control over the actual shipment in the hands of the exporters or manufacturers, while f.o.b. stands for free on board, which leaves control over shipment to the importer.

[99]Marden to WASA, 6 September 1901, No. 37, WASA, V, SAWA.

[100]See, for example, *Morning Herald*, 18 April 1903.

[101]The *Report* failed to mention the competitive rates accepted by the combine for special contracts, such as those for the goldfields water scheme or the W.A. government railways.

[102]*Report of the Royal Commission on Ocean Freights*, 5-6, 8.

[103]*Ibid.*, 12.

The history of the WASA provides considerable insights into the complex process of the transition from sail to steam in the British and American trades to Fremantle and a unique inside account of the prevailing commercial conditions. Its role as an NVOCC chartering tonnage on the open market illuminate a vital stage in the evolution of both shipbroking and liner shipping which has yet received very little attention. Its contribution to our understanding of the dynamics of the conference system lies above all in a comparison of the different experiences of the WASA in its two areas of operation and the agreements and combines which attempted to rule the trades. It needed peace to thrive. Even more than Marden, the directors in Fremantle were unwilling to fight. The well-nigh permanent peace in the London trade, after the WASA had fought its way in, was diametrically opposed to the turbulence in New York. Its investment in the Australind Steam Shipping Company confirms that the changeover to steam was indispensable to its survival as a loading broker,[104] a position which both directors and Marden held to be vitally important if they were to maintain their influence. Where their views differed was that Marden, in order to establish his independence, attempted to obtain a separate position in the Australind Co., to which the directors were resolutely opposed. They thus prevented their manager from turning the WASA into a London-based shipping operator which in due course might well forget its colonial constituents and *raison d'être*.[105] The fact that the WASA continued to operate until well after World War II suggests that at least for its shareholders the "window" strategy was the most effective way of minimising freight costs. Even so, it should not be overlooked that members, who controlled Western Australia's imports, could pass on most of their costs to the consumer. As Royal Commissioner Diamond put it: "[T]he good old milk cow, the working man, has to stand it."[106]

---

[104]Cf. Tredwen's evidence in *Report of the Royal Commission into Shipping Rings*, IV, qq. 14680-95.

[105]Cf. Broeze, "'A Great Frankenstein.'"

[106]*Report of the Royal Commission on Ocean Freights*, q. 1686.

The Making of a Maritime Firm: The Rise of Fearnley and Eger, 1869-1917[1]

Lewis R. Fischer and Anders M. Fon

On 12 February 1869 Thomas Fearnley, a twenty-eight year-old Norwegian recently returned from abroad, dispatched a circular letter to a number of contacts both within and without Norway announcing that he was establishing a "chartering and agency business" in Christiania (Oslo).[2] While the notice did not state explicitly that the new enterprise would specialise in shipping-related activities, prescient observers certainly could have made the inference. One clue was in the two references that Fearnley chose: N.A. Andresen and Company, Christiania bankers who also owned ships, a forwarding agency and a soap factory, and Rücker Offor and Company, London shipbrokers. The second clue had to do with what Thomas Fearnley had been doing for the previous four and one-half years. During that time he had been

[1]This paper is part of two larger projects. The first is a history of Astrup Fearnley, being written in collaboration with Helge W. Nordvik, Gunnar Nerheim and Even Lange. The second is a larger international history of shipbroking being written by the senior author. We would like to thank our colleagues for assistance with some of the conceptual problems relating to this study. In addition, several past and present employees at Fearnleys, especially Birger Nossum, former head of Fearnresearch, have helped in a number of ways. We acknowledge support for this project from both Astrup Fearnley and from the Social Sciences and Humanities Research Council of Canada.

[2]The notice did not mention shipbroking in particular, likely because entrance into this profession in Christiania was restricted by law between 1818 and 1871. See Birger Boquist (ed.), *Norsk Skibsmæglerforbund 1919-1969* (Oslo, 1969), 19.

in London, learning the practice of shipbroking from Rücker Offor and making a number of contacts in the shipping world.[3]

From this modest beginning evolved first Thomas Fearnley, agent, and then Fearnley and Eger, formed in 1874 when Fearnley invited his cousin, Engelhardt Eger, to become a partner. While focusing on shipping, Fearnley and Eger was willing to diversify into any business that promised a reasonable return on investment. Indeed, in the first half-century the company acted as an representative for a variety of life and marine insurance companies,[4] sold shipbuilding and chandlery supplies on commission, and invested in timber and manufacturing industries. Yet its core activities were always maritime. Eventually two separate firms emerged. One was Astrup Fearnley, the parent company of what is today Norway's oldest shipbroking firm and the largest privately-owned maritime brokerage company in the world.[5] Also springing from these roots was Fearnley and Eger, a major shipowning enterprise that was rocked by the shipping crisis of the 1970s and finally succumbed to financial problems in 1991. The two firms were in fact one until 1917, when the broking arm was devolved into a separate entity; indeed, until 1972 the two enterprises,

---

[3]Norwegian Public Record Office (Riksarkivet), Fearnley and Eger Collection (hereafter F&E). Since this collection is currently being organised, no references will be given to box numbers, which are intended to be only temporary.

[4]Fearnley and Eger represented at least four insurance firms before founding its own insurance firm, Fearnley and Egers Assuranceforretning, in 1916. By 1874 the firm had become the Norwegian agent for one of the leading Swedish insurance companies, Sveriges Allmänna Sjöforsäkrings-Aktiebolag; two years later, it became the agent for both Norway and Sweden for the Scottish Imperial Insurance Companies. The firm also came to represent two Norwegian marine insurance companies, Den Gjensidige Dampskibsassuranceforening of Grimstad and Den Vestfoldske Skibsassuranceforening of Tønsberg.

[5]Most large shipbroking firms are in fact owned by the brokers. What makes Fearnleys unique is that even in 1992 it is entirely owned by a single individual, Hans Rasmus Astrup.

while in theory separate, were united by a common board and common ownership.[6]

This paper seeks to explain the growth of the firm from its founding to the formal division of the shipowning and brokerage companies. During these years Fearnley and Eger became one of Norway's most important shipowning and shipbroking enterprises. By the time western Europe erupted into flames in 1914, the firm was Norway's seventh largest shipowner, with shares in nineteen vessels possessing carrying capacities of 32,005 gross tons.[7] It is not possible to be quite so precise about its position in broking, but as early as 1882 the firm had surpassed the most established broker, Ferdinand Breda, in wealth, and the next year exceeded its rival in income.[8] On the eve of World War I, Fearnley and Eger was most likely the largest shipbroker in Christiania.[9]

---

[6]On the shipping company, see especially Gunnar Christie Wasberg and Kaare Petersen, *Fearnley & Eger 1869-1969* (Oslo, 1971).

[7]By the measure of tonnage owned, Fearnley and Eger trailed only Wilhelm Wilhelmsen of Tønsberg, Thomas Fredrik Olsen of Christiania, A.F. Klaveness of Lysaker, Brusgaard, Kiøsterud and Company of Drammen, Det Bergenske Dampskibs-selskab of Bergen, and Otto Thoresen of Christiania. See J.M. Worm-Müller (ed.), *Den norske Sjøfartshistorie* (Oslo, 1951), II, part 3, 357.

[8]Oslo Byarkiv, Likningsprotokoll, various years. These taxation lists provide information on both income and estimated wealth for most years. While they do not enable any precise division between broking and other kinds of income, given that all the brokers about whom we have any information were, like Fearnley and Eger, involved in a number of different activities, the data can be used as a rough guide to the relative importance of various firms.

[9]Since the tax lists only specify income and wealth for firms, and do not show the precise activities that generated them, it is impossible to be completely certain about rank of shipbrokers. All of the Christiania shipbrokers about whom we have any information invested in ships as well as pursuing broking activities; what we do not know is the exact proportion of income and wealth generated by non-broking endeavours. This conclusion is therefore based on our general knowledge of Christiania broking rather than precise quantitative sources.

How did the company manage such a meteoric rise? While the answer to this question is complex, an examination of the process underscores two main characteristics during this phase of expansion. The first was the fairly unique tendency among similar companies to continue to rely upon broking as the backbone of the business. Fearnley and Eger was hardly alone in beginning as both a broker and a shipowner, either nationally or internationally. Indeed, some of Norway's more important shipowners, including Wilhelm Wilhelmsen, the country's largest shipowner on the eve of World War I, began this way.[10] And internationally, the mixing of broking and owning was always typical.[11] Such a strategy was eminently rational, since the barriers to entry in broking--in particular, the capital requirements--were obviously much lower. But the lure of shipowning--and likely the

---

[10]On Wilhelmsen, see Leif B. Lillegaard, *Over alle hav. Wilh. Wilhelmsens rederi* (Oslo, 1986); Kr. Anker Olsen, *Wilh. Wilhelmsen i hundre år* (Oslo, 1962); Jan Petter Syse, *Wilh. Wilhelmsen 1861-1977: A Brief History* (London, 1978).

[11]The scholarly literature on the history of shipbroking is virtually non-existent. The best without question is Peter N. Davies, *Henry Tyrer: A Liverpool Shipping Agent and His Enterprises, 1879-1979* (London, 1979), a book which testifies eloquently to the catholicity of Peter's contribution to maritime history. Yet for the most part this generalisation is based primarily upon popular and commissioned studies of various firms and reminiscences. For this period, in addition to the literature cited elsewhere in this essay, see Arthur Behrend, *Portrait of a Family Firm: Bahr, Behrend and Co. 1793-1945* (London, 1970); George Blake, *Gellatley's, 1862-1962: A Short History of the Firm* (London, 1962); W.M.L. Escombe, *Full and Down: The History of Escombe, McGrath and Company Limited* (London, 1953); *A Century of Ship Agency and Brokerage: Funch, Eyde and Co., Inc., 1847-1947* (New York, 1947); Percy Harley, *My Life in Shipping 1881-1938. An Impression of Some of the Matters and Men I Have Met In It* (London, 1939); Hurford Janes, *Full Ahead. The Story of Brown, Jenkinson and Co. Limited 1860-1960* (London, 1960); Anne and Russell Long, *A Shipping Venture. Turnbull Scott and Company 1872-1972* (London, 1974); Augustus Muir, *Blyth, Jourdain and Company Limited, 1810-1960* (London, 1961); Philip Paul, *City Voyage: The Story of Erlebach and Company Limited, 1867-1967* (London, 1967); and Edward F. Stevens, *A Record of the History of Holder Brothers and Co. Ltd. from 1849-1950* (London, 1950). A marvellously useful handbook on late nineteenth and early twentieth century broking which includes much historical material is J.F. Myrhe, *About Chartering and Shipbroking Business* (Copenhagen, 1917).

potentially high profits that could be earned--convinced most to concentrate upon ownership.[12] By continuing to earn a steady, and sometimes crucial, proportion of its profits from broking, Fearnley and Eger was going against the norm. Both broking and shipowning contributed to the firm's striking growth and were integral components of its operations. Yet we believe that previous historians have fundamentally misinterpreted the relationship between these two maritime activities, concluding that shipowning was the primary endeavour.[13] While the surviving accounting records are not always complete, there is sufficient evidence to demonstrate that this is an oversimplification. That the firm hoped to make substantial profits from ownership is indisputable, but it is equally clear that it relied upon broking income to pay the bills. The fact that previous scholars have missed this is understandable: after all, within the pantheon of maritime occupations shipowning has always been more glamorous than broking. Moreover, because of the continuing interest of most governments, shipowning unquestionably generated more records than any other branch of commerce in the western world. As a result, it has always been easier for historians to study ownership than broking activities. Indeed, the very nature of shipbroking has compounded the difficulties. Shipbrokers, in the nineteenth century as well as the present, have made their fortunes by controlling information flows. Brokers have no visible commodities to sell; in essence, their task is to bring together buyers and sellers. By definition, information that is written down is potentially available to competitors. The tradition of

---

[12]An exception to this generalisation was the large British firm, H. Clarkson and Company. Clarkson was a heavy investor in ships up to 1914, although it would appear that the firm frequently lost money on its ownership activities. The First World War marked a watershed; after 1919, Clarkson concentrated almost entirely on brokerage. See *The Clarkson Chronicle 1852-1952* (London, 1952).

[13]This is true especially of Wasberg and Petersen, *Fearnley & Eger*; and Arne Kildahl, "Fearnley & Egers historie 1869-1944" (Unpublished Mss., F&E). Arne Hartmark, "Norwegian Shipping in the 1990s," in Bård Kolltveit (ed.), *Trade Winds: A History of Norwegian Shipping* (Oslo, 1990), 375, goes a step further, arguing that the shipowning firm continued to own the brokerage house in the 1980s, more than seventy years after the two had separated.

shipbrokers to conduct much of their business orally--or, if done in writing, to destroy the records--has contributed to the dearth of detailed records about their activities. These problems notwithstanding, it is possible to study the broking activities of Fearnley and Eger, if not always in the detail we might like.

A second feature of the firm's expansion underscores the importance of relationships. At every step in its growth, it is possible--indeed, essential--to locate Fearnley and Eger within the nexus of interpersonal relationships that facilitated its success. In a any company, it is axiomatic that decision-makers are of course important. In the case of Fearnley and Eger, for the most part judgments were made by a single individual: Thomas Fearnley. While he has been treated by historians as an excellent example of nineteenth-century Norwegian entrepreneurship,[14] we see little evidence of classical Schumpeterian risk-taking in his maritime activities.[15] Instead, he appears to be a man who was extremely adroit at establishing and nurturing key relationships. To a greater extent than most companies, Fearnley and Eger depended upon the ability of its chief executive to develop and nurture extra-organisational alliances. This ability is never as common as it might appear on the surface--and it was vital in leading the firm to its pre-1917 success.

By any measure, the growth enjoyed by the enterprise up to 1917 was impressive. While Fearnley and Eger was not alone in enjoying substantial expansion in this period, its growth was extraordi-

[14]See, for example, Arne Rygh, "Thomas Nicolay Fearnley," *Norsk Biografisk Leksikon* (Oslo, 1929), IV, 104-105; Nils A. Ytreberg, "Gjennombruddstiden 1881-1900," in Worm-Müller (ed.) *Den norske Sjøfartshistorie*, II, part 3, 316-317.

[15]Joseph Schumpeter, *The Theory of Economic Development: An Inquiry into Profits, Capital, Credit, Interest and the Business Cycle* (Cambridge, MA, 1934); *Business Cycles: A Theoretical, Historical and Statistical Analysis of the Capitalist Process* (New York, 1939); *Capitalism, Socialism and Democracy* (New York, 1950). For an examination of a maritime entrepreneur from an explicitly Schumpeterian perspective, see Lewis R. Fischer, "An Engine, Yet Moderate: James Peake, Entrepreneurial Behaviour and the Shipping Industry of Nineteenth-Century Prince Edward Island," in Lewis R. Fischer and Eric W. Sager (eds.), *The Enterprising Canadians: Entrepreneurs and Economic Development in Eastern Canada, 1820-1914* (St. John's, 1979), 97-118.

nary enough to set it apart. There are a number of ways of demonstrating the growth, but two should suffice to illustrate evolution and its patterns.

Figure 1
Value of Fearnley and Eger's Balance Sheet, 1869-1914
(Current Norwegian Kroner)

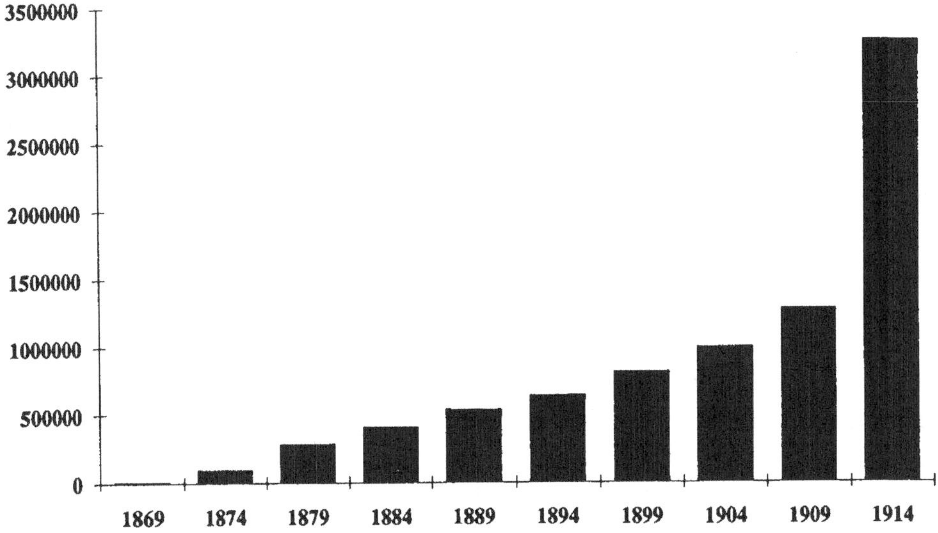

Source: Account Books, Fearnley and Eger Collection, Riksarkivet.

First, we can examine the firm's growth as indicated on its balance sheet (see figure 1). At the end of the first year of operation, the balance sheet reflected a total worth of a modest 8216 kroner (2054 speciedaler).[16] But the rise thereafter was spectacular. Five years later the company's value had expanded eleven-fold to 93,300

[16]Before 1877 the Norwegian unit of currency was the *speciedaler*. To convert *speciedaler* to *kroner*, the currency measure we use throughout this paper, requires multiplication by four. For readers more comfortable with a more "international" currency, *kroner* can be converted to sterling in this period of the fixed exchange rates by dividing by 18.16.

kroner, and by 1879 it had tripled to 285,047 kroner. Growth slowed somewhat in the 1880s, 1890s and the first decade of the twentieth century: the firm's value grew by 1.9, 1.5 and 1.6 times, respectively, in these decades. This slower growth was reversed in the last quinquennium before the war, when the balance sheet swelled an additional 2.5-fold to 3,256,506 kroner. By any measure, this was solid growth.

Figure 2
Fearnley and Eger's Capital Account, 1874-1914
(Current Norwegian Kroner)

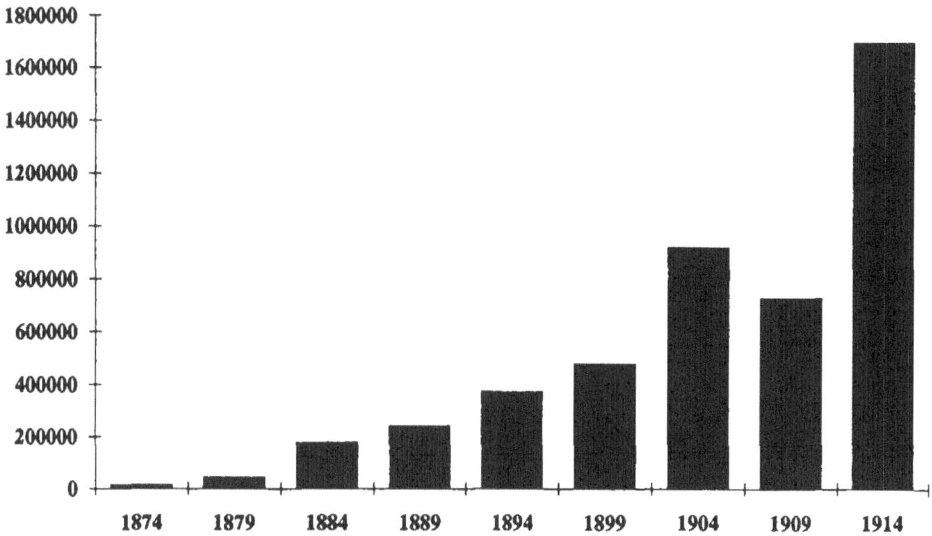

Source: See Figure 1.

But the problem with using a balance sheet in isolation is that it reflects extensive rather than intensive growth. In other words, while it can tell us a great deal about absolute size, at the same time it can obscure a number of factors crucial to a company's health. For example, if a firm borrows heavily to finance investments--something that Fearnley and Eger did, especially to raise funds for investments in vessels in the early years--a myopic focus on gross value may present a misleading picture, since the loans of course inflate its worth without necessarily causing a similar increase in net wealth. Since the state of the financial records do not permit us to compute net wealth for a number of years, we have instead opted to examine Fearnley and Eger's capital account. This is a far better method of simultaneously assessing both the firm's growth and health. In the accounting system used by Fearnley and Eger, the capital account in essence reflected the owners' equity in the enterprise (see figure 2).

Unfortunately, it is not possible given the state of surviving records to calculate the value of this account with any precision prior to 1874. At the end of that year, however, it stood at only 13,488 kroner, which suggests that we have not missed much in the way of growth up to that point. By 1879 owner's equity had tripled. The capital account rose 5.6 times in the 1880s and doubled in the 1890s. By 1904 it had virtually doubled again, but it actually declined between 1904 and 1909, reflecting both the withdrawal of Engelhardt Eger from the firm in 1905 and borrowings to pay for some newly-delivered vessels. Between 1909 and 1914, the capital account grew by 2.3 times, to stand at 1,694,235 kroner.[17]

These two measures supply firm proof that the firm grew rapidly and that expansion was greatest before 1880 and after 1909. Since these two periods also coincided with increasing demand for shipping, this is hardly surprising.[18] Yet the data also show that Fearnley and Eger was able to increase equity faster than gross value in almost every period. Assuming that the owners were not "milking" the company--and there is absolutely no evidence to suggest that they were--the signifi-

---

[17]Balance sheets, F&E, various years.

[18]Helge W. Nordvik, "The Shipping Industries of the Scandinavian Countries, 1850-1914," in Lewis R. Fischer and Gerald E. Panting (eds.), *Change and Adaptation in Maritime History: The North Atlantic Fleets in the Nineteenth Century* (St. John's, 1985), 117-148. The freight rate series in Lewis R. Fischer and Helge W. Nordvik, "Maritime Transport and the Integration of the North Atlantic Economy, 1850-1914," in Wolfram Fischer, R. Marvin McInnis and Jürgen Schneider (eds.), *The Emergence of a World Economy, 1500-1914* (Wiesbaden, 1986), 519-544, confirms the health of the shipping industry in these periods.

cantly steeper rise of the capital account testifies to the health of the enterprise.

The key to attaining (and maintaining) this position was to keep borrowing under control. To gauge Fearnley and Eger's success at doing this, we have calculated a debt/equity ratio; surviving records enable us to do this for all but three years between 1874 and 1914. This time series suggests that the firm was for the most part able to restrain borrowing to reasonable limits (see figure 3). Borrowing was extremely high in the 1870s, but thereafter the long-term secular trend was negative. And most impressively, the ratio stayed below unity in every year save one from 1890 to 1914. Certainly by modern standards the proportion of debt to equity was low for a rapidly-growing company.

Figure 3
Fearnley and Eger's Debt/Equity Ratio, 1874-1914

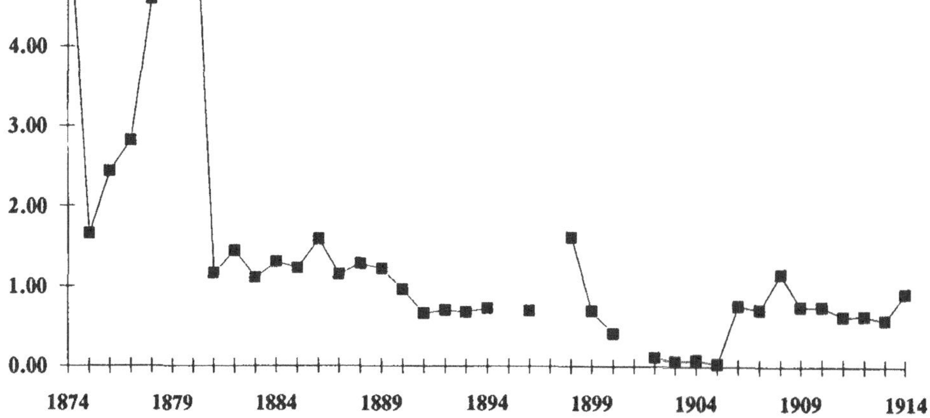

Source: See Figure 1.

Figure 4
The Results of the Chartering Department, 1892-1906
(Current Norwegian Kroner)

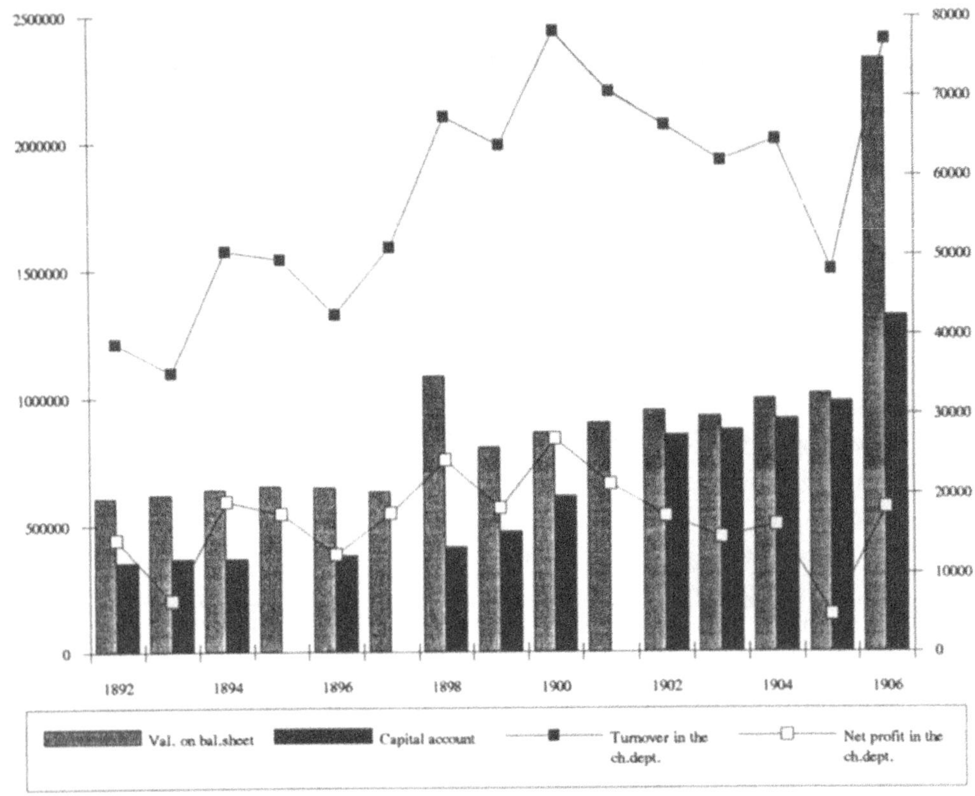

Note: Net profits from chartering are less all the normal deductions for salaries, costs and overhead. They also are less the one-third of profits paid to Carl O. Lie, 1892-1906, and one-sixth to Ole Boe in 1906, as negotiated commissions.

Source: See Figure 1.

How did the firm's two major maritime activities, broking and shipowning, fit into this picture? While the surviving accounting data enable us to answer some questions, it is unfortunately not complete enough to enable any kind of quantitative analysis of the contributions made by various activities to the firm's overall growth for the entire period. Fortunately, there is sufficient evidence for at least a portion of the epoch to suggest strongly the importance of broking to overall development.

We can show this point most clearly for the years 1892-1906 in figure 4, which presents a visual depiction of the importance of broking; in Fearnley and Eger, broking revenues and costs were charged against the chartering department, which was established in 1880. The data in the figure depict both annual turnover and net profit in the chartering department (which should be read on the right-hand axis) and the value on the balance sheet and in the capital accounts (on the left-hand axis). This data graphically suggests the fairly substantial and constant contribution made by brokerage activities to the firm's accounts. Only 1905 stands out as a particularly deviant year.

But because for these years the accounts of the chartering department are available in detail, we can rework these calculations to show even more clearly the importance of broking activities. For the years in which it is possible to make the necessary calculations, table 1 presents the firm's annual net profits along with the share contributed by brokerage activities. To be conservative, the contribution of the chartering department has been deflated by one-third in each year through 1905 to account for the commission paid its head, Carl O. Lie, on gross profits; in 1906 it has been lowered by fifty percent to account for the additional one-sixth paid to his assistant, Ole Boe. The profits from chartering are thus less than they might have been had we elected to charge these commissions to the firm as a whole.

What the table shows supports our contention about the importance of broking to the firm as a whole. In both 1892 and 1894, for example, brokerage activities accounted for more than 100% of the company's profits; to put it another way, without the contribution of the chartering department, the firm would have lost substantial sums in each year rather than generating the small profits that it did. In one additional year, brokerage contributed more than seventy percent of profits, and in two others more than a quarter. Shipowning may have generated immense sums in good years, but broking was a steady and generally reliable way of earning money. To attain the kind of growth it did, Fearnley and Eger needed shipbroking.

Table 1
Contribution of Broking Activities to Net Profits, 1892-1906

Year	Net Profits (NOK)	Chartering (NOK)	% Chartering
1892	9086	14252	156.9
1893	13541	6557	48.4
1894	1245	18978	1524.3
1895		17427	
1896		12314	
1897		17529	
1898		24288	
1899	61686	18131	29.4
1900	137573	26908	19.6
1901		21257	
1902		17192	
1903	20342	14574	71.6
1904	43690	16044	36.7
1905	66602	4793	7.2
1906	338951	18272	5.4

Source: See Figure 1.

To understand the way the firm grew, however, requires not only an appreciation of the importance of broking but also a comprehension of the business relationships into which Fearnley and Eger entered. If Thomas Fearnley had been an entrepreneur in the true sense of the word, it might be reasonable to focus on variables endogenous to the firm, such as quality of service, price, or even "structure" in order to explain its success. But as we shall see below, Fearnley and Eger's early prosperity appears to have derived principally from exogenous relationships developed by its founder.

Everything about Thomas Fearnley's business career suggests a cautious, conservative set of tactics rather than innovation. Consider, for example, his letter to Clarkson in 1869 asking whether his British friends could "suggest any remunerative business or agency that could be carried on in connection with my chartering business."[19] Such a request is hardly the mark of a visionary businessman. An even more telling example can be seen by examining his investment in shipping, especially since it is in this sector that previous writers have argued for entrepreneurial behaviour.[20] Yet Fearnley's pattern of investment was exceedingly conservative: he always purchased shares rather than entire vessels. Indeed, we do not know of a single instance prior to World War I in which the company acquired an entire vessel on its own account. This behaviour, of course, had the advantage of spreading risks in an industry in which the peril of watching helplessly as a valuable asset was lost was always very real. If it placed obvious limits on capital accumulation, it also helped to ensure that the firm would not be imperilled by an unforeseen occurrence. Moreover, this strategy made sense for a firm that was especially interested in shipbroking. While a vessel in which it had a share *might* generate profits, it would *certainly* yield commissions from chartering.

The policy of conservative investment began with the 211-ton brig *Snorre Sturlasson*, in which the firm bought a one-sixteenth interest in August 1870. In 1872 Fearnley purchased a one-eighth share of the 751-ton barque *Marie*, which was mainly operated in the petroleum trade, and a three-thirty-second part of the 604-ton barque *Pallas*. Prior to 1880 we know of ten sailing vessels in which the firm had shares. The proportion of its investment ranged from two to fifty percent. A similar strategy was employed in the purchase of steamers. Its first investment in steam was the paddle steamer *Lara* in 1873; true to its strategy, the firm purchased a one-eighth share. In 1881 it was active in founding the Christiania Dampskibsselskab, in which it had a 6.5% share. The Dampskibsinteressentskabet Garonne, which was established to operate a line to France, was 10.4% owned by Fearnley and Eger. In 1887 the firm (and Thomas Fearnley personally) took a combined 9.4% stake in Dampskibsselskabet Framnæs, the first in a

---

[19]Thomas Fearnley to H. Clarkson and Company, 21 May 1869, Thomas Fearnley Copy Books, F&E.

[20]See the sources cited in note 14.

line of single-ship steamer companies in which it became involved. This was followed by investments in another six similar ventures over the next two decades; in each case Fearnley and Eger subscribed between 11.3 and 36.4% of the share capital.[21]

Given the strategy that Fearnley and Eger pursued, it is obvious that it required the participation of outsiders, at least in the purchase of vessels. But the firm's reliance on external relationships went much further than merely soliciting investors for its vessel syndicates. While all successful firms require alliances, given the tendency of the firm to follow rather than to initiate new behaviours, it is arguable that these were more vital to Fearnley and Eger than to most. At the centre of this complex network of important associations was the principal owner, Thomas Fearnley.[22] While space constraints do not here permit an examination of all of Fearnley and Eger's relationships, to support the point it should be sufficient to discuss the most important of these.[23]

Thomas Nicolay Fearnley's life was hardly a classic tale of "rags to riches." His father was one of Norway's most prominent nineteenth-century painters; although he died while his son was still a child, the Fearnley surname brought with it a recognition factor which must have opened doors within the upper echelons of Norwegian society.[24] His mother, Cecilie Andresen, was the daughter of an important banker. Fearnley was thus born into one of the most prominent families in Christiania, with contacts spread throughout Norwegian society.

---

[21]This account of investments is based upon material in F&E and Kildahl, "Fearnley & Egers historie," I, 22-37 and II, 1-32.

[22]Engelhardt Eger, the other principal after 1874, stayed largely in the background, preferring to leave the day-to-day operations of the firm to Fearnley. Eger's principal contribution would appear to have been as a symbol of the stature of the company, reassuring friends in the Christiania business community of the probity of the transactions undertaken. On Eger's role, see Ole Boe, "Interview," F&E.

[23]For a fuller discussion of these alliances, see chapter 2 of our forthcoming book on Astrup Fearnley.

[24]A. Aubert, *Norsk kultur og norsk kunst* (Christiania, 1917), 146-162.

The Andresen connection was crucial from the start. Indeed, it would not be too strong to suggest that the Andresens shaped the direction of his life. From an early age Fearnley was groomed for a business career. At seventeen, the Andresens sent him to the Leipziger Handelsschule in Germany for two years of commercial training. Upon his return to Norway in 1860, he went to work as a "junior" for his uncle, N.A. Andresen, the proprietor of an important Christiania firm with interests in, among other things, shipowning and forwarding. When Thomas Fearnley launched his agency in 1869, he became the exclusive broker for all Andresen-owned vessels.[25] And when in 1870 Fearnley began investing in vessels, the Andresens were there to assist. Indeed, Johan I. Andresen, a lawyer and another of Fearnley's uncles, lent him 375 speciedaler at six percent interest to purchase a one-sixth share in his first craft, the brig *Snorre Sturlasson*.[26] The link with the Andresens remained important throughout his commercial life; not only was the bank a constant source of capital but the Andresens also participated in one way or another in a number of Fearnley and Eger's shipping investments.

While the Andresens provided a good foundation, they were not really major participants in maritime affairs, the career that Fearnley chose to follow. But they did know people who were more central to shipping and apparently were able to provide him with a number of introductions to prominent businessmen from whom he might further his education. In 1864 he set off for London, the capital of the nineteenth-century shipping world, where one of his letters landed him a job with the large shipbroking house, Rücker Offor and Company. We know little about his responsibilities at Rücker Offor, but we do know that he impressed the partners sufficiently that when he returned to Norway in 1869 to establish his own business, the firm made him its Norwegian agent. While he did not maintain this business relationship

---

[25]Fearnley to Gunder Anton Aas, 17 April 1872, Thomas Fearnley Copy Books, F&E.

[26]Kildahl, "Fearnley & Egers historie," I, 20.

with Rücker Offor for long, it did give him some additional prestige with which to begin his operations in Christiania.

In addition to teaching him something about shipping, Rücker Offor left him with a good deal of spare time. A bright young man like Fearnley would have recognized the opportunities available in the British metropolis, and he proceeded to use his leisure moments to make additional contacts. His most important new friends were associated with a rival London broking establishment, H. Clarkson and Company. The contacts that he made in this firm would lead later to a long-standing arrangement that would prove indispensable to his success. We have no idea how Fearnley made his contacts at Clarkson, but we do know that the choice was fortuitous. By the 1860s the firm was increasingly becoming a specialist in Scandinavian shipping. This was by no means an easy task. In 1860 broking for Norwegian vessels was dominated by two other large British concerns, Charles Northcote and Co. and W.S. Lindsay and Co. Neither firm, however, apparently was as assiduous in courting Norwegian interests as Clarkson. Indeed, Clarkson's offices became a favourite meeting place for Norwegian captains in town while waiting for their vessels to be readied for departure. It is likely that Thomas Fearnley made a number of the contacts upon which he later built in Clarkson's "Captains' Corner."

Central to the development of Clarkson's Scandinavian business were Carl August Granlund, a Swede from Hernösand, and Henry Benham, both of whom later became partners. Fearnley befriended them both. While Granlund appeared to take the young man under his wing, the contact with Benham may have been even more important, since he was on exceedingly good terms with Wilhelm Wilhelmsen, the Tønsberg shipowner who was then beginning his phenomenal rise in Norwegian shipping circles. It is likely that Benham either introduced the two or provided Fearnley with a letter of introduction. Regardless, Wilhelmsen would become one of Fearnley's most loyal customers and for a while a partner in a shipowning venture.[27]

[27]This was Fearnley and Wilhelmsen, a short-lived venture to operate liners, which was founded in 1917.

But the Clarkson connection went even further. For starters, the London company was involved as a partner in a number of the early vessels in which Fearnley invested, beginning with the brig *Snorre Sturlasson* in 1870. Thereafter, the two firms invested together in the sailing vessels *Pallas* (1872) and *Makrina* (1873), as well as the steamer *Lara* (1873). Even more important was a connection in shipbroking. We do not know precisely when Fearnley began working with Clarkson on broking, but it must have been shortly after his return to Christiania.[28] For reasons that are not altogether clear, Fearnley apparently was dissatisfied with his existing relationship with Rücker Offor. At the same time, Clarkson appears to have seen some advantage in working with Fearnley. In the early 1870s, the principal Clarkson connection in Norway seems to have been Ferdinand Breda, at the time the largest broker in Christiania. Yet by 1872 Fearnley had apparently reached some sort of agreement to receive a share of Clarkson's broking business. As he wrote to Gunder Aas at Clarkson in April of that year,

> I can of course not for one moment doubt that you are in earnest regarding the principle of dividing commission as proposed...[yet] you can not class me with your sole and exclusive agents who have a share of everything you do with their respective towns whether they do it direct or indirect even if the business is done through other agents. I believe I have here to compete with Breda, who is placed on perfectly equal terms with me...[29]

Sometime in 1873 Clarkson appears to have agreed that at the beginning of 1874 Fearnley would become its exclusive agent in Christiania.[30] This was confirmed in a revealing letter that Fearnley

---

[28]Fearnley to Clarkson, 21 May 1869, Thomas Fearnley Copy Books, F&E. In this letter, Fearnley indicated that he had succeeded in fixing a Clarkson vessel and noted that the British firm had "booked 1.1/4% to me."

[29]Fearnley to Aas, 17 April 1872, Thomas Fearnley Copy Books, F&E.

[30]Fearnley to Clarkson, 18 September 1873, Thomas Fearnley Copy Books, F&E.

penned to Gunder Aas early in 1874: "Well, henceforth then we begin working exclusively with each other. On condition that you break off with Breda, we agree not to fix direct with any merchants in England."[31] From this point on, Fearnley and Clarkson attempted to dominate the freight market throughout eastern Norway. From Fearnley's perspective, this meant that he would share in any commissions involving Clarkson-chartered vessels trading to or from Norway, whether he actually performed any brokerage services or not. This relationship thus became a guaranteed source of income for Fearnley and Eger and provided the solid base upon which the firm could engage in other activities.

In short, by the mid-1870s Thomas Fearnley had established the most crucial relationships that would foster the success of his firm. The Andresens could supply much of the capital;[32] associations with major shipowners like Wilhelmsen provided the customers; and the working arrangement with Clarkson contributed the international might and the guaranteed income. The second vital stanchion of Fearnley and Eger's success was now in place.

In its early years, Fearnley and Eger was part of the most dynamic sector of the Norwegian economy--shipping--during one of its most important periods of growth. If the country benefitted from its activities, so too did the firm gain from national growth. While never an innovator, in its own cautious way the company did make solid contributions in both shipowning and shipbroking.

Of the two, we believe that it was shipbroking which was in the long-term Fearnley and Eger's most important endowment. While it is indisputable that shipowning contributed the lion's share of revenues in those years in which the firm's profits were especially substantial, it is equally clear that shipowning was the bedrock on which the enterprise was anchored. Indeed, hindsight suggests that one of the

---

[31] Fearnley to Aas, 10 January 1874, Thomas Fearnley Copy Books, F&E.

[32] Fearnley also was able to obtain funds from N.O. Young, who after 1875 became his father-in-law, and the Olsen family, which apparently provided capital during a crisis in 1886 and invested in most of the steamship companies established by Feanrley and Eger after 1880.

most obvious reasons for investing in vessels was to improve the likelihood of earning commissions from brokerage activities. The reasons for this are fairly clear. First of all, broking was a much safer activity than shipowning. If, as we have shown above, Fearnley and Eger was a fairly conservative firm, the security of shipbroking must have held much appeal. Moreover, because it encompassed so many facets, broking offered a myriad of possibilities for making a profit. There were revenues to be garnered in arranging the purchase of the vessel; in its operation, either by chartering it or by acting as a managing owner; in its insurance, especially if you represented a variety of insurance companies, as Fearnley and Eger did; and in its sale. And as a part owner of so many craft, it was only logical that Fearnley and Eger should get the brokerage activities related to them. This was the attraction of broking--it was a safe, yet very lucrative--way of making money.

And it was especially safe and lucrative if an individual possessed the knack that Thomas Fearnley did of cementing vital relationships. Had he been an entrepreneur, Fearnley might have been sufficiently innovative to have developed strategies which would have enabled to firm to prosper virtually unaided. But lacking this gift, the founder instead tried to maximise his return by calling into play his inter-personal skills. The rapid growth of Fearnley and Eger in its first half-century of existence is a testimonial to the skill with which he succeeded.

Entrepreneurship and Risk-Taking in the Norwegian Shipping Industry in the Early Part of the Twentieth Century: The Case of Lauritz Kloster, Stavanger[1]

Helge W. Nordvik

Introduction

The transition from sail to steam in the Norwegian shipping industry has traditionally been described as slow and hesitant.[2] Contrary to the established view in the literature that this was due to entrepreneurial failure, the slow adoption of new steamship technology has recently

[1]The primary sources for this paper consist of the surviving archival material of the Lauritz Kloster Steamship Company and associated companies in the Stavanger Maritime Museum. The former director of the Museum, Arne Bang Andersen, used an unpublished document summarising the surviving accounts and papers of the various Kloster companies written by Sigurd Clausen, a former director of the company during the Second World War, in his 1979 book on the history of Stavanger steam shipping. The original sources upon which Clausen's manuscript was based were apparently not consulted by Andersen. At the request of the then Director of the Stavanger Maritime Museum, Bjørn S. Utne, I went through the records and catalogued them in an inventory dated 24 January 1984. I want to thank Mr. Utne and the present Director of the Museum, Harald Hamre, for permission to copy and use the material. I also want to thank Miss Hege Imseth, research assistant at the Section for Economic History at the Norwegian School of Management, for her assistance in computing the balance sheet and profit and loss accounts of the Lauritz Kloster shipping company, 1915-1916, and Lauritz Kloster's personal accounts. References to the source material, which is registered as Stavanger Maritime Museum manuscript collection no. 4284, is given as SMM 4284 followed by a letter corresponding to the protocol or notebook in my inventory.

[2]This is the traditional view in the Norwegian literature. See, for example, the discussions by N. Ytreberg in J. Worm-Müller (ed.), *Den norske sjøfarts historie*, II, part 3 (Oslo, 1951), and Kaare Petersen, *Norsk Dampskipsfart blir en stormakt på havet* (Trondheim, 1949).

been defended as a case of rational profit-maximizing behaviour.[3] It is well-known that Norwegian owners took advantage of the continuing opportunities offered by sailing technology well into the twentieth century. The transition from sail to steam began late: only after the First World War did the Norwegian fleet assume a structure similar to the other major shipping nations with respect to technology and the tonnage distribution of the merchant fleet.

It is perhaps surprising that most Norwegian shipping historians seem to take for granted that the transition from sail to steam and the preservation of a large and viable merchant shipping industry had to happen. In an international context, it is worth asking why and how it happened at all.[4] Many countries with large investments in sailing vessels, such as Canada and the United States, failed to make the transition in the nineteenth century.[5] By 1914 they had lost their effective presence in the international shipping industry, although they did build up domestic steam fleets to carry goods along their coasts and on inland waterways.[6] There was thus nothing automatic about making the transition from sail to steam. Any explanation which aspires to explain this complex phenomenon would have to include an

---

[3]See Ole Gjølberg, "The Substitution of Steam for Sail in Norwegian Ocean Shipping," *Scandinavian Economic History Review*, XXVIII, No. 2 (1980), 135-146.

[4]I have discussed the Norwegian shipping industry in a comparative Scandinavian context in "The Shipping Industries of the Scandinavian Countries, 1850-1914," in Lewis R. Fischer and Gerald E. Panting (eds.), *Change and Adaptation in Maritime History: The North Atlantic Fleets in the Nineteenth Century* (St. John's, 1985), 117-148.

[5]For a comparative discussion on the growth of the international shipping fleets of major shipping countries before 1914, see Lewis R. Fischer and Helge W. Nordvik, "Maritime Transport and the Integration of the North Atlantic Economy, 1850-1914," in Wolfram Fischer, R. Marvin McInnis and Jürgen Schneider (eds.), *The Emergence of a World Economy 1500-1914* (Wiesbaden, 1986), II, 519-544.

[6]For a comparison of the Norwegian and Canadian experience see Lewis R. Fischer and Helge W. Nordvik, "Floating Capital: Investment in the Canadian and Norwegian Merchant Marines in Comparative perspective, 1850-1914," Scandinavian-Canadian Studies, III (1988), 17-42.

analysis of the absolute and relative costs of labour and capital, the alternative opportunities for investment and employment, attitudes to risk and seafaring, the level of technology in shipbuilding and supply of skilled labour both shipbuilding and shipping management, the role of classification societies, insurance companies and brokerage firms, the role of government policies, and so on.

These wider problems are beyond the scope of the present paper.[7] Instead, I want to focus on the role of the individual shipowner faced with the uncertainties of the international shipping industry. Whether or not we call him an entrepreneur, the individual businessman must remain central to any explanation of the growth and development of Norwegian shipping in the first two decades of the twentieth century. The how rather than the why of Norwegian ship management and shipowning before and during the First World War is really the theme of this paper. In particular, I want to examine how a relatively unknown middle-aged shipping clerk managed to convert his considerable expertise and modest capital resources into a major shipping enterprise.

Shipowning and ship management were intensely competitive activities, carried on in an environment that was characterized by largely competitive markets in the demand and supply of tramp shipping services. The capacity to spot and exploit opportunities, the willingness to take risks and the ability to manage were qualities that were central to the success of any shipping enterprise.[8]

Such attributes were particularly crucial in a period of rapid technological change within the industry. In the 1870s, Stavanger had been one of the major Norwegian shipping centres, with a sailing fleet

---

[7]For a survey of current Norwegian historiography on these aspects of the history of Norwegian shipping, see Helge W. Nordvik, "Norwegian Maritime Historical Research during the Past Twenty Years," *Sjøfartshistorisk Årbok 1990* (Bergen, 1991), 241-278.

[8]For a discussion of an early entrepreneur in the transition from sail to steam in Norway, see Lewis R. Fischer and Helge W. Nordvik, "From Broager to Bergen: The Risks and Rewards of Peter Jebsen, Shipowner, 1864-1892", *Sjøfartshistorisk Årbok 1985* (Bergen, 1986), 37-68.

that in terms of gross tonnage was second only to Arendal.[9] The economic crisis of the 1880s had caused the economic ruin of many large shipowners and led to a substantial reduction in tonnage on registry in Stavanger.[10] The surviving merchant houses and shipowners were slow in making the transition from sail to steam. Most were not wholly committed to the new technology, preferring to have a foot in each camp. Economically, this probably made sense, since sailing vessels remained competitive in many of the long-distance tramp trades in which Stavanger and other Norwegian shipowners had a presence in the 1880s and 1890s.

There were, however, some notable exceptions to the relative lethargy and aversion to risk that characterised many of the established shipowners hurt by the crisis-ridden 1880s. Perhaps the most notable example of a Stavanger shipping entrepreneur was twenty-three year-old Sigvald Bergesen, who in 1887 established an insurance, brokerage and commission business, which he rapidly turned into a major shipowning enterprise. Bergesen hedged his bets by investing in both sailing vessels and second-hand steamers, and by the turn of the century he owned fourteen vessels, the largest steamship fleet in Stavanger.[11]

The Years of Apprenticeship, 1870-1906

The son of a sea-captain, Lauritz Kloster was born in Stavanger on 18 September 1870. After graduating from secondary school in 1887 he

---

[9]See Johs. B. Thue, "Skipsfartsnæring i Stavanger gjennom den siste glansperioden for norsk seglskipsfart," in *Stavanger på 1800-tallet* (Stavanger, 1975), 87-118; Harald Hamre, *Skipsfarten i Stavanger i 1870-åra. En næringsøkonomisk undersøkelse* (Stavanger, 1985).

[10]Rolf Danielsen, "Den store krise," in *Stavanger på 1800-tallet*, 281-316.

[11]See Tore Jørgen Hanisch and Liv Jorunn Ramskjær, *Firmaet Sigval Bergesen Stavanger. Under vekslende vilkår* (Stavanger, 1987), especially 9-50; Arnljot Strømme Svendsen, "Generelle og spesielle vilkår for rederietableringen i 1880-90 årene. Tilfellet Stavanger," *Sjøfartshistorisk Årbok 1990* (Bergen, 1991), 57-94.

started his shipping "apprenticeship" by obtaining a position with the established firm of Holdt and Isachsen. This was fortuitous, since the company proved to be one of the most successful and progressive in Stavanger in the 1880s and 1890s. It was founded in 1873 by Hans G.W. Holdt and I.S. Isachsen, who took over the shipbroking arm of the firm owned by one of the most dynamic shipowners in Stavanger, Ths. S. Falck.[12] Holdt and Isachsen gradually built up a considerable fleet of sailing vessels in the 1870s and 1880s. In the 1890s the firm moved decisively into steam, specialising like many other Bergen and Stavanger shipowners in the West Indian fruit trade to the United States. By the end of 1900 it managed a fleet of nine fairly small steam vessels totalling 6300 gross tons (see table 1).[13]

In addition to his work with the Holdt and Isachsen, where he advanced to the position of chief clerk, Kloster served as agent for several insurance companies on his own account. This business started in 1895, when he secured the agency for the Swedish company Svea in fire and life insurance. The expansion of fish canning in Stavanger opened possibilities for British firms selling tin plate, and from 1896 he operated as sales agent for several U.K. companies. In addition, he also purchased tin scrap, which he resold to Dutch companies.[14] The following year he secured the position as local representative for the firm of Emil G. von Höveling, a specialist Hamburg firm selling anti-fouling paint to the shipping industry. By 1901 this firm delivered paint to 132 Norwegian vessels, fifty of them through the Kloster agency. The previous year Kloster also became the local representative of Swan and Finch Oil Co.; when this firm merged in 1905 with Vacuum

---

[12]L. M. Michaelsen, *Stavanger Sjøfarts Historie* (Stavanger, 1927), 192.

[13]Computed by the author from the list in A.B. Andersen, *Stavanger Sjøfarts historie. Fra seil til damp* (Stavanger, 1983), 238-239. The list is based on the Veritas register.

[14]The development of the Stavanger fish canning industry in the context of the town's industrial development is covered in Anders Haaland and Helge W. Nordvik, "Stavangerindustriens struktur og utvikling 1890-1940", in Rolf Danielsen (ed.), *Stavanger mellom sild og olje. Hermetikkbyen 1900-1940* (Stavanger, 1988), I, 49-167.

Oil Co. of New York, Kloster continued as agent for the new enterprise.

Table 1
Vessels Managed and Controlled by Holdt and Isachsen, 1900

Vessel Name	Place Built	Year Built	Gross Tonnage
Alabama	Fevig	1897	935
Fulton	Stavanger	1891	488
Gyller	Christiania	1892	549
Habil	Stavanger	1896	632
Hiram	Christiania	1890	602
Mercator	Fevig	1899	1083
Sunniva	Stavanger	1892	605
Svithun	Flensburg	1881	668
Utstein	Christiania	1890	765
Total			6327

Note: List reflects vessels owned at the end of the year.

Source: Arne Bang Andersen, *Stavanger Sjøfarts Historie. Fra seil til damp* (Stavanger, 1979), 238-239.

Important as these various business involvements were in enabling him to build a net of business contacts and connections and to expand his capital, the decisive breakthrough for Kloster came in 1906 when he became the representative of the Norwegian insurance company Norske Lloyd. This recently-established organisation was destined to become a leader in marine insurance and it is probable that his position a Norske Lloyd agent gave Kloster the confidence to become his own man. He gave notice to his employers and parted amicably; indeed, Kloster continued to act as a consultant for Holdt and Isachsen.

Lauritz Kloster established his firm on 7 November 1906 at Skagen 10 in Stavanger's central business district. In the notice to the Norwegian Register of Companies the firm was listed as an insurance, agency and shipping business. The opening balance sheet of the firm was not particularly impressive (see table 2). Although Kloster's net worth was listed as close to NOK 50,000, almost a third of his capital was tied up in a warehouse, another two-fifths was invested in shipping shares, while most of the rest was accounted for by furniture and office equipment; his liquid capital was limited to a few hundred kroner in petty cash and an account of around NOK 1500 with a local bank.

Table 2
Balance sheet of Lauritz Kloster, 7 November 1906
(Norwegian Kroner)

Assets:		
Warehouse, Lydersagensgade, 22		16,000.00
Shares in vessels:		
6 shares in D/S *Svidthun*	12,000.00	
2 shares in D/S *Senator*	5,300.00	
2 half shares in D/S *Navigator*	2,000.00	
1 quarter share in D/S *Helen & Katie*	500.00	
1 share in Stavanger Dampskipsselskap	500.00	
9 shares in Ryfylke Dampskipsselskap	75.00	20,375.00
Shares in other companies:		
5 shares in Norske Lloyd	1,000.00	
6 shares in Stavanger Fosfatfabrik	5,000.00	
5 Government Bonds	30.00	6,030.00
Office equipment	6,000.00	
Account with Stavanger Privatbank	1,450.00	
Life insurance policies	2,000.00	
Cash	329.66	
Total assets		52,184.66
Liabilities:		
Creditors (E.G. von Höveling)	2,200.00	
Capital account (Kloster's net worth)	49,984.66	
Total liabilities		52,184.66

Source: Stavanger Maritime Museum (SMM), 4284 E.

Starting a Shipping Business, 1906-1914

Shortly after Kloster started on his own he began negotiations for the purchase of a small wooden steam vessel. On 6 December 1906 he bought the 830-dwt DS *Sjøgutten*, built in Stavanger in 1891, from A.O. Lindvig of Kragerø for NOK 55,000. The first shareholders' meeting in the limited liability company *Damskipsaktieselskabet Sjøgutten* was held in Stavanger on 12 December; the capital was fixed at a sum identical to the purchase price of the vessel, with fifty-five shares issued at NOK 1000 each (see table 3). Kloster held eight shares, financed by a personal loan of NOK 10,000 from his former employer, Hans Holdt, while the ship's captain, Chr. Christophersen, held seventeen shares. This was a common occurrence in Norwegian shipping around the turn of the century--in order to secure command of a vessel a prospective captain often had to take a minority shareholding in a single-vessel limited liability company. The other large shareholder was the *Jadar* Company, while the rest of the shares were held by thirteen small investors, including a British holder of two shares.[15]

The decision to buy the *Sjøgutten* probably represented the least expensive entrance into steam shipping available, and must be interpreted as a very cautious move. Instead of diving into the cold depths of contemporary tramp shipping by committing his available capital, Kloster chose instead to dip his toe in the water by investing a relatively small sum of borrowed money and retaining control of his financial assets. In making this decision, he was probably influenced by two considerations. First, his relatively meagre savings were insufficient to commit most to one venture. Equally important, although he had many years experience in shipping, he was untested as a managing owner, and it seems reasonable to assume that he would have to prove his worth before he could persuade other investors to back him.

The newly-purchased vessel was employed in the North Sea and Baltic bulk trades, chiefly in the ice trade between Norway and the United Kingdom, with return freights of coal, later supplemented by

[15]Stavanger Maritime Museum (SMM) 4284 I (Forhandlingsprotokoll *Sjøgutten*, 1906-1912).

trips to the Baltic for timber and to Iceland with supplies for the herring fishery and return cargoes of salted herring. From June 1907 the vessel was employed on a seven-month time charter to a Norwegian ice-exporting company. In the following years the vessel alternated between time charters in the ice trade for Norwegian shippers and in the Seville fruit trade for the firm of A.C. Wallace of Glasgow. The return cargoes were mostly coal from British ports. The monthly time-charter freights in the ice trade varied from £255 in 1907 to £240 in 1908. The time charter in the fruit trade covered a three-month period from October 1908 to January 1909 and paid £210 for three-quarters of a month, with the vessel free to take return cargoes of coal on the return leg.[16]

Table 3
Companies Managed by Lauritz Kloster, 1906-1918: Paid-In and Repaid Capital
(Norwegian Kroner)

Company	Paid-In Capital	Repaid Capital	Years
A/S *Sjøgutten*	55,000	85,250	5.5
A/S *Smaragd*	110,000	114,400	4.0
A/S *Kong Frode*	125,000	110,000	1.5
A/S *Vestlandet*	125,000	272,125	4.0
A/S *John Wilson*	96,000	243,210	3.5
A/S *Cassiopeia*	309,375	641,250	4.0
A/S *Libra*	300,000	902,400	2.5
A/S *Freda*	100,000	588,500	3.5
A/S Klosters Rederi	1,000,000	21,030,000	2.0
Hercules (partnership)	300,000	7,403,000	2.0
Mia (partnership)	1,000,000	2,008,400	2.0
Mia II (partnership)	368,000	2,000,000	1.0
Total	3,888,375	35,398,535	

Source: SMM, Manuscript entitled "Lauritz Kloster," written by Sigurd Clausen.

[16]SMM 4284 Å (Fartopgavebog).

The modest success of DS *Sjøgutten* in the North Sea tramp trade and the conclusion of a profitable time charter agreement in June 1907 must have sufficiently encouraged Kloster to start looking for additional tonnage with which to expand. In July he agreed to purchase for NOK 60,000 an old Norwegian-built steamer, DS *Krystal*, but the transaction was cancelled when the 650-dwt vessel, built in 1885, was found to have faulty boilers. This somewhat chastening experience led Kloster to look for a more modern vessel. He decided to purchase the eight year-old German-built 600-dwt steamer *Senator Krüger* from Carl Tiede in Wismar for 120,000 German marks or NOK 107,100. The vessel was transferred to the new owners in Bremerhaven on 5 September 1907 after having been inspected by Kloster, the future captain, N. Fr. Lindtner, and the chief engineer, Carl Rosenvold.

Two days earlier the first shareholders' meeting of the new single-ship company *Smaragd* had been held in Stavanger. The share capital was set at NOK 110,000, with each share worth NOK 1,000. The DS *Smaragd* was employed in the North Sea and the Baltic on single-voyage charters, interspersed with short time charters, carrying timber, ice and coal until the vessel was sold in October 1911. The economic results were largely unsatisfactory. The vessel was involved in accidents in 1908 and 1910, necessitating substantial repairs. The shareholders were paid dividends of six percent per annum in 1907-1909 and three percent in 1910. In 1911 they received a 1.5% dividend plus 81.5% of their original investment. A total net return of four percent of the original investment can hardly be considered satisfactory. The opportunity to sell the vessel when second-hand tonnage prices rose sufficiently to recoup the original investment seems wholly understandable in retrospect.

The third vessel purchased and managed by Kloster, the 1300-dwt DS *Kong Frode*, built in Sunderland by W. Doxford and Sons, also proved unsuccessful. After being acquired in December 1907, the single-ship company *Kong Frode* was established in Stavanger on 15 January 1908 with a total share capital of NOK 125,000 divided into one hundred shares of NOK 1250 each. Kloster himself subscribed to sixteen shares, plus one share in the name of his children; the remainder were bought by fifty-one investors, mostly from Stavanger and the surrounding area. There were also some investors from Bergen, as well as one share taken by the firm of Tinwell and Scheel of Blyth.[17]

The vessel was initially occupied in the Spanish fruit trade at a monthly time charter rate of £325, but a series of mishaps led to the charter party being cancelled. After a refit and classification in Cardiff during the autumn of 1908, Kloster succeeded in obtaining a nine-month time charter in the West Indies-US fruit trade at the advantageous rate of £550 per month. After loading coal for the US the vessel started in the fruit trade on 27 March 1908. On 30 April, however, the managing owner received a message that the vessel had stranded two days earlier on Lighthouse Reef outside Belize, British Honduras. As the repairs and refits of vessel had been financed by borrowing NOK 57,000, it had been insured for NOK 175.000. The insurance premium of NOK 12,000 had to be paid in full, and together with other incidental expenses including crew wages, this meant that the shareholders lost about NOK 200 per share, getting back eighty-eight percent of their initial investment.[18]

The setbacks experienced by Kloster and his investors through the misfortunes of the *Smaragd* and *Kong Frode* were potentially serious blows for a recently-established managing shipowner trying to build confidence among local investors. Nonetheless, Kloster had no intention of retiring from the industry. Luckily, the *Sjøgutten* had paid dividends of twenty-one percent in 1907 and eighteen percent the following year, thus maintaining some credibility for Kloster. His experiences with the *Kong Frode* and the trend toward increasing vessel size not only in the tramp trade but also on the North Sea and Baltic routes with which he was most familiar convinced him that he needed a larger vessel.

Through his contacts with the brokerage firm V.T. Thompson in London, Kloster initiated protracted negotiations to purchase the DS *Ella* from the Bridge Dockyard Company in Sunderland. The yard

---

[17]SMM 4284 P (Forhandlingsprotokoll *Frode*).

[18]*Ibid.*, Report from Managing Owner of DS *Frode* to the Shareholders, 10 May 1909.

had acquired the 2680-dwt vessel, built in 1884 by the North of England Shipbuilding Co., as part payment for a newbuilding. The negotiations were successfully concluded in November 1909 after the newly-classified vessel had been inspected by captain S. Sivertsen, and a purchase price of £6750 was agreed. Although more than twenty-five years-old, the vessel was in good condition and the purchase price must be considered something of a bargain. The single-ship company DS *Vestlandet*, formed to take over the vessel in Stavanger on 17 November 1909, had a share capital of NOK 125,000, with many of the same investors who had participated in the *Kong Frode*.

The ship was insured for NOK 160,000 and was initially placed in the Baltic timber trade to Britain and later to Germany. This commerce was an important source of revenue for the growing Norwegian shipping industry in the years before the First World War, as Norwegian owners increasingly out-competed British vessels in this market.[19] Rising freight rates led to quite satisfactory economic results in both 1911 and 1912 and Kloster therefore suggested towards the end of 1912 that the ship be sold. The buyer, Jacob Prebensen, Jr. of Risør, paid NOK 225,000 for the vessel, NOK 125,000 on delivery and NOK 100,000 the next year, secured by a mortgage on the vessel.

The shareholders must have considered the net result satisfactory, since they voted to give the managing owner NOK 5000 as a bonus at the time of the sale. In addition to being paid dividends of between eight and eighteen percent in 1910-1912, the shareholders also were repaid their full investments at the time of the sale, and an additional 77.7% when the buyer redeemed the mortgage in 1913.[20]

In September 1910, the owners of DS *John Wilson*, a 950-dwt steamer built by Bergens Mekaniske Verksteder in 1893, offered to sell

---

[19]Lewis R. Fischer and Helge W. Nordvik, "The Nordic Challenge to British Domination in the Baltic Timber Trade to Britain, 1863-1913," in Lewis R. Fischer, Helge W. Nordvik and Walter E. Minchinton (eds.), *Shipping and Trade in the Northern Seas, 1600-1939* (Bergen, 1988), 74-88.

[20]SMM 4284 Q, Report to the Shareholders in Dampskipsaktieselskabet *Vestlandet* by Lauritz Kloster, 14 November 1913.

the vessel to Kloster for NOK 120,000. The vessel was fitted out for the West Indian fruit trade. While the initial offer was rejected, in March 1911 a renewed offer was made by the owners, A and A. Irgens of Bergen. The vessel was at the time due for a refit and reclassification; after inspection the vessel was finally purchased for NOK 55,000 and towed to Stavanger where it was refitted at a local shipyard, Stavanger Støberi and Dok, for NOK 41,000.

Up to this point, Kloster had taken only minor shareholdings in the vessels for which he was managing owner, but with the *John Wilson* this practice changed. This investment must be regarded as the first example of a business strategy that became characteristic of Kloster during the First World War: speculative investment in vessels with a view to securing profits not through operations but through "asset play." In addition to Kloster, the new company had only two other shareholders: the captain, Chr. Christophersen, and a local wholesale merchant, Sven Haabet. Each shareholder held a third of the 120 shares valued at NOK 1000 each. Since the cost of the vessel was only NOK 96,000 the difference represented an initial write-off of NOK 24,000 (or a hidden reserve, presumably for tax-purposes) on the book value of the vessel. Each of the shareholders borrowed NOK 32,000 from the Stavanger Privatbank to finance the cost of the shares.

The intention of owners was clearly to sell the vessel immediately for profit. It was in fact put on the market for NOK 125,000, but the partners decided instead to accept an offer from the shipbrokers Joachim Grieg to charter the vessel for a year in the Brazil-Argentina fruit trade for £550 per month. After six months the deal turned sour when the Brazilian charterers encountered economic difficulties and were close to bankruptcy. While the charter was cancelled with appropriate compensation, and the shareholders did not in fact lose money on the deal, the vessel was now without employment. Luckily, Grieg found a new time charter, this time with the United Fruit Company in the West Indian-US fruit trade. The vessel continued in this business until the start of the First World War and was eventually sold to a Norwegian shipowner in January 1915 for NOK 115,000. The final accounts showed a total surplus of more than NOK 147,000 during the three and one-half years the vessel was operated by Kloster, representing an average annual net surplus for the partners of forty-four percent.[21]

Kloster's next venture represented another step forward in his slow but steady progress as a shipowner. Captain L. Castberg, the managing owner of DS *Cassiopeia*, a 2600-dwt vessel built at the Nyland Shipyard in Christiania in 1906, wanted to sell his shares in the single-ship company of the same name. Captain Castberg was planning to embark on a whaling expedition to the south Atlantic in the 1911-1912 season, and wanted to sell his 172 shares (of a total of 375), which had a nominal value of NOK 1000 each. The attraction for Kloster was that with Castberg's shareholding came the possibility of usurping his position as managing owner. Kloster eventually acquired the shares for NOK 825 apiece, and at an extraordinary general meeting of the shareholders on 23 November 1911 the sale was approved by the other shareholders. At the same time, the vessel was transferred from the Christiania to the Stavanger ship registry and Kloster was installed as managing owner.

The sale of DS *Smaragd* a month before the purchase of DS *Cassiopeia* meant that Kloster could now spread his risks by offering some of his stock in the latter to ex-shareholders in the former, while still retaining effective control. He kept sixty of his original shares and sold the remainder to investors in the Stavanger area at cost. An existing mortgage of NOK 15,000 held by the Flekkefjord Savings Bank was retained, implying that the book value or full real cost of the vessel to the new ownership company was NOK 324,375. Most of the new shareholders were in fact old investors in the *Smaragd*, including Kloster's associates Sven Haabet and Captain S. Sivertsen. They were also elected joint directors of the company along with Kloster at the first general shareholders' meeting following these transactions. The meeting also decided to pay Kloster an annual managing owner's fee of NOK 1500 plus five percent of the net profits. In addition, all return commissions due on charters and the sale of the vessel were to accrue to the company, corresponding to the contemporary practice in eastern Norway.

---

[21]SMM 4284 O.

The *Cassiopeia* was chiefly employed on time charters in the North Sea and the Mediterranean. In November 1912 a twelve-month charter at £900 per month was agreed with John Bruce and Co. of Glasgow, which chiefly employed her on a regular run between English and Mediterranean ports. When the war began the vessel was in the midst of a six-month time charter with a Viborg firm at £400 per month. Although the agreement still had three months to run, the charterers cancelled the contract and the vessel was thereafter employed in the grain tramp trade between the US and Europe for the remainder of the year.

Rising freights and second-hand prices made the sale of the vessel increasingly attractive; in December 1914 a deal was concluded to sell it to a Christiania shipowner for NOK 450,000. The company paid dividends of 15.2%, 24.2% and 18.2% for the years 1912, 1913 and 1914, respectively. Together with the proceeds from the sale, this meant that the original Christiania shareholders achieved an annual average return of eighteen percent during the four-year period the vessel was managed by Kloster. The new Stavanger shareholders did even better, receiving an annual average return of twenty-seven percent on their investment.[22]

As we have seen, 1912 was a good year for Kloster and his various companies. The favourable economic results must have encouraged him to take the next step on the road to becoming a major player in the local shipping industry. For the first time, Kloster placed a contract for a newbuilding with the Fredrikstad Mek. Verksted. The order, for a steamship of 3050-dwt, was placed in October 1912, with delivery in June/July 1913. The price was stipulated at NOK 485,000, a sum considerably above the previous investments in second-hand vessels made by Kloster's single-ship companies. He therefore adopted a new strategy in the financing and employment of the vessel. Before signing the contract he had already secured a two-year time charter with a Christiania shipowning firm at a monthly rate of £900.

On the strength of this charter he invited investors to purchase shares in the newly formed single-ship company that would own the

---

[22]SMM 4284 M and 4284 Y.

newbuilding. The share capital was set at NOK 300,000, or 120 shares with a nominal value of NOK 2500 each. Kloster himself took thirty shares in the new company; the captain, Chr. Christophersen, purchased twenty shares; and Mr. Sven Haabet bought four shares. The remainder were quickly subscribed by other Stavanger investors, most of whom took one or two shares each. The difference between the cost of the vessel and the share capital was secured by a first mortgage loan with the Amsterdamsche Scheepsverband Bank. The rate of interest was set at five percent per annum, with three percent commission, at least ten percent of the principal to be repaid per year. At the inaugural general meeting of the new company on 2 May 1913 Kloster was voted managing owner on the same terms as agreed for DS *Cassiopeia*. The ship, to be called DS *Libra*, was insured for NOK 500,000.[23]

The success in raising capital for the *Libra*, as well as the continuing good freight market, was probably the deciding factor in Kloster's decision to place an order for a sister ship at the same shipyard in March 1913. The financing was arranged in a similar fashion, but this time Kloster felt sufficiently confident to dispense with the time charter that had been an integral part of the earlier venture. He secured a considerably lower contract price for the new vessel (NOK 436,500), with delivery in May/June 1914. This time the share capital of the new single-ship company was set at NOK 200,000, with Kloster subscribing twenty-five shares at NOK 1000 each. A loan of 160,000 guilders secured by a first mortgage on the vessel was obtained at the Nederlandsche Scheepshypotheekbank in Rotterdam on similar terms as the loan on DS *Libra*. The inaugural general meeting of A/S Gemma (later changed to A/S *Freda*) resolved that Kloster be the managing owner on the same terms and conditions as with the sister vessel. The DS *Freda* was delivered in September 1914.

Thus, immediately after the outbreak of the First World War Kloster was managing owner of four vessels totalling 9650 dwt. By reinvesting his profits he had increased his net worth from around NOK 50,000 in 1906 to almost 212,000 by the end of 1914. Unfortu-

---

[23]SMM 4284 K.

nately, his personal accounts for 1911-1912 are unavailable, but we can reconstruct his personal balance sheet for the years 1906-1911. These show that the returns from his various activities were modest in the initial years. His personal net worth was close to NOK 82,000 at the end of 1911, a year in which he earned a very respectable 28.8% on his investments. The returns on his own capital for the previous years were much more modest, varying between 0.9% in 1908 and seven percent in 1910. The pronounced increase in his personal net worth in 1912-1914 indicates that he likely earned very satisfactory returns in those years, probably comparable to the return on own capital of 24.6% in 1914.[24]

The accounts of the individual vessels indicate that through 1914 most of the income was generated by freight earnings, although the successful sale of DS *Vestlandet* had generated hyper-profits. These kinds of returns stood him in good stead and enabled him to adopt a higher risk strategy. It was from this platform that he was able to make his initial, but unfulfilled attempts at asset play.

The Opportunities of War

After the initial uncertainties in the world shipping markets during the first months after the outbreak of war, it became clear that the conflict would offer unparalleled possibilities for shipowners in neutral countries. Opinion was divided, however, during the first weeks of the conflict. Some observers argued forcefully that as long as Norway stayed neutral, the war would be a time of opportunity for both Norwegian shipowners and exporters. Others disagreed, among them many who voiced their misgivings at a meeting of the Oslo Shipowners Association early in September.[25]

In the first weeks and months of the war many shipowners panicked and sold their vessels, while others hurried to conclude long-

---

[24]SMM 4284 H.

[25]Knut Utstein Kloster, *Krigsår og gullflom. Skibsfarten under verdenskrigen* (Oslo, 1935), 13-15.

term charters at relatively low, but secure, rates. Kloster was offered the option to cancel the three-year time charter just concluded for DS *Freda* through the firm Louis Donald and Co. of Mobile, Alabama on behalf of the Seeberg Line. The vessel was to be employed in the West Indian trade at a monthly freight of £815. On 9 September, the charterers' agent in Mobile cabled Kloster offering to cancel the deal. Kloster replied the next day that "[the] owners will not cancel [the] charter." Two years later he had to pay the charterers US $100,000 in order to get out of the final year of the agreement.[26]

This episode illustrates that Kloster at the time sided with the pessimists. Nonetheless, it did not take long for him to realize that with the tonnage belonging to the belligerents largely occupied in supplying their war needs, Norwegian shipowners were in a good position not only to increase their market share in key trades but also to reap the full benefits of rising freight rates. With soaring freight rates, the prices of second-hand tonnage also rose, and newbuildings looked like an attractive option. Kloster took advantage of the rising second-hand market; as we have already noted, he sold the DS *Cassiopeia* in December 1914 and DS *John Wilson* the following month. This meant that he now only managed two vessels, DS *Libra* and DS *Freda*.

On 7 January 1915 Kloster signed an agreement with Captain Henrik Østervold of Bergen under which he assumed a newbuilding contract at Bergens Mek. Verksted for a 3050-dwt steamship to be delivered the following April. The purchase price was a very reasonable NOK 468,000, while the initial contract price had been NOK 410,000. The very same day Kloster invited interested investors to purchase shares in a new limited liability shipping company entitled Klosters Rederi A/S. The prospective shareholders were informed that the bearer shares of NOK 2500 each would initially finance the purchase of the newbuilding contract, but that Kloster reserved the right to purchase additional vessels on behalf of the company now being formed. Within a few days, the subscribed capital reached NOK 700,000 and Kloster redoubled his attempts to secure more tonnage. At the end of the month he successfully negotiated the purchase of DS

[26]SMM, Clausen manuscript.

Mathilde from its Tønsberg owners for NOK 583,000. The 3600-dwt vessel was built at the Fevig Shipyard in 1908 and was employed on a time charter for the Munson Line in the Gulf of Mexico trade at a monthly rate of £800. A few days after the conclusion of the sale, the charterer offered to renew at £1700 per month, and a few days later Kloster was offered NOK 650,000 for the vessel. Both were refused.

Kloster's ambitions were growing daily and he was amassing a substantial stake in shipping. The first general meeting of Klosters Rederi A/S was held in Stavanger on 23 April 1915. The initial capital of the new company was stipulated at NOK 1,000,000 divided into four hundred shares of NOK 2500 apiece. The managing owner was to have the normal fee of NOK 1500 per year plus a five percent portion of net profits. In addition to Kloster, the board of directors consisted of a long-time investor in various single-ship companies, the Stavanger industrialist John G. Myhre, and Captain Reinert Tørresen, another old business associate. The statutes of the new company contained one innovation which clearly shows that Kloster had plans for an "asset play" investment strategy. In the old single-ship companies, the consent of a majority of shareholders was necessary to buy or sell either vessels or contracts. But under the new rules, the managing owner could make such deals without consulting the shareholders as long as the other two directors agreed. On 28 May 1915 Klosters Rederi A/S was registered as the first multi-ship limited liability company in Stavanger.[27] Its establishment gave Kloster the vehicle he needed to pursue his new strategy in a market of rapidly-escalating freights and ship prices.

Space does not allow a detailed examination of the many business deals in the next three years. A brief description of the investment policy and its economic results will have to suffice. From the list of vessels and newbuilding orders in table 4, it is clear that Kloster was extraordinarily active in the second-hand market during 1915. By the end of November his company had bought eight second-hand vessels and one newbuilding contract. The latter had been quickly sold to the Haugesund shipowner Knut Knutsen at a net profit of NOK 182,000. Three of the second-hand purchases had also been sold, at a

---

[27]SMM 4284 N.

net profit of about NOK 910,000. In addition, the *Hercules* company, owned by Kloster and five business associates, had purchased the DS *Hercules*, a 6600-dwt tramp vessel built in Sunderland in 1903.

Table 4
Vessels Managed by Lauritz Kloster, 1906-1917

Vessel Name	Tonnage (Dwt.)	Purchased	Sold
Sjøgutten	830	Dec. 1906	May 1912
Smaragd	600	Sep. 1907	Oct. 1911
*Kong Frode**	1300	Dec. 1907	Apr. 1909
Vestlandet	2680	Nov. 1909	Nov. 1912
John Wilson	950	Mar. 1911	Jan. 1915
Cassiopeia	2600	Nov. 1911	Dec. 1914
Libra	3050	Oct. 1912	Dec. 1915
Freda	3050	Mar. 1913	Feb. 1917
Newbuilding	3050	Jan. 1915	Jun. 1915
Mathilde	3600	Jan. 1915	Aug. 1915
*Sola***	5000	May 1915	Oct. 1916
Bellatrix	4200	Jun. 1915	Aug. 1916
Etna	6300	Aug. 1915	Sep. 1915
Matti	3650	Aug. 1915	Oct. 1915
Rigel	4700	Sep. 1915	Dec. 1915
Norfolk	6200	Sep. 1915	Jan. 1917
Hercules	6600	Sep. 1915	Sep. 1916
Sirrah	5150	Nov. 1915	Dec. 1915
Mia	7250	May 1916	Sep. 1916
Vesterlund	8800	Mar. 1916	Apr. 1917
Vesterlide	8800	Apr. 1916	Feb. 1917
Vesterlen	8800	Apr. 1916	Feb. 1917
Vestervarde	8800	Aug. 1916	Apr. 1917
Vesterfjell	8800	Aug. 1916	Apr. 1917
Vesterfjord	8800	Aug. 1916	Apr. 1917
Vesterøy	8800	Aug. 1916	Apr. 1917
Vesterdal	8800	Dec. 1916	Apr. 1917
Vesterness	8800	Dec. 1916	Apr. 1917

Notes: Includes Newbuilding orders. * denotes wrecked at sea; ** indicates lost at sea.

Source: See table 3.

The many purchases had stretched the financial resources of the Kloster company in spite of the profit of the sales and solid cash flow from profitable freight contracts. By November 1915 the existing fleet was encumbered by different mortgage loans from various banks totalling NOK 1,850,000. Klosters Rederi A/S had outstanding unsecured loans (so-called "cash credit loans") with Stavangers Privatbank for over NOK three million. In addition, the bank provided an unsecured loan to the *Hercules* partnership of over NOK 800,000. The bank must have realized that its exposure to a single customer was too large, because it demanded that Kloster sell his latest purchase, the DS *Sirrah*, as well as another vessel of his choice in order to reduce his borrowing. His reluctant compliance netted a profit on the two vessels of NOK 860,000.[28] When the accounts for Klosters Rederi A/S were balanced for the year 1915, they showed total assets of NOK 5.4 million against debts of NOK 4.2 million. The total return on capital employed was 21.7%, but the high leverage borrowing resulted in a rate of return on own capital of a whopping 76.3%.[29]

Freight rates and vessel prices continued to rise in the early months of 1916 despite attempts by the British government to control this through various measures, including the refusal of bunker coal to vessels refusing to comply with a set of maximum rates. The Norwegian Shipowners' Association was compelled to send a delegation to London in order to negotiate this dispute. An agreement was reached in September to limit the freight rate in the British coal trade. Eventually the Norwegians were also forced to negotiate a tonnage agreement with Great Britain.[30]

Neither of these developments markedly affected the general level of freight rates, however, nor did they discourage Norwegian and other neutral shipowners from continuing to speculate. By 1916, it was clear that the only country able to satisfy the increasing demand for newbuildings was the United States. Although Norwegian and other

---

[28]SMM 4284, Clausen manuscript.

[29]Computed by the author from information in SMM 4284 H.

[30]Johan Schreiner, *Norsk skipsfart under krig og høkonjunktur* (Oslo, 1963), 123-130.

neutral yards were fully occupied, the limited capacity plus the increasing difficulty of securing shipbuilding materials meant that European newbuildings outside the belligerent countries were almost negligible. Increasingly, ships belonging to neutral countries also fell victim to both mine and submarine warfare.

Kloster signed his first newbuilding contract with an American yard in March 1916, ordering an 8800-dwt tanker vessel from Chester Shipbuilding Co. in Pennsylvania for delivery in August 1917. The price was stipulated at US $100 per ton. The initial payment was ten percent of the price, the remainder to be paid in instalments during the building period. The newbuilding was named *Vesterlund*.

At the same time, the Norwegian shipowner Christopher Hannevig had obtained the agency for the Northwest Steel Company of Portland, Oregon. This yard had developed a standard 8800-dwt general cargo vessel of the so-called "Robert Dollar" type, with turbine engines equipped for either coal or oil. Kloster decided that these looked promising. After receiving information on the company through his bank, he wired Captain Chr. Christophersen, who was in New York with the DS *Hercules* to remain in the USA. He was given power of attorney authorising him to accept contract terms and specifications and to sign contracts for two vessels. The first, to be called *Vesterlide*, was purchased by the Klosters Rederi, while the other was bought by the *Hercules* partnership. The vessels cost US $900,000 each, with ten per cent of the price due immediately and the rest to be paid in monthly instalments during construction. The contracts were signed on 2 April 1916 for delivery in February/April 1917.

In August Kloster signed a contract for four additional newbuildings of the same type with the same yard. The contract was again negotiated through Christopher Hannevig for delivery between September 1917 and February 1918. The price per vessel was US $1,012,000 or $115 dollars per ton. The first and last newbuildings, named *Vestervarde* and *Vesterfjell*, were purchased by Klosters Rederi A/S, while the *Hercules* partnership got number three and a new partnership called *Mia II* acquired the fourth vessel.

The economic results of the Kloster companies at the end of 1916 were impressive. The shipping company showed a net profit of almost NOK 7.2 million. Operating or net profit from the operation of the Kloster fleet amounted to almost NOK 2.3 million, while proceeds from the sale of vessels totalled almost NOK five million. The balance sheet showed assets of NOK 8.8 million, consisting chiefly of instalment payments made on the US newbuildings (NOK 6.8 million). The only remaining vessel operated by the company, DS *Norfolk*, was listed at a book value of NOK 1.6 million. The return on average capital employed by the company was 98.1%, while the return on equity capital amounted to an incredible 175.1%. Kloster's personal accounts for the year 1916, including his share in the partnerships *Hercules* and *Mia I* and *II*, showed that his net worth had increased to over NOK 2.3 million. He had achieved a return on average own capital invested of 150.7%, while the equivalent overall return was 92.7%.[31]

The Sale of the Century

As the beginning of 1917 the Kloster company had six newbuilding contracts in the US and only one ship, the *Norfolk*, actually sailing. The newbuildings were due to be delivered over a period stretching from February 1917 to February 1918. In addition to the payments of NOK 6.8 million already made on the various contracts, another NOK fifteen million was due during the delivery period. On the other hand, the company had virtually no other debts (only a paltry NOK 800,000 at the end of 1916) and a steady cash flow from DS *Norfolk*, which was employed on a profitable time charter to the Holland-America Line through 11 January 1917.

In order to safeguard the company's ability to pay the newbuilding instalments as they came due, Kloster secured a credit line with Norway's largest commercial bank, the Centralbanken for Norge A/S. On 10 January 1917 he obtained a letter granting him a loan for NOK ten million, secured by first mortgages on the six newbuildings as well as a NOK one million mortgage on the DS *Norfolk* and Kloster's personal guarantee. A two percent commission was payable to the bank, and the variable rate of interest was set at one percent above the Bank of Norway discount rate. The loan was to be repaid in

[31]See note 28.

full within two years. The bank also added another condition: as long as the loan was outstanding, the dividend to shareholders in Klosters Rederi A/S was limited to forty percent!

As it transpired, it never became necessary to draw on the loan guarantee from Centralbanken. Kloster and his co-directors agreed that the time was propitious to sell *Norfolk* if the price was right. After a few days of negotiations with the Christiania shipbrokers Winge and Co., acting for the Haugesund shipowner Jacob Ringen, the ship was sold on 16 January for NOK 4.75 million and delivered to the buyer in the Tyne estuary. Since the vessel had been purchased a year and a half previously for NOK 1.7 million, the net sales profit was more than NOK three million. In addition, the net operational profits during the period amounted to NOK 827,000.

After the sale of DS *Norfolk* the remaining real assets of the company comprised its six newbuildings in America. The first, the *Vesterlide*, had been delayed and delivery was now due at the end of April. Building was due to begin on the last vessel, *Vesterfjell*, during February. In spite of the relatively good delivery record of the Northwest Steel Company, it was clear to Kloster and his co-directors that as the war progressed, material shortages and other problems were increasingly likely to retard newbuilding deliveries. Letters from Kloster's captains visiting New York toward the end of 1916 warned of similar delays in yards on the eastern seaboard. Worrying as well were the increasing portents of US entry into the war. The German resumption of unlimited submarine warfare on 1 February increased the likelihood of American involvement. Finally, the risk that newbuildings on order in the US would be confiscated by the American authorities or transferred to US registry could not be ruled out.

The decision was therefore taken to sell the first two newbuildings, one of which was owned by the *Hercules* partnership. After initial negotiations with French buyers in January, the vessels were sold through Joachim Grieg and Co. to the Cunard Line on 26 February for US $4.3 million (NOK 14.5 million). Cunard was also interested in purchasing the remaining five newbuilding contracts owned by the Kloster company, as well as the two contracts owned by the partnership companies *Hercules I* and *Mia II*, respectively.

Negotiations were opened on 28 February when Kloster telegraphed that the total asking price for all seven newbuildings would be NOK forty million. The decision to open negotiations was taken after Kloster had decided that the vessels would not be operationally competitive once the wartime boom ended. Kloster reached this conclusion after consulting with his US representative, Captain Chr. Christophersen, and others.

Negotiations proceeded during March and April, with an initial offer of US $9.5 million from Cunard. On 2 April, Cunard temporarily suspended the talks, but came back with a new offer of US $11.5 million on 11 April. In the interim, Cunard had its annual general meeting on 4 April, and the US had declared war on Germany on 6 April. Kloster countered his previous offer of US $12 million, which was finally accepted by Cunard. After various commissions and transfer fees, the net result for the Kloster companies was US $6.618 million (NOK 22.6 million). The largest portion went to the shareholders in Klosters Rederi A/S, but the associates in the partnerships also made huge profits. The accounts for Klosters Rederi A/S show that each holder of a certificate with a face value of NOK five hundred received NOK 10,215 per share in addition to the annual dividends. Kloster's personal accounts for 1917 show a net worth of NOK 8.4 million. His return on average own capital amounted to 113.5%.[32]

Conclusion

This paper has shown how a forty year-old Norwegian shipping clerk established himself successfully as a shipowner by initially following a cautious investment policy. When the chance to alter his strategy from low to high-risk, increasingly dependent on asset play, arose as a result of the war, Kloster rapidly pursued it vigorously. From 1915, he retained a high degree of control not only of Klosters Rederi A/S but also the associated partnership companies, thus enabling him to respond decisively to changing opportunities. He finally successfully negotiated the sale of the company's assets in time to avoid the fate

[32] *Ibid.*

that befell many other Norwegian shipping companies: having their vessels requisitioned by the US government. In addition to providing large profits for his shareholders and partners, he amassed a large personal fortune.

After a spell as General Director of the Government Shipping Board, Kloster re-entered the shipping industry in 1923, this time based in Christiania. The present-day Kloster companies survived crises both before and during the Second World War, and in the 1970s became major participants in the Miami-based cruise industry. The story of the Kloster enterprises is an outstanding, but not atypical, example of how Norwegian shipping entrepreneurs built substantial enterprises from limited initial economic resources. The Kloster experience from 1906 to 1917 is also a powerful historical reminder that success in shipping is not only about the timing of investment but also about the importance of disposing of real assets in time.

The Harriman-Hamburg-American Line Agreement of June 1920: The Foremost German Shipping Company's Return to the Seas

Lars U. Scholl

In his highly-praised and enthusiastically-welcomed book *The Trade Makers*,[1] Peter Davies cast his eyes over the German lines engaged in the West African trade and observed that they "had made very good progress in the early years after the war."[2] Considering the fact that following the Treaty of Versailles the German mercantile marine had, in the words of John Maynard Keynes, been "swept from the seas,"[3] it was quite remarkable for 102 ships to be in operation again in the West African trade by December 1923, "in spite of the loss of the German colonies which were the basis of their business."[4] While the 444,153 gross tons in the fleet only amounted to one-third of the prewar tonnage of 1,361,628, the emergence of four fleets calling at West African ports was an astonishing achievement only a few years after almost the entire German merchant marine had been surrendered to the Allies.[5]

---

[1]See Walter Minchinton's review in *Mariner's Mirror*, LXII (1976), 405.

[2]Peter N. Davies, *The Trade Makers: Elder Dempster in West Africa, 1852-1972* (London, 1973), 218.

[3]John M. Keynes, "The Economic Consequences of the Peace," *Collected Writings of John Maynard Keynes* (London, 1971), II, 41.

[4]Davies, *Trade Makers*, 218.

[5]For details see Lars U. Scholl, "The German Merchant Marine in the Inter-War Period, 1920-1932," in Lewis R. Fischer and Helge W. Nordvik (eds.), *Shipping and Trade, 1750-1950: Essays in International Maritime Economic History* (Pontefract, 1990), 191-212.

Keynes and many contemporary observers were convinced that the German merchant marine could not "be restored for many years to come on a scale adequate to meet the requirements of her own commerce."[6] Moreover, many of Keynes' British compatriots did not wish to see the Germans return to maritime affairs.

> The idea that, after the last shot was fired, the struggle against Germany must be transferred to the economic sphere had taken firm hold of many minds; in order to avert the danger of new aggression by Germany, German trade must be completely ruined, and German trade could be struck at most effectively through the shipping which carried it.[7]

While the war was still in progress, men like A.M. Samuel and W.S. Holdsworth advocated the reintroduction of the Navigation Acts since "the war had shown that merchant shipping possessed an importance in the realms of supply, of transport, and of actual operations, even greater than had been hither to supposed and no price was too great to pay for supremacy at sea."[8]

The crushing of German trade and the fostering of British shipping were two proposals put forward in the discussion of domestic problems relating to British shipping after the war. Punitive measures against Germany were widely endorsed in France, Great Britain and other countries; the harshness of some of the clauses of the Treaty of Versailles reflected that spirit. It is not the intention of this paper to discuss the rights or wrongs of the Treaty. My aim is to show that capitalists think differently, not letting themselves be governed primarily by nationalistic sentiments but rather by pragmatism. Their main objects are to gain business and to earn profits. If these goals can best be achieved by cooperation with a former enemy, logic demands

---

[6]Keynes, "Economic Consequences," 41.

[7]C. Ernest Fayle, *The War and the Shipping Industry* (London, 1927), 349.

[8]*Ibid.*, 349.

that capitalists grasp the opportunities. This is not to say that capitalists are free from nationalistic ideals or vengefulness. But for the sake of business they are more easily induced to discard ideologies which are detrimental to their objective. This seems to hold true especially for shipowners. As C.E. Fayle put it,

> to shipping, perhaps beyond all other industries, the free play of economic forces and the free growth of exchange between nations is the essential foundation of healthy and permanent prosperity. To such conditions war and the war spirit are alike utterly opposed.[9]

Although Fayle's study was sponsored by the Carnegie Endowment for International Peace, which was intended to "contribute fundamentally toward the aims of an institution dedicated to the cause of international peace,"[10] there is no reason to believe that his analysis was distorted or that his observation about shipowners was erroneous. It is in this context that I want to examine the Harriman-Hamburg-American Line Agreement of 1920.[11]

At the outbreak of World War I the Hamburg-American Line (HAL) owned a fleet of 1,360,360 gross tons, including 194 ocean steamers. More than seventy overseas routes were operated independently or in conjunction with other shipping companies, and HAL vessels called at four hundred major ports on every inhabited continent, with the exception of Australia. In 1913 about 460,000 passengers and roughly 8.3 million tons of cargo had been carried by the com-

---

[9]*Ibid.*, 412.

[10]*Ibid.*, editor's preface, v.

[11]This essay benefitted greatly from the generous permission from Hapag-Lloyd's governing board to examine the archival material presently being catalogued by the Hamburg State Archive. Since Lamar Cecil wrote his biography of Albert Ballin in the 1960s (*Albert Ballin* [Princeton, 1967]), this material had been virtually inaccessible to scholars.

pany's ships.[12] This impressive performance had moved the HAL to the top ranks of the world's shipping companies.

When the hostilities ceased, war losses and subsequent surrenders cost the company 1,235,357 gross tons of shipping, leaving it with insufficient vessels to resume business on even the most moderate scale. Two options confronted the directors: either to leave shipping altogether and make investments in non-maritime fields, a strategy of survival which had been pursued during the war, or to start from scratch. The first option was never discussed or even contemplated seriously, since the shipping hiatus had been caused by the war rather than managerial or other failures. Businessmen and politicians concentrated solely on the resurrection of shipping to its pre-1914 levels. Starting over was the only solution thinkable in a country which believed in its natural right to continue as it had before the war interrupted. National pride, the necessity of feeding a starving nation, and a desire to rebuild a ruined economy demanded the reconstruction of a domestically-owned merchant fleet.

Neither financial manipulations, such as increasing share capital, nor governmental compensations for war losses or public spending on the reconstruction of the merchant fleet can be touched upon here.[13] Instead, the focus will be on a third element in the strategy pursued to reinvigorate the maritime sector. The HAL, like other German shipping companies, sought international cooperation with partners which controlled the ships it so desperately needed.

Keynes, in his widely-read analysis on the economic consequences of the peace, argued that

> no lines will run from Hamburg, except such as foreign nations may find it worthwhile to establish out of their surplus tonnage. Germany will have to pay to foreigners for the carriage of her trade such charges as they may be

---

[12]Teubner, "Der Wiederaufbau der Hamburg-Amerika Linie 1919 bis 1929," *Archiv für Post und Telegraphie*, LVII (1929), 231-245.

[13]Scholl, "The German Merchant Marine," 194-198.

> able to exact and will receive only such conveniences as it may suit them to give her.[14]

Although Germans argued that without domestic ships the transport of food would be difficult, the Allies insisted on the transfer of the greater part of the mercantile marine precisely to safeguard the supply of foodstuffs to Germany. Transporting food to Germany was only one rationale for reviving the fleet; revitalising German ports and commerce was the second objective. Keynes assumed that German shipping companies would seek to bring under their effective influence the Scandinavian and Dutch merchant marines.[15] He was close to prescient; the HAL, for example, tried to come to terms with Norwegian shipping companies.[16] But negotiations broke down in August 1919 and were not resumed.

To Dr. Wilhelm Cuno, director-general of the HAL after Albert Ballin's sudden death in November 1918, it was obvious that German commerce and industry would not recover if trade remained dependent on foreign tonnage. To bolster his position he demanded on many occasions that German shipping companies be granted access to foreign tonnage until newly-ordered ships were available.[17] It is one of the amazing aspects of post-bellum developments that Cuno's strategy was successful. There must have been a strong temptation for allied shipping companies to use the dire straits of the HAL to completely crush their former rival. Grievances against the HAL existed in shipping circles because Ballin had taken so much advantage

---

[14]Keynes, "Economic Consequences," 41-42.

[15]*Ibid.*, 42.

[16]Erich Priester, *Der Wiederaufbau der deutschen Handelsschiff-fahrt. Ein Beitrag zur Wirtschaftsgeschichte der Gegenwart* (Berlin, 1926), 97.

[17]Wilhelm Cuno, *Der Friedensvertrag und die deutsche Schiffahrt* (Berlin, 1920), 14.

of the conference system before the war.[18] Moreover, seamen and public opinion in America and Britain favoured punishment for the damage Germany had inflicted on international shipping between 1914 and 1918. But the opposite occurred: the HAL and other companies received British and American help not for philanthropic but for economic reasons. Despite not having one seaworthy ship of their own, German shipping companies still had something to offer which many allied companies lacked. The HAL, the Norddeutscher Lloyd (NDL) and other German shipping firms possessed outstanding commercial facilities and a good deal of long-term experience in shipping.

To anyone who wanted to usurp the HAL's prewar trading empire, it was essential to gain access to extensive port and commercial facilities and to acquire a sophisticated communication network. Foreign ships calling at German ports needed to use the quays, cranes, warehouses and labour force if they wanted to take advantage of the available opportunities. Without the intimate knowledge of the HAL's employees and overseas partners, any attempt to re-establish old routes from Hamburg likely would have suffered many setbacks or encountered severe economic problems. It was important to tap these assets, because without cooperation it would have been virtually impossible to operate ships effectively on routes to and from Germany.

A nation which was bitterly opposed to what it considered unfair treatment under the Versailles Treaty was easily capable of obstructing shipping, even at the cost of further suffering for the domestic population. Apart from people directly involved in shipping, many industrial workers depended on the smooth supply of raw materials shipped to Germany at freight rates beyond German control. According to contemporary statistics, fourteen million Germans earned their living in shipping, foreign trade or related activities.[19] That passive resistance was more than an ephemeral possibility became apparent during the French occupation of the Ruhr in 1923. Germany

---

[18]Frank Broeze, "Albert Ballin, The Hamburg-Bremen Rivalry and the Dynamics of the Conference System," *International Journal of Maritime History*, III, No. 1 (June 1991), 1-32.

[19]Cuno, *Der Friedensvertrag*, 14.

was an important market within the world economy. It was therefore a matter of sound judgement to seek cooperation with the ex-enemy. A British commercial journal ventured in 1920 that "it will be quite impossible to rule Hamburg out of the running."[20] It was not desirable either. The huge number of vessels handed over resulted in a tonnage glut, and there was not enough cargo available to keep the ships fully employed. Whatever antipathy there may have been, British and American shipping companies were eager to profit from German facilities and expertise. They thus allowed the HAL, the NDL and other firms to get started again while they tried to cope with the imbalance caused by surplus tonnage.

The HAL contacted various shipping companies to offer to act as agents and to create opportunities for re-establishing its former routes. The first agency contract into which the HAL entered was with the Kerr Steamship Co., which started a regular service between Hamburg and New York in June 1919.[21] Later the same year, the Kerr Line commenced operations between Hamburg, Mexico and the River Plate. On the initiative of Alfred Holt and Co. in Liverpool and the Ellerman and Bucknall Steamship Company in London, the HAL early in 1920 agreed to husband their vessels from Hamburg to the Far East; the agreement covered departures and rates. Each shipping company remained independent and all earnings were kept separate. Late in April 1920 the service was opened with British ships. In the same month the HAL was able to send her first steamer, the 1439-ton *Grimm* which had been purchased in Scandinavia, to the West Indies and Mexico to inaugurate a monthly service primarily using chartered ships.

In the long-run the HAL was not satisfied merely to act as an agent for others. The managers in Hamburg wanted more, since they believed that their business needed a broader perspective to ensure the company's future and to maintain its international connections. Their goal--to enlarge the firm's responsibilities and to regain a stronger

---

[20] Quoted in *ibid.*, 17.

[21] Hans-Jürgen Witthöft, *Hapag. Hamburg-Amerika Linie* (Herford, 1973), 63.

foothold in international shipping--coincided with the aim of the US Shipping Board (USSB) to increase the profitability of the rejuvenated American merchant fleet by making use of the HAL's vast experience. Edward Hurley, Chairman of the USSB in 1919, "devised a way, long before the peace treaty was signed, to edge out the Allies and gain control over this shipping bonanza."[22] In April 1919 he asked J.W. Burchard, a vice-president of the General Electric Company and an intimate associate of German commercial leaders, to act as a special commissioner for the USSB. Burchard was sent to Germany in order to "do something in connection with our shipping routes to Hamburg and other plans in connection with our export and import trades."[23] Hurley was convinced that Burchard, who did not have direct shipping connections, would "be able to do things in a quiet way that shipping men who would be more or less checked up by our friends in England could not do."[24] Hurley's plan to establish trade links with Germany before the peace was signed did not materialise, in part because British competitors were in the process of establishing similar contacts. Ultimately, however, as Jeffrey Safford has noted, "only the Shipping Board was willing to take the risk of assuming such a vast responsibility."[25] Consequently the Shipping Board sent a second agent, W.G. Sickel, the HAL's American representative before the war, to Hamburg in the autumn of 1919. When he returned in November he informed the Board that the HAL was very much interested in American cooperation on its old routes. On behalf of the USSB, Sickel arranged a form of contract "enabling the Shipping Board to take over all of the German line's facilities in Hamburg."[26] The matter

---

[22]Jeffrey J.Safford, *Wilsonian Maritime Diplomacy, 1913-1921* (New Brunswick, NJ, 1978), 239.

[23]*Ibid.*

[24]*Ibid.*

[25]*Ibid.*, 240.

[26]*Ibid.*

remained dormant for several months until on 4 March 1920 the Board decided to approach private companies in the United States on the question of negotiating with the HAL.

Only two companies, the International Mercantile Marine Corporation (IMMC) and the American Ship and Commerce Corporation (ASCC), were considered large enough to participate in such an important operation. A week later the Board discussed the matter with P.A.S. Franklin, formerly head of the USSB's ship control committee during the war and currently president of IMMC. He argued against seeking the proposed arrangement with the HAL. Although he admitted that the short-term benefits would be great, in the long-run he predicted great financial disadvantages, since IMMC would have to pay for "giving up its own long established port facilities to take over those of the German line."[27] The Board was not very pleased with Franklin's answer.

Another objection was even more serious. Franklin was strongly opposed to any direct involvement of the USSB in forming a partnership with the HAL. Similarly, Senator Wesley Jones of Washington, chairman of the Senate Committee of Commerce, maintained that it would be preferable to let private companies conduct the negotiations and conclude the contracts for such joint ventures. As long as Germany and America were still formally at war it was not acceptable for an institution of the state like the Board to enter into agreements with the enemy. USSB chairman John Barton Payne reacted swiftly, announcing that the government would not participate in any direct negotiations between the HAL and private enterprises. Under the original plan the USSB was to have arranged a working agreement with the HAL. On 14 March 1920, the *New York Times* published an article entitled "Plan to Operate German Searoutes."[28] The publication followed the approval by the Senate Commerce Committee of a plan "under which American steamship companies would take over and operate the sixty

---

[27] *Ibid.*

[28] *New York Times*, 14 March 1920.

prewar world trade routes of the Hamburg-American Line."[29] The favourable vote passed by a margin of ten to four. The four Senators who voted against the proposal, "were not necessarily opposed to the plan, but...before giving their assent they desired to ascertain more definitely the particulars."[30] There was some disagreement among Committee members as to the exact scope of the plan. Both Jones and Payne assured the Committee that the Board's part "merely would be to furnish the ships either through sale or lease and to lend its co-operation in obtaining this business for American shipping interests."[31] The newspaper was unable to tell its readers "whether the plan originated with the German company or with the Board."[32] From the outset it was clear that any arrangement would be co-operative, subject to the approval of the German company. Chairman Payne promised that:

> 1. No direct arrangement be made by the board with the Hamburg Line;
> 2. It is very desirable that an American company or group of companies make an arrangement by which this business may be secured; and
> 3. The board is prepared to co-operate with an American company or companies in the sale or chartering of ships to enable such American companies to secure this outlet, the terms of any contract which may be made with the Hamburg-American Line being subject to the approval of the board.[33]

---

[29] *Ibid.*

[30] Senators Edge of New Jersey, Lenroot of Wisconsin, Calder of New York and Fletcher of Florida voted against the bill.

[31] *New York Times*, 14 March 1920.

[32] *Ibid.*

[33] *Ibid.*

The USSB was not ready to admit publicly that there had been negotiations with the HAL. But it was obvious that the Germans were interested in entering into a co-operative agreement with American steamship lines. In order to calm any opposition it was stressed that the Board was "not prepared to make any further move in the direction of this development without the approval of the Senate committee, because a technical state of war exists still between the United States and Germany."[34]

Originally, the three members of the HAL's governing board who went to America on 28 March 1920 planned to negotiate a contract with the Board. Following Sickel's preliminary talks with the USSB they were under the impression that this was also the Board's intention. The minutes of the meetings of the HAL's governing board in January 1920 indicate that the company did not want to make any concessions to the ASCC concerning quays in Hamburg as long as negotiations with the USSB were ongoing.

Sickel was instructed to let the USSB know that there was a strong demand for quay space. Therefore, negotiation of a contract with the Board seemed urgent to ensure that dockside facilities were available.[35] Just before they left Hamburg, however, the negotiators were informed that the state of war ruled out this possibility and that the USSB suggested instead discussions with private shipping companies. The Board promise to support such a pact with ships, quay space, and the like.[36]

It is difficult to understand why the HAL's representatives suggested the formation of a German-American shipping company with the USSB as a party to the proposed agreement, since they knew that this opportunity no longer existed. As late as 3 April, the German shipping journal *Hansa* published an official announcement by the HAL telling the public that negotiations were underway to work out details of a plan which enabled the HAL to incorporate her port

[34]*Ibid.*

[35]Staatsarchiv Hamburg (StAH), Hapag I, 2068, 9 and 17 January 1920.

[36]StAH, Hapag I, 1201, 30 July 1920.

facilities and huge shipping assets into the services which the USSB was about to begin.[37]

On their arrival in the United States the Germans started talks with the Kerr Line, their first postwar American business partners. Their counterpart was General George Goethals, president of the ASCC, which controlled the Kerr Navigation Company, a holding company of Kerr Steamships. At first, an agreement seemed possible. But finally negotiations failed because Goethals insisted upon operating old HAL routes with American ships only and was not prepared to withdraw them once the HAL's first newly-constructed ships were ready. Goethals had discussed this plan with the new chairman of the USSB, Admiral William S. Benson, on 24 March.[38] When the German delegation was confronted with this proposal Cuno and his colleagues rejected it outright, since acceptance would have meant an abandonment of the HAL's independence.

In addition to Cuno's refusal it turned out that Goethals was unable to secure the support of the USSB. One of the reasons may have been that the Kerr Steamship Co. had been founded in 1917 by two British subjects, H.F. Kerr and A.E. Clegg; in addition, there was a good deal of Norwegian capital involved.[39] The USSB was committed to an American merchant marine "made up of ships built by Americans, owned by American capital, sailing under the American flag, and carrying the products of this country to all parts of the world."[40] Kerr did not qualify.

Since Franklin and the IMMC were strongly opposed to an agreement with Kerr and to the USSB's support of any arrangement, negotiations were terminated. Later, in an attempt to camouflage this

---

[37]*Hansa*, 3 April 1920.

[38]Priester, *Wiederaufbau*, 99.

[39]Theodor Baldus, "Die Wiederanknüpfung der Verkehrsverbindungen Deutschlands mit Übersee nach dem Weltkrieg 1914/1918," (Unpublished Ph.D. thesis, Universität Köln, 1921), 68.

[40]Safford, *Wilsonian Maritime Diplomacy*, 227.

failure and to conceal that he had misjudged the situation, Cuno declared on his return to Germany that he had never intended to negotiate a contract with the USSB but had made a courtesy call on Admiral Benson to thank him for the invitation and the support he had promised to lend.[41] Be that as it may, the USSB intervened and arranged a meeting with the young financier W. Averell Harriman in New York in May 1920. Before discussing the details of the contract the German managers signed with Harriman a month later, it is necessary to take a brief look at the attempts of the Wilson administration to rebuild an indigenous merchant marine in order to understand why the Americans had such a strong interest in coming to terms with the HAL.[42]

The American merchant marine experienced a dramatic decline after the end of the Civil War. American tonnage registered in overseas commerce plunged from 2.5 millions gross tons before the war to 1.5 millions gross tons in 1865. What followed has been called the "dark age" for the American merchant marine in foreign trade.[43] While in 1860 over seventy percent of the ships calling at American ports from abroad were American, by the end of the century less than ten percent of the U.S. foreign commerce was carried by American bottoms. In 1913, when the Woodrow Wilson took office, the American merchant fleet comprised 1.9 million gross tons, excluding sail and barges.[44]

World War altered this long-term stagnation. By 1920 the capacity of the American merchant fleet had risen more than six-fold to 12.4 million gross tons, and the United States had re-emerged as a major maritime nation. President Wilson had grasped the chances offered by the First World War to engineer the reconstruction of the merchant fleet. Before the Wilsonians came to power there was a

---

[41]StAH, Hapag I, 1201, 30 July 1920.

[42]The following is based upon Safford, *Wilsonian Maritime Diplomacy*.

[43]*Ibid.*, 1.

[44]*Lloyd's Register of Shipping*, statistical tables, various years.

common understanding among progressive Republicans and Democrats that foreign trade expansion was "the *sine qua non* of the nation's economic welfare."[45] The apparent inability of the domestic market to absorb more American products made it "absolutely indispensable" to revitalise the merchant marine. In his speeches during the 1912 campaign, Wilson repeatedly emphasised that "without a great merchant marine, we cannot take our rightful place in the commerce of the world."[46] Once in office Wilson initiated tariff and fiscal reforms which paved the way for the creation of maritime services that would ship American surpluses across the oceans.[47] In August 1914 Congress legalised the registration of foreign ships under the American flag and the Shipping Act of 1916 authorised government ownership and operation of a national merchant fleet, both measures that were regarded as essential for the prosperity of America's domestic economy and foreign trade. A strong merchant marine, it was believed, would not only create opportunities to "capture new markets now necessarily abandoned by British and German interests" but also play a vital role in America's war efforts.[48] Eventually, it was hoped that Great Britain's dominance of the seas could be undermined. By the time that Germany, in a desperate attempt to turn the tides of war, decided to resort to unrestricted submarine warfare, much legislative work had been carried out to launch a massive shipbuilding programme and to acquire, purchase or charter foreign and interned enemy tonnage. When the United States entered the war in April 1917, the merchant marine consisted of roughly 2.7 million gross tons of ships above 1,500 gross tons.

---

[45]Safford, *Wilsonian Maritime Diplomacy*, 17.

[46]*Ibid.*, 21.

[47]Jeffrey J.Safford, "The United States Merchant Marine in Foreign Trade, 1800-1939," in Tsunehiko Yui and Keiichiro Nakagawa (eds.), *Business History of Shipping. Strategy and Structure* (Tokyo, 1985), 91-118, 102-103.

[48]Safford, *Wilsonian Maritime Diplomacy*, 37.

By the end of 1918 over three million tons of shipping had been launched, most of it within the previous six months. In 1919 a further 4.1 million tons emerged from builders' yards and in 1920 another 4.7 million tons were added.[49] Finally, the USSB secured control over 700,000 tons of ships confiscated in American ports. With more than twelve million gross tons at its disposal, the American merchant fleet had become the second largest in the world.

With the return of peace, Anglo-American shipping was aggravated by a commercial "war after the war." In the words of one scholar, Great Britain ruthlessly tried "to capture the lion's share of the world's carrying trade."[50] Admiral Benson, navy chief of staff and in March 1920 Payne's successor as USSB chairman, warned in January 1919 that "if the United States desired to get in the running at all, it would have to get its shipping organized and into competition as quickly and efficiently as possible."[51]

Fourteen months later, just before he left the USSB, Payne was forced to admit that "we have no organization. We have nothing but ships. So far as the operation of ships is concerned, we are infants."[52] And these ships were not all in good condition or suitable for international trade. Huge sums had to be invested in the preparation of confiscated vessels which had suffered from long periods of idleness or had been damaged by their crews. Many wooden vessels which had been rapidly constructed in large series were unable to stand the rigours of ocean commerce. The manning problem was immense as well, since it proved difficult to find enough trained personnel. With malicious joy, Cuno described the crossing of the *Imperator*, which usually took five days but on one occasion lasted thirteen because the crew was unfamiliar with handling the valves, thus causing the engine

---

[49]Baldus, *Wiederanknüpfung*, 61-74.

[50]Safford, *Wilsonian Maritime Diplomacy*, 177.

[51]*Ibid.*

[52]*Ibid.*, 226.

room to flood with water from the swimming pool.[53] While he insinuated that incompetence had caused this accident, it is more likely that it resulted from the ship's long inactivity.

The passage of the Merchant Marine Act of 1920 had two objectives. First, it aimed at the general demobilisation of the fleet; second, it gave the USSB the power to operate "essential trade routes" as governmental enterprises as long as private shipping companies were unable to undertake permanent trade with foreign markets. Ultimately, publicly-operated lines were to be handed over to private owners. One of the matters which occupied Benson as chairman of the USSB was to engineer the transfer of government ships to private companies and to secure for American interests the prewar trade and commercial facilities of the HAL. Trade with Germany had been very lucrative for America before the war, reaching 2.4 thousand million marks in 1913.[54] American exports, amounting to 1.7 thousand million marks, comprised cotton, copper, wheat, oils and fats, crude oil and petrochemical products, timber, barley, maize and hides. German exports, which amounted to seven hundred million marks, consisted of toys, textiles and chemicals. Although the balance of trade was negative for Germany, the country was to compensate for this in other trades. Moreover, there were invisibles, such as shipping earnings, which further lessened the trade deficit. It was in the interest of both countries to re-establish strong commercial relations after the war. As a first step the War Trade Board announced in July 1919 that American citizens were allowed to trade again with Germany.[55]

Immediately several American shipping companies like the Kerr Line, the Pacat Steamship Corp., the Maritime Navigation Co., the Williams, Dimond Co. and the Brooks Steamship Corp. started liner services to Germany calling in Hamburg and Bremen. But they were unable to stand the competition from British and Dutch concerns. It was therefore necessary for the USSB to bring together the leading

---

[53]Cuno, *Friedensvertrag*, 17.

[54]Baldus, *Wiederanknüpfung*, 62.

[55]*Ibid.*, 70-72.

American and German shipping companies if the US merchant fleet were to be employed successfully in highly-competitive maritime commerce.

In May 1920, Cuno and his delegation met in New York with R.H.M. Robinson, L.H. Monk and George S. Dearborn, representatives of the Harriman trust. Harriman had been to Europe in April and studied the shipping situation.[56] In Hamburg he conducted secret talks with HAL officials at their headquarters. He was convinced that if he could come to an agreement with the HAL, "it would be a shipping coup."[57] If provided with the necessary ships, the HAL possessed vast knowledge and experience and still controlled "numerous docking facilities, ticket agencies, and all the paraphernalia so essential to successful competition with Britain."[58] With the USSB's sympathetic support the parties found a way to a mutual understanding which served their interests very neatly.

While talks proceeded Harriman enlarged his foothold in shipping by buying the ASCC (in the process making himself its president), the important shipyards William Cramp and Sons, and the Kerr Navigation Company. These firms were added to the Independent Steamship Company; the American Hawaiian Steamship Company; Livermore, Dearborne and Company; the Shawmut Steamship Company; and the Coastwise Transportation Company, all already under his control.[59] In August 1920, Harriman reorganised his shipping interests, combining all the firms into the United American Lines (UAL). The UAL operated eighty-six ships totalling 600,000 deadweight tons, a third of which had been consigned by the USSB. While Harriman streamlined his shipping interests, the ASCC and the

---

[56]For the details of Harriman's shipping and shipbuilding activities see Larry J. Bland, "W. Averell Harriman: Businessman and Diplomat 1891-1945" (Unpublished Ph.D. thesis, University of Wisconsin, 1972), 23-48.

[57]*Ibid.*, 35.

[58]*Ibid.*

[59]*Ibid.*, 32, 35-36.

HAL drafted the details of an agreement which was signed on 19 June 1920. Although the document referred to the ASCC, the UAL became the actual contracting partner when the agreement was put into operation.

Confusion and furore arose on both side of the Atlantic over the date and scope of the agreement. The preliminary contract was announced on 6 June 1920. The next day a dispatch issued by Reuters informed the German public that "the American Ship & Commerce Corporation had taken over the routes which the HAL had operated before the war."[60] Further details became known on Cuno's return to Cuxhaven on 30 June 1920. In an interview with the *Hamburger Fremdenblatt* Cuno discussed the agreement in broad terms without disclosing any details. The publication of the interview a few days later is probably the reason that 4 July is often cited erroneously as the contract date in the German literature.[61] In a further interview with the Associated Press on 17 July Cuno pointed out that

> the belief is deepening in shipping and financial circles that it [the agreement] constitutes one of the most momentous events for Germany since the war. Through it Germans see the means of regaining touch with the outside world and an opportunity for Hamburg to re-establish a semblance at least of its former position as a great port.[62]

---

[60]*Zeitschrift der Hamburg-Amerika Linie*, XIV (1920), 60-61.

[61]Reinhard Schmelzkopf, *Die deutsche Handelsschiffahrt 1919-1939. Chronik und Wertung der Ereignisse in Schiffahrt und Schiffbau* (Oldenburg, 1974), 31. Arnold Kludas und Herbert Bischoff, *Die Schiffe der Hamburg-Amerika Linie. Vol. 2: 1907-1926* (Herford, 1980), 12. Otto J. Seiler, *Bridge across the Atlantic. The Story of Hapag-Lloyd's North American Liner Services* (Herford, 1991), 41. Teubner, *Wiederaufbau*, 235, even gives May 1920 as a date.

[62]StAH, Hapag I, 1707, 17 July 1920.

But apart from the commercial benefits expected, Germans also attached much political significance to it. "I call your special attention," Cuno said,

> to the fact that our agreement must not only be considered from a purely business point of view but, in the first instance, is to be taken as a trial to re-establish good relation between two countries which, during long years, have been separated by war. The way we have taken will be for the near future the only possible one to go to resume relations between foreign countries and Germany. In its effects the war has left a deep gulf between the governments of the fighting countries and has disorganized the entire economic order. A normal state of things can only be restored if representatives of economic interests endeavor to meet both as men and as business men in order to gain by linking their mutual interests together in a new and more binding connection than was possible in prewar times and which may now be reached through diplomatic ways.[63]

Cuno continued by reminding Germans of the lessons of Versailles. The conference, he observed, had supplied the best proof

> that the co-operation of nations cannot be brought about by the government of the victor dictating a decree to the government of the beaten nation. The experience...of our negotiations in America confirms this conception. Beginning with the first day, we took up discussions with a full knowledge that this first renewal of friendship on an important and vital point would have to be sincere and binding. While expressing my full satisfaction regarding the success of the convention, it has been with a final view of making this agreement the basis for

[63]*Ibid.*

> re-opening peaceful working relations with both countries.[64]

Although pressed by reporters, HAL officials refused to disclose any further details of the agreement than had so far been made public. Since the approval of the USSB was still pending, they preferred that announcements come from the Harriman company. Yet there was a second, more important reason for remaining uncommunicative. The announcement of the tentative contract stirred emotions in the United States, Great Britain and France. Harriman's name was constantly in the press. It was a strange coalition which assembled to attack the agreement for its allegedly pro-German bias.[65] There were rival shipowners like Alfred F. Clegg, vice-president of the Kerr Steamship Company, who called the "Harriman-Hamburg plan a one-sided bargain favorable to Germany."[66] Ship operators and the American Steamshipowners Association accused Harriman of giving German tonnage a better position in American ports than that given America's former Allies. Others maintained that the Germans were favoured at the expense of the American merchant fleet. Harriman's secretary at the ASCC, Kermit Roosevelt, resigned his position in protest.[67] Senator Robert M. LaFolette blamed the Harriman group for harbouring British influences to the detriment of the American merchant marine. The general feeling among those opposed to the agreement was that Harriman was helping the enemy.

In order to create furore in Germany, news was circulated in Paris that the USSB was about to buy the HAL.[68] Much propaganda was also issued against the agreement in Britain. Because of this

---

[64] *Ibid.*

[65] Bland, "Harriman," 37-38.

[66] *New York Times*, 7 October 1920.

[67] *New York Times*, 6 October 1920.

[68] *Hansa*, 10 April 1920.

controversy, Cuno did not feel able to stress in the German press what he believed to be the advantages for the HAL. He therefore advised the HAL's governing board to accept that Harriman was trying to appease domestic opposition when he handed out a one-sided statement to American newspapers extolling the advantages of the agreement to the domestic merchant marine.[69] Cuno recognised that it was important that public opinion in the United States be reconciled to the idea that German and American shipping interests were seeking to solve problems in both countries. In a letter to his brother, Max, a member of the HAL's governing board, Paul M. Warburg cautioned him

> not to try too much at this moment and to be satisfied if active trade relations are established on the most cordial and effective basis possible in the circumstances, and not to care too much about form and prestige at this time. What you want first of all are results. You want ships to come to your part and do business and your people to get to work and be busy. He [Cuno] will have it very difficult here, because there is a very strong propaganda carried on against the particular plan of the Shipping Board which would re-establish intimate connections with the old Hamburg line. Naturally so, because that line was greatly advertised during the war as an active arm of your government. Whether that was true or not, it gives a sufficient argument to the competition to attack any plan that will put the company back in the field. I have my doubts, therefore, whether the Shipping Board, which no doubt shows a great deal of friendly feeling towards the company, not because it loves the company but because it sees the importance of making use of the existing organization in order to make the American marine a success in competing with England, Holland and Japan, will be able to carry out its

[69] StAH, Hapag I, 1201, 9 June 1920.

> present plans and I should not be surprised if your friend would return home with much less of a contract in his pocket than he expected to secure when he sailed. But his strategic position is so delicate and weak that whatever he may bring home is an advantage.[70]

While the Germans were concerned with keeping a low profile, the controversy in the United States continued vigorously. Harriman's only public supporter was Admiral Benson, who argued openly on a number of occasions that he considered the agreement "one of the most important ocean traffic developments brought about since the end of the war."[71] On 17 August, Benson admitted for the first time that a draft of the contract had been "prepared between the Shipping Board and the HAL with the idea of reopening at least some of the trade routes formerly operated by the Hamburg interest, but in a purely American way."[72] What he did not say was that the USSB had been forced to withdraw and let private companies conduct negotiations. "After careful consideration," he went on,

> the Shipping Board, while still favorable to the general idea, decided that it would be better in the long run if the agreement was made between the Hamburg-American Line and a private American company, rather than that the Shipping Board itself be a direct party to such a contract, but at the same time to be prepared to assist the American end if such an arrangement could be consummated. After protracted negotiations Dr. Cuno and his associates, with the knowledge and approval of

[70]StAH, Hapag I, 1571, 13 April 1920.

[71]*New York Times*, 17 August 1920.

[72]*Ibid.*

> the Shipping Board, concluded a contract with the American Ship and Commerce Corporation.[73]

In the same press-release Admiral Benson summarised the main points negotiated and sanctioned by the USSB. Both companies would operate transatlantic passenger and freight services between New York and other American ports and Germany, as well as between Germany and ports outside the United States. Each company would become the agent for the other in their respective countries and put port, office and pier facilities at each other's disposal. The term of the agreement was twenty years. While the first part covered principles, the second detailed the methods of implementation. Ships for the new organisation would be provided by the Shipping Board. The two companies would operate on an equal basis and retain their corporate independence. Benson found it necessary to state that no German money was to be invested in the American end of the business, nor was there "any clause which makes possible German investment in the American part of the enterprise in the future."[74]

Although the financial base was "one hundred percent American," and despite Benson's conviction that the HAL's methods, personnel and experience would inestimably benefit American shipping and commerce, the statement did not pacify the public. The controversy in America continued to rage. On 6 October 1920 Benson praised the agreement again in the *New York Times*. "The very fierceness of the attacks upon the contract indicates its value to American shipping," he declared. And he assured the readers that Harriman was a "full-blooded American citizen."

> It is not necessary for him to risk his fortune to earn a living. It seems to me that every real American should commend him in the risks he is taking in his attempts to develop American shipping. There is no other motive he

---

[73] *Ibid.*

[74] *Ibid.*

> could have in putting his money and efforts into this proposition, and he has the support of the Shipping Board, so far as I am concerned.[75]

While the contract had his personal approval, Benson made it clear, contrary to his earlier statement, that the Board had not yet passed it. But he emphasised that "I shall do what I can to push it."[76]

In a dramatic and highly unusual move, Harriman tried to quell the opposition by publishing the full text of the agreement in the New York newspapers.[77] Yet instead of silencing the critics, publication of the text motivated opponents to begin to scrutinise and object to each individual clause. These new critiques led Harriman to reply in a long statement, which was published alongside Benson's remarks in the *New York Times*.[78] His defense of the deal comprised sixteen points through which he attempted to dismiss all the objections. In the concluding sentence he claimed that "we regard the whole undertaking as a brilliant American opportunity." The following day Alfred Clegg launched a new attack, accusing Harriman of having entered into further agreements "by letters so far kept secret."[79]

A more serious problem which had to be solved before the controversy could ebb was the question of official approval by the new seven-man Shipping Board, which had been established by the new Merchant Marine Act.[80] Since the President had made no appointments, the full Board did not exist. While Benson was quite worried

---

[75] *New York Times*, 6 October 1920.

[76] *Ibid.*

[77] See *The Journal of Commerce* (New York), 17 August 1920. Priester, *Wiederaufbau*, 143-146, has published the German version. StAH, Hapag I, 2358 and 2359 contains preliminary drafts of the agreement and related documents.

[78] *New York Times*, 6 October 1920.

[79] Safford, *Wilsonian Maritime Diplomacy*, 242-243.

[80] *New York Times*, 7 October 1920.

that the whole deal would fall through at the last minute, he recognised that if Harriman commenced operations with non-USSB vessels, no sanction would be required.[81] Harriman took the hint and declared that he would only employ UAL vessels to inaugurate the services. Having dispensed with this final roadblock, Harriman began to accept bookings for the old HAL routes. A week later he was full of praise of the first results at a meeting of the American Manufacturers' Export Association, telling the audience that the trade was already functioning. He said that "although Germany had been given a new lease on maritime life, America was the real winner because it had been afforded an unparalleled opportunity to profit from association with a firm world renowned for its shipping expertise and savvy."[82]

By mid-October the public dispute had ended and the newspapers switched to news about the upcoming elections. In Germany the public did not know much more about the "mysterious" agreement than what Cuno and the HAL had told the press. The only issue with which critics were concerned was the duration of the agreement, arguing that twenty years would obstruct the HAL's future development. But the general feeling was very positive. The *New York Times* correspondent in Berlin reported that "the German press hails the... agreement with particular joy as creating the biggest shipping concern in the world."[83] It "carries the restoration of the German shipping out of the stage of preparation and brings about a distinct improvement in our position," he quoted from the *Berliner Börsenzeitung*. The agreement made "it possible for Germany to enter the sphere of world shipping again and strengthen the back of American against British competition."[84]

At a dinner which opened Merchant Marine Week in Chicago, Benson launched a major attack on the critics of USSB policies "Hidden behind corporate names," he declared,

---

[81]Safford, *Wilsonian Maritime Diplomacy*, 243.

[82]*New York Times*, 15 October 1920.

[83]*Ibid.*

[84]*Ibid.*

> there are Americans basking in the favor of foreign shipping interests, who are creating the impression that ships are a menace to the nation...Now and then their efforts to muddy the waters succeed to the extent of influencing honest opinion against the Shipping Board's policies which aim to upbuild a permanent merchant marine...Those who worry most about our entrance in her ocean commerce must be our cousins overseas--the British...It is essential that the world should understand that we, who fully appreciate the service rendered by other nations, are now ship-independent in the development of our ocean carrying trade. We mean to play our part in a manly American fashion and have done so from the start. I pledge myself to help see that not only my own, but other governments be brought to a point where they fully agree to retire absolutely from ocean carriage which could only mean uneven competition with the private owner. We are endeavoring to do this as quickly as possible and the law demands it.[85]

Together with the Merchant Marine Act, the Harriman-HAL agreement represented Benson's "crowning achievement" as chairman of the USSB.[86] Yet only a few months later Harriman's operation began to stagger and he fell out with the Board.

The Harriman-HAL arrangement had a promising start. In early September 1920 the dispatch of the steamer *Mar Del Norte* ended the HAL's cooperation with the Kerr Line.[87] On 15 September the steamer *Beursplein*, chartered in the Netherlands, opened a weekly HAL/UAL freight service between Hamburg and New York. In January 1921 the steamer *Mount Clay*, formerly the German *Prinz Eitel Friedrich*, inaugurated the joint passenger service, followed by the

---

[85]*New York Times*, 16 October 1920.

[86]Safford, *Wilsonian Maritime Diplomacy*, 242.

[87]Witthöft, *Hapag*, 65-66.

steamers *Mount Carrol* and *Mount Clinton* in April/May. In the autumn of 1921 the HAL brought its first newly-built steamers, *Bayern* and *Württemberg*, into operation. Both vessels were especially designed for carrying third-class passengers.[88]

It was the steerage passenger trade on the north Atlantic, HAL's dominant business before the war, upon which Harriman concentrated his efforts, "hoping to capitalize on renewed tourism and immigration, and to replace the Germans in this trade."[89] In April/May 1922 the UAL sent their two twenty thousand-ton ships, *Resolute* and *Reliance*, vessels which had been built for the HAL's passenger trade to South America in 1914, on their maiden voyages from Hamburg and Southampton to New York. The third UAL ship, *Cleveland*, an ex-HAL vessel of the same name, joined the service in October 1923. On the German side the steamers *Albert Ballin*, *Deutschland*, *Thuringia*, *Westphalia* and *Hannover*, were put into operation in 1923/24, while the *Bayern* and *Württemberg* were transferred to other duties. With insufficient third-class traffic to America, the *Mount Clay*'s cabin accommodation was enlarged from six to 110 in 1923.[90] The UAL's *Mount Carroll* and *Mount Clinton* made their last crossings from Hamburg to New York in July/September 1923; only on one voyage in September 1922 had arrived at New York almost fully booked. Both ships had their third-class accommodation capacities increased to 1,050 in 1921. While the joint-services operated smoothly, external factors which clouded the relationship. In mid-summer of 1920, it become increasingly difficult to obtain sufficient cargo. After an eighteen-month shipping boom following the end of the war, a depression set in. The USSB was forced

---

[88]Arnold Kludas, *Die Geschichte der deutschen Passagierschiff fahrt. Vol. IV.: Vernichtung und Wiedergeburt 1914 bis 1930* (Hamburg, 1989), 49-61.

[89]Bland, "Harriman," 36-37.

[90]Noel R.P. Bonsor, *North Atlantic Seaway* (Jersey, 1979), IV, 1502-1508.

to lay-up more than twenty-five percent of its vessels in February 1921. A month later the figure had risen to thirty-five percent.[91]

A great scramble for cargo began in the United States, Great Britain, Japan and Germany. Compared to a world tonnage of 45.4 million gross tons in June 1914, by June 1921 the figure had soared to 61.9 million gross tons. An increased capacity of thirty-five percent was much more than the international shipping market could bear. Overcapacity caused freight rates to plummet. Coinciding with severe pressures on the international exchange market, this caused the postwar shipping bonanza to come to an end.

To compound matters, the American Immigration Act of 1921 worsened the crisis.[92] Compared to 1.1 million immigrants who entered the United States in 1913, the new law limited entrants to only 357,000 people per annum. The quota of German immigrants was fixed at sixty-seven thousand. The result was a sharp fall in the number of people sailing to New York. In 1924 about 458,000 passengers, less than half of the 1913 level, crossed the Atlantic. The combined shares of the HAL and the NDL dropped from 35.5 to 6.8%. Due to the exhaustion of the US immigration quota, the steamer *Deutschland*, which was delivered in December 1923, was laid-up until the end of March 1924. In addition to the Immigration restrictions, German hyper-inflation had caused the value of the dollar to soar to the astronomical exchange rate of 4,200 billion marks, a value which did not entice many Germans into crossing the Atlantic. Harriman's hopes to make money with third-class passengers withered. In an attempt to find an alternative to the troubled immigrant business to the United States, the HAL/UAL in February 1924 initiated a joint-service to Canada, where farmers, farm labourers and female domestic servants were much in demand.[93]

Harriman gradually lost interest in shipping and began to dismantle his empire. On the basis of the short postwar boom he had

---

[91]Safford, *Wilsonian Maritime Diplomacy*, 246.

[92]Scholl, "The German Merchant Marine," 200.

[93]Kludas, *Geschichte*, 59-60.

miscalculated the opportunities for an American merchant marine. American exports dropped by two-thirds between 1920 and 1921 and remained at that low level for several years. The immigration restrictions ruined his "carefully assembled third class steamer operation."[94] He failed to assess correctly the American readiness "to subsidize an overpriced...and technically outmoded merchant marine. He also failed to gauge accurately the great lengths to which the British were willing to go to protect their own maritime power."[95] When he realised that his plans were "unsound," he was ready to sell his part of the passenger business in 1926.

At the end of February 1926 Cuno met representatives of the Harriman group in London for talks concerning the reorganisation of business relations. Since the HAL had surpassed the UAL in every respect, Cuno felt that the fifty-fifty agreement no longer served both ends adequately; he therefore proposed to cancel the twenty-year contract. The meeting resulted in the *Resolute*, *Reliance* and *Cleveland* being sold to the HAL. The vessels retained their names and continued to sail between Hamburg, Southampton, Cherbourg and New York. The following statement was given to the press.

> As is known, six years ago Harriman and the Hapag concluded a community of interests agreement for 20 years, which provided that each partner should participate in the proportion of 50:50 on the Lines operated by the Hamburg-American Line before the war. The course of the development of both parties gave rise to a desire for the agreement, which worked to the satisfaction of both sides, to be remodelled to suit the changed conditions, the most expedient solution of which appeared to be the transfer of the ships in exchange for granting Harriman a financial interest. In this connection it lay in the interest of both parties not only fully to preserve the

---

[94]Bland, "Harriman," 48.

[95]*Ibid.*

> purely German character of the Hamburg-American Line, but also to assure a continuance of the advantages of international co-operation. To this end it was agreed that the voting power of the Hapag shares to be given Harriman should remain with the Hapag and that the American business friends, including Mr. W.A. Harriman, will retain their seats on the Board of Directors of the United American Lines, which have also been taken over by the Hamburg-American Line which will continue to act as General Agents of the Hamburg-American Line in the United States. With this new arrangement, which is the result of experience gained in common work, it is to be expected that the agreement now made in place of the old contract will prove of advantage to both parties.[96]

All told the HAL paid thirty-two million marks to regain full control over all shipping operations.[97] A total of 1.5 million dollars was to be handed over in cash immediately, while an additional four million dollars were guaranteed by debenture bonds and shares, worth ten million marks. The voting power remained with the HAL. This arrangement ended Harriman's direct control over the German shipping company and all negotiable property was put at the HAL's disposal. The lease of pier facilities was taken over by the Germans as well. The Hamburg-American Line had reached total independence again. Six years after the armistice had left the HAL on the verge of extinction, the foremost German shipping company had re-emerged as one of the world's leading maritime enterprises. When the second Harriman-HAL-agreement came into effect in July 1926 the German and American press reacted positively. The *New York Herald Tribune* called the postwar development of the HAL one of the most astonish-

---

[96]A photocopy of this statement was supplied by my colleague Arnold Kludas.

[97]Newspapers in Hamburg and Berlin reported that the figure was variously thirty-five and thirty-eight million marks. See *Zeitschrift der Hamburg-Amerika Linie*, XX (31 July 1926), 86-87.

ing restorations in the history of world shipping. The *New York World* predicted that the HAL was on the way to becoming a serious rival to British shipping interests,[98] something which Harriman and the UAL had failed to achieve.

In only two generations before World War One, Germany had been transformed from an agrarian to an industrial state. While she was able to feed forty million inhabitants on the basis of her agricultural economy, industrialised Germany, with sixty-seven million people, had to import foodstuffs amounting to about twelve million tons in 1913. At the outbreak of war a total of fourteen million people secured their living through foreign trade, shipping and the provision of foreign raw materials. In terms of money, imports exceeded exports by thirty-three million. Taking the average of the five years ending in 1913, the figure was substantially higher, amounting to seventy-four million. In the Treaty of Versailles Germany had lost her foreign property, overseas investments and her mercantile marine, assets which had covered her prewar trade deficit. In order to transport badly needed foodstuffs and to ensure the livelihood of millions of people, one of the main objectives of German politicians and managers involved in maritime trade was to rebuild the domestic fleet. Despite having been stripped of their ships, they still possessed important expertise which was invaluable to those who now had an abundance of vessels. For the German shipping companies survival hinged on the ability to overcome the "deflection of post-bellum policy by war aims and war sentiment"[99] in Great Britain and the United States and to seek international cooperation with British and American shipowners, many of whom proved to be more interested in maritime business than in nurturing hostile feelings against their prewar rivals.

In this essay I have focused on one incident to show how economic motivations were able to pave the way for a working agreement between two shipping companies which clearly saw the

---

[98]*Ibid.*, 88.

[99]Fayle, *War*, 412.

advantages in merging their interests and to bridge the Atlantic.[100] The Harriman-HAL agreement served both companies well for a time and was only abrogated prematurely because conditions in America had changed and because Harriman's maritime efforts "had opened his eyes to new worlds to conquer."[101] Friendly relations continued even after Harriman abandoned his shipping business on the north Atlantic. While Harriman and Admiral Benson did not achieve their goals of gaining a permanent foothold in maritime trade and compete successfully with British shipping companies, for a short time it made economic sense to cooperate with the former enemy's leading shipping company despite much opposition in the US. When the rationale behind this decision became outdated, Harriman agreed to end the arrangement and remained a passive stockholder for years to come.

The Hamburg-American Line, however, was able to use Harriman's help to rebuild its business after the war, eventually ensuring the company's complete independence from its American partners, an accomplishment which seemed impossible at the outset. Paul Warburg was judging the situation correctly when he wrote to his brother in 1920: "As I say, my own feeling is that the main thing is to get started and to re-establish relations and not be to finicky about the future and about prestige. That will take care of itself when once the relations are established."[102]

In February 1923 Cuno made a remarkable statement in Breslau. In reviewing the postwar reconstruction of international shipping, he concluded that

> Politicians should not be the only ones who determine the relations between nations, it is the businessmen's task to find ways and create the basis for international cooperation in a world where all countries are economi-

---

[100]The Norddeutscher Lloyd in Bremen entered into similar agreements with American and British companies.

[101]Bland, "Harriman," 48.

[102]StAH, Hapag I, 1571, 13 April 1920.

cally dependent on each other...Businessmen and not politicians led the way to economic understanding. The extent to which economy is the true pacemaker for politics can be demonstrated by the Harriman-HAL agreement which was signed long before the state of war between Germany and the United States had come to an end.[103]

[103] StAH, Hapag I, 539, 17 February 1923.

Peter Neville Davies: A Bibliography

Compiled by Andrew Armitage

BOOKS

The Trade Makers: Elder Dempster in West Africa, 1852-1972. London: George Allen and Unwin, 1973.

Trading in West Africa. London: Croom Helm, 1976. (editor).

Sir Alfred Jones: Shipping Entrepreneur Par Excellence. London: Europa Publications, 1978.

Henry Tyrer: A Liverpool Shipping Agent and his Enterprise, 1879-1979. London: Croom Helm, 1979.

The Sutcliffes of Grimsby: The Family and the Firm. Grimsby: Graphic Press, 1987.

The Japanese Shipping and Shipbuilding Industries: A History of their Modern Growth. London: Athlone Press, 1990. (with Tomohei Chida).

Fyffes and the Banana: Musa Sapientum--A Centenary History, 1888-1988. London: Athlone Press, 1990.

The Man Behind the Bridge: Colonel Philip Toosey and the River Kwai. London: Athlone Press, 1991.

CONTRIBUTIONS TO BOOKS

"The African Steam Ship Company." In J.R. Harris (ed.). *Liverpool and Merseyside: Essays in the Economic and Social History of the Port and Its Hinterland*. London: Frank Cass, 1969, pp. 212-238.

"Group Enterprise: Strengths and Hazards. Business History and the Teaching of Business Management." In Sheila Marriner (ed.). *Business and Businessmen: Studies in Business, Economic and Accounting History*. Liverpool: Liverpool University Press, 1978, pp. 141-168.

"The Development of the Liner Trades." In Keith Matthews and Gerald Panting (eds.). *Ships and Shipbuilding in the North Atlantic Region*. St. John's: Maritime History Group, 1978, pp. 173-206.

"Nautical Archaeology in Wales." In *Proceedings of the 12th Annual Conference on Nautical Archaeology*. New Orleans: Society for Historical Archaeology, 1982, pp. 38.

"Commentary on the Methodology and Results of the Atlantic Canada Shipping Project." In Lewis R. Fischer and Eric W. Sager (eds.). *Merchant Shipping and Economic Development in Atlantic Canada*. St. John's: Maritime History Group, 1982, pp. 55-59.

"Edward Wathen Fyffe." In D.J. Jeremy and C. Shaw (eds.). *Dictionary of Business Biography: A Biographical Dictionary of Business Leaders Active in Britain in the Period 1860-1980*. London: Butterworths, 1984, Vol. II, pp. 452-455.

"Sir Alfred Jones and the Provision of Shipping Services for the Congo Free State." In *Proceedings of the Symposium of the Royal Academy of Science, Brussels, for the Centenary of the Congo Free State*, 1985, pp. 477-492.

"Sir Alfred Lewis Jones." In D.J. Jeremy and C. Shaw (eds.). *Dictionary of Business Biography: A Biographical Dictionary of Business Leaders Active in Britain in the Period 1860-1980*. London: Butterworths, 1985, Vol. III, pp. 527-530.

"The British Contribution to the Economic Development of the Canary Islands." In *Proceedings of the VI Conference on the History of the Canary Islands and America*. Las Palmas, 1984, pp. 355-374.

"British Shipping and World Trade: Rise and Decline, 1820-1939." In Tsunehiko Yui and Keiichiro Nakagawa (eds.). *Business History of Shipping: Strategy and Structure*. Tokyo: University of Tokyo Press, 1985, pp. 39-85.

"Japanese Merchant Shipping and the Bridge over the River Kwai." In C.G. Reynolds (ed.). *Global Crossroads and the American Seas*. Missoula, Montana: Pictorial Histories Publishing Company, 1988), pp. 197-219.

"The Development of the Japanese Shipping Industries in the Post-War Era." In H.M. Hignett (ed.). *A Second Merseyside Maritime History: Transactions and Research*. Heswall: Liverpool Nautical Research Society, 1991, pp. 53-64.

ARTICLES

"Lord Kylsant and the Royal Mail." *Business History*. Vol. XIV, No. 2 (July 1972), pp. 102-123. (with A.M. Bourn).

"The Discovery of the *Mary*, Charles II's Yacht." *International Journal of Nautical Archaeology and Underwater Exploration*. Vol. II, No. 1 (March 1973), pp. 59-60.

"An Expedition to Identify and Survey the Wreck of the Paddle Steamer *Lady Lansdowne*." *Transactions of the Liverpool Nautical Research Society*. Vol. X (1973), pp. 22-27.

"The Impact of the Expatriate Shipping Lines on the Economic Development of British West Africa." *Business History*. Vol. XIX, No. 1 (January 1977), pp. 3-17.

"Sources for West African Economic and Business History." *African Research and Documentation*. Vol. XV (1977), pp. 4-6.

"The Discovery and Excavation of the Royal Yacht *Mary*." *Maritime Wales*. Vol. IV (March 1979), pp. 25-32.

"Business Success and the Role of Chance: The Extraordinary Philipps Brothers." *Business History*. Vol. XXIII, No. 2 (July 1981), pp. 208-232.

"The Rise of Japan's Modern Shipping Industry." *The Great Circle*. Vol. VII, No. 1 (April 1985), pp. 45-56.

"Recent Publications and Developments in the Study of Maritime Economic History." *Journal of Transport History*. Vol. IX, No. 1 (March 1988), pp. 93-108. (with Sheila Marriner).

"The First Hundred Years: Fyffes and the Banana." *Fruit Trades Journal*, 9 September 1988, special supplement, pp. 1-40.

"G.K.N. Axles/Salisbury Division: 50 Years in Birmingham." *Birmingham Post*, 12 December 1988, special supplement, pp. 1-8.

"The Japanese Shipping and Shipbuilding Industries." *International Journal of Maritime History*. Vol. II, No. 2 (December 1990), pp. 241-245. (with Tomohei Chida).

"The Transfer of Shipbuilding Technology: The Case of National Bulk Carriers and the Kure Shipyard." *Hiroshima Shudo University Research Review*. Vol. VII (1991), pp. 87-97.

"The Development of the Japanese Shipping Industries in the Post-War Era." *Collectanea Maritima*. Vol. V (1991), pp. 181-197.

"The Role of National Bulk Carriers in the Advance of Shipbuilding Technology in Post-War Japan." *International Journal of Maritime History*. IV, No. 1 (June 1992), pp. 131-143.

Printed and bound by CPI Group (UK) Ltd, Croydon, CR0 4YY
06/08/2026
14937425-0009